THE BEST TEST PREPARATION FOR THE

GRE®

LITERATURE IN ENGLISH

James S. Malek, Ph.D.
Chairperson and Professor of English
DePaul University
Chicago, Illinois

Thomas C. Kennedy, Ph.D.
Professor of English
Washburn University
Topeka, Kansas

Pauline Beard, Ph.D.
Instructor of English
Portland State University
Portland, Oregon

Robert Liftig, Ed.D.
Adjunct Professor of English
Fairfield University
Fairfield, Connecticut

Bernadette Brick
University of Rochester
Rochester, New York

Research & Education Association
61 Ethel Road West
Piscataway, New Jersey 08854

**The Best Test Preparation for the
GRE LITERATURE IN ENGLISH**

Copyright © 2004, 2001 by Research & Education Association, Inc. All rights reserved. No part of this book may be reproduced in any form without permission of the publisher.

Printed in the United States of America

Library of Congress Control Number 2004094056

International Standard Book Number 0-87891-346-7

REA® is a registered trademark of Research & Education Association, Inc., Piscataway, New Jersey 08854.

REA supports the effort to conserve and protect environmental resources by printing on recycled papers.

CONTENTS

ABOUT RESEARCH & EDUCATION ASSOCIATION

Research & Education Association (REA) is an organization of educators, scientists, and engineers specializing in various academic fields. Founded in 1959 with the purpose of disseminating the most recently developed scientific information to groups in industry, government, high schools, and universities, REA has since become a successful and highly respected publisher of study aids, test preps, handbooks, and reference works.

REA's Test Preparation series includes study guides for all academic levels in almost all disciplines. Research & Education Association publishes test preps for students who have not yet completed high school, as well as high school students preparing to enter college. Students from countries around the world seeking to attend college in the United States will find the assistance they need in REA's publications. For college students seeking advanced degrees, REA publishes test preps for many major graduate school admission examinations in a wide variety of disciplines, including engineering, law, and medicine. Students at every level, in every field, with every ambition can find what they are looking for among REA's publications.

Unlike most test preparation books—which present only a few practice tests that bear little resemblance to the actual exams—REA's series presents tests that accurately depict the official exams in both degree of difficulty and types of questions. REA's practice tests are always based upon the most recently administered exams, and include every type of question that can be expected on the actual exams.

REA's publications and educational materials are highly regarded and continually receive an unprecedented amount of praise from professionals, instructors, librarians, parents, and students. Our authors are as diverse as the fields represented in the books we publish. They are well-known in their respective disciplines and serve on the faculties of prestigious high schools, colleges, and universities throughout the United States and Canada.

ACKNOWLEDGMENTS

*In addition to our authors,
we extend special thanks to the following people:*

Anita Davis, Ed.D., and Dan Newman
for technically editing the review and practice tests;

David Gracer, Christopher Hubert, and Brian Walsh
for their significant contributions in creating and assessing
new practice test material;

Dominique Won
for copyediting the book in its final production stages;

Ellen Gong for proofreading the manuscript;

and

Michael C. Cote for typesetting the book.

*We would also like to thank the following people
for their special efforts:*

Larry B. Kling, Manager, Editorial Services,
for his supervision of revisions;

Gianfranco Origliato and Diane Goldschmidt,
for coordinating revisions of this book;

Pam Weston, Production Manager,
for ensuring press readiness;

Kristin M. Rutkowski and Catherine Battos,
for coordinating the development of this book;

Nisha Aidasani, Lia Daniels, and Craig Pelz
for their editorial contributions;

and

Christine Saul, Senior Graphic Artist,
for designing the cover of this book.

Introduction

ABOUT THE TEST

The GRE (Graduate Record Examination) Literature in English Test is taken by students applying to graduate programs in English. Most programs require that applicants submit scores for both the GRE General Test and the GRE Literature in English Test. Both tests are offered by ETS (Educational Testing Service) and administered at test locations throughout the country and abroad. You can obtain a test registration booklet from your college or by contacting ETS directly.

The test is usually administered 3 times a year and contains approximately 230 questions, which you have two hours and fifty minutes to answer. Unlike the General Test, the Literature in English Test is not divided into sections, so you can answer the questions in any order. However, keep in mind that *there are no breaks* in this examination. Each of the 230 questions is worth the same amount, one point. Also unlike the General Test, there is a penalty for wrong answers which serves to correct for "guessing." For each wrong answer, one-quarter of a point is deducted from your score. Unanswered questions are not counted either way.

Questions on the GRE Literature in English can be loosely categorized into two types:

Critical – These questions test your ability to distinguish aspects of literature such as voice, tone, mood, theme, form, structure and literary methods from a given literature passage (usually an excerpt from a larger work or a short poem).

Factual – These questions are a straightforward testing of specific facts. You are asked to recall and recognize information regarding authors and literary works (often based on brief passages written by or about the authors); substance and styles of writing; historical and biographical information; and details such as plot, character, and setting.

When you register for the test, you will receive a booklet about the types of questions you will be asked to answer. These question types are as follows:

- ✔ Literary Analysis (40-55%)
- ✔ Identification (15-20%)
- ✔ Cultural and Historical Contexts (20-25%)
- ✔ History and Theory of Literary Criticism (10-15%)

These questions test the following literatures:

- ✔ Continental, Classical, and Comparative Literature through 1925 (5-10%)
- ✔ British Literature to 1660 (including Milton) (25-30%)
- ✔ British Literature from 1660-1925 (30–35%)
- ✔ American Literature through 1925 (15-25%)
- ✔ American, British, and World Literatures after 1925 (20-25%)

You should keep in mind, however, that ETS's classification of questions may not be the same as your own. Therefore, we suggest you focus primarily on knowing how to answer ID questions. Refresh your memory of the big names in literature, their better known works, and the time periods they come from. You should also study the review and practice tests in this book, which cover the material that most often appears on administrations of the GRE Literature in English Test, and study actual past administrations of the test published by ETS.

HOW TO STUDY FOR THE TEST

Use the review at the beginning of this book to refresh your knowledge of the subject matter. This review covers authors and works most often seen on the GRE Literature in English Test. However, not everything covered in the review will be on every administration of the test and not everything on the test will be a part of any review. If you are unfamiliar with any authors, works, or terms covered in the review, you should be sure to look them up in reference books such as the *Norton Anthology of English Literature* or *The Oxford*

Companion to English Literature. If you have time, you should also consult the works themselves. This is especially important for an author like Chaucer. Although our review and the above reference books can give you summaries of the most important of *The Canterbury Tales,* only by actually reading a few of the tales will you be able to recognize Middle English and Chaucer's distinctive style when you must identify a line on the test.

After studying REA's review and additional reference materials, take the practice tests in this book. When you take our GRE Literature in English practice tests, be sure to simulate testing conditions: sit at a table in a quiet room free of distractions and time yourself. Doing this will make you less nervous the day of the actual test and, more importantly, you will develop a sense of pacing. After timing yourself for all of the practice tests, you will have a very good idea of how much time you can spend on each question during the actual test.

In addition to doing the practice tests in this book, we encourage you to purchase a book of actual GRE Literature in English tests published by ETS. The tests included in the ETS book are several years old and therefore have fewer questions about non-traditional authors than more recent administrations; however, the GRE changes little from year to year and the types of questions on the exam remain the same. You can purchase a book of actual tests from most bookstores or you can order one directly from ETS.

Most importantly, be sure to check over your practice tests. Look up any questions you got wrong in the explanations. Use reference books and the works themselves for further review. Only by studying what you miss will you be able to get it right on the actual GRE.

TEST-TAKING STRATEGIES

Although you will probably have to take both the General and the Subject Test, try to avoid taking them on the same day. Taking any test is stressful, and after sitting for one extremely long standardized test, you will hardly be at your best for the second exam.

Be sure to register for testing dates several months before the due date to ensure that the graduate schools you designated will receive your scores by the application deadlines. Most schools will not consider an incomplete application.

Because the test is not divided into sections, you are completely responsible for budgeting your own time. All of the questions are worth the same amount of points, so you should not spend too much time on any one question. The GRE Literature in English Test attempts to cover a broad range of authors and works. It is unlikely that you will have read all of the works ETS includes, or even most of them; therefore, some questions will be substantially easier for you than others. It is important that you do not spend too much time on questions you find difficult at the expense of working on questions that are easier for you.

The time constraints are such that, on average, a little over a minute is allotted for each question. Thus, it is unlikely that you will have time to answer all 230 questions; however, you can still receive an excellent score without answering all of them. Because the questions are in no particular order, we recommend making a complete pass through all the questions on the test. Answer the ones that are immediately easy for you and mark ones that you want to come back to. Once you have answered all of the easier questions, you can use the remaining time to go back through the test a second time and work on the harder questions that require a greater amount of your time. In this way you ensure that you have the chance to answer all the questions you are likely to get correct, instead of spending time on difficult questions near the beginning of the test and leaving easy questions at the end of the test unanswered.

The penalty for wrong answers should not deter you completely from guessing. If you have no clue what the answer might be, by all means leave the question unanswered. However, if you can eliminate one or two of the five choices, it is to your advantage to make an educated guess. Statistically, guessing randomly among the five choices would give you the possibility of guessing correctly 1/5 of the time. (This is what the 1/4 point deduction for wrong answers is designed to balance.) Being able to eliminate three of the choices as wrong answers means that guessing between the two remaining choices would give you a better chance of being correct.

SCORING THE TEST

Each correct answer receives one "raw score" point, each incorrect answer deducts 1/4 of a point, and any omissions will not be counted. Use the formula below to calculate your raw score.

$$\underline{\hspace{2cm}} - (\underline{\hspace{2cm}} \times \tfrac{1}{4}) = \underline{\hspace{2cm}} \text{ (round to nearest whole number)}$$

# of questions correct   # of questions wrong

Now find your raw score on the Conversion Chart below to determine your scaled score range.

Score Conversion Chart

Raw Score	Scaled Score
216 – 230	770 – 800
201 – 215	750 – 770
186 – 200	690 – 750
171 – 185	650 – 690
156 – 170	610 – 650
141 – 155	580 – 610
126 – 140	530 – 580
111 – 125	490 – 530
96 – 110	450 – 490
81 – 95	430 – 450
66 – 80	390 – 430
51 – 65	360 – 390
36 – 50	340 – 360
21 – 35	270 – 340
6 – 20	220 – 270
< 5	< 220

Note: Due to the statistical formulas used by ETS, your performance on our practice tests will strongly *approximate* your performance on the actual GRE.

STUDY SCHEDULE

The following study schedule allows for thorough preparation for the GRE Literature in English Subject Test. Although it is designed for eight weeks, it can be condensed by covering two weeks' worth of preparation in just one week. But no matter which study schedule works best for you, the more time you spend studying, the more prepared and relaxed you will feel on the day of the exam.

Week	Activity
1	Study the review in this book. Be sure to answer all of the drill questions. If you have particular trouble with any of those questions, go back and study the corresponding section of the review.
2	Take Practice Test 1, and after scoring your exam, carefully review the answer explanations for the questions you had trouble with.
3 – 4	Locate and review any notes you might have from previous literature classes. Be sure to spend extra time on material you haven't looked at in a while.
5	Take Practice Test 2, and after scoring your exam, carefully review the answer explanations for the questions you had trouble with.
6 – 7	Look through our Suggested Reading List for other poems, plays, and essays to familiarize yourself with. Try to get a sense of the authors' particular styles and content.
8	Take Practice Test 3, and after scoring your exam, carefully review the answer explanations for the questions you had trouble with.

Review

General Overview
for the
GRE Literature in English

GRE Literature in English Review

LITERATURE

Classical Literature

Classical literature has exerted a strong influence over English literary history. You will need a solid foundation in the major works of Greek and Roman letters for the GRE Literature in English Subject Test.

In addition to the brief outline of the works we present below, it will be useful for you to become acquainted with some of the conventions of the epic form. An important convention that can be traced to Classical literary practice is beginning the action *in medias res*—Latin for "in the midst of things." For instance, instead of being told chronologically, *The Odyssey* begins with Odysseus' adventures with the nymph Calypso; the earlier action is told in flashback. Another convention of English authors, particularly those of the Early Modern Period, is to introduce the poem with the epic invocation, a request for aid from the Muses.

HOMER

ETS draws the majority of Classical literature questions from Homer's *The Iliad* and *The Odyssey*. Reputed to be a blind man living in Greece circa the eighth century B.C., Homer is probably the most famous of the ancient poets. It is strongly recommended that you read or thoroughly familiarize yourself with both of these works.

The Iliad

Homer's poem, *The Iliad*, deals with events from nearly 300 years before his own time. The basic story revolves around the titanic war between the city of Troy and several Greek city-states. When Paris, son of the Trojan King Priam, abducts the beautiful Helen, wife of Menelaus, the war begins. Menelaus' brother Agamemnon, the Spartan king, leads the Greek forces against the Trojans, who are led by Priam's son Hector. Throughout the poem, the gods on Olympus take sides in the conflict, elevating the chaos and destructiveness of the war.

The most powerful Greek warrior, the proud Achilles, sits on the sidelines refusing to fight because of a feud with Agamemnon. With the Trojans on the verge of victory, the Greek commanders implore Agamemnon to make peace with Achilles. This fails, but Achilles' dear friend Patroclos does enter the battle wearing Achilles' suit of armor. The Trojans are pushed back, but Hector kills Patroclos and provokes Achilles to a wild rage. He enters the fray in a suit of armor obtained through his mother, the demi-god Thetis, and kills Hector. In his rage he drags the Trojan hero's body through the dirt with a chariot. Priam's pleas move Achilles to return Hector's body.

The Odyssey

Homer's second major work picks up from the end of the Trojan War and traces the adventures of the Greek commander Odysseus and his troubled journey home to Ithaca. The complicated plot is told largely in a series of flashbacks that deal with Odysseus's adventures, including his encounter with the Cyclops; his visit to the enchanted isle of Circe, a sorceress who turns his men into pigs; and his perilous journey through the dangerous straits of the sea monsters Charybdis and Scylla. A second major component of the poem concerns Odysseus's wife Penelope, who waits for her husband and fends off the hordes of suitors who are pressing for her hand in marriage. His son, Telemachus, escapes the malicious designs of the suitors, and when his father finally reaches Ithaca, helps him slaughter them *en masse*. Odysseus resumes his place in Ithaca with his faithful wife.

GREEK TRAGEDY

Greek drama is not as popular with ETS as Homer's epic poems, but you should be familiar with the major tragedians and some of their more important works. The three major Greek tragedians are Sophocles, Aeschylus, and

Euripides. Sophocles is best known for his Oedipus cycle: *Oedipus the King*, *Antigone*, and *Oedipus at Colonus*. *Oedipus the King* and *Antigone* are the major plays of the trilogy, particularly the former, telling the story of the doomed Oedipus, who solves the riddle of the sphinx and becomes King of Thebes. He has already unknowingly killed his father, the former King of Thebes, and upon assuming the throne, unknowingly marries his mother according to the Oracle's prophecy. When the truth is revealed, Oedipus, in horror, blinds himself, while his mother/wife Jocasta hangs herself in despair. *Antigone* tells the story of Oedipus's children. His daughter, the title character, defies the civil authority of Creon, Ruler of Thebes, who refuses to allow her brother's body to be properly buried.

Aeschylus is best known for his trilogy *The Oresteia*: *Agamemnon*, *Choeporoe* (or *The Libation Bearers*), and *Eumenides*. These plays tell of the cursed house of Atreus. Agamemnon is murdered upon his return from the Trojan War by his wife Clytemnestra and her lover Aegisthus. Agamemnon's son Orestes vows revenge and eventually kills his mother and her lover. The Furies, the horrifying divinities of revenge for intra-family murders, then pursue him. He is tormented to the point of madness until he is granted a trial, at which Athena votes in his favor, bringing an end to the family curse.

Euripides is not as important ultimately as Sophocles and Aeschylus; his major plays include *Medea* and *Phaedra*.

VIRGIL

The Roman poet Virgil (sometimes spelled Vergil), particularly his epic *The Aeneid*, is a cornerstone of Western literature. Virgil began his career with *The Eclogues*, a series of pastoral poems that were widely imitated in England and throughout Europe during the Renaissance. From *The Eclogues*, Virgil moved on to *The Georgics*, poems that dealt mainly with farming methods. The crowning achievement of Virgil's career was *The Aeneid*; the trajectory from pastoral poet to epic poet, known as the Virgilian career, was thought by many English authors to be the model for poets to follow.

The Aeneid

As with Homer's epic poems, the Trojan War is central to *The Aeneid*. The story follows the fate of the Trojan hero Aeneas and his quest to found a new Troy after the fall of his city. The theme of the epic ultimately is a patriotic one, culminating in the founding of a city that will eventually become Rome.

During the course of his adventures, the goddess Juno continually vexes Aeneas. Notable episodes in the poem include Aeneas becoming the lover of the Carthaginian Queen Dido, who kills herself when Aeneas must return to his quest for a new home, and his journey to the underworld, where he converses with the shades of past heroes and relatives. This particular episode is an important model for Dante's *Inferno*.

Drill Questions

1. Both *The Iliad* and *The Odyssey* begin
    - (A) *in medias res.*
    - (B) with an epic metaphor.
    - (C) with an epic simile.
    - (D) at Colonus.
    - (E) at Thebes.

2. The author of the *Oresteia* trilogy is
    - (A) Atreus.
    - (B) Aeschylus.
    - (C) Homer.
    - (D) Sophocles.
    - (E) Agamemnon.

CONTINENTAL INFLUENCES

Non-English-language authors are not widely represented on the Subject Test, but you should be prepared for a few questions on some of the bigger names that tend to be mentioned. Probably the most important is Dante, whose *Divine Comedy*, written in the fourteenth century, is a major work in world literature. *The Comedy* is divided into three sections: *Inferno*, *Purgatorio*, and *Paradiso*. *Inferno* is by far the most famous, and you should try to be as familiar with it as possible. Although it is sometimes translated into English in prose, in its proper form it is poetry, in *terza rima* (lines of eleven syllables arranged in groups of three and in rhyming pattern of *ababcbcdc*). This form and the theme of divine retribution, wherein the punishment fits the crime, make *Inferno* fairly easy to spot.

The Spanish author Cervantes and his major seventeenth-century work *Don Quixote* may appear on the test. The tone of this work is mock heroic and satirical, dealing with an idealistic but somewhat simple-minded knight who goes on a quest to duel with windmills.

The great seventeenth-century French playwright Molière is known for his sharp wit and his memorable characters, including those in *The Misanthrope* and *The Imaginary Invalid*. In addition to these, you should become familiar with another of his works, *Tartuffe*.

Other figures likely to make an appearance on the Subject Test are novel writers from the nineteenth and twentieth centuries. The most important nineteenth-century figures from ETS's perspective are the Russian authors Dostoyevsky and Tolstoy, and the French writers Verne and Flaubert. The latter's *Madame Bovary* is an important work that is worth skimming. Charles Baudelaire is another author you should be familiar with. His poetry is distinctive for its dark power and bleak view of humanity. In the twentieth century, non-European authors like Nigerian Chinua Achebe and his work *Things Fall Apart* are popular with ETS. *Things Fall Apart* is a short, quick read, and it is a good idea to familiarize yourself with it. Other twentieth-century authors that ETS may refer to include Jean-Paul Sartre, Albert Camus, and Jorge Luis Borges.

Anglo-Saxon Period

The major Anglo-Saxon work you need to know for the GRE Literature in English is *Beowulf*. *Beowulf* is an ancient poem that was transmitted orally by Anglo-Saxon bards for centuries before it was written down sometime in the eighth century. It is important to have some general knowledge of the formal qualities that distinguish Old English verse. Remember that it is organized largely by alliteration rather than rhyme, and that it is driven primarily by stressed syllables rather than regular alterations between stressed and unstressed.

The basic plot outline that follows should help you answer questions regarding *Beowulf*, but it is strongly advised that you take a look at the poem in the original Old English so that you have a greater sense of how the poetry operates and what the words look like.

The plot follows the adventures of Beowulf, a Swedish hero who is enlisted by the Danish King Hrothgar to kill the monster Grendel. Grendel's mother seeks revenge but is also slain by Beowulf, who then becomes King of the Geats. Renowned for his bravery and strength, he is called out of retirement years later to fight a dragon, which he kills. Beowulf is mortally wounded, but names the young Wiglaf as his successor.

 Drill Questions

1. **The Danes and the Geats are the subject of**
    (A) *Beowulf.*
    (B) *The Dream of the Rood.*
    (C) *Ecclesiastical History of the English People.*
    (D) *Piers Plowman.*
    (E) *The Canterbury Tales.*

2. **The character Grendel in *Beowulf* is**
    (A) the monster.
    (B) the monster's mother.
    (C) Beowulf's closest friend.
    (D) Beowulf's mother.
    (E) Beowulf's father.

The Middle Ages

CHAUCER AND HIS CONTEMPORARIES

Geoffrey Chaucer is by far the most significant figure from this period. However, you should also know the other important Middle English authors listed here and what they wrote, if only to be able to eliminate them as possible answers for questions that deal with later periods.

The Canterbury Tales are Geoffrey Chaucer's central achievement and are written in Middle English. The date of composition is usually given as circa 1387. These tales exert a strong influence on the English literary imagination, and it is recommended that you read some of the major tales that are likely to be referenced by ETS. At a minimum, you should spend some time looking over excerpts of the text in order to become familiar with Chaucerian diction and spelling. He alternates between different verse forms and prose, but most of the major tales are written as poetry. "The General Prologue" outlines the major characters and sets the basic scene: a group of travelers are making a pilgrimage to Canterbury and decide to pass the time by engaging in a story-telling contest. The major tales are summarized below.

The Knight's Tale

A long, elaborate tale concerning the rivalry between Arcite and Palamon for the love of Emelye, a woman neither has met. After a convoluted series of events and changes of fortune, the young men stage a duel for Emelye's hand. Arcite prays to Mars and Palamon to Venus. A dispute erupts among the gods, and in the end each man is granted his wish: Arcite wins the duel, but dies immediately afterward, so that Palamon weds Emelye.

The Miller's Tale

It is important to know that generically "The Miller's Tale" is considered a fabliau, as are several other tales, including "The Reeve's Tale." "The Miller's Tale" is a bawdy tale of sexual misadventure between a carpenter's wife and a young student, Nicholas. Through a series of deceptions, the young lovers manage to force the carpenter into hiding in anticipation of a second great flood while they spend the night together. In a classic instance of Chaucerian ribaldry, they also manage to trick a foppish would-be suitor of the young wife into kissing her buttocks in the darkness. The enraged suitor gets his revenge against Nicholas with a hot poker, though, sending everything into chaos and bringing the carpenter bumbling back into the scene.

The Wife of Bath's Prologue and Tale

The Wife of Bath is a remarkable figure. The prologue, in which she gives her personal history, is probably just as important as her tale itself. The Wife of Bath is a surprisingly frank woman who is open about the joy she takes in sex. She has been married five times, and sexual partners other than her husbands are also alluded to. She is a popular figure for thinking about gender roles in the period: on the one hand, she is an example of the sexually voracious and permissive woman of misogynist discourse; on the other hand, the assertive stance she takes on her right to enjoy sex and her refusal to be submissive to a husband are sometimes read as articulations of a kind of proto-feminism. Her tale continues this double posture. In it, a knight is sent on a mission to answer the question "What do women really want?" as punishment for raping a maiden. A hideous old woman promises the answer in exchange for marriage. He reluctantly agrees, and she supplies him with the answer: sovereignty. She then transforms into a beautiful young woman.

The Pardoner's Tale

The Pardoner is androgynous and his sexuality is ambiguous. His tale is an allegory of greed and treachery. Three young drinking partners go in search of Death, which they find in the form of buried treasure. They agree to share the loot but quickly contrive to murder each other in order to increase their personal shares, and in the end they do find death—at each other's hands.

The Nun's Priest's Tale

This tale is most significant from ETS's perspective because of its form: it is a beast fable that follows the adventures of the cock Chanticleer and the wily fox that beguiles him.

WILLIAM LANGLAND

Langland, a contemporary of Chaucer, wrote *Piers Plowman* in alliterative verse, a throwback to earlier works like *Beowulf. Piers Plowman* is a series of allegorical visions wherein a protagonist, Will, seeks Truth.

JOHN GOWER

Gower is another contemporary of Chaucer. He is less likely to appear on the test, but it is useful to be able to place him as an important Middle English writer who produced the *Confessio Amantis*, a long discourse on the fortunes of lovers, told with a strong moral didacticism.

SIR THOMAS MALORY

Despite the French title of his major work, *Le Morte D'Arthur*, Malory's epic telling of the story of King Arthur is written in Late Middle English. It is an important work that can be differentiated from the many other famous Arthurian tales likely to be on the exam (such as Tennyson's *Idylls of the King* and parts of Spenser's "The Faerie Queene") because it is written in prose rather than poetry.

 Drill Questions

1. **Which of the following tales is a beast fable?**
    (A) "The Knight's Tale"
    (B) "The Nun's Priest's Tale"
    (C) "The Miller's Tale"
    (D) "The Pardoner's Tale"
    (E) "The Wife of Bath's Tale"

"Now let's be silent," said Truth. "It seems to me I see

Out of the nip of the north, not far from here,

Righteousness come running—let's wait right here,

For she knows far more than we—she was here before us both."

"That is so," said Mercy, "and I see here to the south

Where Peace clothed in patience comes sportively this way."

2. **This modernized passage is taken from**
    (A) William Langland's *Piers Plowman*.
    (B) *Sir Gawain and the Green Knight*.
    (C) Chaucer's "The Reeve's Tale."
    (D) Chaucer's "The Knight's Tale."
    (E) Sir Thomas Malory's *Le Morte D'Arthur*.

The Renaissance

The literature of the English Renaissance holds an important place in the English literary canon, and will take up a significant portion of the Subject Test. Below, we list several of the major figures and their best-known works. Most of these writers are primarily lyric poets so it is not possible to adequately summarize their works here—you will need to review the poets and poems we suggest in order to get a proper feel for the stylistic achievements of the period.

EDMUND SPENSER

Spenser is best known for his epic poem "The Faerie Queene." You should know that this project was never completed, and that it was largely a paean to Queen Elizabeth. "The Faerie Queene" is divided into six books, and is an allegory that follows the adventures of various knights, each representing a moral virtue. For instance, *Book I* tells the story of the Redcrosse Knight, the Knight of Holiness, while *Book V* tells the story of Artegall, the Knight of Justice. Loosely organizing the disparate tales is the figure of Prince Arthur, who makes brief appearances in each book and represents Magnificence, the perfection of mastering all the virtues.

Identifying Spenser is easy if you remember a few important things. First, you should keep in mind that for aesthetic reasons, Spenser deliberately wrote in archaic language, using Chaucerian diction and spelling. Also, Spenser developed what we now call the Spenserian stanza, a form that ETS often asks test-takers to identify. Spenserian stanza has been imitated by subsequent authors, but Spenser is almost always easy to spot because of his unusual spelling and word choice. The Spenserian stanza consists of nine lines that follow an *ababbcbcc* rhyme pattern. You should also be able to recognize that the Spenserian stanza ends with an alexandrine, a line in iambic hexameter, meaning that there are six syllables per unit rather than the five that comprise the iambic pentameter of the first eight lines.

CHRISTOPHER MARLOWE

Marlowe did not produce many plays or poems, but his work exerted a strong influence over his contemporaries, particularly Shakespeare. Marlowe was bold in both style and content. He employed blank verse to such effect in his plays that it became the dominant mode of stage poetry. His long poem

"Hero and Leander" retells a famous legend of tragic Greek lovers, while his *Dr. Faustus* tells the powerful story of a man who sells his soul to the devil. "The Passionate Shepherd to His Love" is a brief lyrical poem with which you should familiarize yourself. You should be able to recognize the basic plot of *Dr. Faustus* and the name Mephistopheles, the satanic agent with whom Faustus deals.

DONNE, JONSON, HERBERT, AND HERRICK

Except for Ben Jonson, who also produced several noteworthy plays, these are primarily lyric poets. John Donne, in particular, is an important figure and we suggest you carefully read all of the following poems, as well as any other Donne works you have time to look over: "The Canonization," "The Flea," "A Valediction: Forbidding Mourning," "The Sun Rising," and "Air and Angels." You should also take a look at some of his *Holy Sonnets*, in particular number 14, "Batter my heart." Donne is famous for his use of the metaphysical conceit—the witty comparison of unlike things. He is a highly intellectual poet, and his works can often be identified for his frequent allusions to science and alchemy. Donne's "Batter my heart" also shows a masterful use of *caesura*. Defined as a pause in the middle of a line of poetry, caesura brings variety to a poem's rhythm and adds emphasis to the words it surrounds. Read the following two lines from this sonnet as an example.

> That I may rise and stand, o'er throw me and bend
> Your force to break, blow, burn, and make me new.

Jonson's "To the Memory of My Beloved Master William Shakespeare" is a popular poem with ETS. You should read and remember its famous lines, in particular "He was not of an age, but for all time!" Jonson's poem "To Penshurst" is also worth reading as an example of the country-house genre of poems popular in the early seventeenth century. ETS occasionally will refer to his play *Volpone*, a comedy about a diverse group of scoundrels all out to swindle each other, and how the chief swindler, the title character (which means "fox") gets his just desserts at the end.

George Herbert wrote exclusively religious poems. He makes frequent use of metaphysical conceit, and his poems are often elaborate comparisons between objects or conditions and the relationship between humans and God. Read "The Pulley," "The Collar," and the "Prayer" poems. You should also be able to visually recognize his famous "shaped" poems: "The Altar," and "Easter Wings."

Robert Herrick is most famous for the line "Gather ye rosebuds while ye may" from his poem "To the Virgins, To Make Much of Time." Look at his "Corrinna's Going A-Maying" for further work with the *carpe diem* theme. You should also become familiar with his several "Julia" poems, which were widely imitated by his successors.

ANDREW MARVELL

Marvell is best known for his poem "To His Coy Mistress." You should study this poem carefully, as well as his "Mower" poems and his poem in praise of Milton's *Paradise Lost.*

JOHN MILTON

Milton has a few famous sonnets and lyric poems, but ETS is most concerned with *Paradise Lost. Paradise Lost* is one of the most frequently alluded to works in English literature. Its influence is enormous and you should be familiar with it. If you can't read all of it, we strongly recommend that you read the first two books to get a feel for Milton's style and diction, both of which are unusual. Milton is famous for his frequent use of Latinate and Greek words and for his sometimes confusing word order. *Paradise Lost* is Milton's epic of the fall of Adam and Eve in the Garden of Eden, as well as the titanic war in heaven and the expulsion of Satan and the rebel angels. Adam, Eve, Satan, God, Jesus, and the angel Raphael all make appearances.

WILLIAM SHAKESPEARE

At the center of the English literary canon is William Shakespeare. It is absolutely necessary that you be familiar with Shakespeare's work, although ETS does tend to concentrate on his better-known plays, so that an ability to recognize some names and plots can take the place of trying to make it through the entire Shakespeare canon. In addition to getting to know the plays listed here, you should become familiar with Shakespeare's sonnets, as well. They are popular with ETS as identifications, and in terms of form and content have exerted a strong influence over subsequent poets.

Hamlet

The most famous of Shakespeare's plays, *Hamlet*, is the story of a young man whose uncle has murdered his father and married his mother. The murdered father's ghost has visited Hamlet and demands revenge. The major characters are Hamlet, his father Old Hamlet, his uncle Claudius, his mother Gertrude, the advisor Polonius, Polonius's daughter Ophelia, Hamlet's friend Horatio, and the bumbling agents of the king, Rosencrantz and Guildenstern. You should read this play and be familiar with some of the major soliloquies, such as "To be or not to be," and "Oh that this too too sullied flesh would melt."

King Lear

A popular play with ETS, this tragedy concerns the old King's decision to divide his kingdom between his three daughters, Regan, Goneril, and Cordelia. Lear rashly banishes Cordelia because of her refusal to engage in hyperbolic flattery, and divides the kingdom between the two remaining daughters. The division of the kingdom is a disaster, and King Lear finds himself alienated from Cordelia and at odds with Regan and Goneril. Accompanied by his Fool and Poor Tom (a nobleman named Edgar in disguise), he goes mad and takes up residence in a desolate heath. Cordelia, ever loyal, returns with her husband, the French King, and an army to retake the land from her sisters and to rescue her father. The invasion fails and she is killed at the order of the bastard Edmund. Lear dies of grief.

Othello

Another tragedy, *Othello* tells the story of a Moor who marries a white Venetian noblewoman, Desdemona, against the wishes of her father. The action is then moved to Cyprus, where the sinister Iago, one of Shakespeare's most famous and compelling figures, poisons Othello's mind against his new wife. Through a series of coincidences and intricate plots set by Iago, Othello becomes convinced that Desdemona has been unfaithful to him with his officer Cassio. He then strangles her in her bed. Iago's treachery is revealed and the Moor kills himself, pronouncing that he has loved "not wisely, but too well."

Henry IV, Part I

A popular play among Shakespeare scholars, *Henry IV* contains one of Shakespeare's most popular characters, the fat knight Falstaff. Falstaff is an eloquent and witty figure who also happens to be a notorious liar and coward. Falstaff is a frequent answer to identification questions on the Subject Test—

you can usually identify him by his sarcastic and yet articulate rationalizations of his own shameful behavior. The play's other main figures are the young Prince Hal, the king's prodigal son and Falstaff's boon companion who eventually comes into his own as the "true prince," and Hal's rival Hotspur, who is leading a rebellion against the king. Hotspur is killed and the main part of the rebellion is put down as the play ends.

The Merchant of Venice

This play is famous for two characters in particular, the bold and intelligent heroine, Portia, and the compelling old Jew, Shylock. The plot revolves around Shylock's attempts to extract a cruel debt—a pound of flesh—from Antonio, a Venetian merchant. Portia, engaged to Antonio's best friend Bassanio, saves the day by going in disguise as a lawyer and turning the tables on Shylock in a dramatic court scene. In the end, Shylock is forced to convert to Christianity and forfeit his fortune, which he values above all things with miserly delight. The play is difficult because of the simultaneously sympathetic and anti-Semitic portrait it renders of Shylock and because it perennially vexes definitive interpretation. Was Shakespeare, like virtually all of his contemporaries, convinced of the inherent depravity of Jews and using his play as a vehicle to reiterate this commonplace, or was he attempting to make audiences question such practices? Particularly important for this debate is Shylock's famous speech in Act III, Scene i that begins "Hath not a Jew eyes?" Read and remember these lines. They are famous in and of themselves, and are often alluded to as a way of commenting on the things that unite all human beings. Equally famous and worth reviewing is Portia's "The quality of mercy" speech from Act IV, Scene i.

The Tempest

This is an increasingly popular play due to the growing interest in the history of European imperialism and postcolonial theory. The main characters are the exiled Duke of Milan, Prospero, his daughter Miranda, and a "deformed slave," Caliban. Prospero, Miranda, and Caliban are the sole inhabitants of an enchanted island, where Prospero practices magic and schemes to regain his dukedom by orchestrating the shipwreck of his usurping brother. By the play's end, he does regain his position and marries his daughter to the son of the King of Naples. Caliban is native to the island, and in a few important formulations, makes an early, eloquent case against colonialism.

Drill Questions

From you have I been absent in the spring,
When proud-pied April (dress'd in all his trim)
Hath put a spirit of youth in every thing,
That heavy Saturn laugh'd and leapt with him.
Yet nor the lays of birds, nor the sweet smell   5
Of different flowers in odor and hue,
Could make me any summer's story tell,
Or from their proud lap pluck them where they grew;
Nor did I wonder at the lily's white,
Nor praise the deep vermillion in the rose,   10
They were sweet, but figures of delight,
Drawn after you, you pattern of all those.
Yet seem'd it winter still, and, you away,
As with your shadow I with these did play.

1. **The referent of "these" in line 14 is**
    (A) birds.
    (B) stories.
    (C) flowers.
    (D) colors.
    (E) winter and spring.

2. **The author of this poem also wrote**
    (A) **"The Faerie Queene."**
    (B) *Paradise Lost.*
    (C) *Pamphilia to Amphilanthus.*
    (D) *The Winter's Tale.*
    (E) **"To His Coy Mistress."**

The Restoration and Eighteenth Century

This period is notable for its stage comedies and for its great works of satire. The major figures are John Dryden, Jonathan Swift, Alexander Pope, and Samuel Johnson, but we also mention a few other notable writers who have surfaced on past administrations of the Subject Test.

WYCHERLY AND CONGREVE

Exemplars of the Restoration comedy, William Wycherly and William Congreve produced comedies of manners and witty language use, highly charged with sexual and scatological innuendo. Wycherly is best known for *The Country-Wife*, and Congreve for *The Way of the World*. You should familiarize yourself with one of these to enable you to recognize the tone of these plays, as well as the type of character name that is often a give-away of this genre. Examples include Mrs. Pinchwife in *The Country-Wife* and Mincing in *The Way of the World*.

JOHN WILMOT, EARL OF ROCHESTER

Although he wrote on a number of subjects, Rochester is best known for his sexual poems that are shockingly explicit even by today's standards. It is unlikely that ETS would actually quote from him because of this, but he is significant as an example of the "court wits" that surrounded Charles II, and as an indicator of the decadence that characterizes much of the lore about the Restoration period.

JOHN DRYDEN

Dryden was a prolific writer, but ETS is mainly concerned with his poem "Absalom and Achitophel." Look over this poem to get a feel for its verse style and its content. It is a complex political allegory that uses biblical figures and events to stand in for a political crisis current in Dryden's time. His other work popular with ETS is "Mac Flecknoe," a mock epic that attacks Dryden's contemporary, the poet Thomas Shadwell. You should be able to identify the mock epic as a form, and be able to recognize this poem in particular. The mock epic (employed by Pope for "The Rape of the Lock,") is characterized by use of elaborate and grandiose language typical of the epic to describe mundane things and trivial events.

JONATHAN SWIFT

Swift is best known for two works: the satirical tract *A Modest Proposal*, and his longer work, *Gulliver's Travels. A Modest Proposal* is easy to recognize; in a precise and confident tone, it advocates the wholesale slaughter and consumption of poor children in Ireland. *Gulliver's Travels* is best remembered in association with these key names: the Lilliputians, who are very small; the Brobdignags, who are very large; the Houyhnhnms, very smart horses; and the Yahoos, brutish subhumans. It would be wise to look over at least the first two books of *Gulliver's Travels* to get a feel for Swift's incomparably witty prose style.

ALEXANDER POPE

Pope is one of the finest craftsmen in English poetics. His verses are polished and painstakingly wrought, and his wit rivals that of Swift. He writes almost exclusively in heroic couplets, so his work is often easy to spot. Read his "Essay On Man" to get a sense of his style, but spend the most time reviewing "The Rape of the Lock," the most famous mock epic in English. The story concerns an unappreciated haircut given to a lady by a lord at a high-society gathering and the chaos that ensues. Pope carefully follows the accepted epic conventions, and the result is a comedic and artistic achievement that stands out as one of the best-known works of the period.

ADDISON AND STEELE

Joseph Addison had a major hit with his tragedy *Cato*, but he is probably still best known in conjunction with Richard Steele and their periodical *The Spectator*. Addison and Steele's journalistic endeavors are important in the history of periodical publication and in the emerging category of the public intellectual in the eighteenth century. Looking over excerpts from *The Spectator* probably isn't worth the time and trouble, but you should know who these men are and be able to place them in this period.

JOHNSON AND BOSWELL

Although he authored a few poems, most notably "The Vanity of Human Wishes," produced a famous edition of Shakespeare's works, and is responsible for the first comprehensive English language dictionary, Samuel Johnson is best known to us through the work of his biographer, James Boswell. It is in Boswell's *Life of Samuel Johnson* and in his *Journal of a Tour of the Hebrides* that we get a taste of Johnson's enormous intellect, wit and eccentricity, fixing Johnson as one of the great minds in English literary history.

THE EARLY NOVELISTS: DEFOE, RICHARDSON, AND FIELDING

The novel has a long and complex history that involves developments in European and Classical literature, but generally speaking the English novel emerged in the beginning of the eighteenth century with the works of Daniel Defoe, Henry Fielding, and Samuel Richardson. You should be familiar with their positions as the first English novelists and with the themes and stylistic conventions that mark their respective works.

Daniel Defoe

Defoe is best known for *Robinson Crusoe*, although *Moll Flanders* has been known to appear on the Subject Test. *Robinson Crusoe*, of course, is the story of a man's solitary existence on an island following a shipwreck, the world he builds for himself there, and the native he eventually enlists as his servant, Friday. Defoe is known for his plain prose style and his journalistic style of reporting realistic details.

Samuel Richardson

Richardson's expansive works *Pamela* and *Clarissa* are landmarks of the early novel. They both concern the moral life of young women in England. In *Pamela*, as the subtitle tells us, virtue is rewarded when the young heroine, after a long resistance to the lascivious advances of her employer, Mr. B., is rewarded by his reformation and his sincere love. In contrast, *Clarissa* is a tragedy in which the morally upright heroine is raped by the rakish Lovelace and eventually slips into madness and death. Both novels take as a theme the importance of female chastity and virtue as a guiding force of morality in the face of rampant sexual vice. Richardson's novels are all epistolary in form, meaning that they are written as a series of letters to, from, and about the major characters involved. His writing is marked by attention to precise details of transcribed conversations and a sometimes intimidating length.

Henry Fielding

Fielding is best known for *Tom Jones*, a rollicking story about a man of mysterious origins who gets involved with various love affairs, fights, and controversies in pursuit of his true love, Sophia. Fielding and Richardson were bitter rivals and critics of each other's work. Fielding's style is marked by his conscious attempt to break away from Richardson's model of writing. Fielding does not write in the epistolary form, but instead creates a vigorous prose that is as ironic and skeptical as Richardson's work is pious and naive. *Shamela: Joseph Andrews* is Henry Fielding's parody of Richardson's *Pamela*, which he published one year after the original was released. In Fielding's version, Shamela is not as virtuous as she seems and the story of assailed virtue is changed to one of calculation.

Drill Questions

Mrs. Millamant: O, aye, letters—I had letters—I am persecuted with letters—I hate letters.—Nobody knows how to write letters; and yet one has 'em, one does not know why.—They serve to pin up one's hair.

Witwoud: Is that the way? Pray, madam, do you pin up your hair with all your letters? I find I must keep copies.

Mrs. Millamant: Only with those in verse, Mr. Witwoud. I never pin up my hair with prose. I think I tried once, Mincing.

Mincing: O mem, I shall never forget it.

1.   **The passage appears in**
      (A)   *The Way of the World.* ✓
      (B)   *Love for Love.*
      (C)   *The Importance of Being Earnest.*
      (D)   *A Midsummer Night's Dream.*
      (E)   *The Country-Wife.*

2. **Which of the following authors is known for producing epistolary novels?**

(A) John Dryden

(B) Jonathon Swift

(C) Daniel Defoe

(D) Henry Fielding

(E) Samuel Richardson ✓

The Romantic Era 1800 - 1830

Poems from the Romantic Era are popular among educators for their imaginative quality and for the invitation for close reading and interpretation that they offer. Many of the poems we list here make frequent appearances on Identification portions of the Subject Test, so you should take the time to familiarize yourself with them. The Romantic Era is usually said to cover roughly 1800 to 1830 or so, although the first major Romanticist, Blake, is a bit earlier. The period is characterized by a strong interest in nature, folk traditions, and the poetic rendering of interior, subjective emotions. There is also a strong undercurrent of political sentiment mainly pertaining to the French Revolution of 1792 and its aftershocks.

WILLIAM BLAKE

Blake is an extraordinary and unusual poet. His more complex works, such as *Milton* and *The Marriage of Heaven and Hell* will most likely not be on the Subject Test, but you should take the time to look through his *Songs of Innocence and Experience*, paying special attention to "Tyger." In his poem "Jerusalem," Blake writes, "I must Create a System or be enslav'd by another Man's," a fitting epigram for his career. His writing is characterized by his deeply personal theology and his unique philosophy, which is fairly consistent throughout his works. He protested against conservative theology and promoted a radical interpretation of Christianity that emphasized Christ's radical stance on social issues and his rebellious nature, and believed in embracing sexuality as ennobling and uplifting.

WILLIAM WORDSWORTH

Wordsworth is probably the preeminent figure of this period. His *Lyrical Ballads* should be studied closely, particularly because of his interest in rural settings and simple people. *Preface to Lyrical Ballads* outlines the essential elements of Romantic poetry. ETS also likes to extract famous passages from his enormous epic *The Prelude*, in which he traces the development of his poetic sensibility. This work is much too long and complicated to read for the test, but in addition to looking over several shorter pieces in *Lyrical Ballads*, you should be sure to look at the following excerpts from *The Prelude*: in Book First, read the passage that begins "One summer evening" and describes a childhood adventure in a small boat; from Book Sixth, look at the passage that describes crossing the Alps and the stanzas immediately following that begin "Imagination–here the powers so called." Finally, spend a little time skimming through most of Book Eighth, in which Wordsworth reviews his first 21 years as a way to understand his intellectual and emotional development.

SAMUEL TAYLOR COLERIDGE

Coleridge, Wordsworth's close friend and sometime collaborator, is best known for his *Biographia Literaria*, a collection of his aesthetic principles and lectures on literature, and "The Rime of the Ancient Mariner," his mystical, allegorical poem of sin and redemption. Glance over a few sections of the *Biographia* just to get a sense of the tone and style—excerpts will often appear in identification sections. Read "The Rime of the Ancient Mariner" and be able to identify its key symbols, particularly the albatross.

GEORGE GORDON, LORD BYRON

Byron has a strong style and a distinctive aesthetic charisma that will become familiar to you through consultation with a few key works. *Childe Harold's Pilgrimage* follows the course of the traveler Harold as he moves from a libertine existence of sin and pleasure to the revelations and realizations, both personal and universal, that he gains through his wanderings in Europe. Harold is important as an example of the "Byronic" hero, a figure characterized by contempt for conventional morality and a general sense of defiance coupled with a capacity for deep and strong emotional attachments. *Don Juan,* a very long, unfinished epic satire, is probably Byron's most famous work. Read excerpts in order to be able to recognize its form (ottava rima) and to familiarize yourself with the biting humor that saturates this work. Famous episodes include a shipwreck that leads to an incident of cannibalism, and the sale of the hero into slavery in the Ottoman Empire.

PERCY BYSSHE SHELLEY

Shelley's poetry is highly political and like many Romantic poets, deeply influenced by German philosophy. His great works include *Alastor, Prometheus Unbound,* and *The Triumph of Life.* Shelley's poetry is extremely dense and difficult to master in brief surveys. The best strategy is to look at excerpts from *Alastor* to familiarize yourself with his pithy verse style, and to read a few of his shorter pieces, including "The Cloud" and "To A Skylark." For a taste of his political radicalism, see the brief, acerbic "England in 1819."

JOHN KEATS

Keats' "Odes" have been widely influential and are perennial favorites with ETS for identification questions: "Ode to a Nightingale," "Ode on Melancholy," and the most famous, "Ode on a Grecian Urn," which includes the oft-quoted closing lines "'Beauty is truth, truth beauty' – that is all / Ye know on earth, and all ye need to know." The poems are short and worth a careful examination.

MARY SHELLEY

Mary Shelley is best known for her gothic novel *Frankenstein,* which explores the Faustian theme of human inquiry that infringes on divine prerogatives. The novel is saturated with Romantic themes, particularly in its long descriptions of the Swiss Alps and surrounding countryside, and is rich in allusions, particularly to Milton's *Paradise Lost.* It is a short book and a good example of both certain forms of the Gothic novel and the Romantic sensibility, and worth reading in preparation for the Subject Test.

Drill Questions

1. The albatross is a major figure in which of the following Romantic poems?
   - (A) Coleridge's "Rime of the Ancient Mariner" ✓
   - (B) Byron's *Childe Harold's Pilgrimage*
   - (C) Shelley's "The Cloud"
   - (D) Keats' "Ode to a Nightingale"
   - (E) Blake's "Tyger"

O Attic shape! Fair attitude! with brede

Of marble men and maidens overwrought,

With forest branches and the trodden weed;

Thou, silent form, dost tease us out of thought

As doth eternity: Cold Pastoral!

When old age shall this generation waste,

Thou shalt remain, in midst of other woe

Than ours, a friend to man, to whom thou say'st

"Beauty is truth, truth beauty," —that is all

Ye know on earth, and all ye need to know.

2. This stanza addresses
   - (A) men and maidens.
   - (B) Pastoral.
   - (C) youth.
   - (D) old age.
   - (E) a grecian urn. ✓

The Victorian Age

The literature of the Victorian Era is reflective of the profound changes that were taking place in England in the nineteenth century. Some of these changes include the industrial revolution and its effects, rapid urbanization, growing class tensions, and movements for wide-scale political reform.

JANE AUSTEN

Austen is one of the most important novelists of the nineteenth century. Her insights into the concerns and outlook of the upper classes and the petty gentry in peril of losing their fortunes revolve in particular around the social position of women and the complexities of marriage in the period. *Pride and Prejudice, Persuasion*, and *Sense and Sensibility* are her best-known works, and a thorough acquaintance with one of them should be sufficient for the Subject Test. Pay attention to her interest in financial arrangements and social status, as well as her dry humor and witty prose style.

ALFRED, LORD TENNYSON

Tennyson is probably the dominant poet of the Victorian period, possibly sharing this distinction with Robert Browning (see next page). Tennyson's interest in history and legend is evident in his epic *Idylls of the King*, and in the very important and influential poem "The Lady of Shallot." You should read the latter carefully, paying attention to its versification, and also look through his expansive poem *In Memoriam A.H.H.*, which contains the famous lines "It is better to have loved and lost, than to have never loved at all." You should also read his "The Charge of the Light Brigade" and "Mariana" to become familiar with his shorter works.

ELIZABETH BARRETT BROWNING

Elizabeth Barrett Browning is best known for her *Sonnets from the Portuguese*, especially sonnet 43 ("How do I love thee? Let me count the ways"). Read over a few and note their formal qualities.

ROBERT BROWNING

Browning is an important stylist whose vivid language and innovative use of the dramatic monologue in his poetry mark him as a strong and distinctive voice in English literature. His poems are complex and even the shorter ones often contain surprisingly pithy narratives. It is worth spending time working through a few Browning poems. In particular, you should read "My Last Duchess," "Porphyria's Lover," "Love Among the Ruins," and "The Last Ride Together."

JOHN RUSKIN

Ruskin is famous for his books and essays on art and architecture, and was considered one of the preeminent critics and lecturers of his time. He developed a strong, anti-modern philosophy that he promulgated in his writing and speaking, and which created a great deal of controversy. It would be difficult and unnecessary to do a comprehensive survey of Ruskin's work, but we would suggest looking through some excerpts from his *Modern Painters*, a multi-volume work that includes in Volume III, Part IV a celebrated discussion of the "pathetic fallacy," a literary term Ruskin coined to describe the poetic device wherein natural objects are given human emotions and capabilities, as in *Paradise Lost* when the earth groans from the transgression of Eve.

THE BRONTË SISTERS

Charlotte and Emily Brontë are responsible for two of the most celebrated novels of the nineteenth century: *Jane Eyre* and *Wuthering Heights*, respectively. Both books are very well-known and have exerted an enormous influence on subsequent novels in English. We recommend that you read one or both thoroughly.

Jane Eyre is the story of a young woman who survives a gloomy and abusive childhood to become a governess at the house of the mysterious Mr. Rochester, with whom she eventually falls in love. On the day of their proposed marriage, it is revealed that Mr. Rochester already is married to a mad woman, Bertha, who lives in the attic of his estate. Jane leaves Rochester and is taken in by the Rev. St. John Rivers and his sisters, who turn out to be Jane's cousins. St. John nearly convinces Jane to marry him and aid him in his missionary work in India before she returns to Mr. Rochester to find that he has been blinded and maimed in an attempt to rescue his wife from a fire in which she perishes. Jane marries him and as the novel ends, they have a child and Rochester's sight is partially restored.

Wuthering Heights is an emotionally charged novel told in a complicated series of time shifts and flashback narrations. The story revolves around the painful and passionate love between Catherine and the wild, violent Heathcliffe. Catherine cannot marry Heathcliffe, largely because of his uncertain origins, and instead marries the banal Linton as Heathcliffe flees. Heathcliffe returns three years later and embarks on a dark and at times sadistic path of revenge against everyone he feels has wronged him. By the novel's end, Catherine and her husband are dead and Heathcliffe longs to die to be reunited with his one true love. The story is at times morbid and bleak, but the ending suggests that the union of new generations of the families involved in the story will renew and heal the destructiveness of the previous ones.

CHARLES DICKENS

Dickens, in many respects, stands at the center of the Victorian period. In some critical assessments, he is as towering a figure for the nineteenth century as Shakespeare is for his period. Identifying Dickens' prose is not difficult if any characters are mentioned—he is famous for such unusual names as Murdstone, Magwitch, Pip, Uriah Heep, and Micawber, to name just a few. His major works include *Oliver Twist*, *A Tale of Two Cities*, *Great Expectations*, *David Copperfield,* and *Bleak House.* Dickens is known for his prolixity: *David Copperfield* and *Bleak House* are both very long books. You should try to read some of his work so that you are familiar with his distinctive style. We suggest *Great Expectations.* In addition, it is a good idea to look over the opening lines of a few of his novels—they are generally famous (in particular, *A Tale of Two Cities*) and ETS has been known to use them in identification questions. In general, Dickens favors themes about the hardships of working-class families and societal outcasts, evincing a strong interest in debtors prisons, workhouses, and dirty factories, while evincing a strong interest in the law. He is known for his surprise plot twists, often involving the introduction of long-lost or newly revealed relatives and unexpected inheritances.

MATTHEW ARNOLD

Arnold was both a poet and a critic. ETS is more interested in his poetry, in particular his famous lyric "Dover Beach," which you should be sure to read.

You should also remember Arnold as the person who first coined the phrase "sweetness and light" to describe the civilizing effect of aesthetic pleasure.

CHRISTINA ROSSETTI

Rossetti is a distinctive voice in Victorian poetics. Her most famous work is probably the long allegorical poem "Goblin Market," which explores issues of temptation, sin, and redemption in gothic language that is highly charged with sexual overtones. "A Birthday" is perhaps her next best-known work, and is short enough for thorough familiarization.

WALTER PATER

Pater's *Studies in the History of the Renaissance*, or simply *The Renaissance*, is one of the most important and influential books of the period. It is comprised of a series of essays on figures such as Leonardo da Vinci and Botticelli, and it played a pivotal role in the aesthetic movement of the later nineteenth century. Skim over the essay on Leonardo da Vinci, paying particular attention to his descriptions and analyses of the *Mona Lisa*.

CHARLES DARWIN

The Victorian Age as a period is highly tinctured by the influence of Darwin's theories of evolution as promulgated in his *The Descent of Man*. You should know the basics of Darwinism and the ways it was interpreted in the period as a useful context in which to think about Victorian literature.

OSCAR WILDE

Wilde is as well-known for his personality as he is for his literary accomplishments. His legion of witty aphorisms have survived into the present, and he is closely associated with the aesthetic movement that was popular in England at the close of the nineteenth century. His most famous works are probably the stage comedy *The Importance of Being Earnest* and the novel *The Picture of Dorian Gray*, a melodramatic allegory of sin, guilt, and obsession with beauty and youth.

Drill Questions

She cried "Laura," up the garden,

"Did you miss me?

Come and kiss me.

Never mind my bruises,

Hug me, kiss me, suck my juices

Squeezed from goblin fruits for you,

Goblin pulp and goblin dew.

Eat me, drink me, love me;

Laura, make much of me:

For your sake I have braved the glen

And had to do with goblin merchant men."

1. **This stanza is from a poem by the same author as**
    - (A) **"Dover Beach."**
    - (B) **"The Lady of Shallot."**
    - (C) **"A Birthday."** ✓
    - (D) ***Sonnets from the Portuguese.***
    - (E) **"The Bishop Orders His Tomb at Saint Praxed's Church."**

2. **Jean Rhys's novel *Wide Sargasso Sea* takes as its subject a character from another novel, the madwoman Bertha, from**
    - (A) **Charles Dickens' *Bleak House.***
    - (B) **Charles Dickens' *Great Expectations.***
    - (C) **Matthew Arnold's "Dover Beach."**
    - (D) **Emily Brontë's *Wuthering Heights.***
    - (E) **Charlotte Brontë's *Jane Eyre.*** ✓

Pre-Twentieth Century American Authors

American literature is still considered a kind of younger sibling to English literature, and this bias is reflected on the Subject Test. This does not mean, however, that you can skip studying American authors altogether. You do need to have a sense of who the major figures are and be familiar with their works and periods.

NATHANIEL HAWTHORNE

Hawthorne is best known for his novels *The House of the Seven Gables* and *The Scarlet Letter*. Questions on the Subject Test will most likely address the latter. You should read this book and be familiar with the major characters and its setting in a Puritan community in colonial America: Hester Prynne, a woman who is ostracized for having a child out of wedlock and refusing to reveal the name of the father; her baby girl, Pearl; Roger Chillingsworth, her estranged husband who returns after she has had her baby and covertly seeks to discover and take revenge on the man who dishonored him; and Dimmesdale, the young and seemingly upright minister who is later revealed to be the father.

WALT WHITMAN

Whitman is one of the most important figures in all of American literature. His style is distinctive and his subject matter can generally be reduced to a few themes that make it easier to identify him: democracy, self, sensuality (including, at times, explicit homoeroticism) and transcendental philosophy. His major work is *Leaves of Grass*, a collection of poems that he continued to expand and revise throughout his entire career. In particular, you should read and become familiar with "Song of Myself."

EMILY DICKINSON

Dickinson is recognizable by her blunt, clipped versification and frequent use of the dash. Her poems are short and once you've read a few you will have little trouble recognizing her work on identification questions. In particular, look at "Because I could not stop for Death," "Bee! I'm Expecting You," and "Hope is the Thing With Feathers."

HERMAN MELVILLE

Melville's massive novel *Moby Dick* is considered one of the great achievements of American literature. If you have not already read it, you probably will not have time to in preparation for the Subject Test. We suggest you do take time to read through some parts of the book, however. It is a generically unstable work that alternates between a first-person narrative, drama (complete with stage directions), and chapters on whaling. The central figure is the fanatical Captain Ahab who destroys his ship, *The Pequod,* and all but one of his crew in his furious pursuit of the whale Moby Dick who has chewed off Ahab's leg. The sometime narrator and sole survivor is Ishmael, who famously begins the book by announcing his name: "Call me Ishmael." Other important characters include Starbuck, Father Marple, who delivers a stirring sermon to the crew, and the harpooner, Queequeg.

MARK TWAIN

Mark Twain is the pen name of Samuel Langhorne Clemens. The famous American humorist and writer is most celebrated for his novels *The Adventures of Tom Sawyer* and *The Adventures of Huckleberry Finn*, which describe Mississippi frontier life. *The Innocents Abroad* is about American tourists, *The Prince and the Pauper* is about a democratic switch in places between the two title characters, and *A Connecticut Yankee in King Arthur's Court* is a satirical look at history and Twain's contemporary society. *Puddn'head Wilson* concerns itself with questions of race.

Drill Questions

Her breast is fit for pearls,

But I was not a "Diver"—

Her brow is fit for thrones

But I have not a crest.

Her heart is fit for home—

I—Sparrow—build there
Sweet of twigs and twine
My perennial nest.

1. **The author of the above poem also wrote**
    (A) **"Song of Myself."**
    (B) **"Because I could not stop for Death."** ✓
    (C) **"The Imaginary Iceberg."**
    (D) **"The Emperor of Ice-Cream."**
    (E) **"Song for a Red Nightgown."**

I hear America singing, the varied carols I hear,
Those of mechanics, each one singing his as it should be
    blithe and strong,
The carpenter singing his as he measures his plank or beam,
The mason singing his as he makes ready for work, or
    leaves off work,

2. **The author of the above excerpt also wrote**
    (A) **"Song of Myself."** ✓
    (B) **"Because I could not stop for Death."**
    (C) **"The Imaginary Iceberg."**
    (D) **"The Emperor of Ice-Cream."**
    (E) **"Song for a Red Nightgown."**

The Twentieth Century

CHARLOTTE PERKINS GILMAN

An ardent feminist and political activist, Charlotte Perkins Gilman is best remembered for her short story *The Yellow Wallpaper*, which tells the story of a young writer who, after the birth of her first child, is forbidden by her physician husband to see the baby or to write because of her "nervousness." Confined to an attic room, without the release of writing which she repeatedly craves, the woman begins to believe she sees a woman trapped behind the intricate pattern of the wallpaper in her room, and quickly spirals into complete madness.

Perkins Gilman's novel, *Herland*, tells the story of a utopic world of women, in which they live in harmony with each other and their environment. The present patriarchal system of the world is implicitly criticized through this alternative vision and the narration of the story by a male visitor who contrasts this utopian world with the one from which he comes.

THOMAS HARDY

Hardy's best-known novels are *Jude the Obscure* and *Tess of the D'Urbervilles,* both of which elicited stinging negative reviews upon their publication in the 1890s. *Jude the Obscure* centers around the life of Jude Fawley and his intellectual ambition to study at a prestigious university. He marries the barmaid Arabella, then falls in love and lives with his unconventional cousin, Sue Bridehead. After the tragic death of their children, Sue leaves him to return to her husband and the church, and Jude goes back to Arabella and dies an early death.

Tess of the D'Urbervilles tells the story of a poor girl whose father is descended from the D'Urbervilles. She is seduced by Alec D'Urberville, and the product of this seduction dies soon after birth. Tess becomes a dairymaid and falls in love with Angel Clare. On their marriage night, Tess confesses her history to him, and although he too has had past sexual experience, he hypocritically leaves Tess. Tess and her family are again thrown into poverty, and to alleviate her family's suffering, Tess becomes Alec's mistress once again. Angel Clare repents his behavior and returns from abroad to find Tess and Alec living together. Tess goes mad and stabs Alec to death. After being briefly reunited with Angel, Tess is arrested, tried, and hanged.

GEORGE BERNARD SHAW

Shaw was a freethinker, feminist, socialist, and vegetarian whose more than 50 plays dealt with social issues of his day. His more famous plays include *Arms and the Man*, *Man and Superman*, *Major Barbara*, and *Pygmalion*. Shaw's witty plays concentrate on the conflict between thought and belief.

JOSEPH CONRAD

Conrad was born in Ukraine of Polish parents; he became a British citizen when he was about thirty. He published his first novel in English, his third language, when he was 38. Conrad had been a sailor for twenty years, and most of his novels and short stories are set at sea. Conrad's most widely taught novel is *Heart of Darkness*, which concerns itself with the inhumanity and corruptibility of man in telling the story of the British ivory trade in Africa. Marlowe, the narrator, relates his experience in Africa to his fellow sailors and gives his listeners a portrait of the agent Kurtz, who has degenerated during his reign of absolute power over the village in Africa.

The Secret Agent of this title is Verloc, who runs a pornographic magazine shop as a cover for his spying for the British government on the ineffectual anarchists of London. In an attempt to discredit the anarchists, Verloc inadvertently causes the death of his wife's brother, Stevie. Winnie, who had only married Verloc in order to secure the future of her brother and her mother, is overcome with grief and anger and stabs Verloc to death, and eventually commits suicide.

WILLIAM BUTLER YEATS

An Irish nationalist poet, Yeats' poems are short enough that you should read through his most well-known poems, such as "The Lake Isle of Innisfree," "Who Goes With Fergus," "The Man Who Dreamed of Faeryland," "The Wild Swans at Coole," "Easter 1916," "The Second Coming," "A Prayer for My Daughter," "Sailing to Byzantium," "Leda and the Swan," and "Crazy Jane Talks with the Bishop."

E. M. FORSTER

Forster's most famous novels are *A Room With A View*, *Howard's End*, *A Passage to India*, and *Maurice*. *Howard's End* tells the story of the clash between lifestyles: the Schlegel siblings care for music, literature, and conversation, while the Wilcox family values the business world and practicality. The interactions between the two families take place in Howard's End, the ancestral home of the gentle and dignified Mrs. Wilcox. *A Passage To India* concerns itself with society in India under British rule. The protagonist is Dr. Aziz, a Muslim doctor who pursues relationships with the British until the racist assumptions of the British cause a crisis in relations between the communities. *A Room With A View* portrays the experiences of English tourists in Italy. Forster wrote *Maurice* circa 1913 but arranged that it be published posthumously because of the homosexual content.

VIRGINIA WOOLF

Woolf is considered one of the foremost Modernist writers because of her innovative, experimental style and her involvement in the literary world; she not only wrote important novels but also wrote literary criticism and essays, and, along with her husband, founded the Hogarth Press.

The most well-known of Virginia Woolf's novels is *Mrs. Dalloway*, which portrays a day in the life of a society woman. As Clarissa Dalloway spends the day preparing for a party she is giving that evening, she repeatedly recalls moments of her past, rendering for the reader a story of female development. Clarissa focuses on the romantic friendships she had with Sally Seton and Peter Walsh and her ultimate decision to sublimate her feelings for Sally and to refuse Peter's marriage proposal in favor of a union with the safe and sedate Richard Dalloway. Other characters include the Dalloways' daughter, Elizabeth; Elizabeth's tutor, Miss Kilman; and Septimus Warren Smith, a shell-shocked veteran of the World War and his Italian wife, Rezia. Woolf's innovative use of interior monologue and stream-of-consciousness technique in the telling of the story has made it a classic of Modernist writing.

To the Lighthouse (1927) portrays the Ramsays (Mrs. Ramsay is maternal while Mr. Ramsay is self-centered), their children, and their guests. The novel is divided into three parts, the first part describes a vacation during which Mr. Ramsay prevents the group of his family and friends from taking a desired trip to the lighthouse. The second part reports the death of Mrs. Ramsay and also the death of one of the sons in the war. The last part of the novel describes the arrival of some of the original guests and the trip made to the lighthouse by Mr. Ramsay and some of the children. An important character is the guest Lily Briscoe, who illustrates the struggles of female artists and the problems of same-sex desire in her frustrated attempts to paint and to express her love for Mrs. Ramsay.

The novel *Orlando* is styled as a biography and tells the story of Orlando's life, which spans several centuries and two genders. Woolf considered an androgynous mind to be ideal, and this idea is played out when Orlando changes sex yet remains essentially the same person.

Also well known is Woolf's essay *A Room of One's Own*, in which she argues that women need financial independence and a workspace (a room of one's own) in order to become writers. Woolf details the disadvantages that have kept women from becoming writers in the past and honors the women in history who managed to become successful writers despite these disadvantages.

JAMES JOYCE

The most famous novel of this famed Irish Modernist is *Ulysses*, which centers on one day in the life of Leopold Bloom and Stephen Dedalus. The novel is set in Dublin and employs stream-of-consciousness technique as well as many other experiments in language in the telling of the story. Stephen Dedalus is also the protagonist in *A Portrait of the Artist as a Young Man*, which is an autobiographical work telling the story of Stephen's development into a young intellectual. *Dubliners* is a collection of short stories, and *Finnegan's Wake* tells the story of a Dublin barkeeper, Humphrey Chimpden Earwicker, through the representation of his thoughts during one night of sleep.

D. H. LAWRENCE

Lawrence's major novels are *Sons and Lovers*, *The Rainbow*, *Women in Love*, and *Lady Chatterly's Lover*. *Sons and Lovers* tells the story of the working-class Morel family in a coalmining village. *The Rainbow* tells the story of the Brangwen family, the passionate marriage of the parents and the development of the children, especially Ursula. Ursula has an intimate relationship with a female teacher which ends with the teacher's marriage. Ursula decides to earn her living as a teacher and enrolls in college. She then has a passionate relationship with a man which she eventually breaks off. The stories of the Brangwen daughters Ursula and Gudrun are the focus of *Women in Love*. In *Women in Love*, Ursula is established as a teacher at the grammar school while Gudrun completes her own studies and has an affair with Gerald. Gudrun and Gerald's relationship is destructive, and Ursula's boyfriend offers to have an intimate relationship with Gerald, but Gerald declines. Ursula and Birkin marry and grow increasingly closer while Gudrun becomes involved with a sculptor and Gerald lays down in the snow and dies. *Lady Chatterly's Lover* concerns itself with a woman who leaves her husband for her lover. The writing is sexually explicit and was not published in England until 1960. As a whole, Lawrence's work portrays the mystical and cyclical qualities of sexual relationships against a backdrop of industrialism. Because of the content, Lawrence's works were repeatedly charged with obscenity by the authorities.

T. S. ELIOT

Eliot's most famous poem is "The Waste Land," which conveys the feeling of postwar society. Also well known is the humorous poem "The Love Song of J. Alfred Prufrock." Eliot is considered one of the foremost Modernist writers; you should familiarize yourself with these two poems for the GRE Literature in English. Eliot was also a well-known and influential literary critic—it is a good idea to skim through some of his essays to become familiar with his opinionated and erudite scholarship.

SAMUEL BECKETT

Beckett is known for his innovative novels and stage plays. His best-known work is *Waiting for Godot*—it is a good idea to read this over. It will give you a taste for his style and, more importantly, introduce you to some of his recurring themes, namely a bleak outlook on existence and a predilection for writing dramas about the failure of anything to ever really take place.

W. H. AUDEN

Auden is one of the most gifted poetic stylists of this century. His poems evince a technical virtuosity that is rare among modern writers. Look at a few of his better-known poems to get a sense of his style and diction: "In Memory of W. B. Yeats," "Musée des Beaux Arts," and "In Praise of Limestone."

DYLAN THOMAS

Thomas, a Welshman, is best known for two works: "Fern Hill" and "Do

Not Go Gentle Into That Good Night." You should read both of these poems carefully and pay attention to his Romantic and rhetorical style.

LANGSTON HUGHES

Hughes wrote poetry, novels, essays, and plays about the African-American experience. His most famous poem is "Harlem," in which he wonders aloud about what happens to a dream (and the dreamer) when a dream remains unfulfilled.

GWENDOLYN BROOKS

Gwendolyn Brooks, a prolific poet, is closely associated with the Black Arts Movement of the 1960s–1970s, especially in Chicago, her hometown. Brooks' style varies widely; she writes in both traditional forms and free verse, both dramatic and narrative poetry. The subject matter of her poems also varies widely; two of her most famous poems are "The Mother," about abortion, and "Gay Chaps at the Bar."

JAMES WALDEN JOHNSON

James Walden Johnson was an important figure in the Harlem Renaissance who, as poet and editor, took part in literary debates of the time. He is best known for his only novel, *The Autobiography of an Ex-Colored Man*, and his book of poems, *God's Trombones, Seven Negro Sermons in Verse*.

 Drill Questions

No! I am not Prince Hamlet, nor was meant to be;

Am an attendant lord, one that will do

To swell a progress start a scene or two,

Advise the prince; no doubt, an easy tool,

Deferential, glad to be of use,
Politic, cautious, and meticulous;
Full of high sentence, but a bit obtuse;
At times, indeed, almost ridiculous—
Almost, at times, the Fool.

1.   The speaker of this poem compares himself to
     (A)   Hamlet.
     (B)   Shakespeare.
     (C)   Polonius.
     (D)   Claudius.
     (E)   the Fool.

2.   The stanza is excerpted from
     (A)   "The Waste Land."
     (B)   "The Love Song of J. Alfred Prufrock." ✓
     (C)   "The Lake Isle of Innisfree."
     (D)   "Who Goes with Fergus?"
     (E)   "In Memory of W. B. Yeats."

Note: This review is by necessity incomplete. It is impossible for us to go into great detail about individual authors or to be all-inclusive, just as it is impossible for you to study all of English literature in preparation for this test. We encourage you to refer to the more exhaustive list that follows as a general reference. And as a further aid, we have marked with an asterisk those titles in our MAXnotes® series of literary digests.

SUGGESTED READING LIST

Achebe, Chinua. *Things Fall Apart*

Adams, Henry. *The Education of Henry Adams*

Addison, Joseph. *The Pleasures of the Imagination*, "Tulips"

Aeschylus. *The Libation Bearers, Oresteia*

Algren, Nelson. *The Man with the Golden Arm*

Amis, Kingsley. *Lucky Jim*

Angelou, Maya. *I Know Why the Caged Bird Sings* *

Anouilh, Jean. *The Lark*

Aristophanes. *Lysistrata*

Aristotle. *On the Art of Poetry, Poetics*

Arnold, Matthew. "Dover Beach," "The Scholar-Gypsy," *The Study of Poetry*, "Thyrsis," "To Marguerite – Continued"

Atwood, Margaret. *The Handmaid's Tale, Lady Oracle*

Auden, W.H. "In Memory of W.B. Yeats," "Musée des Beaux Arts"

Auerbach, Eric. *Mimesis: The Representation of Reality in Western Literature*

Austen, Jane. *Emma,* * *Northanger Abbey, Pride and Prejudice,* * *Sense and Sensibility*

Baldwin, James. *Go Tell it On the Mountain, Notes of a Native Son*

Baraka, Amiri (Leroi Jones). "Poem for Half White College Students"

Barth, John. *Lost in the Funhouse*

"The Battle of Maldon"

Beckett, Samuel. *Murphy, Waiting for Godot* *

Bede. *Historia Ecclesiastica Gentis Anglorum*

Behan, Brendan. *The Hostage*

Behn, Aphra. *Oroonoko: Or, the Royal Slave*

Bellow, Saul. *Henderson the Rain King, Seize the Day*

Beowulf *

Bishop, Elizabeth. "One Art"

Blair, Robert. "The Grave"

Blake, William. "The Lamb," "London," *The Marriage of Heaven and Hell*, "The Tyger"

Booth, Wayne C. *The Rhetoric of Fiction*

Borges, Jorge Luis. *The Garden of Forking Paths*

Boswell, James. *The Life of Samuel Johnson, LL.D.*

Brecht, Bertolt. *The Caucasian Chalk Circle, St. Joan of the Stockyards, The Threepenny Opera*

Brode, Anthony. "Breakfast with Gerard Manley Hopkins"

Brontë, Charlotte. *Jane Eyre* *

Brontë, Emily. *Wuthering Heights* *

Brooks, Gwendolyn. "We Real Cool"

Browne, Sir Thomas. *Religio Medici*

Browning, Elizabeth Barrett. "Aurora Leigh," *Sonnets from the Portuguese*

Browning, Robert. "The Bishop Orders His Tomb at Saint Praxed's Church," "Fra Lippo Lippi," "The House Holder," "My Last Duchess," "Porphyria's Lover"

Bryant, William Cullen. "The Death of Lincoln"

Bunyan, John. *The Pilgrim's Progress*

Burke, Edmund. *Speech on Conciliation with the Colonies*

Burney, Fanny. *Evelina*

Burns, Robert. "A Red, Red Rose," "Tam o' Shanter," "To a Louse [On Seeing One on a Lady's Bonnet at Church]"

Burton, Robert. *Anatomy of Melancholy*

Butler, Samuel (1612-1680). "Hudibras"

Butler, Samuel (1835-1902). *Erewhon, The Way of All Flesh*

Byrd, William. *The History of the Dividing Line*

Byron, George Gordon, Lord. *Childe Harold's Pilgrimage, Don Juan, Manfred,* "She Walks in Beauty"

Campion, Thomas. "When to Her Lute Corinna Sings"

Camus, Albert. *The Myth of Sisyphus, The Stranger* *

Carlyle, Thomas. *Characteristics, On Heroes, Hero Worship, and the Heroic in History, Portrait of His Contemporaries, Sartor Resartus*

Carroll, Lewis. *Alice's Adventures in Wonderland,* "Jabberwocky"

Cather, Willa. *Death Comes to the Archbishop, My Antonia* *

Centlivre, Susanna. *A Bold Stroke for a Wife, The Busie Bodie*

Cervantes, Miguel de. *Don Quixote*

Chaucer, Geoffrey. *The Canterbury Tales,* * *Troylus and Criseyde*

Chekhov, Anton. *The Cherry Orchard, The Darling*

Chopin, Kate. *The Awakening,* * *The Story of an Hour*

Cibber, Colley. *Love's Last Shift*

Coleridge, Samuel Taylor. *Biographia Literaria,* "Frost at Midnight," "On Donne's Poetry," "The Rime of the Ancient Mariner," *Table Talk*

Congreve, William. *The Way of the World*

Conrad, Joseph. *Heart of Darkness,* * *Lord Jim, The Secret Sharer*

Cooper, James Fenimore. *The Deerslayer, The Pioneers*

Cortazar, Julio. *Blow-Up*

Crabbe, George. "The Village"

Crane, Stephen. "The Open Boat," *The Red Badge of Courage*

Cullen, Countee. "From the Dark Tower"

Cumberland, Richard. *The West Indian*

cummings, e.e. "A salesman is an it that stinks Excuse"

Dante Alighieri. *The Divine Comedy I: Inferno* *

Declaration of Independence

Defoe, Daniel. *Moll Flanders,* * *Robinson Crusoe*

De Quincey, Thomas. "Confessions of an English Opium Eater"

Dickens, Charles. *Bleak House, David Copperfield, Great Expectations,* * *Hard Times,* * *The Pickwick Papers*

Dickinson, Emily. "Because I could not stop for Death," "I reason, earth is short," "If I can stop one heart from breaking," "That after Horror – that 'twas us"

Donne, John. "The Bait," *Devotions Upon Emergent Occasions,* "The Flea," "The Sun Rising," "A Valediction Forbidding Mourning"

Dos Passos, John (Roderigo). *The Big Money*

Dostoyevsky, Fyodor. *Crime and Punishment*

Douglass, Frederick. *The Narrative Life of Frederick Douglass*

Drayton, Michael. "Since there's no help, come let us kiss and part"

Dreiser, Theodore (Herman Albert). *An American Tragedy, Sister Carrie*

Drummond, William. *Notes on Ben Jonson*

Dryden, John. "Absalom and Achitophel," "Alexander's Feast," *All For Love, The Conquest of Granada,* "Epigram on Milton," *Essay of Dramatic Poesy, An Evening's Love,* "Mac Flecknoe," "Ode to Mrs. Anne Killigrew," "A Song for St. Cecilia's Day"

Edwards, Jonathan. *Personal Narrative, Sinners in the Hands of an Angry God*

Eliot, George. *Adam Bede, Middlemarch,* * *Silas Marner*

Eliot, T.S. *Hamlet and His Problems,* "The Love Song of J. Alfred Prufrock," *Tradition and the Individual Talent,* "The Waste Land"

Ellison, Ralph. *Invisible Man* *

Emerson, Ralph Waldo. "Brahma," *Divinity School Address, Journals,* "Nature," "Poet," "Self-Reliance," "Two Rivers"

Erik's Saga

Etherege, Sir George. *The Man of Mode*

Euripides. *Iphigenia at Aulis, Medea* *

Everyman

Farrell, James T. *Studs Lonigan*

Faulkner, William. *As I Lay Dying,* * "The Bear," "A Rose for Emily," *The Sound and the Fury* *

Fielding, Henry. *Joseph Andrews, Tom Jones*

Finch, Anne. "Adam Pos'd"

Fish, Stanley. *Is There a Text in This Class?*

Fitzgerald, F. Scott. *Babylon Revisited, The Great Gatsby* *

Flaubert, Gustave. *Madame Bovary*

Fleming, William. *Arts and Ideas*

Fletcher, Phineas. *The Purple Island*

Ford, John. *'Tis Pity She's a Whore*

Forster, E. M. *Aspects of the Novel, Howard's End, A Passage to India,* * *The Road to Colonus, A Room With a View, What I Believe, Where Angels Fear to Tread*

Foster, Hannah Webster. *The Coquette*

Fowles, John. *Wormholes*

Franklin, Benjamin. *Autobiography*

Freneau, Philip (Morin). "The House of Night"

Frost, Robert. "Design," "Meeting and Passing," "Mending Wall," "Mowing," "The Road Not Taken"

Frye, Northrop. *Anatomy of Criticism*

Gay, John. *The Beggar's Opera*

Gide, Andre. *The Counterfeiters*

Ginsberg, Allen. "Howl"

Godwin, William. *Caleb Williams*

Goethe, Johann Wolfgang von. *Faust, The Sorrows of Young Werther*

Gogol, Nikolai. *The Diary of a Madman*

Goldman, Emma. *In Jail*

Goldsmith, Oliver. "The Deserted Village," *National Prejudices, She Stoops to Conquer, The Vicar of Wakefield*

Gower, John. *Confessio Amantis*

Gray, Thomas. "The Bard on a Pindaric Ode," "Elegy Written in a Country Churchyard," "Ode on the Death of a Favourite Cat, Drowned in a Tub of Gold Fishes," *The Progress of Poesy*

Greene, Henry Graham. *Monsignor Quixote, The Quiet American*

Halle, Morris. *The Rules of Language*

Hardy, Thomas. "Ah, Are you Digging on my Grave?" *Far From the Madding Crowd,* "Hap," *Jude the Obscure,* * *Neutral Tones, The Return of the Native, Tess of the D'Urbervilles* *

Hawthorne, Nathaniel. *The Minister's Black Veil—A Parable, My Kinsman, Major Molineux, The Scarlet Letter,* * *Young Goodman Brown*

Hazlitt, William. *My First Aquaintance with Poets, On the Pleasure of Hating*

Heller, Joseph. *Catch-22*

Hemingway, Ernest. *A Clean, Well-Lighted Place, For Whom the Bell Tolls, Hills Like White Elephants, The Killers, The Old Man and the Sea, The Short Happy Life of Francis Macomber, The Sun Also Rises* *

Herbert, George. "The Altar," "Easter Wings," "The Pulley"

Herrick, Robert. "To the Virgins, to Make Much of Time," "Upon Julia's Clothes"

Hesse, Hermann. *Siddartha*

Heywood, Thomas. *A Woman Killed With Kindness*

Hobbes, Thomas. *Leviathan*

Holmes, Oliver Wendell. "The Chambered Nautilus," "Elsie Venner," "My Aunt"

Home, John. *The Fatal Discovery*

Homer. *The Iliad,* * *The Odyssey* *

Hopkins, Gerard Manley. "Carrion Comfort," "Pied Beauty," "Spring and Fall," "Thou art Indeed Just, Lord, If I Contend," "The Windhover"

Horace. *Art of Poetry, Epistles*

Housman, A.E. "To an Athlete Dying Young," "When I Was One-and-Twenty"

Howells, William Dean. *Criticism and Fiction*

Hughes, James Langston. "Harlem"

Hume, David. *Of Tragedy, Of the Standard of Taste*

Hurston, Zora Neale. *Their Eyes Were Watching God* *

Huxley, Aldous. *Brave New World,* * *Point Counter Point, Science and Culture*

Huxley, Sir Julian Sorell. *Memories*

Ibsen, Henrik. *A Doll's House, An Enemy of the People, The Wild Duck*

Ionesco, Eugene. *The Chairs, The Lesson, Rhinoceros*

Irving, Washington. *The Golden Reign of Wouter Van Twiller, Rip Van Winkle, The Sketch Book of Geoffrey Crayon, Gent*

James, Henry. *The Ambassadors, The Art of Fiction, The Aspern Papers, The Beast in the Jungle, The Golden Bowl, The Portrait of a Lady,* * *What Maisie Knew*

Johnson, Samuel, Dr. *Life of Cowley, The Lives of the English Poets,* "Of Bashfulness," "The Preface to Shakespeare," *Rasselas, The Vanity of Human Wishes*

Jonson, Ben. *Discoveries,* "Ode on the Death of Sir H. Morison," "On My First Son," "Perfection in Small Things," "Pleasure Reconciled to Virtue," "To the Reader," *Volpone or The Fox*

Joyce, James. *Dubliners,* * *A Portrait of the Artist as a Young Man,* * *Ulysses*

Kafka, Franz. *A Hunger Artist, The Metamorphosis* *

Keats, John. "Endymion," "The Eve of St. Agnes," *Isabella*, "La Belle Dame sans Merci," *The Letters*, "Ode on a Grecian Urn," "Ode on Melancholy," "Ode to a Nightingale," "On First Looking into Chapman's Homer"

Kempe, Margery. *Book of Margery Kempe*

Kerouac, Jack. *On the Road* *

Kitto, H.D.F. *Form and Meaning in Drama*

Koch, Kenneth. "Variations on a Theme by William Carlos Williams"

Kyd, Thomas. *Spanish Tragedy*

Lactantius Caecilius (or Caelius) Firmanus. *Divinae Institutiones*

La Fontaine, Jean de. "The Acorn and the Pumpkin"

Langland, William. *Piers Plowman*

Lardner, Ring. "Haircut"

Lawrence, D. H. *Edgar Allan Poe*, "The Horse Dealer's Daughter," *John Galsworthy, The Rainbow*, "The Rocking-Horse Winner," *Sons and Lovers, Surgery for the Novel -Or a Bomb, Thomas Hardy, Thomas Mann, Why the Novel Matters, Women in Love*

Leibniz, Gottfried Wilhelm. *Monadologie*

Leonard, William Ellery. *Two Lives*

Le Sage, Alain-Rene. *Histoire de Gil Blas de Santillane*

Lessing, Doris. *The Golden Notebook, Sunrise on the Veld*

Lessing, G.E. *Laokoon*

Lewis, C.S. *The Allegory of Love*

Lillo, George. *The London Merchant*

Lindsay, Vachel. "The Leaden-Eye'd"

Locke, John. *An Essay Concerning Human Understanding*

Longfellow, Henry Wadsworth. *Keats, The Song of Hiawatha, Evangeline*

Longinus. *On the Sublime*

Lovelace, Richard. "To Althea, From Prison"

Lowell, Amy. *Tendencies in Modern American Poetry*

Lowell, James Russell. *The Biglow Papers, A Fable for Cities, The Present Crisis, Thoreau*

Lowell, Robert. "For the Union Dead," "Mr. Edwards and the Spider," "The Quaker Graveyard in Nantucket"

Lubbock, Percy. *The Craft of Fiction*

Lyly, John. *Campaspe, Euphues: The Anatomy of Wit*

Machiavelli, Niccolo. *The Prince*

Mackenzie, Henry. *The Man of Feeling*

MacLeish, Archibald. "Ars Poetica"

Macpherson, James. *Fingal, Temora*

Magna Carta

Malory, Sir Thomas. *Le Morte D'Arthur*

Mansfield, Katherine. *Bliss, The Garden Party*

Marlowe, Christopher. *Doctor Faustus,* "The Passionate Shepherd to His Love," *Tamburlaine the Great*

Marvell, Andrew. "Damon the Mower," "The Garden," "To His Coy Mistress"

Mather, Cotton. *Magnalia Christi Americana, Manuductio and Ministerium*

Maturin, Charles Robert. *Melmoth the Wanderer*

The Mayflower Compact

Melville, Herman. *The Apple Trees, Bartleby the Scrivener, Benito Cereno, The Encantadas, Moby Dick* *

Mencken, H.L. *The American Language, The Novel*

Meredith, George. *The Egoist*

Middleton, Thomas. *Women Beware Women*

Mill, John Stuart. *Autobiography, On Liberty, What is Poetry?*

Miller, Arthur. *All My Sons, The Crucible,* * *Death of a Salesman* *

Milton, John. *Areopagitica, Comus,* "How Soon Hath Time,"

"Lycidas," *Of Education,* "On Shakespeare," "On the Late Massacre in Piedmont," *Paradise Lost,* * *Samson Agonistes,* "When I Consider How My Light Is Spent"

Molière. *Le Bourgeois Gentilhomme, Tartuffe*

Moody, William Vaughn. "An Ode in Time of Hesitation"

More, Sir Thomas. *Utopia*

Morris, William. "The Defense of Guenevere"

Morrison, Toni. *Beloved,* * *Song of Solomon* *

Nabokov, Vladimir. *Pale Fire*

Naipaul, V.S. *The Mystic Masseur, A House for Mr. Biswas*

Newman, John Henry. *Apologia pro vita sua, The Idea of a University*

Newton, Sir Isaac. *Light and Colors*

O'Casey, Sean. *Innocence and Experience*

O'Connor, Flannery. "The Life You Save May Be Your Own"

O'Connor, Frank. *Guests of the Nation*

O'Neill, Eugene. *Desire Under the Elms, The Hairy Ape, The Iceman Cometh, Long Day's Journey Into Night, Mourning Becomes Electra*

Orwell, George. *1984,* * *Animal Farm,* * *Coming Up for Air, Dying Metaphors, The Problem of the Golden Rule, Shooting an Elephant*

Osborne, John. *Look Back in Anger*

Owen, Wilfred. "Anthem for Doomed Youth," "Dulce et Decorum Est"

Paine, Thomas. *The Age of Reason*

Parker, Dorothy. "But the One On the Right"

Parnell, Thomas. "A Night-Piece on Death"

Pater, Walter. *Leonardo DaVinci, The Renaissance*

Peacock, Thomas Love. *Nightmare Abbey*

Philips, Ambrose. "The First Pastoral"

Philips, John. *The Splendid Shilling*

Pinero, Sir Arthur Wing. *The Second Mrs. Tanqueray*

Pinter, Harold. *The Caretaker, The Homecoming*

Plath, Sylvia. *The Bell Jar,* "Daddy," "Mirror"

Plato. *The Beast and the God in Man, The Republic* *

Plautus. *Menaechmi*

Poe, Edgar Allan. *Annabel Lee, The Murders on the Rue Morgue,* "The Raven"

Pope, Alexander. "Eloisa to Abelard," "Epistle to Miss Blount, on Her Leaving the Town after the Coronation," "An Essay on Criticism," "An Essay on Man," "The Rape of the Lock," "To a Lady"

Pound, Ezra. "The Lake Isle," "A Pact," "The River-Merchant's Wife: A Letter"

Proust, Marcel. *Remembrance of Things Past*

Pynchon, Thomas. *The Crying of Lot 49*

Quinn, Michael. *Form and Intention*

Radcliffe, Mrs. Ann. *The Italian, The Mysteries of Udolpho*

Raleigh, Sir Walter. "The Author's Epitaph, Made by Himself," "The Nymph's Reply to the Shepherd," "Sir Walter Raleigh to His Son"

Rand, Ayn. *Atlas Shrugged, Fountainhead*

Ransom, John Crowe. "Bells for John Whiteside's Daughter," "Janet Waking," "Piazza Piece"

Reynolds, Sir Joshua. *Discourse XIII*

Rice, Elmer. *The Adding Machine*

Richardson, Dorothy Miller. *Pilgrimage*

Richardson, Samuel. *Pamela: or Virtue Rewarded*

Rodin, Auguste. *Art in Life*

Roethke, Theodore. "The Bridge," "My Papa's Waltz"

Rossetti, Christina. "Goblin Market," "Remember"

Rossetti, Dante Gabriel. "The Blessed Damozel," *The House of Life,* "A Superscription"

Rousseau, Jean-Jacques. *Confessions, The Social Contract*

Rowe, Nicholas. *The Fair Penitent*

Ruskin, John. *The Society of Books, The Stones of Venice*

Salinger, J.D. *The Catcher in the Rye* *

Sandburg, Carl. "Chicago," "Fog"

Sartre, Jean-Paul. *Nausea, No Exit, The Respectful Prostitute*

Schiller, Johann. *The Maid of Orleans*

Scott, Sir Walter. *Waverly Novels*

"The Seafarer"

The Second Shepherd's Play

Shakespeare, William. *Antony and Cleopatra,* * As You Like It,* * Cymbeline, The Comedy of Errors, Hamlet,* * Henry IV Part I,* * Henry IV Part II, Henry V,* * Henry VI, Julius Caesar,* * King Lear,* * Macbeth,* * The Merchant of Venice,* * Othello,* * Pericles, Romeo and Juliet,* * "Sonnet 18," "Sonnet 55," "Sonnet 75," "Sonnet 116," "Sonnet 130," The Tempest,* * Twelfth Night,* * The Winter's Tale*

Shaw, George Bernard. *Arms and the Man, A Dramatic Realist to His Critics, Major Barbara, Mrs. Warren's Profession, Pygmalion, Saint Joan*

Shelley, Mary. *Frankenstein* *

Shelley, Percy Bysshe. "Adonais," "Mont Blanc," "Ode to the West Wind," "Ozymandias," *Prometheus Unbound,* "To a Skylark," "To Wordsworth"

Sheridan, Richard Brinsley. *The Rivals, The School for Scandal*

Sidney, Sir Philip. *Astrophel and Stella, The Defence of Poesie*

Simpson, Louis. "Walt Whitman at Bear Mountain"

Sinclair, Upton. *The Jungle*

Singer, Isaac Bashevis. *Gimpel the Fool*

Sir Gawain and the Green Knight *

"Sir Patrick Spens"

Skelton, John. "Colin Clout"

Smith, Captain John. *Report of the Newfound Land of Virginia*

Smith, Stevie. "Mother, among the Dustbins"

Smollett, Tobias. *The Adventures of Peregrine Pickle, The Expedition of Humphrey Clinker*

Sophocles. *Antigone,* * Oedipus the King* *

Spenser, Edmund. *Amoretti,* "Epithalamion," "The Faerie Queene," *Shepheardes Calendar*

Stafford, Jean. *Bad Characters*

Steele, Sir Richard. *The Conscious Lovers*

Stein, Gertrude. *Composition and Exposition, Three Lives*

Steinbeck, John. *The Grapes of Wrath* *

Sterne, Laurence. *Tristram Shandy*

Stevens, Wallace. "Anecdote of the Jar," "The Snow Man"

Stevenson, Robert Louis. *Kidnapped, Strange Case of Dr. Jekyll and Mr. Hyde*

Stoppard, Tom. *Rosencrantz and Guildenstern Are Dead*

Stowe, Harriet Beecher. *Uncle Tom's Cabin**

Strindberg, August. *Miss Julie*

Stuart, Jesse. *The Thread that Runs So True*

Surrey, Henry Howard, Earl of. "The Soote Season"

Swift, Jonathan. *The Battle of the Books*, "Cadenus and Vanessa," "A Description of a City Shower," *Gulliver's Travels,** *A Modest Proposal*, "Verses on the Death of Dr. Swift, D.S.P.D., Occasioned by Reading a Maxim in Rochefoucauld"

Synge, John M. *The Playboy of the Western World, The Shadow of the Glen*

Tennyson, Alfred, 1st Baron. "Break, Break, Break," *In Memoriam A.H.H.*, "King Arthur's Order of Chivalry," "The Lady of Shalott," "The Lotos-Eaters," "Mariana," Songs from *The Princess*, "To E. FitzGerald," "Ulysses"

Terence. *Andria*

Thackeray, William Makepeace. *Vanity Fair*

Theocritus. *Idylls*

Thomas, Dylan. "Do Not Go Gentle into That Good Night," "Fern Hill"

Thoreau, Henry David. *Civil Disobedience, Walden*

Thucydides. *History of the Peloponnesian War*

Thurber, James. *The Secret Life of Walter Mitty*

Tolstoy, Leo. *Anna Karenina, War and Peace, What is Art?*

Toomer, Jean. "Blood-Burning Moon"

Twain, Mark (Samuel Clemens). *The Adventures of Huckleberry Finn,** *Advice to Youth, Tom Sawyer*

Updike, John. "The Bulgarian Poetess"

Vanbrugh, Sir John. *The Relapse*

Villiers, George, Duke of Buckingham. *The Rehearsal*

Villon, François. "Ballad of Dead Ladies"

Virgil. *The Aeneid,** *Eclogues*

Voltaire. *Candide*

Vonnegut, Kurt Jr. *Slaughterhouse-Five**

Walker, Alice. *The Color Purple,** "Everyday Use"

Waller, Edmund. "Of English Verse," "On a Girdle," "Song"

Walpole, Horace. *The Castle of Otranto*

Warren, Robert Penn. *All the King's Men,* "Blow West Wind"

Webster, John. *Duchess of Malfi*

Welty, Eudora. *Delta Wedding,* "Why I Live at the P.O."

Wharton, Edith. *The Age of Innocence, Ethan Frome*

Wheatley, Phillis. "On Being Brought from Africa to America," "To the University of Cambridge in New England"

Whipple, Edwin. *Literature and Life*

White, E.B. "Once More to the Lake"

Whitman, Walt. *Democratic Vistas,* "Pioneers! O Pioneers!," "Song of Myself," "When I Heard the Learn'd Astronomer," "When Lilacs Last in the Dooryard Bloom'd"

"Widsith"

Wilde, Oscar. *The Ballad of Reading Gaol, The Critic as Artist, The Importance of Being Earnest, The Picture of Dorian Gray*

Williams, Tennessee. *Cat on a Hot Tin Roof, The Glass Menagerie, A Streetcar Named Desire*

Williams, William Carlos. "Asphodel, That Greeny Flower," "This is Just to Say"

Wilson, John. *Noctes Ambrosianae of "Blackwood"*

Winstanley, William. *Lives of the Most Famous English Poets*

Wollstonecraft, Mary. *A Vindication of the Rights of Woman*

Woolf, Virginia. *The Common Reader, Mrs. Dalloway,* To the Light-house **

Woolman, John. *Journal*

Wordsworth, William. *The Excursion,* "It Is a Beauteous Evening (Calm and Free)," "My Heart Leaps Up (When I Behold)," Preface to *Lyrical Ballads, The Prelude,* "She Dwelt among the Untrodden Ways," "Tintern Abbey," "The World Is Too Much with Us"

Wright, Richard. *Black Boy, Native Son**

Wycherley, William. *The Country-Wife*

Yeats, William Butler. "Crazy Jane and the Bishop," "The Dolls," "The Lake Isle of Innisfree," "Leda and the Swan," "Sailing to Byzantium," "The Second Coming," "When You Are Old," "The Wild Swans at Coole"

Young, Edward. "Night Thoughts"

LITERARY CRITICISM

This section will give you an overview of the major schools of literary criticism and their representative critics. This broad general knowledge will serve you well for the few questions on literary theory included in each administration of the exam. You will be asked not for extended theoretical engagement but rather for the ability to match literary theorists with characteristic passages or schools of theory. In other words, you do not need to be able to use literary theory so much as you need to know it when you see it.

RUSSIAN FORMALISM

Russian Formalism is characterized by a concern with the text itself, and the literary aspects of the text. Interesting to the formalists were the words and literary devices rather than the meaning of the words. This school of theory was prevalent in the U.S.S.R. from about 1915 to about 1930, although its influences can be felt in the New Criticism which emerged in the U.S. in the mid-twentieth century. The formalists saw literary texts as art and as fundamentally different from everyday speech and objects, and were interested in what made them so. Two important functions of literature for formalists are defamiliarization of life through its representation in literature and exposure of the way literature functions by calling attention to literary forms and conventions. Important critics for this school include Roman Jakobson and Mikhail Bakhtin.

MARXISM

Marxist forms of literary analysis have had a profound impact on the study of literature. There are many kinds of Marxist criticism, and its tenets are numerous and deeply complex. Luckily, ETS tends to ask questions about Marxist approaches to literature that are relatively easy to identify. Any example of Marxist criticism that you will find on the Subject Test will invariably be very explicit about economics and class relationships. Signal words to look for when identifying Marxist criticism include *dialectics, materialism, bourgeoisie,* and *proletariat.* There are far too many notable Marxist critics to note here, but some important figures are Georg Lukacs, Walter Benjamin, and Terry Eagleton.

NEW HISTORICISM/CULTURAL MATERIALISM

Like Marxism, New Historicism and its British counterpart Cultural Materialism are concerned with the conditions in which works of literature are produced and consumed. These schools of analysis argue that works of art are embedded within a cultural system specific to the moment of their creation, and that they need to be read in terms of their historical moment rather than as transcendent, "timeless" works that speak universal truths. New Historicism and Cultural Materialism are both essentially ideological forms of criticism—that is, through a careful examination of literature and the period from which it emerges, both methodologies are attempts to uncover the true relations of power in a given society that the dominant classes attempt to mystify and conceal. Subversion is an important buzzword for New Historicists—these critics are interested in finding voices of subversion and examining what strategies power structures employ to contain these voices. The most important name in New Historicism is Stephen Greenblatt and, to a lesser extent, Louis Adrain Montrose. Peter Stallybrass is an important figure in Cultural Materialism.

PSYCHOANALYSIS

Psychoanalysis differs sharply from Marxist and Historicist/Materialist criticism by emphasizing universal conditions over particular historical moments. Like Marxism, psychoanalysis has a long and complex history, and takes many different forms. However, as with Marxism, Psychoanalysis is generally reduced by ETS to a few basic principles with keywords that make it easy to identify on the Subject Test. Look for words like *repression, id* and *ego, Oedipal Complex, trauma, subconscious* and *unconscious, death drive, phallus, desire, lack,* and anything that emphasizes mothers and early childhood experiences. Jacques Lacan is a towering figure for psychoanalysis, along with Julia Kristeva, and to a certain extent, Harold Bloom.

STRUCTURALISM

Structuralism holds that meaning is produced by the structuring of units within systems. Language is a system, and is analyzed for its semiotic components. Look for words like *sign* and *signifier* as an indication of a structuralist critique. Structuralists also tend to set up binary oppositions, but this is a common practice in post-structuralism, or deconstruction as well. The French critics Saussure, Barthes, and Levi-Strauss are important Structuralist figures.

POST-STRUCTURALISM/DECONSTRUCTION

Post-Structuralism refers to a series of critical movements that draw on structuralist principles and attempt to go beyond it in some aspects. Deconstruction, associated most closely with the French philosopher Jacques Derrida, is sometimes referred to as if it were interchangeable with post-structuralism. This is not completely accurate, but it ultimately is not important for the Subject Test—any question ETS asks about post-structuralist theory will invariably be a question asking you to identify an example of deconstruction. Deconstruction emphasizes the fundamental disorder and instability of signs and signifiers, and the way authors play, consciously or unconsciously, with meaning and metaphor. Deconstruction, in its crudest formulation, emphasizes the points at which works of literature seem to contradict themselves, the point at which they "deconstruct," leaving the critic to construct the meaning of these moments of contradiction. Look for words like *text*, *textuality*, *discourse*, *dissemination*, *difference*, and *logocentrism*. Besides Derrida, Jonathan Culler and Paul de Man are major figures in deconstruction.

FEMINIST CRITICISM

Most obviously, feminist forms of criticism are concerned with the position of women in works of literature. More specifically, feminist criticism seeks to elucidate the workings of patriarchy and gender oppression, with special attention to the way society constructs identities for men and women and punishes those who do not conform to these identities. *Patriarchy* is, of course, an important term to look out for, as are *misogyny*, *essentialism*, *constructivism*, and *gender*. Elaine Showalter, Helene Cixous, and Luce Irigaray are major figures in feminist criticism.

READER-RESPONSE CRITICISM

This methodology, associated with Stanley Fish, is primarily concerned with the experience of reading and the effect that a work has on its readers. In essence, reader-response critics argue that the real "event" of literature is the production of meaning by individual readers. Important terms include *implied* and *ideal* reader.

LITERARY TERMS

If you've been out of school for awhile, you may need to be reminded of the difference between a metaphor and a simile. The list below reviews common literary terms that you may encounter on the GRE Literature in English.

Allegory

> a story in which the characters and actions make literal sense as well as signify a second story

Alliteration

> the repetition of sounds, especially beginning consonants in a sequence of words

Apostrophe

> a direct address to either a person or entity; many odes begin by addressing the subject of the poem

Assonance

> the repetition of the same or similar vowel sounds in a sequence of words

Aubade

> a song meant to be played or sung in the morning

Ballad

> a song, transmitted orally, which tells a story

Bildungsroman

> a novel of education that tells the story of the protagonist's growth into adulthood

Breton Lay

(fourteenth-century) poems written in the style of Marie de France; Chaucer's "The Franklin's Tale" is an example

Cacophony

language that sounds harsh and unmusical to the ear

Caesura

a strong pause which occurs within a line of poetry

Conceit

an extended comparison of two dissimilar things, used for poetic effect

Connotation

the thoughts and feelings associated with a word outside of its dictionary meaning

Consonance

the repetition of consonants in a sequence of words

Courtly Love

an aristocratic code of love, wherein love was viewed as a religious passion. The devoted love between the knight and the beloved lady was ennobling and forever unfulfilled. (There is still debate on whether courtly love was actually practiced or whether it existed in literature only.) Chaucer's *Troylus and Criseyde* is a well-known work in which the conventions of courtly love can be seen.

Denotation

the dictionary definition of a word, its primary meaning

Enjambment

> in poetry, when the syntax of the poem carries over the end of the verse line, so that the thought being expressed does not end at the end of the line but is continued in the next line

Euphony

> language that is musical and pleasing to the ear

Fable

> a short story told to illustrate a moral

Fabliau

> a comic short story about middle- or working-class characters; this form was popular in medieval times and is often bawdy

Feminine Rhyme

> a rhyme of two syllables in which the first syllable is stressed

Flat Character

> a character not given very much individuation by the author; this character is usually used to illustrate an idea

Free Verse

> a form of poetry that does not follow traditional meter or rhyme schemes

Kunstlerroman

> a type of Bildungsroman about the development of the protagonist into an artist

Leitmotif, or Motif

an element that recurs frequently in literature, or within a single work of literature

Malapropism

the mistaken use of a word in place of another that it resembles, resulting in a comic effect. This term comes from the character Mrs. Malaprop in Richard Sheridan's *The Rivals*.

Masculine Rhyme

a rhyme of one accented syllable

Metaphor

a figure of speech where one word is used to describe another without making an explicit comparison

Meter

the rhythmic pattern of verse. Formal rhythmic patterns are discussed in terms of feet: the combination of a stressed syllable with one or more unstressed syllables makes up a foot. In describing the meter of a line, the foot is named and then the number of feet in the line, for example, iambic pentameter. Types of feet:

Iambic

an unstressed syllable followed by a stressed syllable

Anapestic

two unstressed syllables followed by a stressed syllable

Trochaic

a stressed syllable followed by an unstressed syllable

Dactylic

a stressed syllable followed by two unstressed syllables

Spondaic

a stressed syllable followed by an equally stressed syllable

Pyrric

an unstressed syllable followed by an equally unstressed syllable

The names of the lines in ascending order of feet are: monometer, dimeter, trimeter, tetrameter, pentameter, hexameter, heptameter, and octameter.

Metonymy

something is evoked by an associated term; for example, *the crown* can refer to a queen or king or royalty in general.

Morality Play

late medieval morality plays dramatize moral instruction by allegorically personifying vices and virtues.

Objective Correlative

a phrase coined by T. S. Eliot to describe the concept that a poet must communicate emotion by finding a concrete situation that corresponds to, or evokes the emotion

Onomatopoeia

a word whose sound mimics the sound it means, like *buzz* or *screech*

Ottava Rima

an Italian stanza of eight eleven-syllabled lines with rhyme *ababbcc*

Paean

a song of praise, joy, triumph, or thanks sometimes directed at a god

Parable

a story told to illustrate a moral or religious lesson

Pastoral

a poem portraying a city poet's nostalgia for the idealized country life

Pathetic Fallacy

a term invented by John Ruskin identifying the practice of personification

Personification, or Prosopopeia

an inanimate object or an idea given human attributes

Picaresque

a narrative that portrays in a realistic, and sometimes satiric, manner the adventures of a rogue-hero

Round Character

a character who is complex and individuated

Simile

a comparison between two different things using the words *like* or *as*

Sonnet

a poem of fourteen lines of rhymed iambic pentameter; different rhyme schemes differentiate the Petrarchan sonnet, Shakespearean sonnet, and the Spenserian sonnet

Stream-of-Consciousness

the representation of the flow of a character's psychic processes, including the intermingled thoughts, memories, associations, and feelings of the mind

Synecdoche

a part of something stands in for the whole, or the whole stands in for a part

Answers to Drill Questions

Classical Literature

1.   **(A)**   Both epics begin in the middle of the action, *in medias res*, and give background information as the narrative progresses. They do not begin with epic metaphors (B) or epic similes (C), although both epics do contain epic similes. The places Colonus (D) and Thebes (E) are part of the Oedipus tragedies written by Sophocles.

2.   **(B)**   Aeschylus wrote the *Oresteia* trilogy. The trilogy is about the curse on the house of Atreus (A). Homer (C) wrote *The Iliad* and *The Odyssey*. Sophocles (D) wrote the Oedipus tragedies. Agamemnon (E) is a character in the *Oresteia* trilogy.

Anglo-Saxon Period

1.   **(A)**   While *Beowulf* is in English, it tells the story of the earlier Germanic tribes (the Danes and the Geats) from whom the English are descended. *The Dream of the Rood* (B) is a religious poem. *Ecclesiastical History* (C) is primarily concerned with the spread of Christianity. *Piers Plowman* (D) takes as its subject allegorical figures. *The Canterbury Tales* (E) concerns itself with a group of pilgrims.

2.   **(A)**   Grendel is the monster, described as a giant worm. His mother (B) doesn't have a name. (C), (D), and (E) are not part of the story; be sure to familiarize yourself with the plot of *Beowulf* if you got this question wrong.

The Middle Ages

1.   **(B)**   "The Nun's Priest's Tale" is a beast fable in which the main character is the cock, Chanticleer. "The Knight's Tale" (A) is a more elevated story of courtly love in keeping with the status of its teller. "The Miller's Tale" (C) is classified as a fabliau. "The Pardoner's Tale" (D) is an allegory about greed. "The Wife of Bath's Tale" is notable for asking the question: what do women want most?

2.   **(A)**   You should identify *Piers Plowman* by the allegorical personification of Truth, Righteousness, and Peace. *Sir Gawain and the Green Knight* (B) can be eliminated because it is written in alliterative verse and the main characters are the two named in the title. Choices (C) and (D) can be eliminated because Chaucer's Middle English is accessible enough that it is not often modernized. Also, you should familiarize yourself with the most popular of Chaucer's tales. Choice (E) can be eliminated because *Le Morte D' Arthur* is a work of prose, not poetry.

The Renaissance

1.   **(C)**   The flowers are named in line 6. (A), (B), (D), and (E) are all mentioned in the sonnet, but are not the referent in line 14.

2.   **(D)**   *The Winter's Tale* is a play by Shakespeare; the poem is his Sonnet 98, written in a form we now call the Shakespearean sonnet. "The Faerie Queene" (A) was written by Edmund Spenser, who also wrote sonnets in a form now referred to as the Spenserian sonnet. *Pamphilia to Amphilanthus* (C) is a Petrarchan sonnet sequence written by Lady Mary Wroth. "To His Coy Mistress" (E) is a poem (not in sonnet form) written by Andrew Marvell.

The Restoration and Eighteenth Century

1.   **(A)**   William Congreve's Restoration comedy, *The Way of the World,* is recognizable by the witty speeches and descriptive characters' names. *Love for Love* (B) is also a play by Congreve. *The Importance of Being Earnest* (C) is a witty play by Oscar Wilde. *A Midsummer Night's Dream* (D) is a Shakespearean comedy. *The Country-Wife* (E) is a Restoration comedy by William Wycherly.

2.   **(E)**   Richardson wrote the early novels *Pamela* and *Clarissa* in epistolary form, meaning that they are made up of a series of letters between the characters. Dryden (A) is primarily known for his poetry. Swift (B), Defoe (C), and Fielding (D) wrote prose, but not in epistolary form.

The Romantic Era

1.   **(A)**   The albatross is the famous symbol in this well-known poem; if you answered incorrectly be sure to read the poem. Although choices (B) through (E) are also Romantic poems, none of them use the albatross as a symbol.

2.   **(E)**   This passage from Keats' "Ode on a Grecian Urn" addresses the urn itself. Even if you didn't recognize the poem, the stanza itself gives enough information that you can tell it is a Grecian marble object. On the urn are depicted men and maidens (A) and a pastoral scene (B). The poem does not so much deal with youth (C) and old age (D) as it does with the transitory quality of life and the more permanent quality of art.

The Victorian Age

1.   **(C)**   Christina Rossetti is the author of "A Birthday" and "Goblin Market," from which the stanza is excerpted. You can identify the poem as "Goblin Market" by its references to goblins and the character Laura. The tone and subject matter of "Goblin Market" differ completely from those of Matthew Arnold's lyric, "Dover Beach" (A); Alfred, Lord Tennyson's poem, "The Lady of Shalott" (B); Elizabeth Barrett Browning's volume of poetry, *Sonnets from the Portuguese* (D); and Robert Browning's poem, "The Bishop Orders His Tomb at Saint Praxed's Church" (E).

2.   **(E)**   Bertha is Mr. Rochester's mad first wife in *Jane Eyre*. *Wide Sargasso Sea* creates a story and background for the character, Bertha, who is locked in the attic of Mr. Rochester's house in *Jane Eyre*. Both of Dickens' novels (A and B) have female characters who are considered to be mad, but neither of them are named Bertha. "Dover Beach" (C) is a poem, not a novel, so you should have been able to immediately discard this choice. The two main characters in Emily Brontë's *Wuthering Heights* (D) are Catherine and Heathcliff.

Pre-Twentieth Century American Authors

1.   **(B)**   Emily Dickinson is easily identifiable because of her distinctive use of the dash and her sparse language. "Because I could not stop for Death" is one of her most famous poems. "Song of Myself" (A) is one of

Walt Whitman's most famous poems in *Leaves of Grass*. Elizabeth Bishop is the author of "The Imaginary Iceberg" (C); Wallace Stevens wrote "The Emperor of Ice-Cream" (D); and Anne Sexton is the author of "Song for a Red Nightgown" (E). The poems comprising choices (C), (D), and (E) are twentieth-century works, while Dickinson and Whitman wrote in the nineteenth century.

2.   **(A)**   "Song of Myself" is one of Walt Whitman's most famous poems in *Leaves of Grass*; the excerpt quoted is from "I Hear America Singing," also found in *Leaves of Grass*. Whitman is recognizable by his patriotic themes and embracing impulse toward all he describes. Emily Dickinson wrote "Because I could not stop for Death" (B); Elizabeth Bishop is the author of "The Imaginary Iceberg"(C); Wallace Stevens wrote "The Emperor of Ice-Cream" (D); and Anne Sexton is the author of "Song for a Red Nightgown" (E). The poems comprising choices (C), (D), and (E) are twentieth-century works, while Dickinson and Whitman wrote in the nineteenth century.

The Twentieth Century

1.   **(C)**   Polonius is the attendant lord in *Hamlet* who is 'full of high sentence, but a bit obtuse.' The speaker asserts he is not Prince Hamlet (A); that he is not at the center of action, but a peripheral character. The play the speaker alludes to was written by Shakespeare (B) but the speaker in no way compares himself to the author. The speaker's view of himself as a supporting character makes it similarly impossible for him to compare himself to the king (D), and there is no allusion to Claudius in any case. Although the speaker, in comparing himself with Polonius, indicates that his character sometimes almost crosses over into the Fool (E), he is not comparing himself with the Fool.

2.   **(B)**   This stanza is from T. S. Eliot's "The Love Song of J. Alfred Prufrock," which you can identify by the self-deprecating tone of the speaker. "The Waste Land" (A) is also a famous poem by Eliot, but the subject matter and the speakers of the poem are far different from "Prufrock." Choices (C) and (D) are both poems by Yeats, again with a far different voice and tone. Choice (E) is a poem written by W. H. Auden about Yeats.

Practice Test 1

We have left the spaces below for you to record your scores on this Practice Test. Please refer to the Scoring section in the front of this book for how to compute your raw score and convert it into a scaled score. By comparing your scores on each Practice Test, you will be better able to mark your progress.

Raw Score   _____

Scaled Score   _____

GRE LITERATURE
IN ENGLISH

PRACTICE TEST 1

DIRECTIONS: Choose the best answer for each question and mark the letter of your selection on the corresponding answer sheet. Answer sheets can be found in the back of this book.

---

1. "One must commit oneself to a conjunction with the other — forever. But it is not selfless — it is a maintaining of the self in mystic balance and integrity — like a star balanced with another star."

    The above description of love is stated by

    (A) Heathcliff in *Wuthering Heights.*

    (B) Birkin in *Women in Love.*

    (C) Rochester in *Jane Eyre.*

    (D) Stephen Dedalus in *A Portrait of the Artist as a Young Man.*

    (E) George Emerson in *A Room with a View.*

Questions 2 – 4 refer to the following passage.

"Son of heaven and earth,
Attend: that thou art happy, owe to God;
That thou continu'st such, owe to thyself,
That is to thy obedience; therein stand.
This was that caution giv'n thee; be advised.
God made thee perfect, not immutable;
And good he made thee, but to persevere
He left it in thy power, ordained thy will
By nature free, not overruled by fate
Inextricable, or strict necessity;
Our voluntary service he requires,
Not our necessitated, such with him
Finds no acceptance, nor can find, for how
Can hearts, not free, be tried whether they serve
Willing or no, who will but what they must
By destiny, and can no other choose?
Myself and all th' angelic host that stand
In sight of God enthroned, our happy state
Hold, as you yours, while our obedience holds;
On other surety none; freely we serve,
Because we freely love as in our will
To love or not; in this we stand or fall:
And some are fall'n, to disobedience fall'n,
And so from heav'n to deepest hell; O fall
From what high state of bliss into what woe!"

2.   In the above passage, the narrator and narratee are

(A)   the Angel Michael and Eve.

(B)   the Angel Gabriel and Mary.

(C)   the Angel of Death and Virgil.

(D)   the Angel Raphael and Adam.

(E)   the Angel Gabriel and Dante.

3.   The narrator suggests

   (A)   man's continued happiness depends on God.

   (B)   man's continued happiness depends on the angels.

   (C)   man cannot change his state.

   (D)   man has no free will.

   (E)   man must serve God voluntarily.

4.   Which of the following best describes the narrator's tone?

   (A)   Patronizing and didactic

   (B)   Wise and instructive

   (C)   Jolly and humorous

   (D)   Gloomy and bad-tempered

   (E)   Threatening and vindictive

5.   　　　Who should come to my lodge this morning but a true Homeric or Paphlagonian man — a Canadian, a wood chopper and post maker, who can hole 50 posts in a day, who made his last supper on a woodchuck which his dog caught.

   Whose lodge does the wood chopper visit?

   (A)   Rousseau's   (D)   Homer's

   (B)   Thoreau's   (E)   Frost's

   (C)   Wordsworth's

Questions 6 – 8 refer to the following stanza.

> Heard melodies are sweet, but those unheard
> Are sweeter; therefore, ye soft pipes, play on;
> Not to the sensual ear, but, more endear'd,
> Pipe to the spirit ditties of no tone:
> Fair youth, beneath the trees, thou canst not leave
> Thy song, nor ever can those trees be bare;
> Bold Lover, never, never canst thou kiss,
> Though winning near the goal — yet, do not grieve;
> She cannot fade, though thou hast not thy bliss,
> For ever wilt thou love, and she be fair!

Keats
Ode to
a Grecian
Urn

6.   Which of the following best describes the theme of this stanza?

(A) Music refreshes the soul.

(B) Youth has every advantage.

(C) Art is immortal.

(D) Imagination enhances life.

(E) Art destroys life.

7.   In which literary era was the entire poem written?

(A) The Elizabethan   (D) The Victorian

(B) The Postmodern   (E) The Modern

(C) The Romantic

8.   Which of the following best describes the philosophy of this era?

(A) Delight in the Immortality of Nature bringing man closer to God

(B) Despair in the failure of man to create the perfect world

(C) Distrust in the new technology

(D) Fear of fragmentation in the world as a result of a loss of belief in God

(E) Triumph in man's ability to overcome nature

Questions 9 – 13 refer to the following passage.

> now were getting at it you seem to regard it merely as an experience that will whiten your hair overnight so to speak without altering your appearance at all you wont do it under these conditions it will be a gamble and the strange thing is that man who is conceived by accident and whose every breath is a fresh cast with dice already loaded against him will not face that final man which he knows beforehand he has assuredly to face without essaying expedients ranging all the way from violence to petty chicanery that would not deceive a child until some day in very disgust he risks everything on a single blind turn of a card no man ever does that under the first fury of despair or remorse or bereavement he does it only when he has realized that even the despair or remorse or bereavement is not particularly important to the dark diceman and i temporary and he it is hard believing to think that a love or a sorrow is a bond purchased without design and which matures willynilly and is recalled without warning to be replaced by whatever issues the gods happen to be floating at the time no you will not do that until you come to believe that even she was not quite worth despair perhaps and i will never do that nobody knows what i know and he i think youd better go on to cambridge right away you might go up into maine for a month you can afford it if you are careful it might be good thing watching pennies has healed more scars than jesus and i suppose i realize that you believe i will realize up there next week or next month and he then you well remember that for you to go to harvard has been your mothers dream since you were born and no compson has ever disappointed a lady

9.   What literary technique does the above passage illustrate?

    (A)   Enjambment

    (B)   Dream of the unconscious

    (C)   Stream-of-consciousness

    (D)   Extended metaphor

    (E)   Dislocation of time

10.   By what means does the author achieve the effect?

(A) Poetic language

(D) Lack of meaning

(B) Use of nuance

(E) Lack of punctuation

(C) Extended metaphor

11.   What is the subject under discussion?

(A) Coloring one's hair

(D) Courtesy to women

(B) Killing oneself

(E) Going away to college

(C) Killing one's dream

12.   Which of the following most closely expresses the main speaker's point of view?

(A) Life is not worth living.

(B) Man's life is determined and cannot be altered.

(C) People let you down and love destroys in the end.

(D) Man has free will and should exercise it.

(E) In the game of life, man always wins.

13.   The author of the passage is

(A) Thomas Hardy.

(D) Kurt Vonnegut, Jr.

(B) Henry James.

(E) William Faulkner.

(C) Theodore Dreiser.

---

14.   _____ looked vacantly at the richly carpeted floor. A new light was shining upon all the years since her enforced flight. She remembered now a hundred things that indicated as much. She also imagined that he took it on her account. Instead of hatred springing up there was a kind of

Sister Carrie

sorrow generated. Poor fellow! What a thing to have had hanging over his head all the time.

Supply the name that completes the first sentence.

(A) Emma

(D) Carrie

(B) Tess

(E) Maggie

(C) Milly

15.
Come my friends
Tis not too late to seek a newer world
Push off and sitting well in order smite
The sounding furrows; for my purpose holds
To sail beyond the sunset, and the baths
Of all the Western stars, until I die.

The speaker is

(A) Achilles.

(D) Ishmael.

(B) Jason.

(E) Ulysses.

(C) Ahab.

Questions 16 – 18 refer to the following passage.

Their society, for instance, is stoic in appearance. They accept such inevitable calamities as death calmly; they eat, sleep and exercise wisely; they believe in universal benevolence as an ideal, and accordingly have no personal ties or attachments. The family is effectively abolished; marriage is arranged by friends as "one of the necessary actions in a reasonable being"; husband and wife like one another, and their children just as much and as little as they like everyone else. Sex is accepted as normal but only for the purpose of procreation...They have no curiosity: their language, their arts and sciences are purely functional and restricted to the bare necessities of harmonious social existence.

16.   This society is featured in

(A) *Animal Farm.*   (D) *Gulliver's Travels.*

(B) *Slaughterhouse-Five.* (E) *Brave New World.*

(C) *1984.*

17.   Which best describes such a book?

(A) A travelogue   (D) A fable

(B) A Utopia novel   (E) A satire

(C) An anti-Utopia novel

18.   Who lives in the society described?

(A) Midgets   (D) Pigs

(B) Tralfamadorians   (E) Horses

(C) Giants

Questions 19 – 22 refer to the opening stanza below.

> Busie old foole, unruly Sunne,
> Why dost thou thus
> Through windowes, and through curtaines call on us?
> Must to thy motions lovers seasons run?
> Saucy pedantique wretch, goe chide
> Late school boyes, and sowre prentices,
> Goe tell Court-huntsmen, that the King will ride,
> Call country ants to harvest offices;
> Love, all alike, no season knowes, nor clyme,
> Nor houres, dayes, months, which are the rags of time.

19.   This impudent address of the sun is

(A) anti-heroic.   (D) anti-Miltonic.

(B) anti-Shakesperean.   (E) anti-cleric.

(C) anti-Spenserian.

20. Which is the name for an address to daybreak?

    (A) An ode   (D) An aubade

    (B) An elegy   (E) A sestina

    (C) A sonnet

21. Which best describes the poem's meaning?

    (A) The two lovers are all sufficient to each other.

    (B) The two lovers prefer the night.

    (C) The two lovers want to share their love with the sun.

    (D) The two lovers do not want others to know of their love.

    (E) The two lovers want the sun to shine forever on their bed.

22. Which best explains the metaphor of time?

    (A) Love is eternal and does not recognize units of time.

    (B) Love lasts forever and does not need to be measured in mere fragments of time.

    (C) Love does not last forever so there is no point in measuring time.

    (D) Measurements of time are useless when trying to hang on to love.

    (E) Hours, days, months simply show how love is passing by with time.

---

23. Do not begrudge us oracles from birds,
        or any other way of prophesy
        within your skill; save yourself and the city,
        save me; redeem the debt of our pollution
        that lies on us because of this dead man.

    Who is the dead man?

    (A) King Lear   (D) King Priam

    (B) King Alonzo   (E) King Creon

    (C) King Laius

24.   Perhaps it is only a game. Modern women like Sarah exist and I have never understood them.

Sarah exists in

(A)   Beckett's *Endgame.*

(B)   Joyce's *Ulysses.*

(C)   Dickens's *Great Expectations.*

(D)   John Fowles' *The French Lieutenant's Woman.*

(E)   Pynchon's *V.*

25.   The thing that hath been, it is that which shall be; and that which is done is that which shall be done; and there is no new thing under the sun.

The quote is from

(A)   Ecclesiastes.   (D)   *The Iliad.*

(B)   Isaiah.   (E)   *The Symposium.*

(C)   *The Odyssey.*

Questions 26 – 28 refer to the following passage.

We picture the world as thick with conquering and elite humanity, but here, with the bugles of the tempest pealing, it was hard to imagine a peopled earth. One viewed the existence of man then as a marvel, and conceded a glamour of wonder to these lice which were caused to cling to a whirling, fire-smitten, ice-locked, disease-stricken, space-lost bulb. One was a coxcombe not to die in it.

26.   Which best describes this world-view?

(A)   Man's life is futile and farcical.

(B)   Man is a wonderful creation.

(C)   Man's life is no more important than an insect's.

(D)   Man is at the center of the universe.

(E)   Man's place in the world is to create light.

27.   In context, which best defines "coxcombe"?

(A) A conceited fool   (D) A wastrel

(B) A tragic hero   (E) A dandy

(C) A moron

28.   The author of this passage also wrote

(A) *The Stranger.*

(B) *Breakfast of Champions.*

(C) *The Red Badge of Courage.*

(D) *The Crying of Lot 49.*

(E) *Tess of the D'Urbervilles.*

---

29.   And round it was upon a hill
      It made the slovenly wilderness
      Surround that hill

      The wilderness rose up to it,
      And sprawled around, no longer wild.

      By "it," the poet means

(A) a blackbird.   (D) a plum.

(B) death.   (E) nature.

(C) a jar.

Questions 30 – 31 refer to the following passage.

As to what that exile and that longing for reunion meant, Rieux had no idea. But as he walked ahead, jostled on all sides, accosted now and then, and gradually made his way into less crowded streets, he was thinking it has no importance whether such things have or have not a meaning; all we need consider is the answer given to men's hope.

30. What has just ended "that exile"?

(A) The Holocaust

(D) An epidemic

(B) The Russian Revolution

(E) The winter

(C) The French Revolution

31. What term best describes the author's philosophy?

(A) Determinism

(D) Quietism

(B) Negativism

(E) Nihilism

(C) Existentialism

---

32. "The most heterogeneous ideas are yoked by violence together."

Who said this about which sort of poetry?

(A) Bacon on Shakespeare's love sonnets

(B) Dryden on love poetry

(C) Milton on epic poetry

(D) Samuel Johnson on metaphysical poetry

(E) Ben Jonson on religious sonnets

33. Which of the following best defines the term "comedy of manners"?

(A) A play or novel in which strong, moral values are hidden by trite appearances

(B) A comedy where etiquette is seriously followed

(C) A play or novel in which etiquette is uproariously parodied

(D) A play in which odd and witty people make fun of other odd and witty people

(E) A novel in which unconventional behavior shocks conventional people

Questions 34 – 36 refer to the following works.

(A) "Ode to Autumn"

(B) Ecclesiastes

(C) "Fern Hill"

(D) "Spring and Fall: To a Young Child"

(E) "Mending Wall"

34. Which represents the poet and a neighbor as an apple orchard and a pine tree?

35. Which contains the following lines?

Leaves like the things of man, you
With your fresh thoughts care for, can you?

36. Which is adapted in the following?

To everything
Turn, turn, turn
There is a season
Turn, turn, turn.

Questions 37 – 39 refer to the following dialogue.

"I realize," the girl said. "Can't we maybe stop talking?"

They sat down at the table and the girl looked across at the dry side of the valley and the man looked at her and at the table.

"You've got to realize," he said, "that I don't want you to do it if you don't want to. I'm perfectly willing to go through with it if it means anything to you."

"Doesn't it mean anything to you? We could get along."

"Of course it does. But I don't want anyone else. And I know it's perfectly simple."

"It's all right for you to say that, but I do know it…. Would you do something for me now?"

"I'd do anything for you."

"Would you please please please please please please please stop talking?"

He did not say anything but looked at the bags against the wall of the station. There were labels on them from all the hotels where they had spent nights.

37.   What is the main point of the discussion?

(A) Seduction   (D) Vacation

(B) Abortion   (E) Repetition

(C) Accusation

38.   What does the "dry valley" reflect in the relationship?

(A) Dryness   (D) Passion

(B) Finality   (E) Heat

(C) Sterility

39.   Which best explains the significance of the details of the bags?

(A) The couple have traveled extensively.

(B) The couple love traveling, not each other.

(C) The couple are on vacation.

(D) The couple have a restless physical relationship.

(E) The couple share their luggage and their emotional love.

Questions 40 – 41 refer to the following passage.

The plot of such novels usually involved an amazingly virtuous and beautiful heroine in all kinds of terrifying adventures, generally in a foreign land — Italy was popular because of the "banditti." Murders, sadistic villains, old ruins, haunted buildings, long lost children, explanatory documents hidden in secret drawers — all that could shock and horrify the reader were part of the trappings of these novels.

40.   The novels referred to are known as

    (A)   Italian novels.   (D)   Naturalistic novels.

    (B)   Gothic novels.   (E)   Detective novels.

    (C)   Realistic novels.

41.   Which one of the following is a burlesque of such a novel?

    (A)   *Northanger Abbey*   (D)   *Frankenstein*

    (B)   *The Mysteries of Udolpho*   (E)   *Evelina*

    (C)   *The Italian*

Questions 42 – 45 refer to the following passage.

As to my own part, having turned my thoughts for many years upon this important subject and maturely weighed the several schemes of other projectors, I have always found them grossly mistaken in their computation. It is true a child just dropped from its dam may be supported by her milk for a solar year with little other nourishment, at most not above the value of two shillings, which the mother may certainly get, or the value in scraps, by her lawful occupation of begging; and it is exactly at one year old that I propose to provide for them in such a manner as instead of being a charge upon their parents or the parish, or wanting food and raiment for the rest of their lives, they shall, on the contrary, contribute to the feeding and partly to the clothing of many thousands.

42.   The tone of the passage is

(A)   reasonable and mathematical.

(B)   angry and threatening.

(C)   religious and reverent.

(D)   hypocritical and sanctimonious.

(E)   mature and sensitive.

43.   What is the proposal the writer suggests later?

(A)   To ship out the nursing mothers to America

(B)   To use the babies' hair for thread for weaving

(C)   To use the babies' carcasses as meat and soft gloves

(D)   To impose a tax on mothers with more than one child

(E)   To impose harsh penalties on nursing mothers found begging

44.   Which of the following defines such writing?

(A)   Realism   (D)   Modernism

(B)   Satire   (E)   Hedonism

(C)   Irony

45.   A contemporary of the writer was

(A)   John Donne.   (D)   Henry James.

(B)   Milton.   (E)   Cyril Tourneur.

(C)   Henry Fielding.

Questions 46 – 49 refer to the following excerpt.

> Sir, 'twas not
> Her husband's presence only, called that spot
> Of joy into the Duchess' cheek; perhaps
> Fra Pandolf chanced to say, "Her mantle laps
> Over my lady's wrist too much," or "paint
> Must never hope to reproduce the faint
> Half-flush that dies along her throat." Such stuff
> Was courtesy, she thought, and cause enough
> For calling up that spot of joy. She had
> A heart-how shall I say? — too soon made glad,
> Too easily impressed; she lik'd whate'er
> She looked on, and her looks went everywhere.
> Sir, 'twas all one! My favor at her breast,
> The dropping of the daylight in the West,
> The bough of cherries some officious fool
> Broke in the orchard for her, the white mule
> She rode with round the terrace…

46. The poem is an example of

(A) a satiric dialogue.

(B) a sonnet.

(C) a parody.

(D) dramatic irony.

(E) a dramatic monologue.

47. The men are looking at

(A) a statue of a sea horse.

(B) a landscape.

(C) a portrait.

(D) a book of favors.

(E) designs for an orchard.

48. The speaker reveals himself as

(A) proud and egotistical.

(B) weak and effete.

(C) angry and inane.

(D) approving and amiable.

(E) old and unreasonable.

49. The Duchess is revealed as

    (A) one who flirts with all men.

    (B) one who takes delight in simple things.

    (C) one who knows how beautiful she is and plays on it.

    (D) one who delights in rank and jewels.

    (E) one who has had many affairs.

Questions 50 – 53 refer to the following lines.

> This fellow's of exceeding honesty,
> And knows all qualities, with a learned spirit
> Of human dealings. If I do prove her haggard,
> Though that her jesses were my dear heartstrings
> I'd whistle her off and let her down the wind   5
> To prey at fortune. Haply for I am black
> And have not those parts of conversation
> That chamberers have, or for I am declined
> Into the vale of years—yet that's not much—
> She's gone. I am abused, and my relief   10
> Must be to loathe her...
>   Yet 'tis the plague to great ones;
> Prerogatived are they less than the base.
> 'Tis destiny unshunnable, like death.
> Even then this forked plague is fated to us   15
> When we do quicken. Look where she comes.

50. "This fellow" is

    (A) Cassio.   (D) Iago.

    (B) Bassanio.   (E) Horatio.

    (C) Mercutio.

51.   Which best defines the metaphor in lines 3–7?

(A)   If I find she is old and deteriorating, I'll lock her up.

(B)   If I find as she gets older she becomes more witch-like, I'll banish her.

(C)   If I find that she is like a hawk gone wild, I'll let her fly free.

(D)   If I find she is like a mare grown old, I'll whistle to her to come to me and love her.

(E)   If I find she is dishonest, I'll let her find her own fortune on her own.

52.   What is significant about the word "forked" in line 15?

(A)   Split in two—the sign of the devil

(B)   Horned—the sign of the cuckold

(C)   Poisoned—by a contaminated fork

(D)   Deceived—by a liar with a forked-tongue

(E)   Obsessed—with a whore

53.   In context, what is the meaning of "quicken" in line 16?

(A)   Die   (D)   Fall ill

(B)   Are born   (E)   Rush love too quickly

(C)   Fall in love

---

54.   The power of the novel is precisely what made it such a dangerous book in the opinions of most early reviews. _____ did not seem to use her power to condemn the action of Edna Pontellier as Flaubert condemned Emma Bovary in the novel to which it is most often compared.

Which author's name completes the passage?

(A) Jane Austen

(D) Kate Chopin

(B) George Eliot

(E) Emily Brontë

(C) George Sand

55. The title of the Shaw play *Arms and the Man* echoes the first lines of

(A) *The Aeneid.*

(D) *The Iliad.*

(B) *Beowulf.*

(E) *The Inferno.*

(C) *Paradise Lost.*

Questions 56 – 57 refer to the following passage.

And it was at this moment, as I stood there with the rifle in my hands, that I first grasped the hollowness, the futility of the white man's dominion in the East. Here was I, the white man with his gun, standing in front of the unarmed native crowd— seemingly the leading actor of the piece; but in reality I was only an absurd puppet pushed to and fro by the will of those yellow faces behind. I perceived in this moment that when the white man turns tyrant it is his own freedom that he destroys.

56. The white man is

(A) E.M. Forster.

(D) Rudyard Kipling.

(B) Ernest Hemingway.

(E) Frank O'Connor.

(C) George Orwell.

57. The incident takes place in

(A) India.

(D) Africa.

(B) Burma.

(E) Vietnam.

(C) China.

58. Upon which literary tradition are the names Billy Pilgrim, Goodman Brown, and Willy Loman based?

    (A) Pilgrims' stories along a journey as in Chaucer's *Tales*

    (B) Historical character names as in the Holinshed *Chronicles*

    (C) Vice and Virtue names as in Medieval morality plays

    (D) Famous men's names as in Plutarch's *Lives*

    (E) Concepts and principles as in Aristotle's *Poetics*

59.   The mind receives a myriad impressions — trivial, fantastic, evanescent, or engraved with the sharpness of steel. From all sides they come, an incessant shower of innumerable atoms...Life is not a series of gig lamps symmetrically arranged; but a luminous halo, a semi-transparent envelope surrounding us from beginning of consciousness to the end.

    Which best describes the meaning here in regard to the development of the novel?

    (A) The novel should be as fragmented as experience.

    (B) The novel's time structure should be linear like life.

    (C) The novel's structure should reflect the randomness of experience.

    (D) The novel should be free from pattern but must follow conventional life.

    (E) The novel should be vague and hazy like a mist, not symmetrically patterned.

60.   But now Fortune, fearing she had acted out of Character, and had inclined too long to the same Side, especially as it was the Right side, hastily turned about: For now goody Brown, — whom Zekiel Brown caressed in his Arms; nor he alone, but half the Parish besides; so famous was she in the Fields of Venus, nor indeed less in those of Mars.

The author employs the technique of

(A) mock heroism.

(B) hubris.

(C) dramatic irony.

(D) pathetic fallacy.

(E) intentional fallacy.

61.   It is a beauteous morn, opinion grants.
       Nothing remains of last night's Summer Formal
       Save palms and streamers and the wifely glance
       Directed with more watchfulness than normal,
       At listless mate who tugs his necktie loose,
       Moans, shuns the light and gulps tomato juice.

The poem parodies

(A) Coleridge.

(B) Byron.

(C) Frost.

(D) Wordsworth.

(E) Dylan Thomas.

Questions 62 – 64 refer to the speeches that follow.

62.   Which lines are spoken by Volpone?

63.   Which by Shylock?

64.   Which by Falstaff?

(A) Methinks my moiety, north from Burton here
     In quantity equals not one of yours.

(B) A diamond gone cost me two thousand ducats in Frankfort!
     The curse never fell on our nation till now; I never felt it till now.

(C) Let good Antonio look he keep his day,
     Or he shall pay for this.

(D) Good morning to the day; and next my gold!
     Open the shrine, that I may see my saint.

(E) I would to God thou and I knew where a commodity of good names
     were to be bought.

Questions 65 – 67 refer to the following passage.

On a table in the middle of the room was a kind of lovely crockery basket that had apples and oranges and peaches and grapes piled up in it which was much redder and yellower and prettier than real ones is but they warn't real because you could see where pieces had got chipped off and showed the white chalk or whatever it was underneath....There was some books too, piled up perfectly exact, on each corner of the table. One was a big family Bible, full of pictures. One was *Pilgrim's Progress*, about a man that left his family it didn't say why. I read considerable in it now and then. The statements was interesting, but tough. Another was "Friendship's Offering," full of beautiful stuff and poetry but I didn't read the poetry.

65.   The narrator of this passage is

(A)   David Copperfield.   (D)   Huckleberry Finn.

(B)   Dreiser's Carrie.   (E)   Lambert Strether.

(C)   Crane's Maggie.

66.   Which best explains the significance of the false fruit?

(A)   The narrator is starving.

(B)   The narrator has never seen fake fruit before, emphasizing the innocence of the character.

(C)   The fruit looks amusing and the narrator has a keen sense of humor.

(D)   The fruit symbolizes the deprivation in the narrator's life.

(E)   The fruit symbolizes the false front put up by the family who owns it.

67.   Why are the books used ironically here?

(A)   The narrator cannot read.

(B)   The family is not peace-loving.

(C)   The family cannot read.

(D)   The narrator loves reading but not poetry.

(E)   The family is not pilgrims.

Questions 68 – 70 refer to the following poetry by T. S. Eliot.

68.   Which is an example of Eliot's symbolism?

69.   Which demonstrates Eliot's poetic paradox?

70.   Which demonstrates Eliot's probing the unconscious for his imagery?

(A)   For I have known them all already, known them all:
       Have known the evenings, mornings, afternoons,
       I have measured out my life in coffee spoons.

(B)   NO! I am not Prince Hamlet, nor was meant to be;
       Am an attendant Lord, one that will do
       To swell a progress, start a scene or two,
       Advise the prince…

(C)   I do not know much about gods, but I think that the river
       Is a strong brown God.

(D)   The stair was dark
       Damp, jagged, like an old man's mouth drivelling
           beyond repair,
       Or the toothed gullet of an aged shark.

(E)   What we call the beginning is often the end
       And to make an end is to make a beginning
       The end is where we start from

Questions 71 – 72 refer to the following passage.

   A volume of _____'s poems lay before him on the table. He opened
it cautiously with his left hand lest he should waken the child and began
to read the first poem in the book:

       Hushed are the winds and still the evening gloom,
           Not e'en a Zephry wanders through the grove,
       Whilst I return to view my Margaret's tomb
           And scatter flowers on the dust I love.

   He paused. He felt the rhythm of the verse about him in the room.
How melancholy it was! Could he, too, write like that, express the
melancholy of his soul in verse? There were so many things he wanted to

describe; his sensation of a few hours before on Grattan Bridge for example...The child awoke and began to cry.

71. The volume of poems is written by

    (A) Gerard Manley Hopkins.   (D) Wallace Stevens.

    (B) Wordsworth.   (E) Lord Byron.

    (C) Tennyson.

72. The author of the above passage also wrote

    (A) *Sons and Lovers.*

    (B) *To the Lighthouse.*

    (C) *The Damnation of Theron Ware.*

    (D) *Ulysses.*

    (E) *Jude the Obscure.*

---

73. _____ world is not ours, and perhaps we are too neglectful of the graces by which he sets such store. But when a man threatens his young son that spies report to his father on his conduct, and advises him to have affairs only with women of quality, who will combine adultery with polishing his manners, we may well consider him an unpleasant mixture of Polonius and Pandarus.

    Whose world is described here?

    (A) Richardson's   (D) Sterne's

    (B) Addison's   (E) Chesterfield's

    (C) Swift's

74. In which literary work does Pandarus feature?

    (A) *A Midsummer Night's Dream*

    (B) Chaucer's "The Miller's Tale"

    (C) Chaucer's *Troylus and Criseyde*

(D) Bolt's *A Man For All Seasons*

(E) Eliot's *Murder in the Cathedral*

75. Which best describes a pander's role?

(A) He sacrifices his own interests for other people's.

(B) He acts as a go-between in political matters.

(C) He acts as a liaison in sexual intrigues.

(D) He sends important messages between people.

(E) He flatters people and helps them get on in business.

Questions 76 – 78 refer to the following stanzas.

And he to me: "The whole shall be made known;
        Only have patience till we stay our feet
        On yonder sorrowful shore of Acheron."

Abashed, I dropped my eyes; and, lest unmeet
        Chatter should vex him, held my tongue, and so
        Paced on with him, in silence and discreet.

76. "he to me" (line 1) are

(A) Ulysses to Patroklus.

(B) God to Adam.

(C) Adam to Eve.

(D) Homer to Odysseus.

(E) Virgil to Dante.

77. Who journeys on the river Acheron?

(A) The souls of the joyous going to heaven

(B) The bodies of soldiers going to rest

(C) The souls of unbaptized children going to Limbo

(D) The souls of the damned going to Hell

(E) The souls of the saved going to Purgatory

78.	Which best paraphrases the second stanza?

(A)	Angry, I glared at him, accepted his taunt and continued seething silently.

(B)	Ashamed, I avoided his glance, and in case my useless talking angered him, I silently walked by his side.

(C)	Embarrassed, I turned away and wanting to meet others, left him standing there silent and angry with me.

(D)	Awkward, I looked down, and not wanting to anger him further with my chit-chat, walked on ahead of him in silence.

(E)	Bored, I looked away and thought it was unseemly of me to talk, so I walked by his side silently and apart.

Questions 79 – 81 refer to the following dialogue.

"'His last word — to live with'" she insisted. "'Don't you understand
I loved him — I loved him — I loved him.'"
I pulled myself together and spoke slowly.
"'The last word he pronounced was — your name.'"

79.	The narrator is

(A)	the Director.

(B)	Marlow.

(C)	Dr. Rieux.

(D)	Edith Summerson.

(E)	Ishmael.

80.	The true last words were

(A)	"Ah! My angels!"

(B)	"I don't complain of none, dear boy."

(C)	"The sun... the sun."

(D)	"The horror! The horror!"

(E)	"Dear old Flo! Master wouldn't hurt you. Come here!"

81. Which of the following explains why the narrator lies?

    (A) The woman is the dead man's wife and the narrator tells her what she wants to hear.

    (B) The woman is the dead man's mistress who left him for another man.

    (C) The woman is the dead man's fiancee who loves flattery.

    (D) The woman is the dead man's fiancee who believes in the man's goodness—the narrator knows the man's innate evil.

    (E) The dead man had had many affairs—his last words were not this woman's name but another's.

---

82.   The function of the older son is to contrast the father's attitude to him, the loyal steadfast one, and the younger wastrel son. If the father had had only the one son the jubilation of his return would be more understandable. A deep-rooted sibling rivalry perhaps sparks the outcry of the older son.

In the above story, why does the father rejoice to see the younger son return?

    (A) This boy is the father's favorite.

    (B) The father cannot tolerate the rivalry between the two boys and teaches the older one a lesson.

    (C) The younger son represents the sinner welcomed back into God's forgiveness.

    (D) The younger son represents the Oedipal complex which the father has forgiven.

    (E) The younger son failed and is now back in the power of the father.

Questions 83 – 84 refer to the following two stanzas excerpted from a longer poem.

> I have looked upon those brilliant creatures,
> And now my heart is sore.
> All's changed since I, hearing at twilight,
> The first time on this shore,
> The bell-beat of their wings above my head,
> Trod with a lighter tread.
>
> Unwearied still, lover by lover,
> They paddle in the cold
> Companionable streams or climb the air;
> Their hearts have not grown old;
> Passion or conquest, wander where they will,
> Attend upon them still.

83. The stanzas embody which aspect of the poet's world view?

   (A) That the world is in a constant state of flux, which he hates

   (B) That man can never achieve happiness in this world

   (C) That man can never be as free and happy as the birds who stay the same always

   (D) That man needs love and companionship

   (E) That man changes and grows old but Nature renews herself and appears constant

84. "Those brilliant creatures" are

   (A) peacocks.   (D) geese.

   (B) swans.   (E) doves.

   (C) ducks.

Questions 85 – 86 refer to the following dialogue.

In the meantime let's try and converse calmly, since we're incapable of remaining silent.
You're right, we're inexhaustible.
It's so we won't think.
We have that excuse.
It's so we won't hear.
We have our reasons.

85. The two speakers are

(A) Ponzo and Lucky.

(B) Molloy and Moran.

(C) Vladimir and Estragon.

(D) Clov and Hamm.

(E) Biff and Happy.

86. What does the dialogue reveal?

(A) The two are bored with each other and hide their boredom in idle chatter.

(B) The characters wish to hide their fear of life by listening to one another.

(C) The two enjoy chatting with one another.

(D) The two hope to forget their fear of life by talking.

(E) The characters are strangers and have nothing vital to say.

Questions 87 – 88 refer to the following passage.

In this book the hero is just arriving at manhood with the freshness of feeling that belongs to that interesting period of life, and with the power to please that properly characterizes youth. As a consequence he is loved; and, what denotes the real waywardness of humanity, more than it corresponds with theories and moral propositions, he is loved by one full of art, vanity and weakness, and loved principally for his sincerity, his modesty, and his unerring truth and probity.

87. Which hero does this preface to the novel describe?

    (A) Tom Jones

    (B) Heathcliff

    (C) The Deerslayer

    (D) The Reverend Dimsdale

    (E) Theron Ware

88. A contemporary of the author of the preface is

    (A) Samuel Richardson.

    (B) Henry Fielding.

    (C) Edgar Allan Poe.

    (D) Charles Brockden Brown.

    (E) Samuel Langhorne Clemens.

Questions 89 – 90 refer to the following passage.

> Marlow is terrified of well-bred women, although he has no problem with "females of another class." His shyness—certainly an absurd foible for a young man about town in this day and age—is soon demonstrated when he meets Miss_____.

89. Supply the name that completes this criticism.

    (A) Hardcastle

    (B) Earnshaw

    (C) Booby

    (D) Andrews

    (E) Teazle

90. The play referred to in the above criticism is

    (A) *Venice Preserv'd.*

    (B) *The Rover.*

    (C) *The Way of the World.*

    (D) *She Stoops to Conquer.*

    (E) *The Winter's Tale.*

91.   "An 'Image' is that which presents an intellectual and emotional complex in an instant of time. I use the word 'complex' rather in the technical sense employed by the newer psychologists."

The "I" here is

(A) T. S. Eliot.

(B) Wyndham Lewis.

(C) Ezra Pound.

(D) Archibald MacLeish.

(E) Robert Lowell.

Questions 92 – 93 refer to the passages that follow.

92.   Which did Pound write?

93.   Which did Robert Lowell write?

(A)   There is a moment when we lie
Bewildered, wakened out of sleep,
When light and sound and all reply
That moment time must tame and keep.

(B)   So far for what it's worth
I have my background;
And you had your background.

(C)   One dark night,
my Tudor Ford climbed the hill's skull;
I watched for love-cars. Lights turned down,
they lay together, hull to hull,
where the graveyard shelves on the town...

(D)   I am moved by fancies that are curled
Around these images and cling:

(E)   I too am a rare
Pattern. As I wander down
The garden paths.

94. Lady Sneerwell, Mrs. Candour, Sir Oliver Surface, Snake, and Careless are all characters from which Restoration play?

    (A) *The Beaux Stratagem*   (D) *School for Scandal*

    (B) *All for Love*   (E) *Love's Last Shift*

    (C) *The Way of the World*

95. Such names as above are based on which dramatic tradition?

    (A) The Greek Chorus   (D) Deus ex machina

    (B) The Furies   (E) The Peripeteia

    (C) The Humours

96. Dryden said, "'Tis sufficient to say, according to the proverb, that here is God's plenty."

    According to Dryden, where is God's plenty?

    (A) In the Bible

    (B) In a book of Proverbs

    (C) In Dryden's essays

    (D) In Chaucer's *The Canterbury Tales*

    (E) In Shakespeare's history plays

97.   He told Hawthorne that his book has been broiled in hell-fire and secretly baptized not in the name of God but in the name of the Devil. He named his tragic hero after the Old Testament ruler who "did more to provoke the Lord God of Israel to anger than all the Kings of Israel that were before him."

    This tragic hero is

    (A) Ahab.   (D) Lucifer.

    (B) Ishmael.   (E) Job.

    (C) Isaiah.

Questions 98 – 102 refer to the following lines taken from a longer poem.

> Two Handmaids wait the Throne: Alike in Place,
> But diff'ring far in Figure and in Face.
> Here stood Ill-nature like an ancient Maid,
> Her wrinkled Form in Black and White array'd;
> With store of Pray'rs, for Mornings, Nights and Noons,   5
> Her Hand is fill'd; her Bosom with Lampoons.
> There Affectation with a sickly Mien
> Shows in her Cheek the roses of Eighteen,
> Practis'd to Lisp and hang the Head aside,
> Faints into Airs, and languishes with Pride;   10
> On the rich Quilt sinks with becoming Woe,
> Wrapt in a Gown for Sickness and for Show.
> The Fair-ones feel such Maladies as these,
> When each new Night-Dress gives a new Disease.

98. The stanzas are written in

(A) free verse.

(B) couplets.

(C) heroic couplets.

(D) blank verse.

(E) octosyllabic couplets.

99. Which best paraphrases the second half of line 6?

(A) Her bosom is arrayed with exotic flowers.

(B) Her bosom overflows with political tracts written to flatter a politician.

(C) Her bosom is stuffed with anadromous fishes allegorizing love.

(D) Her bosom is filled with satirical writings which ridicule an enemy.

(E) Her bosom rested against a Grecian lamp.

100. The "Fair-ones" feel such "maladies" (line 13) because

(A) ladies then never received enough air or exercise and were often sickly but still wanted to look fashionable in bed.

(B)   the Plague was rampant at this time and fashionable nightdresses were made in which ladies received visitors discreetly.

(C)   ladies often received company in their bedrooms, so they became "ill" when they had a new nightdress to show off.

(D)   the fashion was so highly corseted then ladies often fainted and had to wear loose flowing nightdresses.

(E)   fashion was so elaborate then that ladies "fell ill" to avoid seeing people they did not want to see.

101.   In context, which word best replaces "Mien" in line 7?

(A)   Bent   (D)   Gait

(B)   Posture   (E)   Appearance

(C)   Pallor

102.   The poet's purpose is

(A)   to vent his misogyny.

(B)   to show male superiority in his day.

(C)   to ridicule the fashionable world of his day.

(D)   to hurt a woman he once loved, who scorned him.

(E)   to take revenge for a trivial trick played on him.

Questions 103 – 106 refer to the following description.

The scene was a plain, bare, monotonous vault of a schoolroom, and the speaker's square forefinger emphasized his observations by underscoring every sentence with a line on the schoolmaster's sleeve. The emphasis was helped by the speaker's square wall of a forehead, which had his eyebrows for its base, while his eyes found commodious cellarage in two   5
dark caves, overshadowed by the wall. The emphasis was helped by the speaker's mouth, which was wide, thin, and hard set. The emphasis was helped by the speaker's voice, which was inflexible, dry, and dictatorial. The emphasis was helped by the speaker's hair, which bristled on the skirts of his bald head, a plantation of firs to keep the wind from its shining   10

surface, all covered with knobs, like the crust of a plum pie, as if the head had scarcely warehouse-room for the hard facts stored inside. The speaker's square carriage, square legs, square shoulders—nay, his very neckcloth, trained to take him by the throat with an unaccommodating grasp, like a stubborn fact, as it was—all helped the emphasis.　　15

103. The speaker's name is Mr. Gradgrind—how does the repetition in the passage add to the name's connotation?

   (A) The word *emphasis* repeated adds to the harshness of the name.

   (B) The repetition of *speaker* emphasizes how important the name is.

   (C) The repeated *square* emphasizes how old-fashioned the speaker is.

   (D) The repeated *square* adds to the name by suggesting how harsh reason will grind everyone down.

   (E) The repeated *square* suggests how hard facts in schooling will grind down reason and make for nonsense.

104. Which term best describes the author's language?

   (A) Descriptive   (D) Symbolic

   (B) Allegorical   (E) Prosodic

   (C) Metaphorical

105. Which figures of speech do lines 10–12 contain?

   (A) A metaphor and a simile

   (B) Two metaphors

   (C) Oxymoron and a simile

   (D) Pastoral and a metaphor

   (E) Paradox and a simile

106. The author of this passage also wrote

   (A) *The Way of All Flesh.*

   (B) *Fathers and Sons.*

(C) *Villette.*

(D) *The Mystery of Edwin Drood.*

(E) *Adam Bede.*

---

107. Which did George Bernard Shaw write?

(A) She takes the Captain by the arm and coaxes him down into the chair, where he remains sitting dully. Then she takes the straitjacket and goes behind the chair.

(B) Same room. Beside the piano the Christmas tree now stands stripped of ornament, burned down candle stubs on its ragged branches.

(C) The laughter is loud now, and he moves into a brightening area at the left, where THE WOMAN has come from behind the scrim and is standing, putting on her hat, looking into a mirror and laughing.

(D) The office of the old professor, which also serves as a dining room. To the left, a door opens onto the apartment stairs; upstage, to the right, another door opens onto a corridor of the apartment. Upstage, a little left of center, a window, not very large, with plain curtains; on the outside sill of the window are ordinary potted plants.

(E) A lady's bedchamber in Bulgaria, in a small town near the Dragoman Pass, late in November in the year 1885. Through an open window with a little balcony a peak of the Balkans, wonderfully white and beautiful in the starlit snow, seems quite close at hand, though it is really far away.

Questions 108 – 109 refer to the following passage.

"Well, old chap... it do appear that she had settled the most of it, which I mean ter say tied it up on Miss Estella. But she had wrote out a little coddleshell in her own hand a day or two afore the accident, leaving a cool four thousand to Mr. Matthew Pocket."

108. The speaker is

   (A) Joseph in *Wuthering Heights.*

   (B) Joe Gargery in *Great Expectations.*

   (C) Mr. Western in *Tom Jones.*

   (D) Mrs. Malaprop in *The Rivals.*

   (E) Porfiry in *Crime and Punishment.*

109. In context of the above passage, what is the meaning of the word "coddleshell"?

   (A) A small bi-valve seashell

   (B) The opening lines of a will

   (C) The closing lines of a will

   (D) An appendix to a will

   (E) A small piece of shell-pink paper attached to a will

---

110. Which three elements best define Post-Modernism?

   (A) Randomness, excess, discontinuity

   (B) Flashback, fragmentation, humor

   (C) Nature, faith, solidity

   (D) Immorality, sense of loss, meaninglessness

   (E) Montage, metaphor, absurdity

Questions 111 – 113 refer to the following passages.

111. Which did Matthew Arnold write?

112. Which did Coleridge write?

113. Which did T. S. Eliot write?

(A)   Finally, GOOD SENSE is the BODY of poetic genius, FANCY its DRAPERY, MOTION its Life and IMAGINATION the soul that is everywhere and in each; and forms all into one graceful and intelligent whole.

(B)   They (The Greeks) regarded the whole; we regard the parts. With them the action predominated over the expression of it; with us the expression predominates over the action.

(C)   It is essential that a work of art should be self-consistent, that an artist should consciously or unconsciously draw a circle beyond which he does not trespass: on the other hand, actual life is always the material…

(D)   What made Wordsworth's poems a medicine for my state of mind, was that they expressed, not mere outward beauty, but states of feeling, and of thought coloured by feeling, under the excitement of beauty.

(E)   What can we expect this Aristocracy of Nature to do for us? They are of two kinds: the speculative, speaking or vocal; and the practical or industrial, whose function is silent.

Questions 114 – 117 refer to the following passage.

His head leaned back so far that it rested against the face of a defunct mantelpiece clock, and from this position his distraught eyes stared down at Daisy, who was sitting, frightened but graceful, on the edge of a stiff chair… his lips parted with an abortive attempt at a laugh. Luckily the clock took this moment to tilt dangerously at the pressure of his head, whereupon he turned and caught it with trembling fingers and set it back in its place…

"I'm sorry about the clock," he said.

"It's an old clock," I told them idiotically.

I think we all believed for a moment that it had smashed in pieces on the floor.

"We haven't met for several years," said Daisy, her voice as matter-of-fact as it could ever be.

"Five years next November."

114. Who narrates this dialogue?

    (A) Nick Carraway

    (B) Ernest Hemingway

    (C) Ford Maddox Ford

    (D) The Goat Boy

    (E) Italo Calvino

115. What do the details about the defunct clock and its falling reveal about these people?

    (A) Time is dead as far as these people are concerned.

    (B) The narrator is just killing time with these people.

    (C) Time has not mattered before but is beginning to matter now as the three become involved in a love triangle.

    (D) Time is gradually being destroyed for the two lovers who have been apart for five years.

    (E) Time is becoming short as the narrator tries to write the story of these people.

116. Who says the last line and why is the detail important?

    (A) The narrator, because he has known the couple five years

    (B) The other man, because the exact time has been important to him if not to Daisy

    (C) The other man, who has hated Daisy for five years and counted the time to revenge himself on her

    (D) The narrator, because it seems as if the couple has been there with him for five years

    (E) Daisy's husband, who took her away from the other man five years before

117. The author also wrote

    (A) *Nightwood.*

    (B) *Tender is the Night.*

    (C) *The Magus.*

    (D) *A Dance to the Music of Time.*

    (E) *A Burnt Out Case.*

118. Arnold's poem follows a linear progression from moonlit tranquility, through recognition of the loss of faith, to a view of the world as "a darkling plain."

The poem is

(A) "Ode to Immortality."   (D) "Dover Beach."

(B) "Two in the Campagna."   (E) "Endymion."

(C) "Kubla Khan."

Questions 119 – 121 refer to the following poem.

> I met a traveler from an antique land
> Who said: Two vast and trunkless legs of stone
> Stand in the desert...Near them, on the sand,
> Half sunk, a shattered visage lies, whose frown
> And wrinkled lip, and sneer of cold command,   5
> Tell that its sculptor well those passions read
> Which yet survive, stamped on these lifeless things,
> The hand that mocked them, and the heart that fed:
> And on the pedestal these words appear:
> "My name is Ozymandias, king of kings: 10
> Look on my works, ye Mighty and despair!"
> Nothing beside remains. Round the decay
> Of that colossal wreck, boundless and bare
> The lone and level sands stretch far away.

119. Which most closely describes the poet's meaning?

(A) The British Empire will one day tumble like the statue Ozymandias built.

(B) The Egyptian Empire was great but it was destroyed by one man's lust for power.

(C) The ruined statue and the sand's reclamation exemplify the futility of man's life on earth.

(D) No man, no matter how great, has the right to set himself up as immortal.

(E)   The ruined statue shows that men should not build "graven images" to celebrate their power.

120.   What do lines 4–7 suggest about Ozymandias?

(A)   He was a lifeless old man.

(B)   He was conceited and arrogant.

(C)   The sculptor captured the man's coldness and arrogance.

(D)   The sculptor hated him and so executed a perfect likeness.

(E)   The sculptor outlived the model.

121.   The poet also wrote

(A)   "To a Skylark."

(B)   "Cristabel."

(C)   "Ode on a Grecian Urn."

(D)   "Elegy Written in a Country Churchyard."

(E)   "The Magi."

---

122.   Readers feel the same lack of credibility with the too sweet heroine, _____, of *A Room With A View*. Mr. Emerson, her "guardian," guides her into the correct choice of love. Readers grasp the "physical" message of the novel, the scene in the violets and the bathing pool make it clear but the rest of the novel does not support the thesis, especially when the other "guardian," _____, turns out to be on the lovers' side after all!

Complete the passage with the ladies' names.

(A)   Lucy Honeychurch and Mrs. Allen

(B)   Caroline Abbott and Mrs. Moore

(C)   Jordan Baker and Daisy Buchanan

(D)   Caroline Abbott and Mrs. Fairfax

(E)   Lucy Honeychurch and Miss Bartlett

123. Which of the following words does E. M. Forster use to express the puzzlement of life in most of his novels?

    (A) Chaos

    (B) Riddle

    (C) Muddle

    (D) Confusion

    (E) Mayhem

Questions 124 – 129 refer to the following lines from a longer poem.

And they, as storms of snow descend to the ground incessant
on a winter's day, when Zeus of the counsels, showing
before men what shafts he possesses, brings on a snowstorm
and stills the winds asleep in the solid drift, enshrouding
the peaks that tower among the mountains and the shoulders out-jutting,
and the low lands with their grasses, and the prospering work of men's hands,
and the drift falls along the grey sea, the harbours and beaches,
and the surf that breaks against it is stilled, and all things elsewhere
it shrouds from above, with the burden of Zeus' rain heavy upon it;
so numerous and incessant were the stones volleyed from both sides,
some thrown on Trojans, others flung against the Achaians
by Trojans, so the whole length of wall thundered beneath them.

124. Name the poet and work.

    (A) Homer's *The Odyssey*

    (B) Homer's *The Iliad*

    (C) Tennyson's *Idylls of the King*

    (D) Chaucer's "The Knight's Tale"

    (E) T. S. Eliot's *Murder in the Cathedral*

125. Who are the Achaians?

    (A) The Greeks

    (B) The Barbarians

    (C) An ancient race of Britons

    (D) The Romans

    (E) The Goths

126. Who is the hero on each side of the battle?

    (A) Beowulf and Hrothgar   (D) Achilles and Patroklos

    (B) Boadicea and Caesar   (E) Achilles and Hector

    (C) Jason and Priam

127. Which best defines the way the entire simile functions?

    (A)   The stones come down like snow without causing damage, like snow which hushes, not harms — the simile works through likeness.

    (B)   The stones are like snow because they descend in an infinite quantity but the difference between the two, soft and brutal, in reality is a shock — the simile works through contrast.

    (C)   The stones are as white as snow and multiply so they look like snowflakes — the snow simile works visually.

    (D)   The stones hurtle down like snow and cause death just as snow deadens all the countryside — the simile works through likeness.

    (E)   The stones crash down unlike snow which softens all the countryside — the simile works through contrast.

128. Which best describes the effect of the snow description?

    (A) It shows that men are powerless in the hands of the gods.

    (B) It distances the reader from the horror of the battle.

    (C) It gives the writer a chance to pause before describing the horrors of the battle.

    (D) It universalizes the experience so that the reader can empathize with both sides of the battle.

    (E) It adds a serene beauty to what might otherwise be a gruesome scene.

129. Which modern writer uses a similar effect of rain or snow in which work?

    (A) Robert Frost in "Stopping by Woods On a Snowy Evening"

    (B) T. S. Eliot in *Preludes*

(C)   James Joyce in *The Dead*

(D)   Robert Creeley in "The Rain"

(E)   Sartre in *Nausea*

130.   … thanks to the limited desire for its company expressed by the step-parent, the law of its little life, its being entertained in rotation by its father and its mother, wouldn't easily prevail. Whereas each of these persons had at first vindictively desired to keep it from the other, so at present the remarried relative sought now rather to be rid of it — that is to leave it as much as possible, and beyond the appointed times and seasons, on the hands of the adversary…

This is Henry James's preface to which of his novels?

(A)   *The American*   (D)   *What Maisie Knew*

(B)   *The Bostonians*   (E)   *The Golden Bowl*

(C)   *The Turn of the Screw*

Questions 131 – 134 refer to the following excerpted second stanza of a poem.

Now I am a lake. A woman bends over me,
Searching my reaches for what she really is.
Then she turns to those liars, the candles or the moon.
I see her back and reflect it faithfully.
She rewards me with tears and an agitation of hands.   5
I am important to her. She comes and goes.
Each morning it is her face that replaces the darkness.
In me she has drowned a young girl, and in me an old woman
Rises toward her day after day, like a terrible fish.

131.   Which best defines the "I" of the initial metaphor?

(A)   The lake is a mirror to reflect back the woman's true image of herself.

(B)   The lake is the mirror to be rewarded for giving back a soothing image.

(C)   The lake acts as a portrait which flatters the woman.

(D)   The lake is too deep to give back a true image, so it lies.

(E)   The lake waits for the young woman to drown herself in it.

132.   Why are candles or the moon liars in line 3?

(A)   They give a flattering softening light so the picture they reflect is not "true."

(B)   They change so much that the reflection they give back in the mirror can never be true.

(C)   They cannot reflect light as a mirror does, so there is no image.

(D)   Their light is too shadowy or milky to give a good reflection.

(E)   The mirror is jealous of their brightness.

133.   Which is the closest paraphrase of lines 8–9?

(A)   The mirror has changed and refuses to give the young woman the reflection she ought to have.

(B)   Over time the young girl has grown old with the mirror which reflects the true image of a face now wrinkled and aged.

(C)   The woman feels as useless as a fish and thus wishes to drown herself in her rightful milieu, the lake.

(D)   The young girl is desperately unhappy, like a fish out of water, but hates to see this reflected in the mirror.

(E)   The mirror has lost its silver backing and reflects only scaled fragments of the young girl.

134.   The poet is

(A)   Emily Dickinson.   (D)   Sylvia Plath.

(B)   Amy Lowell.   (E)   Wallace Stevens.

(C)   Ted Hughes.

Questions 135 – 136 refer to the following passage.

"When I was writing the *Shadow of the Glen* some years ago, I got more aid than any learning could have given me from a chink in the floor of the old Wicklow house where I was staying, that let me hear what was being said by the several servant girls in the kitchen. This matter I think is of importance, for in countries where the imagination of the people, and the language they use is rich and living, it is possible for a writer to be rich and copious in his words and at the same time to give the reality, which is the root of all poetry, in a comprehensive and natural form."

135.   Who is the "I" in this passage?

(A)   James Joyce   (D)   Frank O'Connor

(B)   John Millington Synge   (E)   W. B. Yeats

(C)   Sean O'Casey

136.   In the above passage, which best explains the writer's defense of language?

(A)   Writers should be allowed to use any language they like.

(B)   Writers should choose only the language of the working people.

(C)   Writers should choose only a living, vibrant language because it can express reality.

(D)   Writers should use only bright, creative words.

(E)   Writers should be allowed to use creative words even if they are "dirty" or in dialect.

Questions 137 – 139 refer to the passages that follow.

137.   Which is from *The Sound and the Fury?*

138.   Which is from *Go Tell It On The Mountain?*

139.   Which is from *Coming Up For Air?*

(A) "This may be the last time I pray with you,
This may be the last time I pray with you."
As they sang they clapped their hands, and John saw that Sister McCandless looked about her for a tambourine.

(B) The sweet corpsy smell, the rustle of Sunday dresses, the wheeze of the organ and the roaring voices, the spot of light from the hole in the window creeping lowly up the nave...

(C) She had risen from one of the side seats, and speaking as she walked, she moved forward til she stood within the altar rail, immediately under the pulpit. The phrases were all familiar enough — Jesus a very present help — Sprinkled by the blood — but it was as in the case of her singing: the words were old; the music was new.

(D) The church had been decorated, with sparse flowers from kitchen gardens and hedgerows, and with streamers of coloured crepe paper. Above the pulpit hung a battered Christmas bell, the accordion sort that collapses. The pulpit was empty, though the choir was already in place, fanning themselves though it was not warm.

(E) The light of the lamps of the church fell upon an assembly of black clothes and white collars, relieved here and there by tweeds, on dark mottled pillars of green marble and on lugubrious canvasses. The gentlemen sat in the benches, having hitched their trousers slightly above their knees and laid their hats in security. They sat well back and gazed formally at the distant speck of red light which was suspended before the high altar.

---

140. Anna waits for a "real man" to come down like a deus ex machina to heal and help her.

Whose Anna is this?

(A) Tolstoy's Anna Karenina

(B) Arnold Bennet's Anna of the Five Towns

(C) Doris Lessing's in *The Golden Notebook*

(D) Sartre's Anna in *Nausea*

(E) Little Cloud's in *Dubliners*

141. In current usage, the term *deus ex machina* means

    (A) a device that descends from the top of the stage to lower a god from the "heavens."

    (B) a Puck-like character who causes mischief and complications in the plot.

    (C) a character who begins with evil intent but softens as the plot unfolds.

    (D) a character who intervenes opportunely to avoid disasters in the plot.

    (E) a device for helping other characters descend into the "earth" below stage.

---

142.   She is similar to unlikely writers such as Kafka and Faulkner but what is horrifying about _____ is that she creates terror amidst the hurry and flurry of females as they perform their "duties." In *Delta Wedding* an impetuous girl prepares for her wedding, harrassed and bullied by the people she loves and who love her.

    The author's name is

    (A) Flannery O'Connor.   (D) Joyce Carol Oates.

    (B) Jane Austen.   (E) George Eliot.

    (C) Eudora Welty.

Questions 143 – 144 refer to the following passage.

       The disemboweled are put back together and the dead resurrected. Victims are raped or flogged, or cut into pieces so quickly the readers have no time to sympathize.

143. The work described is

    (A) Vonnegut's *Slaughterhouse–Five*.

    (B) Gulliver's chapter on the Brobdingnagians.

(C) Chaucer's "The Miller's Tale."

(D) Margaret Atwood's *The Handmaid's Tale.*

(E) Voltaire's *Candide.*

144. Identify the famous word or catch-phrase from the last work.

(A) "Something will turn up!"

(B) "In the best of possible worlds"

(C) "And so on"

(D) "Live!"

(E) "I'm ever so 'umble"

145.　　　　Man has ideas that come not through the five senses or the powers of reasoning; but are either the result of direct revelation from God, his immediate inspiration or his immanent presence in the spiritual world.

Which is the term for the philosophy thus outlined?

(A) Pragmatism

(B) Humanism

(C) Behaviorism

(D) Transcendentalism

(E) Spiritualism

Questions 146 – 147 refer to the passages that follow.

146. Which did William James write?

147. Which did Emerson write?

(A)　　　　I do not wish to look with sour aspect at the industrious manufacturing village, or the mart of commerce. I love the music of the water wheel; I value the railway; I feel the pride which the sight of a ship inspires; I look on trade and every mechanical craft as education also. But let me discriminate what is precious herein. There is in each of these works an act of invention, an intellectual step, or short series of steps taken; that act or step is the spiritual act; all the rest is mere repetition of the same a thousand times.

(B)   I would say that learning to know dread is an adventure which every man has to affront if he would not go to perdition either by not having known dread or by sinking under it. He therefore who has learned rightly to be in dread has learned the most important thing... Dread is the possibility of freedom.

(C)   Through the process of evolution, human beings have put on sense organs — specialized areas where special types of stimuli are most effective — such as the eye, the ear, the nose, the tongue, the skin and semi-circular canals.

(D)   The universe is a system of which the individual members relax their anxieties occasionally, in which the don't care mood is also right for men, and moral holidays in order that if I mistake not, is part, at least, of what the Absolute is "known as," that is the great difference in our particular experiences which his being true makes for us, that is his cash value when he is pragmatically interpreted.

(E)   Even when I looked at things, I was miles from dreaming that they existed: they looked like scenery to me. I picked them up in my hands, they served me as tools, I foresaw their resistance. But that all happened on the surface... all of a sudden, there it was, clear as day: existence had suddenly unveiled itself.

Questions 148 – 152 refer to the following passage.

I' the Commonwealth I would (by contraries)
Execute all things: for no kind of traffic
Would I admit: no name of magistrate:
Letters should be not known: riches, poverty,
And use of service, none: contract, succession,   5
Bourn, bound of land, tilth, vineyard none
No use of metal, corn, or wine, or oil:
No occupation, all men idle, all:
And women too, but innocent and pure:
No sovereignty.   10
        … … …
All things in common Nature should produce

Without sweat or endeavour: treason, felony,
Sword, pike, knife, gun, or need of any engine
Would I not have: but Nature should bring forth
Of its own kind, all foison, all abundance   15
To feed my innocent people.

148.   The speaker is

(A)   a garrulous old fool who talks in riddles.

(B)   a garrulous old statesman whose paradoxes describe a utopia.

(C)   a wise old counselor whose riddles advocate an ideal communism.

(D)   a sad old politician who is losing his memory.

(E)   an interesting old courtier intent on making himself ruler of a
       commonwealth.

149.   In context, what do the words "bourn," "bound," and "tilth" mean in line 6?

(A)   Rights of way, acre of land, and taxes

(B)   Stream, boundary of land, and cultivation

(C)   Valley, acreage, and taxes

(D)   Boundaries, rights of property, and land cultivation

(E)   Stream, public property rights, and soil

150.   In context, what does the word "foison" mean in line 15?

(A)   Plentiful crop   (D)   Fish

(B)   Harvest   (E)   Fodder

(C)   Poison

151.   This commonwealth contradicts which Bible teaching?

(A)   Man should honor his neighbor.

(B)   Man produces by the sweat of his brow.

(C)   Man should employ his best talents.

(D) God separates the sheep and the goats.

(E) Woman shall bear pain in childbirth.

152. Which author owes a debt to whom for this commonwealth ideal?

(A) Ben Jonson to William Perry

(B) Shakespeare to Montaigne

(C) Voltaire to Rousseau

(D) Pope to Locke

(E) Swift to Hume

Questions 153 – 156 refer to the following passage.

Summertime, oh, summertime, pattern of life indelible, the fade-proof lake, the woods unshatterable, the pasture with the sweetfern and the juniper forever and ever, summer without end; this was the background, and the life along the shore was the design, the cottages with their innocent and tranquil design, their tiny docks with the flagpole and the American flag floating against the white clouds in the blue sky, the little paths over the roots of the trees leading from camp to camp and the paths leading back to the outhouses and the can of lime for sprinkling, and at the souvenir counters at the store the miniature birch-bark canoes and the postcards that showed things looking a little better than they were.

153. As E. B. White recalls a childhood summer, why does he employ one very long sentence?

(A) To highlight the waste he feels now as an old man

(B) To try to capture the past with a rambling "old man style," not pausing for breath, but piling incident on incident

(C) To give the reader an idea of the haze of the past

(D) To capture the breathless existence of those summers with so much to see and do

(E) To capture how excited he was then and how sad he is now reminiscing

154. Which term best defines the opening three lines?

    (A) Oratory

    (B) Rhetoric

    (C) Celebration

    (D) Religious

    (E) Incantation

155. Which best explains why the author uses such lines?

    (A) To express his joy with those past summers

    (B) To show how important those summers were to him

    (C) To show how deeply moved he is by the remembrance of those summers

    (D) To show how those summers seemed eternal to him then

    (E) To show that the summers work in a healing way for him now

156. Which best defines the metaphor at work in the last few lines?

    (A) The metaphor of the past

    (B) The metaphor of design

    (C) The metaphor of a painting

    (D) The metaphor of summer

    (E) The metaphor of a portrait

---

157.   He once called her his basil plant; and when she asked for an explanation, he said that basil was a plant which had flourished wonderfully on a murdered man's brain.

Which author owes a debt to which poet for this allusion?

    (A) Joseph Conrad to Edgar Allan Poe

    (B) Graham Greene to Yeats

    (C) George Eliot to Keats

(D) George Sand to Tennyson

(E) H.G. Wells to Blake

Questions 158 – 159 refer to the following passage.

Under his pillow lay the New Testament. He picked it up mechanically. The book belonged to her; it was the same book from which she had read the raising of Lazarus to him. At the beginning of his prison life he had feared that she would drive him frantic with her religion, that she would talk constantly about the gospels, and would force her books on him. But, to his amazement, she had never spoken to him about it, and had not even offered him the New Testament. He had asked for it himself shortly before his illness. He had never opened it till now.

158. The "he" referred to is

(A) Pierre in *War and Peace.*

(B) Jude in *Jude the Obscure.*

(C) Raskolnikov in *Crime and Punishment.*

(D) Vronsky in *Anna Karenina.*

(E) Dick Diver in *Tender is the Night.*

159. In the above passage, why is the reference to Lazarus important?

(A) The man has recently found religion and is now a believer like Lazarus.

(B) The man has ignored God and might be struck down as Lazarus was.

(C) The man is on death row but may gain a reprieve as Lazarus did.

(D) The man has recently undergone a form of resurrection of spirit and feels new life as Lazarus did.

(E) The man has recently been ill and now feels raised from the dead as Lazarus was.

Questions 160 – 161 refer to the author's Preface below.

This middle-class notion about the immobility of the soul was transplanted to the stage, where the middle-class element has always held sway. There a character became synonymous with a gentleman fixed and finished once for all — one who invariably appeared drunk, jolly, sad. And for the purpose of characterization nothing more was needed than some physical deformity like a club-foot, a wooden leg, a red nose; or the person concerned was made to repeat some phrase like "That's capital!" or "Barkis is willin'," or something of that kind.

160.   The author is

(A)   stating that characters are drawn too much from the middle-class and that does not mean real life.

(B)   criticizing playwrights who concentrate on the physical and not the psychological aspects of character.

(C)   suggesting that Naturalist playwrights do not know how to convey realistic characters.

(D)   arguing that characters should not be stock types, but show the full range of human variety.

(E)   suggesting that characters should be shown in the process of change.

161.   Whose character says "Mr. Barkis is willin'"?

(A)   Dickens' in *David Copperfield*

(B)   Thackeray's in *Vanity Fair*

(C)   Shaw's in *Major Barbara*

(D)   Samuel Butler's in *The Way Of All Flesh*

(E)   Sterne's in *Tristram Shandy*

Questions 162 – 163 refer to the following passage.

Chaucer's story describes three rogues who set out to find Death. An old man directs them to a pile of gold florins over which they quarrel and kill one another, thus indeed finding death. However, the greatest irony of the story involves the pilgrim who recounts it.

162.   The tale is

(A)   the Merchant's.

(B)   the Pardoner's.

(C)   the Miller's.

(D)   the Wife of Bath's.

(E)   the Host's.

163.   Which best describes the irony behind the above storyteller?

(A)   He rants against the evils of money but is very wealthy himself.

(B)   He preaches against physical love but bears a motto: "Love Conquers All."

(C)   He preaches against avarice but has revealed how he himself cheats the common folk out of their money.

(D)   He is a successful businessman, yet his tale advocates the idle life of the inns.

(E)   He preaches against carousing in inns but is a prodigious drinker himself.

164.   Which did Virginia Woolf write?

(A)   [The] queen, mindful of customs, gold-adorned, greeted the men in the hall; and the noble woman offered the cup first to the keeper of the land...

(B)   "Put it down there," she said, helping the Swiss girl to place gently before her the huge brown pot in which was the Boeuf en Daube... And she peered into the dish, with its shiny walls and its confusion of savoury brown and yellow meats and its bay leaves and its wine, and thought. This will celebrate the occasion...

(C)   The Professor was not a very strict Hindu — he would take tea, fruit, soda-water, and sweets, whoever cooked them, and vegetables and rice if cooked by a Brahman; but not meat, not cakes lest they contained eggs, and he would not allow anyone else to eat beef: a slice of beef upon a distant plate would wreck his happiness.

(D)   Then delicacies and dainties were delivered to the guests,
Fresh food in foison, such freight of full dishes
That space was scarce at the social tables
For the several soups set before them in silver
On the cloth

(E)   Leela was taken away and Ganesh was left alone to face the kedgeree-eating ceremony the next morning.
    Still in all his bridegroom's regalia, satin robes, and tasselled crown, he sat down on some blankets in the yard, before the plate of kedgeree. It looked white and unpalatable, and he knew it would be easy to resist any temptation to touch it.

Questions 165 – 168 refer to the following lines excerpted from a longer poem.

Thou then take my brand Excalibur,
Which was my pride: for thou rememberest how
In those old days, one summer noon, an arm
Rose up from out the bosom of the lake,
Clothed in white samite, mystic, wonderful,   5
Holding the sword — and how I row'd across
And took it, and have worn it, like a king:
And, wheresoever I am sung or told
In aftertime, this also shall be known.
But now delay not: take Excalibur,   10
And fling him far into the middle mere:
Watch what thou seest, and lightly bring me word.

165.   Who is speaking to whom?

(A)   King Arthur to Sir Galahad

(B)   Sir Gawain to Gringolet

(C) King Arthur to Sir Bedivere

(D) Sir Lancelot to Guinevere

(E) Hrothgar to Beowulf

166. Which best explains the word "samite" in line 5?

(A) Heavily gem-encrusted armor

(B) Silver gossamer-like material

(C) Highly decorated damask

(D) Silk material interwoven with gold and silver thread

(E) Simple white muslin interwoven with heraldic devices

167. What happens to the speaker?

(A) He dies and three gloriously apparelled women lead him to the underworld.

(B) The white samite-clad arm draws him down into the Lake of Forgetfulness.

(C) He falls asleep and dreams that a barge drawn by swans takes him away from the battle ground.

(D) A barge with weeping queens on board takes him and the other man into the Vale of Avalon.

(E) He dies and a funeral barge with three weeping queens takes him to the island valley of Avalon.

168. The author of the passage is

(A) Wordsworth.

(B) Malory.

(C) Yeats.

(D) John Gardner.

(E) Tennyson.

Questions 169 – 171 refer to the following.

> And I said his opinion was good:
> What shold he study and make himselven wood
> Upon a book in cloistre alway to pure
> Or swinken with his handes and laboure
> As Austin bit? How shall the world be served?
> Let Austin have his swink to him reserved!

169. Because of the vowel shift in the fifteenth century, Chaucer's pronunciation of "how" and "be" in line 5 would be closest to the modern pronunciation of

    (A) "who" and "buy."   (D) "hoe" and "buy."

    (B) "hoe" and "bay."   (E) "who" and "bay."

    (C) "hah" and "bah."

170. In this passage, Chaucer is describing

    (A) the Parson.   (D) the Clerk.

    (B) the Pardoner.   (E) the Friar.

    (C) the Monk.

171. In context, the passage could best be described as

    (A) ridiculing hypocrisy.

    (B) anti-intellectual.

    (C) attacking religion.

    (D) a Protestant attack on Catholicism.

    (E) an expression of Lollardism.

Questions 172 – 173 refer to the following poem.

HARLEM

What happens to a dream deferred?

Does it dry up
like a raisin in the sun?
Or fester like a sore—
And then run?
Does it stink like rotten meat?
Or crust and sugar over —
like a syrupy sweet?

Maybe it just sags
like a heavy load.

<u>Or does it explode?</u>

172. The principal rhetorical device used in this poem is

(A) antithesis.

(B) irony.

(C) simile.

(D) personification.

(E) understatement.

173. The topic of the poem is

(A) Freudian dream theory.

(B) adolescent frustration.

(C) pollution of Nature.

(D) the transience of love.

(E) the consequences of racism.

174. The phrase "nature red in tooth and claw" is from

(A) Wordsworth's "Tintern Abbey."

(B) Tennyson's *In Memoriam A.H.H.*

(C)   Blake's *The Marriage of Heaven and Hell.*

(D)   Yeats' "Sailing to Byzantium."

(E)   T. S. Eliot's "The Waste Land."

Questions 175 – 177 refer to the following passage.

> A man can hold land if he can just eat and pay taxes; he can do that.
> Yes, he can do that until his crops fail one day and he has to borrow money from the bank.
> But — you see, a bank or a company can't do that, because those creatures don't breathe air, don't eat side-meat. They breathe profits; they eat the interest on money. If they don't get it, they die the way you die without air, without side-meat.
> — Steinbeck, *Grapes of Wrath*

175.   The repetition of "he can do that" and the use of the second person pronoun

(A)   are errors in grammar, showing the speaker is illiterate.

(B)   are colloquial.

(C)   represent dialect.

(D)   are ironic, showing that the author is actually ridiculing the ideas being expressed.

(E)   are stylistic devices that add emphasis.

176.   Events referred to in the passage are associated with what historical period?

(A)   The economic depression of the 1930s

(B)   The frontier in the nineteenth century

(C)   The gold rush in California

(D)   Slavery in the antebellum South

(E)   The pre-revolutionary colonies

177. The ideas underlying the text show the influence of

(A) Henry David Thoreau.

(D) Sigmund Freud.

(B) Rousseau.

(E) John Stuart Mill.

(C) Karl Marx.

---

178. But I may not stand, mine head works so. Ah Sir Launcelot,
said King Arthur, this day have I sore missed thee: alas,
that ever I was against thee, for now have I my death, whereof
Sir Gawaine me warned in my dream. Then Sir Lucan took up
the king the one part, and Sir Bedivere the other part, and
in the lifting the king swooned; and Sir Lucan fell in a swoon
with the lift, that the part of his guts fell out of his body,
and therewith the noble knight's heart brast.
    — Malory, *Le Morte D'Arthur*

In context, the above passage could best be classified as

(A) an example of verbal irony.

(B) mock epic.

(C) a tragic and heroic passage from a romance.

(D) estates satire.

(E) a parody of medieval literature.

Questions 179 – 180 refer to the following.

In Brueghel's *Icarus*, for instance: how everything turns away
Quite leisurely from the disaster; the ploughman may
Have heard the splash, the forsaken cry,
But for him it was not an important failure;
    — Auden

179. The Greek myth referred to above is the source also for the name of a central
character in

(A) Joyce's *A Portrait of the Artist as a Young Man.*

(B)   Shaw's *Man and Superman.*

(C)   Shaw's *Pygmalion.*

(D)   O'Neill's *Mourning Becomes Electra.*

(E)   Chaucer's "The Knight's Tale."

180.   Auden's theme can best be paraphrased as

(A)   only someone educated in the classics would recognize an allusion to Greek mythology.

(B)   the archetypes of mythology are universal.

(C)   in their immediate context, heroic events often seem insignificant.

(D)   the tragic hero is punished for trying to go beyond human limitations.

(E)   true happiness lies in attending to the business of everyday life, instead of trying to be a hero.

181.   Which of the following works best exemplifies "courtly love"?

(A)   *Beowulf*

(B)   Chaucer's *Troylus and Criseyde*

(C)   Shakespeare's *Henry IV Part 2*

(D)   Milton's *Paradise Lost*

(E)   Pope's "The Rape of the Lock"

182.   Which of the following best exemplifies allegory?

(A)   Chaucer's "The Reeve's Tale"

(B)   Shakespeare's *Richard II*

(C)   Milton's *Samson Agonistes*

(D)   Spenser's "The Faerie Queene"

(E)   Wycherley's *The Country-Wife*

Questions 183 – 184 refer to the following stanza.

> Our two souls, therefore, which are one,
>   Though I must go, endure not yet
> A breach, but an expansion,
>   Like gold to airy thinness beat.

183.   The versification of the above lines may be described as

(A)   iambic pentameter.

(B)   iambic tetrameter.

(C)   blank verse.

(D)   Alexandrine.

(E)   alliterative.

184.   The stanza is from a poem by

(A)   Donne.

(B)   Keats.

(C)   Chaucer.

(D)   Ben Jonson.

(E)   Tennyson.

Questions 185 - 187 refer to the following sonnet.

> Let me not to the marriage of true minds
> Admit impediments; love is not love
> Which alters when it alteration finds,
> Or bends with the remover to remove.
> O, no, it is an ever-fixed mark   5
> That looks on tempests and is never shaken;
> It is the star to every wand'ring bark,
> Whose worth's unknown, although his height be taken.
> Love's not Time's fool, though rosy lips and cheeks
> Within his bending sickle's compass come;   10
> Love alters not with his brief hours and weeks,
> But bears it out even to the edge of doom.
> If this be error and upon me proved,
> I never writ, nor no man ever loved.

185.   "Impediment" (line 2) refers to

    (A)   a barrier or wall that channels water.

    (B)   a military barricade.

    (C)   a legal restriction.

    (D)   encumbering baggage or equipment.

    (E)   a speech obstruction, a stammer, or stutter.

186.   "Mark" (line 5) refers to

    (A)   a navigational beacon.

    (B)   wrinkles or scars on the face.

    (C)   writing.

    (D)   a distinguishing trait or quality.

    (E)   a rating, an assessment of merit or ability.

187.   The sonnet was written in the

    (A)   fifteenth century.   (D)   eighteenth century.

    (B)   sixteenth century.   (E)   nineteenth century.

    (C)   seventeenth century.

---

188.   "Art for art's sake" best characterizes the aesthetic philosophy of

    (A)   Plato.   (D)   Alexander Pope.

    (B)   Oscar Wilde.   (E)   Horace.

    (C)   T. S. Eliot.

Questions 189 – 191 refer to the following passage.

> Thou, nature, art my goddess; to thy law
> My services are bound. Wherefore should I
> Stand in the plague of custom, and permit
> The curiosity of nations to deprive me,
> For that I am some twelve or fourteen moonshines   5
> Lag of a brother? Why bastard? wherefore base?
> When my dimensions are as well compact,
> My mind as generous, and my shape as true,
> As honest madam's issue? Why brand they us
> With base? with baseness? bastardy? base, base?   10
> Who, in the lusty stealth of nature, take
> More composition and fierce quality
> Than doth, within a dull, stale, tired bed,
> Go to the creating a whole tribe of fops,
> Got 'tween asleep and wake? Well, then,   15
> Legitimate Edgar, I must have your land;

189. The above passage, taken in context, is an example of

(A) a dramatic monologue by Robert Browning.

(B) an eclogue.

(C) the use of a persona in the Anglo-Saxon elegiac tradition.

(D) an Elizabethan soliloquy.

(E) a mock-epic invocation.

190. The theme of the passage can best be paraphrased as

(A) illegitimate children are the responsibility of the society as a whole and should be cared for by the state.

(B) it is perfectly acceptable for men to have adulterous affairs, but not for women.

(C) the rights of inheritance are imposed by artificial and unnatural customs.

(D) adultery and the consequent illegitimate offspring are violations of the natural order of society.

(E)   lechery is one of the consequences of humanity's alienation from God.

191.   The speaker could best be classified as

(A)   Machiavellian.   (D)   a personification.

(B)   an anti-hero.   (E)   the protagonist.

(C)   a foil.

---

192.   My mistress' eyes are nothing like the sun;
       coral is far more red than her lips' red;
       If snow be white, why then her breasts are dun;
       If hairs be wires, black wires grow on her head.

This passage could best be classified as

(A)   Petrarchan.   (D)   mock epic.

(B)   anti-Petrarchan.   (E)   surreal.

(C)   Romantic.

193.   The Baroque is a style following the Renaissance, characterized by content by intense religious experience, personal emotion, and expressiveness, and characterized in form by vitality, movement, and magnificence.

Which of the following literary works would best illustrate the Baroque as defined above?

(A)   Chaucer's *The Canterbury Tales*

(B)   Ben Jonson's *Volpone*

(C)   Milton's *Paradise Lost*

(D)   Pope's "An Essay on Man"

(E)   Wordsworth's *The Prelude*

194.   Altogether the scene was somewhat peculiar, at least to Captain Delano, nor, as he saw the two thus postured, could he resist the vagary, that in the black he saw a headsman, and in the white a man at the block. But this was one of those antic conceits, appearing and vanishing in a breath, from which, perhaps, the best regulated mind is not always free.
— Melville, *Benito Cereno*

As illustrated in the passage quoted above, Melville creates irony in *Benito Cereno* by using which of the following narrative techniques?

(A)   Omniscient third-person narration

(B)   Limited third-person point of view

(C)   First-person narration

(D)   Stream-of-consciousness

(E)   Allegorical personification

Questions 195 – 196 refer to the following passage.

Neither a borrower nor a lender be,
For loan oft loses both itself and friend,
And borrowing dulls th'edge of husbandry.
This above all, to thine own self be true,
And it must follow as the night the day
Thou canst not then be false to any man.

195.   What is happening in the above passage?

(A)   Hamlet, at the conclusion of the play, is summing up the significance of the tragedy, drawing a moral.

(B)   Portia is lecturing Shylock in the trial scene.

(C)   Polonius is giving advice to his son before Laertes returns to France.

(D)   Henry IV, shortly before his death, is giving advice to his son, Prince Hal.

(E)   Iago is giving hypocritical advice to Othello.

196.   The versification in the above passage could best be classified as

    (A) free verse.   (D) terza rima.

    (B) blank verse.   (E) heroic couplets.

    (C) alliterative verse.

Questions 197 – 198 refer to the following passage.

> Some to conceit alone their taste confine,
> And glitt'ring thoughts struck out at ev'ry line;
> Pleased with a work where nothing's just or fit,
> One glaring chaos and wild heap of wit.
> Poets, like painters, thus unskilled to trace   5
> The naked nature and the living grace,
> With gold and jewels cover ev'ry part,
> And hide with ornament their want of art.

197.   In the first line, "conceit" refers to

    (A) pride.   (D) abstraction.

    (B) narcissism.   (E) metaphor.

    (C) hyperbole.

198.   The poetry referred to in the above passage might best be classified as

    (A) mock heroic.   (D) Victorian.

    (B) Romantic.   (E) allegorical.

    (C) metaphysical.

Questions 199 – 200 refer to the following poem.

> My heart leaps up when I behold
>   A rainbow in the sky:
> So was it when my life began;
> So is it now I am a man;
> So be it when I shall grow old,   5

Or let me die!
The Child is father of the Man;
And I could wish my days to be
Bound each to each by natural piety.

199.   The best paraphrase for line 7 is

(A)   children do not realize it, but they grow up to be parents themselves and have to discipline their own children.

(B)   parents have difficulty communicating with their children because the children lack experience.

(C)   children have difficulty communicating with their parents because adults tend to be set in their ways.

(D)   the personality of the adult is determined by the experiences he or she had as a child.

(E)   the experiences of the child are determined by the adult society in which he or she grows up.

200.   By "natural piety" (line 9), the poet means

(A)   the appreciation of nature.

(B)   the recognition of the rainbow as the biblical symbol of God's covenant with Noah and his descendants.

(C)   the worship of God through the study of His Creation.

(D)   the belief that the universe is a mechanical device like a clock, created by God but then allowed to run on its own without further intervention.

(E)   the worship of gods and goddesses personifying natural forces and phenomena.

---

201.   "Better to reign in hell, than serve in heav'n."

The above line summarizes the point of view of

(A)   John Milton.

(B)   Satan in Milton's *Paradise Lost.*

(C) Dr. Faustus in Marlowe's *Dr. Faustus*.

(D) Machiavelli.

(E) Othello in Shakespeare's *Othello*.

202. Quoth the Raven, "Nevermore."

Identify the author of the above refrain.

(A) William Wordsworth   (D) Edmund Spenser

(B) Edgar Allan Poe   (E) Alfred Lord Tennyson

(C) William Shakespeare

Questions 203 – 205 refer to the following sonnet.

How soon hath Time, the subtle thief of youth,
Stolen on his wing my three and twentieth year!
My hasting days fly on with full career,
But my late spring no bud or blossom show'th.
Perhaps my semblance might deceive the truth,
That I to manhood am arrived so near,
And inward ripeness doth much less appear,
That some more timely-happy spirits endu'th.
Yet be it less or more, or soon or slow,
It shall be still in strictest measure even
To that same lot, however mean or high,
Toward which Time leads me, and the will of Heaven;
All is, if I have grace to use it so,
As ever in my great Taskmaster's eye.

203. This sonnet reveals that the author wrote in conformance with
_____ models.

(A) Shakespearean   (D) Italian

(B) Phrygian   (E) Romanesque

(C) Spenserian

204. This sonnet is characterized by each of the following with the *exception* that the author

    (A) avoids the final couplet.

    (B) uses enclosed instead of alternating rhyme in the octave.

    (C) does not make a sharp distinction between octave and sestet.

    (D) does not follow a pattern of *abba, abba, cdedce.*

    (E) alters meter and line requirements.

205. This sonnet was written by

    (A) William Shakespeare.   (D) Petrarch.

    (B) John Milton.   (E) Thomas Wyatt.

    (C) Edmund Spenser.

---

206. All of the following are Miltonian works EXCEPT

    (A) *Areopagitica.*   (D) *Il Penseroso.*

    (B) *Paradise Regained.*   (E) *Samson Agonistes.*

    (C) *Manuductio and Ministerium.*

207. If it were done when 'tis done, then 'twere well
    It were done quickly: if the assassination
    Could trammel up the consequence, and catch
    With his surcease success; that but this blow
    Might be the be-all and the end-all here,
    But here, upon this bank and shoal of time,
    We'd jump the life to come.

    The character speaking here is contemplating the murder of

    (A) Caesar.   (D) Cassius.

    (B) Claudius.   (E) Gloucester.

    (C) Duncan.

Questions 208 – 209 refer to the following selection.

> That darksome cave they enter, where they find
> That cursed man, low sitting on the ground,
> Musing full sadly in his sullein mind;
> His griesie lockes, long growen, and unbound,
> Disordred hong about his shoulder's round,   5
> And hid his face; through which his eyne
> Lookt deadly dull, and stared as stound;
> His raw-bone cheekes through penurie and pine
> Were shronke into his jawes, as he did never dine.

208.   The word "pine" in line 8 means

(A) pain.

(B) a mournful look.

(C) peakedness.

(D) starvation.

(E) poverty.

209.   The lines were written by

(A) Christopher Marlowe.

(B) Geoffrey Chaucer.

(C) Sir Philip Sidney.

(D) Edmund Spenser.

(E) Thomas Campion.

Questions 210 – 212 refer to the following works.

(A) John Winthrop, *Journal*

(B) Benjamin Franklin, *Autobiography*

(C) John Woolman, *Journal*

(D) William Byrd, *Secret Diary*

(E) Jonathan Edwards, *Personal Narrative*

210. Which is a Quaker spiritual autobiography?

211. Which is a Puritan chronicle of the Massachusetts Bay Colony?

212. Which is a Puritan autobiography that recounts the experience of spiritual conversion?

---

213. Which is an autobiographical novel written by an escaped slave?

(A) Aphra Behn, *Oroonoko; Or, the Royal Slave*

(B) Harriet Beecher Stowe, *Uncle Tom's Cabin*

(C) Harriet Jacobs, *Incidents in the Life of a Slave Girl*

(D) Zora Neale Hurston, *Mules and Men*

(E) Constance Robertson, *Fire Bell in the Night*

214. Which refers to Jonathan Edwards?

(A)
        … but none can say
That Lenten fare makes Lenten thought
Who reads your golden Eastern lay,
Than which I know no version done
    In English more divinely well;
A planet equal to the sun
    Which cast it, that large infidel
Your Omar; and your Omar drew
    Full-handed plaudits from our best
In modern letters …

(B)

Others abide our question. Thou art free.
We ask and ask — Thou smilest and art still,
Out-topping knowledge. For the loftiest hill,
Who to the stars uncrowns his majesty.

(C)   O weary Champion of the Cross, lie still:
Sleep thou at length the all-embracing sleep;
Long was thy sowing day, rest now and reap:
Thy fast was long, feast now thy spirit's fill.
Yea take thy fill of love, because thy will
        Chose love not in the shallows but the deep:
        Thy tides were spring tides, set against the neap
Of calmer souls: thy flood rebuked their rill.

(D)   What are we in the hands of the great God?
It was in vain you set up thorn and briar
        In battle array against the fire
        And treason crackling in your blood; ...
You play against a sickness past your cure.
How will the hands be strong? How will the heart endure?

(E)   The young Endymion sleeps Endymion's sleep;
        The shepherd-boy whose tale was left half told!
        The solemn grove uplifts its shield of gold
        To the red rising moon, and loud and deep
The nightingale is singing from the steep ...

215.   Skeltonic verse can best be described as

(A)   undignified, close to doggerel.

(B)   a highly artificial form derived from French models.

(C)   an attempt to emulate the plain but dignified style of the Bible.

(D)   a self-conscious attempt to elevate further the epic style.

(E)   an attempt to capture the natural rhythms of daily speech in verse.

216.   All of the following wrote works in which Arthurian legend plays a significant role EXCEPT

(A)   Thomas Malory.   (D)   Alfred Tennyson.

(B)   John Milton.   (E)   Mark Twain.

(C)   John Dryden.

217. Which is spoken by the narrator of Henry James' *The Beast in the Jungle?*

(A)   Personally I wouldn't never leave a person shoot a gun in the same boat I was in unless I was sure they knew somethin' about guns. Jim was a sucker to leave a new beginner have his gun, let alone a half-wit. It probably served Jim right, what he got. But still we miss him round here. He certainly was a card.

(B)   One could not stand and watch very long without becoming philosophical, without beginning to deal in symbols and similes, and to hear the hog-squeal of the universe. Was it permitted to believe that there was nowhere upon the earth, or above the earth, a heaven for hogs, where they were requited for all this suffering?

(C)   Philip looked away, as he sometimes looked away from the great pictures where visible forms suddenly became inadequate for the things they have shown to us. He was happy; he was assured that there was greatness in the world. There came to him an earnest desire to be good through the example of this good woman.... . Quietly, without hysterical prayers or banging of drums, he underwent conversion. He was saved.

(D)   It was a thing of the merest chance— the turn, as he afterwards felt, of a hair, though he was indeed to live to believe that if light hadn't come to him in this particular fashion it would still have come in another. He was to live to believe this, I say, though he was not to live, I may not less definitely mention, to do much else. We allow him at any rate the benefit of the conviction, struggling up for him at the end, that, whatever might have happened or not happened, he would have come round of himself to the light.

(E)   Description of physical appearance and mannerisms is one of several standard methods of characterization used by writers of fiction. It is also important to "keep the senses operating"; when a detail from one of the five senses, say visual, is "crossed" with a detail from another, say auditory, the reader's imagination is oriented to the scene, perhaps unconsciously.... The brown hair on Ambrose's mother's forearms gleamed in the sun like. Though right handed, she took her left arm from the seat-back to press the dashboard cigar lighter for Uncle Karl.

218.   Which satirizes Puritans?

(A)   Thomas Love Peacock, *Nightmare Abbey*

(B)   T .S. Eliot, "The Waste Land"

(C)   Samuel Butler, "Hudibras"

(D)   John Dryden, "Mac Flecknoe"

(E)   William Wycherley, *The Country-Wife*

219.   Frederick Douglass is the author of

(A)   pastoral poetry.

(B)   a slave narrative.

(C)   the first American novel.

(D)   numerous sermons.

(E)   an early American comedy.

220.   Which describes Christopher Marlowe's *Tamburlaine*?

(A)   A duke (1) poisons his wife because he is enamoured of another married woman (2); the married woman's brother (3) kills his brother and contrives the death of her (2) husband, and also kills their virtuous brother; the married woman (2) is tried for adultery and murder, the duke (1) is poisoned by his dead wife's brother, whose dependents kill the married woman (2) and her brother (3) (who earlier murdered his brother and his brother-in-law).

(B)   The play's hero rises from shepherd to emperor of Persia and supreme ruler of all Asia. He conquers the Turkish emperor, placing him and his empress in a cage and taunting them until they die, vaunts himself in the playwright's "mighty line," and defeats the Arabian king and the Soldan of Egypt, whose life he spares out of love for the Soldan's captive daughter.

(C)   Pregnant by her brother, the heroine marries one of her suitors. Her brother stabs her to thwart the husband's plan of vengeance, kills the husband, and is himself killed.

(D)   A husband discovers his otherwise "perfect" wife in the arms of a house-guest, and sends her to live in comfort in a remote manor-house, only prohibiting her from seeing him and her children again. The wife dies of remorse after having received forgiveness from her husband on her death-bed.

(E)   The heroine, an orphan, is loved by both of the twin sons of her guardian. She secretly marries one; the other takes his twin's place during an assignation in the dark with the heroine. When the truth is discovered, the brothers kill themselves and the heroine takes poison.

Questions 221 – 223 refer to the following poem.

One day I wrote her name upon the strand,
But came the waves and washéd it away:
Agayne I wrote it with a second hand,
But came the tyde, and made my paynes his pray.
"Vayne man," sayd she, "that doest in vaine assay,   5
A mortall thing so to immortalize,
For I my selve shall lyke to this decay,
And eek my name bee wypéd out lykewize."
"Not so," quod I, "let baser things devize
To dy in dust, but you shall live by fame: 10
My verse your vertues rare shall eternize,
And in the heavens wryte your glorious name.
Where whenas death shall all the world subdew,
Our love shall live, and later life renew."

221.   The primary theme of the poem is the

(A) brevity of life.   (D) immortality of true love.

(B) permanence of poetry.   (E) vanity of human wishes.

(C) indifference of nature.

222.   This poem can best be described as

(A) an Italian sonnet.   (D) a narrative poem.

(B) an English sonnet.   (E) a villanelle.

(C) a Spenserian sonnet.

223. A poem that expresses the same theme is

    (A) Wyatt's "Whoso List to Hunt."

    (B) Herrick's "To the Virgins, to Make Much of Time."

    (C) Surrey's "Alas! So All Things Now Do Hold Their Peace."

    (D) Raleigh's "What Is Our Life."

    (E) Shakespeare's Sonnet 55 ("Not marble, nor the gilded monuments").

Questions 224–230. For each of the following passages, identify the author or the work. Base your decision on the content and style of each passage.

224. The king sits in Dumferling toune,
    Drinking the blude-reid wine:
    "O whar will I get guid sailor,
    To sail this schip of mine?"

    (A) *Beowulf*

    (B) *Sir Gawain and the Green Knight*

    (C) *Lord Randall*

    (D) "Sir Patrick Spens"

    (E) *Le Morte D'Arthur*

225. A belt of straw and ivy buds,
    With coral clasps and amber studs—
    And if these pleasures may thee move,
    Come live with me and be my love.

    (A) Sir Philip Sidney

    (B) Andrew Marvell

    (C) Christopher Marlowe

    (D) Robert Herrick

    (E) Lord Byron

226. But we by a love so much refined
That our selves know not what it is,
Inter-assuréd of the mind,
Care less, eyes, lips, and hands to miss.

Our two souls therefore, which are one,
Though I must go, endure not yet
A breach, but an expansion,
Like gold to airy thinness beat.

(A) Henry Howard, Earl of Surrey

(B) Thomas Campion

(C) John Donne

(D) John Milton

(E) William Shakespeare

227. 'Twas mercy brought me from my Pagan land,
Taught my benighted soul to understand
That there's a God, that there's a Saviour too:
Once I redemption neither sought nor knew.

(A) Anne Bradstreet   (D) Langston Hughes

(B) Phillis Wheatley   (E) Theodore Roethke

(C) Philip Freneau

228. …Hail, horrors! hail,
Infernal world! and thou, profoundest Hell,
Receive thy new possessor: One who brings
A mind not to be changed by place or time.
The mind is its own place, and in itself
Can make a Heaven of Hell, a Hell of Heaven.

(A) Edmund Spenser   (D) S. T. Coleridge

(B) John Milton   (E) Robert Browning

(C) John Dryden

229. Them that rule us, them slave-traders,
    Haint they cut a thunderin' swarth
    (Helped by Yankee renegaders),
    Thru the vartu o' the North!
    We begin to think it's nater
    to take sarse an' not be riled;—
    Who'd expect to see a tater
    All on eend at bein' biled?

    (A) Edward Taylor   (D) Frederick Douglass

    (B) Philip Freneau   (E) Gwendolyn Brooks

    (C) James Russell Lowell

230. That after Horror—that 'twas us—
    That passed the mouldering Pie—
    Just as the Granite Crumb let go—
    Our Savior, by a Hair—

    (A) Edgar Allan Poe   (D) Stephen Crane

    (B) Walt Whitman   (E) William Carlos Williams

    (C) Emily Dickinson

GRE LITERATURE
IN ENGLISH

Practice Test 1
Answer Key

1.	(B)	26.	(C)	51.	(C)	76.	(E)
2.	(D)	27.	(A)	52.	(B)	77.	(D)
3.	(E)	28.	(C)	53.	(B)	78.	(B)
4.	(B)	29.	(C)	54.	(D)	79.	(B)
5.	(B)	30.	(D)	55.	(A)	80.	(D)
6.	(D)	31.	(C)	56.	(C)	81.	(D)
7.	(C)	32.	(D)	57.	(B)	82.	(C)
8.	(A)	33.	(A)	58.	(C)	83.	(E)
9.	(C)	34.	(E)	59.	(C)	84.	(B)
10.	(E)	35.	(D)	60.	(A)	85.	(C)
11.	(B)	36.	(B)	61.	(D)	86.	(D)
12.	(B)	37.	(B)	62.	(D)	87.	(C)
13.	(E)	38.	(C)	63.	(B)	88.	(C)
14.	(D)	39.	(D)	64.	(E)	89.	(A)
15.	(E)	40.	(B)	65.	(D)	90.	(D)
16.	(D)	41.	(A)	66.	(E)	91.	(C)
17.	(E)	42.	(A)	67.	(B)	92.	(B)
18.	(E)	43.	(C)	68.	(B)	93.	(C)
19.	(C)	44.	(B)	69.	(E)	94.	(D)
20.	(D)	45.	(C)	70.	(D)	95.	(C)
21.	(A)	46.	(E)	71.	(E)	96.	(D)
22.	(B)	47.	(C)	72.	(D)	97.	(A)
23.	(C)	48.	(A)	73.	(E)	98.	(C)
24.	(D)	49.	(B)	74.	(C)	99.	(D)
25.	(A)	50.	(D)	75.	(C)	100.	(C)

101.	(E)	136.	(C)	171.	(A)	206.	(C)
102.	(C)	137.	(D)	172.	(C)	207.	(C)
103.	(E)	138.	(A)	173.	(E)	208.	(D)
104.	(A)	139.	(B)	174.	(B)	209.	(D)
105.	(A)	140.	(C)	175.	(B)	210.	(C)
106.	(D)	141.	(D)	176.	(A)	211.	(A)
107.	(E)	142.	(C)	177.	(C)	212.	(E)
108.	(B)	143.	(E)	178.	(C)	213.	(C)
109.	(D)	144.	(B)	179.	(A)	214.	(D)
110.	(A)	145.	(D)	180.	(C)	215.	(A)
111.	(B)	146.	(D)	181.	(B)	216.	(B)
112.	(A)	147.	(A)	182.	(D)	217.	(D)
113.	(C)	148.	(B)	183.	(B)	218.	(C)
114.	(A)	149.	(D)	184.	(A)	219.	(B)
115.	(D)	150.	(A)	185.	(C)	220.	(B)
116.	(B)	151.	(B)	186.	(A)	221.	(B)
117.	(B)	152.	(B)	187.	(B)	222.	(C)
118.	(D)	153.	(D)	188.	(B)	223.	(E)
119.	(C)	154.	(E)	189.	(D)	224.	(D)
120.	(C)	155.	(D)	190.	(C)	225.	(C)
121.	(A)	156.	(C)	191.	(A)	226.	(C)
122.	(E)	157.	(C)	192.	(B)	227.	(B)
123.	(C)	158.	(C)	193.	(C)	228.	(B)
124.	(B)	159.	(D)	194.	(B)	229.	(C)
125.	(A)	160.	(D)	195.	(C)	230.	(C)
126.	(E)	161.	(A)	196.	(B)		
127.	(B)	162.	(B)	197.	(E)		
128.	(D)	163.	(C)	198.	(C)		
129.	(C)	164.	(B)	199.	(D)		
130.	(D)	165.	(C)	200.	(A)		
131.	(A)	166.	(D)	201.	(B)		
132.	(A)	167.	(E)	202.	(B)		
133.	(B)	168.	(E)	203.	(D)		
134.	(D)	169.	(E)	204.	(D)		
135.	(B)	170.	(C)	205.	(B)		

GRE LITERATURE
IN ENGLISH

Detailed Explanations
of Answers

1. **(B)**

D. H. Lawrence believed in a "star-equilibrium" love, with the woman not as a satellite to the male but the two in balance. ("Mino" chapter – *Women in Love*). Consider the alternatives: Heathcliff's love (A) is "of the earth and rocks." Rochester's love (C) is total possession. Stephen's love (D) of the "bird-girl" is of "profane joy." George Emerson's love (E) is "of the body."

2. **(D)**

Raphael tells the story of the Fall of the Angels to Adam in Book V of John Milton's *Paradise Lost*. The first line gives a clue: "Son of heaven and earth." From the context, eliminate Michael to Eve (A) and Gabriel to Mary (B). The Angel of Death does not appear to Virgil (C). The Angel Gabriel talks to Dante (E), but only to repeat the Annunciation to Mary.

3. **(E)**

The art here is to read the passage intently, eliminating the obvious from context. The angel stresses that continued happiness depends "on thyself," thus eliminating (A) and (B). Man was made "perfect, not immutable"—be careful with the Miltonic negative "not unchangeable"—he can thus change (C). The angel stresses that man's will (D) is by nature "free."

4. **(B)**

Consider carefully the alternatives and eliminate the obviously faulty: the tone is certainly not jolly (C); it is somewhat gloomy especially in the last lines, but not bad-tempered (D). It is not vindictive (E); it could be didactic but not coupled with patronizing (A)— the angel seems willing to be on a level with the man.

5.   **(B)**

The Canadian woodchopper figures largely in Thoreau's *Walden* as the "true savage." If you do not know the work, consider the other authors. All loved Nature and the rustic life, but certainly poets like Homer (D) and Frost (E) never mention visitors like the Canadian who symbolizes for Thoreau all that he himself searches for in the simple life.

6.   **(D)**

You should recognize Keats' "Ode on a Grecian Urn." From this stanza alone, eliminate the other possibilities. Music does refresh the soul (A), but that is not the central point. Youth does have some advantage (B) but not every advantage. Art is immortal (C) but only because the imagination holds the images in time. Nowhere does the stanza say that art destroys life (E).

7.   **(C)**

If you do not know Keats' poem, eliminate the other possibilities by style and tone: the enjambment would be unusual for Elizabethan poetry (A). The style is too "collected" for the fragmentation of the Post-modern (B). The tone might be early Victorian (D), but the imagination theme is Romantic. The tone is too uplifting for the Modern (E).

8.   **(A)**

If you know the poem, this is simpler. If you are relying on the text alone, go back and read carefully. Nowhere is there a suggestion of despair (B), distrust (C) or fear (D). There is an element of triumph (E), but it involves triumph in the imagination. This leaves (A), which sums up the gist of the poem and the philosophy of the era.

9.   **(C)**

If you have not read *The Sound and the Fury,* be aware of the technique of placing the reader within the protagonist's brain, here reliving a conversation from the past. Eliminate the poetic term enjambment (A) and the dream notion (B); the extended metaphor (D) does not sustain the entire passage. Time is dislocated (E), but that is a structural device, not a technique.

10.   **(E)**

Neither the poetic language (A), nor the nuance (B), nor the extended metaphor (C) of the game of chance achieve the effect of a mind in turmoil. Certainly there is lack of meaning (D) on first reading, but analyze how that is achieved. The lack of punctuation forces the reader to find the speech rhythms and, hence, the meaning.

11.   **(B)**
       If you know the novel, the answer is clear—Quentin and his father are discussing suicide. If not, eliminate: white hair (A) is mentioned once—as how Mr. Compson thinks his son conceives of death. He mentions the mother's dream of the boy at Harvard but not killing that dream (C). Courtesy to women (D) and going away to college (E) are evident but not the main point of discussion.

12.   **(B)**
       Even if you know the novel, the speaker's philosophy needs careful thought. The clue is given in the metaphor of the game of chance: dice loaded against men. Eliminate (D) and (E); the passage contradicts these. The idea of life not worth living (A) is negated in men hanging on to "expedients" to keep alive. The text does not state that love destroys (C).

13.   **(E)**
       If you do not know the passage, eliminate the obvious through tone, style, or era of writing. Hardy's tone (A) is gloom and doom, but he is too early to use this technique, as was Henry James (B). Dreiser's sentence structure (C) eliminates him. Vonnegut's zany style (D) and his attitude to death and fate eliminates him.

14.   **(D)**
       If you do not recognize Dreiser's *Sister Carrie*, eliminate the others. Jane Austen's Emma (A) rarely has pity for anyone, nor does anyone take anything on her account; nor for Hardy's Tess of the D'Urbervilles (B), James' Milly (C) of *Wings of a Dove,* or Crane's Maggie or George Eliot's Maggie Tulliver in *Mill on the Floss* (E).

15.   **(E)**
       If you do not know Tennyson's "Ulysses," which tells of the aged Ulysses setting out with his old crew for a new life, think of the other sailors here, thus eliminating Achilles (A) of *The Iliad*. Jason (B) would have mentioned his exciting venture and young crew; Melville's sailors, Ahab (C) and Ishmael (D), would be described in prose.

16.   **(D)**
The Fourth Book of *Gulliver's Travels* describes the Houyhnhnms, the horses who have canceled all feeling from their lives in favor of Reason, fighting against the Yahoos, feeling carried to the other extreme! Eliminate the others through style—all too modern for the sentence structure and high seriousness demonstrated here.

17.   **(E)**
Gulliver's Travels is famous for tricking readers into thinking it is all of these options. It is a travel book—it satirizes travel accounts (A) well loved in the eighteenth century. It describes other societies which appear to be utopias, but then are proved not through satire [(B) and (C)]. The animals would suggest a fable (D), but the satire is stronger than the moral weight that fables carry.

18.   **(E)**
If you do not know the Fourth Book, eliminate through what you do know. The Liliputians and the Brobdingnagians are from the same work [(A) and (C)] but with different philosophies from the Houyhnhnms. Vonnegut's little plumbers' friends (B) view death stoically but not so coldly, and Orwell's pigs (D) run *Animal Farm*, but are more like the Yahoos.

19.   **(C)**
Whether deliberate or not, Donne mocks the Spenserian poetry so popular in his day, especially the addresses to the Sun. If you do not know Donne's poem, see what you recognize in the other possibilities and cancel out the obvious. (B) is a possibility but the poetry has the same liveliness as Shakespeare's—the mockery would not be effective enough.

20.   **(D)**
If you do not know the names of certain types of poems, learn to recognize them. (A) is an address often to a "lofty" subject, (B) a lament, (C) 14 lines of poetry with set patterns (Petrarchan, Shakespearean) which should be learned, and (E) six stanzas of six lines of poetry in a strict pattern.

21.   **(A)**
Read the poetry carefully and choose through analysis of context. The lovers do not need the sun to make their love wonderful or complete (E). There is no mention of non-sharing [(C) and (D)] or preferring the night (B). If you

know the poem, think of the last stanza where the poet admits his love is all worlds to him; thus the sun shines everywhere when shining on their bed.

22. **(B)**
The key word is "rags"—a striking image from metaphysical poetry where time is referred to as worthless fragments rather than the all-important subject Spenser or Marlowe considered it. The lover claims his love is eternal and has no need to be measured by an inconsequential element like time.

23. **(C)**
If you have established the speaker as Oedipus (and discounted the Shakespeare characters) [(A) and (B)], think of the Sophocles story. The "dead king" is his father whom he killed, thus fulfilling the prophecy at his birth. King Priam (D) is king of the Greeks dealing with the "Helen Problem." Creon (E) is Jocasta's brother who becomes king after Oedipus blinds himself.

24. **(D)**
The two key words are "modern" and "Sarah"—John Fowles' mysterious heroine. Eliminate the Dickens novel (C) because of the "modern," and the others because of the names of the heroines or lack of heroines. Pynchon's *V* has a number of women's names—Rachel, Esther, Victoria, but no Sarah (E).

25. **(A)**
If you do not recognize the Bible passage, eliminate the others through style and content, particularly (C) and (D) which would be more poetic, dealing with specific subjects. (E) is a dialogue and is much clearer in its expression, without the technique of paradox. Isaiah (B) also has its own content and distinctive style.

26. **(C)**
This is one of Crane's most famous passages which reflects his realistic world view. If you do not know Crane, look carefully at the harshness of the middle sentence, with the hyphenated adjectives. The word "lice" comes across very bitterly. Through context, eliminate the other possibilities as too gentle and trivial.

27. **(A)**
If you do not know the word through Chaucer and Shakespeare studies, eliminate the others through the context. The bitter tone must accompany a

ridicule-worthy noun. Otherwise, think of Chaucer's tale of Chanticleer, and the word "coxcombe" carries connotations of both foolishness and arrogance. The other possibilities do not capture the almost sneering tone of the last sentence.

28.   **(C)**

Thomas Hardy (E) does have a passage similar to this where Tess and a companion toil like insects across a field, but here the sentence structure is too short and cryptic for Hardy. Vonnegut (B) and Pynchon (D) would be much lighter and more humorous. The opposite would be true for (A); Camus' tone and style are darker than Crane's.

29.   **(C)**

"Anecdote of the Jar" by Wallace Stevens is well known for the central position of an inconsequential object. He does the same for blackbirds, but not just one (A). Death (B) and nature (E) are too general. William Carlos Williams wrote a poem about plums (D), but again, not just one, and not with such an important status in the poem.

30.   **(D)**

The key words are "exile" and the name Rieux. If you have read *The Plague* by Albert Camus you will recall that the exile was caused by bubonic plague. Rieux is the doctor who survives the epidemic and learns about existence in the process. If you are unfamiliar with the work, think of other works that deal with periods of exile and what causes them, which will limit your choice.

31.   **(C)**

Again, if you know Camus the philosophy will follow naturally. Both *The Plague* and *The Stranger* show men battling the problems of existence. From the context of the passage, gather the idea that the character is deeply meditating on the notion of life's meaning and the possibility of hope, and this should lead you to eliminate the other negative choices.

32.   **(D)**

This is the most famous criticism of metaphysical poetry such as that of Donne (the pair of compasses illustrates the point). If you do not know the author, eliminate by thinking of the types of poetry listed, none of which have particularly "violent" images. Do not be confused by Jonson/Johnson—the former wrote at approximately the same time as Donne—but does not comment on religious poetry.

33.   **(A)**
Oscar Wilde's plays are famous for this type of comedy. If you do not know the term or the type of play or novel, think of the choices. (B) is too specific. (C) could be applied to many works. (D) is a possibility but could be applied to most comedies, as (E) could be applied to many novels. Novels of Jane Austen and E. M. Forster perfectly define the term, "comedy of manners."

34.   **(E)**
Frost's famous poem outlines his neighbor's efforts to keep a wall between them. Frost's image captures the poet as a genial, nature-loving, integral-to-nature man, as "fertile" and adaptable as an apple tree. The neighbor is as trenchant, solid, and unchanging as the pine tree. He insists on rebuilding the wall between them.

35.   **(D)**
Gerard Manley Hopkins' poetry is easily recognizable for its sprung rhythm, a counterpoint to the normal English rhythm. If you do not recognize the title, go back to the poetry—the second line should reveal the difference from the usual in poetry.

36.   **(B)**
Ecclesiastes lends itself into being adapted to various poems and songs because of its rhythms and paradoxes. "Ode to Autumn" and "Fern Hill" are equally as rhythmic but without the same resonance of meaning—one dealing with death of a season, the other the death of youth.

37.   **(B)**
If you do not recognize Hemingway's *Hills Like White Elephants*, analyze the passage carefully. What is it the male thinks is so easy and the female is so reluctant to discuss?—not simply (A) or (D). There is accusation (C) and repetition (E), but they are not the main point of the discussion.

38.   **(C)**
Simply from context, the word sums up the relationship gathered from the desultory conversation, a relationship without love, commitment, or un-

derstanding between the man and the woman. When an author as sparse in description as Hemingway includes a detail such as this, you know it is there for a specific reason.

39. **(D)**
Two key elements help here: the amount of labels on the luggage and the point of the "nights" spent together, not days or vacations or weeks, but specifically, nights. This suggests a purely physical relationship which can be gathered from the conversation also, and the labels suggest the restlessness of a couple constantly packing bags and moving on.

40. **(B)**
If you do not know the Gothic novel, eliminate through analyzing the other types of novels. Italian novels (A) is meant to mislead you; realistic novels (C) tended to be about the trials of working-class life; naturalistic novels (D) would not be about "haunted buildings"; and detective novels (E) usually have the detective as the hero/heroine rather than a virtuous young woman.

41. **(A)**
Parodies and burlesques grow out of serious novels, poems, or plays. Jane Austen used *The Mysteries of Udolpho* in her novel (the two "heroines" and "hero" discuss the plot) to poke fun at the type and show the nature of real evil in the world. The other choices here have elements of the Gothic, but none makes a burlesque like Austen's novel.

42. **(A)**
Swift's trick in his *A Modest Proposal* is to convince the reader he is a reasonable man who has done research into the problem of the poor. The other suggestions are not relevant to this passage—if you know the whole tract, leave it at a distance to analyze this particular piece of information.

43. **(C)**
If you know the whole document, you will know the exact proposal for the starving Irish that is under consideration. If not, read the passage carefully to see in which direction the writer is heading. (A), (D), and (E) would be financially crippling in the implementation, and imagine the collection time for suggestion (B)!

44.   **(B)**

Swift is famous for his satirical writing, especially this piece, which original readers took very seriously and became outraged at the suggestion of eating babies. The other suggestions can be eliminated by referring again to context: certainly not realistic (A), too harsh for irony (C), too serious and calm for Modernism (D), and certainly too unpleasant for hedonism (E).

45.   **(C)**

This is a good test to see if you know the author and, more importantly, can place him in the correct era. Think of how early (A), (B), and (E) were written, and how much later and in a much softer style is Henry James. Think of works by Fielding in a similar vein, poking fun at the Establishment-mock-heroic, yet with serious consideration of the plight of the poor.

46.   **(E)**

Browning perfected the technique of the dramatic monologue, a poem in which a speaker addresses a silent listener—not to be confused with the soliloquy in which the speaker addresses thin air, a thinking-aloud process. If you are not familiar with the form, eliminate through what you recognize; none of the others apply.

47.   **(C)**

If you do not know the poem "My Last Duchess" and the situation (showing a portrait of the dead Duchess to an ambassador for the next duch-ess!), catch the clue about the paint and the painter and the subject of the painting—not a landscape (B), designs (E), or a book (D), but a portrait of the lady under discussion. Later, the two men look at the sea horse sculpture (A).

48.   **(A)**

Again, read closely and analyze through tone. What is the Duke saying about the lady? He disliked her simply because she enjoyed simple earthly pleasures which, he suggests, he does not. His tone is not weak (B), certainly, nor is it angry (C); it is not approving (D) nor is it unreasonable (E). There is an element of both pride and egoism.

49.   **(B)**

A good dramatic monologue reveals as much about the subject as the speaker. The lady is revealed as sweet and pleasure loving—enjoying the simpler things of life. There is no hint here, or in the rest of the poem that she is flirtatious (A), licentious (E), avaricious or interested in rank (D), yet her husband has her executed, as revealed later in the poem.

50.   **(D)**
       Othello has just listened to Iago's hints about Desdemona's infidelity, and his pleas to "Beware jealousy!" Pay close attention to Shakespearean names which can sound similar. (A) is the courtier accused of sleeping with Desdemona; (B) is from *The Merchant of Venice*; (C) is from *Romeo and Juliet*; and (E) is from *Hamlet*.

51.   **(C)**
       Most Shakespeare editions give a detailed explanation of this metaphor, which would need no explanation for the Elizabethans: a haggard is a partly trained hawk gone wild. The jesses are straps that attach the hawk to the trainer's wrist. If Desdemona is unfaithful, like a hawk gone wild, then Othello will release her and allow her freedom.

52.   **(B)**
       Horns were supposedly the sign of a man whose wife was unfaithful. Othello is beginning to believe Iago's lies about Desdemona's adultery; he is being cuckolded. Later when she wishes to bind Othello's head for a headache, he insists the handkerchief (the handkerchief that is so vital to the plot) is too small, i.e., the horns are beginning to grow!

53.   **(B)**
       If you are not familiar with the word, think of the religious phrase "the quick and the dead"—the living and the dead. In context, derive the meaning: great ones are susceptible to adulterous affairs—they are as inevitable as death—as soon as they are born. Thus, Othello makes the contrast between the living and the dead.

54.   **(D)**
       Kate Chopin is well known for her short stories. Her main novel, *The Awakening*, is less favored but well worth reading for its similar theme to *Madame Bovary*, but with more sympathy for the heroine. It is a feminist novel written in the late 1800s. If you do not know the novel, think of the heroines of the authors listed here. None of them relates to Flaubert's character.

55. **(A)**

Shaw's play parodies the Greek concept of heroism in battle and gallantry to women. The so-called hero Sergius is brave in battle but weak in life. The so-called coward Bluntchi runs away from battle but is morally brave. Think of the first lines of the epics listed and eliminate those whose contexts do not fit Shaw's title.

56. **(C)**

In *Shooting an Elephant*, Orwell crystallizes all the conflicts and fears involved in colonialism. The other writers listed write of colonialism, but none were so directly and personally involved as Orwell, nor express themselves with such feeling. Orwell served as a policeman in Burma.

57. **(B)**

If you know the passage and Orwell's life, the answer is clear. If not, read the passage for clues. "Dominion in the East" rules out (C), (D), and (E) (the rifle shows the era for the latter). The yellow faces and the white man's uneasiness rules out India—very little of the literature in this age shows white men uneasy with their roles in India.

58. **(C)**

The Medieval writers or singers frequently name their characters for the vices or virtues they displayed, so that the simple country folk watching a play would identify a character immediately. Later this device became more sophisticated. Thus, Everyman represents every human being. John Bunyon's Christian, in *Pilgrim's Progress*, is every Christian.

59. **(C)**

This is a famous statement on the novel in *The Common Reader* by Virginia Woolf, who recommends that novels not be straight, linear, A to B chronologies, but reflect the randomness of life's experience. Woolf experimented in stream-of-consciousness writing which shows not fragmentation, but life-like accounts of how life is passed in the brain.

60. **(A)**

Henry Fielding pokes fun at society in the Age of Reason (or the Augustan Age, named after Augustus who brought culture to his age) for worshipping all aspects of Greek life. The "battle," not between great Greek heroes but a simple village girl and her neighbors, bears allusions to Venus and Mars, which should provide clues for your answer.

61. **(D)**

The poet is parodying Wordsworth's "It is a beauteous evening," written after experiencing a transcendental moment with his daughter. Here the poet "lowers the tone" as the wife watches the husband with a hang-over. You may recognize the original poem for the parody but not the poet. Think of famous poems by the other poets listed and eliminate.

62. **(D)**

The famous opening lines of Jonson's play, spoken by Volpone himself, make a sacrilegious parody of the prayer to God at the opening of a new day. If you are not familiar with the play, analyze the style and tone of the other possibilities, all to do with money or possessions. Distinguish the Shakespearean style from the Jonsonian.

63. **(B)**

Do not be confused with Salonio's speech (C) where Antonio's debt to Shylock is directly mentioned. In *The Merchant of Venice*, Shylock's speeches are frequently in the normal speech patterns of conversation, not in blank verse or rhyme. Salonio, as a friend of the rich merchant Antonio, maintains the speech patterns of the upper-class.

64. **(E)**

Again, to establish a character of the lower class, Shakespeare gives Falstaff the speech patterns of prose, unlike Hotspur's speech (A). Notice that when Prince Hal speaks to Falstaff he adopts the lower-class speech. When he talks to his peers he reverts to blank verse. In this speech Falstaff begins the wish process for a change of identity.

65. **(D)**

If you do not recognize the speech patterns of Huck Finn, start eliminating the names you do know. David Copperfield's tone and style of speech (A) are much more elevated than Strether's (E), and he is not the narrator, nor are Carrie and Maggie, (B) and (C), whose speech patterns are as colloquial but not as harsh.

66. **(E)**

If you recognize the passage, you will recognize the Grangerford house. On the surface the family is orderly and civilized, yet underneath the surface lies a hypocrisy: the morbidity of the dead young girl obsessed with death when alive, the feuding with the Shepherdsons for thirty years. They are not what they seem, just like the fake fruit.

67. **(B)**
Look closely at the titles of the books: The Bible, *Pilgrim's Progress*, *Friendship's Offering*, and the fact that they are piled up exactly, i.e., never read! Even if you do not know the family and their feuding, the titles suggest an irony, and the other possibilities can be eliminated in context.

68. **(B)**
Frequently Eliot's symbolism can be detected only in the poem seen as an integral whole. In "Prufrock" the allusions to characters from the past, characters such as Lazarus and John the Baptist and here, Hamlet, become central symbols for the poem. Do not be confused with (C) from "The Dry Salvages" which personifies the river as a god.

69. **(E)**
"Little Gidding" shows the poet wrestling with words and meaning and returning exactly where he began, to begin all over again, a process the poet saw as part of the life-cycle of man. The entire opening movement of the poem builds upon poetic paradox: "We die with the dying: We are born with the dead."

70. **(D)**
Eliot writes of worlds in despair, fragmented, ruined—the imagery for such worlds demands delving into the subconscious, the night-world of dreams and nightmares. Often the probing produces surrealistic images of madness, debris, waste, and of course, drought, as in "The Waste Land." Here the nightmare image prevails.

71. **(E)**
Lord Byron's poems mean a great deal to the protagonist, Little Cloud. Trapped in a non-Romantic setting, he yearns for the profound loves and exotic adventures of Byron. If you do not know the poetry excerpt in Joyce's short story, eliminate (A), (C), and (D) through style, then try to recall a Wordsworth poem addressed to Margaret.

72.   **(D)**

Again, if you do not know the piece, eliminate through style. (A) is a possibility, considering D. H. Lawrence's short stories, but not this particular novel. (B) and (C) are too modern for the style depicted here, and Hardy's style (E) is too distinct to be confused with Joyce. Do not neglect Joyce's short stories, which are well worth studying.

73.   **(E)**

Lord Chesterfield wrote letters to his son, letters which seem outrageous in some parts to modern readers, but give an interesting insight into the lifestyles of the age. His world was Richardson's (A) and Fielding's who fictionalize the time's mores. Addison (B) and Chesterton developed the essay and epistolary art.

74.   **(C)**

Pandarus features slightly in *The Iliad*, but Chaucer develops the character into a scoundrel to whom readers react differently. He does "procure" Criseyde for Troylus but also brings humor and fun to the story, querying whether Troylus is a man or a mouse in his virginal attitude to women.

75.   **(C)**

There is an element of all these possibilities in the definition, but the main point of a pander's role is the sexual dimension. You can pander to someone's wants and desires by giving in too easily, but the true role involves procuring the sexual favors of one human being for another.

76.   **(E)**

Virgil is conducting Dante to Hell, *Inferno*, Canto III, lines 76–81. If you do not know Dante, then eliminate through style. The Bible [(B) and (C)] and *Paradise Lost* would be in more elevated language. Homer never engages in conversation with Odysseus (D). This passage establishes the relationship between Master and Disciple, something none of the other works develop.

77.   **(D)**

If you do not know Dante or the mythical terms for the journey to Hell, eliminate through context. The words "sorrowful shore" eliminate (A) and (E). As Virgil is taking Dante, neither a soldier nor a child, eliminate (B) and (C). The passage suggests that we all have the potential to cross the river into Hell.

78. **(B)**

The key to understanding the passage are the words "abashed" and "unmeet," and deriving from the context the relationship between master and disciple, the leader and the led. The paraphrase should capture the shame and the humility on the part of the narrator. Eliminate the options that suggest anger on the narrator's part.

79. **(B)**

Death scenes are very important in novels and plays. These last words from Kurtz in *Heart of Darkness* are perhaps the most well known as they reveal the dying man's whole personality. (A) is from the same novel. Dr. Rieux (C) in *The Plague* has too many victims for him to recall last words. (D) and (E) come close to death but do not narrate last words.

80. **(D)**

Kurtz's last words reveal the innate evil of the man and the Hell which is receiving him. (A) is Balzac's Old Goriot thinking of his daughters to the end. (B) is Dickens's Magwitch from *Great Expectations*, (C) is Osvald from Ibsen's *Ghosts* before sinking into insanity, and (E) is Flory to the dog he shoots before killing himself in Orwell's *Burmese Days*.

81. **(D)**

You need to know the plot for the relationship between the fiancee and Kurtz. Marlow cannot reveal to a good, innocent woman the horrifying evil of the man she loved. The man's last words would instantly reveal that Kurtz was not thinking of her or any human thing at that moment, but slipping into evil as horrifying as that which he had perpetrated on earth.

82. **(C)**

The Parable of the Prodigal Son illustrates one of the central premises of Christianity: that sinners will be forgiven and welcomed back, more loved than before, into God's fold. If you do not know the parable, some of the other possibilities could be considered, but there is always a deeper meaning to the seemingly simple stories.

83. **(E)**

A favorite theme of Yeats and the Romantic poets, Coleridge and Wordsworth, was the constancy of nature. The birds come back each year as if they were the same birds. Trees seem to die each year but come back, as if resurrected, in the spring, a feat which man cannot achieve.

84. **(B)**

There are clues in the stanzas even if you do not know the poem: peacocks (A) and doves (E) do not "paddle in the cold/Companionable streams"; ducks (C) and geese (D) seem infinitely less ethereal than swans, and think of the well-known poem of Yeats, "Leda and the Swan," a bird of interest to him.

85. **(C)**

Vladimir and Estragon feature in the play *Waiting for Godot*, frequently performed these days and well worth reading. The other characters are also from Beckett's works with the exception of Biff and Happy (E), who sound like Beckett people but in fact are Arthur Miller's from *Death of a Salesman*.

86. **(D)**

If you know the play, be careful distinguishing between (B) and (D). The characters do not listen to each other, which is one of Beckett's main points about the lack of human communication in the modern age. Eliminate (A) because the boredom is not apparent here. Eliminate (E) as the feeling is strong that they know each other well and can relax with one another.

87. **(C)**

In the preface to *The Deerslayer*, Fenimore Cooper sets the story behind the strange attraction of Judith for his hero. If you do not know the story, analyze the other heroes and "plug into" the relationship described. (A), (B), and (D) do not fit the description of the hero. (E) begins well, but no Judith exists in the story.

88. **(C)**

Although he lived for a shorter span than Cooper, Edgar Allan Poe (1809–1849) wrote at approximately the same time. Charles Brockden Brown (D), often considered the first American novelist, was much earlier, as were Richardson (A) and Fielding (B) in England. Mark Twain (E) comes later. While studying specific authors, be aware of their time and contemporaries.

89. **(A)**

Do not confuse Goldsmith's Marlow with Conrad's—different genres and different literary periods. *She Stoops to Conquer* is a Restoration comedy, frequently performed and very amusing to read. Analyze the other choices: (B) is Catherine's name from *Wuthering Heights*. (C) and (D), Booby and Andrews, are from *Joseph Andrews* and, (E) is Teazle is from *The Rivals*.

90.   **(D)**

A late play in the Restoration period, *She Stoops to Conquer* has softened some of the outright farce of the true Restoration play, like a Congreve, or a Wycherley play. There is more fun in Goldsmith and Sheridan and less cruelty than in the earlier plays, but the period is still considered Restoration.

91.   **(C)**

Ezra Pound's explanations of modern poetry and his work within the movement are worth studying. A number of writers including T. S. Eliot are in debt to him not only for influence but also for personal friendship and help in publishing. The other poets/critics listed rarely express themselves quite so clearly or so emphatically.

92.   **(B)**

Much of Pound's writing is complex and difficult to grasp on first reading because of the internalized symbolism, as in T. S. Eliot's case. However, often as in this excerpt, a cryptic tone comes across which reflects the man's approach to life: a modern take-me-for-what-I-am attitude which antagonized even his friends.

93.   **(C)**

Do not confuse this with Amy Lowell (E) who was influenced by Pound and the French symbolists; her internalizing of images can make for difficult reading. Robert Lowell is more straightforward in the imagery and verse patterns. The picture here of the "hill-skull" and the graveyard extending the metaphor is typical of Robert Lowell, along with his love and death images.

94.   **(D)**

The Sheridan play stands out from the others, which are all early Restoration plays. Sheridan places more symbolic weight on his characters' names. His famous Mrs. Malaprop gave birth to the word "malapropism." Like Goldsmith's, Sheridan's plays tone down the cruelty of the early plays and become semi-realistic comedies.

95.   **(C)**
    The Humours developed from the morality plays where the characters took on the attributes of their names, often associated with sins: Sloth, Gluttony, etc. Ben Jonson developed the technique for attributes of personality, and Sheridan polished it so that without seeing the play we know that Lady Sneerwell will be a snob and Snake is not to be trusted.

96.   **(D)**
    Dryden's criticism is frequently neglected, but he does have interesting insights and writes in clear, succinct prose. Eliminate the obvious from (A), (B), and (C), especially the latter where he would hardly praise his own work so lavishly, and think of the range and diversity in Chaucer's tales versus Shakespeare's history plays.

97.   **(A)**
    If you do not know biblical names, ponder the "he" talking to Hawthorne. Eliminate Isaiah (C) and Job (E) as non-tragic figures not involved with someone who knew Hawthorne. Lucifer (D) in Milton's hands became a tragic figure, but Milton lived centuries before Hawthorne. Ishmael (B) was not an Old Testament ruler, which leaves Melville's tragic hero, Ahab.

98.   **(C)**
    Alexander Pope took the heroic couplet to new heights, splitting the lines at the caesura, developing a two-by-five stress rather than the plodding iambic or octosyllabic line. If you do not know the poem or the poet's technique, cancel out the obvious (A) and (D) and distinguish between the different types of couplets.

99.   **(D)**
    The key word here is in fact omitted, but, in context, mentally add the verb "filled." Your vocabulary should include the word "lampoon," especially if you have studied this era when the lampoon was a very popular means of attacking one's enemy.

100.   **(C)**
    (A) and (B) are possibilities, but from the context analyze why the "Fairones" become ill in the first place. Capture the tone of the poetry and the mockery behind it. There were plenty of reasons for women to fall ill in Pope's day, but in this case, the advent of a new nightdress that they could show off in their rooms provoked diseases.

101. (E)

Again, your working vocabulary should help you, but the meaning can be gauged from the stanzas. If possible, read aloud and fit each word into the sentence. (C) is a possibility, but why use two words that mean the same? (D) suggests movement with affectation that is not demonstrated in Pope's mock heroic presentation of emblems.

102. (C)

The last lines provide the clue if you do not know the whole poem, which was written to ridicule two families quarrelling over a trivial incident: the theft of a lock of hair. Pope, in "The Rape of the Lock," builds the incident into a ridiculous Epic, mocking the epic traditions and more importantly, the foolishness of society around him.

103. (E)

The key is to look carefully at the name and its connotations. There is a harshness, but the "grinding" down sound gives a notion also. There is a notion of wearing down, reducing, and in the end, the passage suggests a nonsense process behind the name. If you know the novel *Hard Times*, then the philosophy of the speaker adds to the passage.

104. (A)

If you recognize Dickens as the author, you will know his reputation for purely descriptive writing: adjective piled upon adjective in a balanced structure. There is no allegorical (B) writing here. Metaphorical (C) writing exists, but that term does not encompass the language in use, nor does symbolic (D), although symbols are at work. Prosodic (E) refers to a particular type of verse—not in use here.

105. (A)

The speaker's hair is likened to a plantation of firs but the author does not use the words *like* or *as*—the figure of speech is a metaphor. However, Dickens then follows the notion with the idea of the speaker's head looking *like* the crust of a plum pie—a simile. Know the terms for figures of speech for poetry as well as prose.

106. (D)

Hard Times is a lesser-known Dickens novel instructive in its criticism of England's educational system. You might surmise from the description that the author is Charles Dickens. If you are not aware of his unfinished novel *The Mystery of Edwin Drood*, analyze those you know: Samuel Butler (A), Turgenev (B), Charlotte Brontë (C) and George Eliot (E), and recall if this passage derives from those.

107. **(E)**
Shaw is renowned for the fully detailed stage directions which add to the realism of the plays. You may recognize the Bulgarian setting for *Arms and the Man*. If not, the pure wealth of detail should lead you to think of Shaw. In your study of drama, take careful note of the different styles of stage directions.

108. **(B)**
The grammar would suggest a lower-class character, a servant perhaps like Joseph (A) or a rough diamond squire like Mr. Western (C). However, the names Estella and Matthew Pocket should reveal *Great Expectations*. If you do not know this book, think of the other choices, none of which contain an Estella or a Matthew Pocket.

109. **(D)**
Joe Gargery is a veritable Mr. Malaprop. The word meant is very similar in sound to "coddleshell"—a codicil (D), not a cockleshell (A). Read the passage closely and eliminate why he should be talking about (A) in the context of a will or why shell-pink paper (E) would be attached to an official document. Your working vocabulary should sift the rest.

110. **(A)**
Post-Modernism is becoming more widely understood, both as a means of literature and criticism, since the works of such writers cum critics as David Lodge simplify the jargon and explain the philosophies of early proponents such as Jacques Derrida. The other choices have elements of Post-Modernism, but often one element counteracts another as in humor (B).

111. **(B)**
Hellenism became part of Matthew Arnold's world-view and produced a very important essay. Look at Arnold's essays as well as his poetry for excellent insights into the thinking of the nineteenth century, especially in regard to education and England's relationship with America.

112. **(A)**

Read Coleridge's *Biographia Literaria* for his thoughts on the mind and imagination. Like Mill, Coleridge sees magical, almost mystical healing powers in the imagination. Recognize work by Coleridge in this field by the key words Imagination and Fancy, which are always capitalized. The criticism aids in the understanding of Coleridge's poetry.

113. **(C)**

Even if you do not know T. S. Eliot's essays (the most important mentions the "objective correlative" in his criticism of *Hamlet*), you will recognize the calm, balanced tone of the prose. Contrast with the strident, almost querulous, tone of Carlyle (E). Key concerns for Eliot are the integrity of the writer and writing as a state of art.

114. **(A)**

Nick Carraway, the most intriguing of narrators, simply relates the dialogue between Gatsby and Daisy. If you do not know *The Great Gatsby*, or do not recall this particular passage, think of the other narrators listed. (B) and (C) do not involve themselves as narrators as (D) sometimes does. (E), Barth's Giles or George, relates stranger dialogues than this.

115. **(D)**

It is as if the stopped clock is smashed to pieces as the time between the lovers' meetings is gradually being destroyed. Gatsby and Daisy should have married five years ago; the time between has been wasted time emotionally, if not financially, for Gatsby, who builds his empire to regain the only woman he has ever loved.

116. **(B)**

The other man, of course, is Gatsby, who has counted the minutes in a classically Romantic way since losing Daisy, and has put his time to "good" use in building a fortune. From the tone of the conversation the other choices can be eliminated, especially (E), Tom Buchanan, who is not mentioned here and indeed knows nothing of the meeting.

117. **(B)**

If you recognize *The Great Gatsby* and know F. Scott Fitzgerald's work, this is straightforward. If not, think of the authors of these novels involving time: Djuna Barnes (A), John Fowles (C), Anthony Powell (D), Graham Greene (E), and eliminate by those you do know.

118. (D)

Even if you do not know the poem, the phrase "darkling plain" should resurrect the association of "Dover Beach" where a love-regret develops into a world-view. Analyze the other titles and decide if any of them have the progression described, or, decide which poet wrote which poem: Wordsworth (A), Browning (B), Coleridge (C), Keats (E).

119. (C)

The poet meditates on not only the destruction of empires, but on man's status on earth—the futility of countries building empires or men building statues to themselves because, in time, all vestiges of man's stay on earth will be hidden, as if by the sands of time. Ozymandias spoke truer than he knew when instructing "Look on my works… and despair!"

120. (C)

The face of the mammoth statue still retains the frown, wrinkled lip, and sneer of command of the ruler—all words that suggest coldness and arrogance. The poet reveals nothing about the sculptor's attitude to his model, other than that he captured the likeness well. Read the three lines carefully so that you capture the adjectives and the sculptor's role.

121. (A)

If you do not know the poet, Percy Shelley, go through the choices to analyze who you do know: Coleridge (B), Keats (C), Gray (D), T. S. Eliot (E). Then go one stage further and think of the range of the poets and whether "Ozymandias" belongs to that poet. This tests whether you can recognize the poet's range. In this case, the two poems are in direct contrast.

122. (E)

If you do not know *A Room With A View*, eliminate from the choices of heroines and chaperones the right heroine, the wrong chaperone (A)—Mrs. Allen is from Austen's *Northanger Abbey*, Caroline Abbott (B) from Forster's *Where Angels Fear to Tread* and Mrs. Moore of *A Passage to India*, (C) from *The Great Gatsby*, and Mrs. Fairfax (D) from *Jane Eyre*.

123. (C)

You need to know Forster's works for this word, repeated in *A Room With A View* and featured in his novels and short stories. However, recalling the humanism of Forster you would discount the strength of (A) and (E) and the exaggeration of (B) and (D). The author wishes human beings simply "to connect" and "muddle" gets in the way.

124.   **(B)**

If you do not know the work, you might be confused by the choices, which all involve war-like passages. However, if you read the passage closely and detect the long heroic simile, you will narrow the choice to (A) and (B). Think then of *The Odyssey's* tales, all much lighter in tone than *The Iliad*, even when death is involved.

125.   **(A)**

Even without knowledge of this particular text and the name for the Greeks, you will recall the war between Greece and Troy for a hundred years starting with the abduction of Helen by Paris. The others, except perhaps the Romans, do not figure in large eloquent pieces of description such as this, nor did they worship Zeus, a clue from the passage itself.

126.   **(E)**

Again if you are not sure of the battle, analyze the choices: (A) are on the same side; Boadicea (B), a British heroine, fights the Romans, not one particular hero; Jason (C) lived in the generation prior to Priam; Achilles and Patroklos (D) were dearest friends—the death of the latter restores Achilles to the battle where he cruelly slaughters Hector.

127.   **(B)**

Frequently a Homeric simile will begin describing one aspect and, after its lengthy run, end up with a totally different focus. The effect is still striking. Here the first image is of the softness of snow, but the last lines contrast that softness with the image of "stones volleyed," "thrown," "flung" and the idea of the noise of the stones as "thunder."

128.   **(D)**

There are elements of each choice that are viable but the main effect of the snow causing a haze over the works of man and bringing all into uniformity universalizes the scene. The armies then could be any armies; the soldiers are all men. Homer's listeners felt, and today's readers feel, for humanity in the struggle.

129. **(C)**
Perhaps the most famous of Joyce's stories captures the same effect at its close. Snow is falling over all of Ireland but the effect is universal. We feel not simply for the protagonists but for humanity. The other choices deal with similar effects of rain or snow, but do not move into the realm of universalizing an experience.

130. **(D)**
The main character is unique in James' work in that she is a child, and the narrative is unique in the art of the novel because the events are seen through a child's consciousness. The idea came from a real case where the child became a shuttlecock between changing sets of parents. If you do not know the novel, analyze those familiar to you—none centers around one child.

131. **(A)**
Sylvia Plath's "The Mirror" begins with the woman's mirror at home "speaking." In the second stanza there is still a mirror, but this time the woman sees her reflection in a lake, another mirror refusing to give an untrue image of the woman. She can destroy that image by agitating the water. You do not need to know the poem to derive the meaning from context.

132. **(A)**
Once you have established the metaphor of the lake as mirror and the fact that the woman does not want her real, true image, you will derive the meaning of the "liars," the soft, flattering lights that people use so that they can hide the wrinkles and the sagging flesh of the aging face.

133. **(B)**
The mirror refuses, indeed is incapable of, reflecting the young girl who has "gone down" with age. It must show the truth, the aging woman with her disappointments and scaling, old wrinkled skin. The lake metaphor does not stretch far enough for the woman to feel like a fish [(C) and (D)]; mirrors don't change (A); and the mirror's silver backing (E) is not addressed by the poem.

134. **(D)**
The poet is obviously a woman. It would take an ingenious male poet to capture the woman's feelings at aging—eliminate (C) and (E). Emily Dickinson's style (A) is distinctive; her poetry is instantly recognized by structure alone. Amy Lowell's (B) would contain repeated symbolism.

135. **(B)**

The title *Shadow of the Glen* or the content of the passage should reveal the playwright, for Synge was involved with the Abbey Theater group who wanted to revitalize the Irish language and prove that natural speech was suitable for the stage. Analyze the other Irish names listed, the body of work of each, and whether the passage's title fits.

136. **(C)**

You do not need to know Synge's theories. Derive the meaning from the passage. If he learned from listening to Wicklow servant girls, then obviously he was interested in the speech and rhythms of the simple country folk. He adds a rider for the use of the language if that language is "rich and copious," not "bright" or "dirty."

137. **(D)**

This scene in the last section of *The Sound and the Fury* is crucial to the whole structure. Here, Dilsey recognizes the "first and the last" of the Compson family and time, symbolized by the Christmas bell, even though the time is Easter: birth and resurrection. If you do not know the passage, the heat and the sparseness of the scene would suggest a Southern, Faulknerian church.

138. **(A)**

The names may well reveal the novel. If not, the song, the audience participation, and the tambourine would reveal the church as James Baldwin's. The stiff, deathly church scenes in (B) and (E) would discount them. (C) is a possibility, but the refrains from the hymns establish a white Presbyterian service from *The Damnation of Theron Ware*.

139. **(B)**

George Bowling reminisces about his childhood church in passages replete with memories. Time has given the church scene an aura of mystery. If you do not know the Orwell novel, you may confuse the scene with (E) from James Joyce's *Grace,* but that church is established as very proper—hints being the way men are dressed and the "high altar"—not an Orwellian church scene.

140. **(C)**

Increasingly popular, Lessing's novel is well worth studying. If you do not know the work, think of the other "Annas" listed. (D) and (E) are, in fact, "Annies" so they can be eliminated. If you know the other two, you know they did not want or wait for a deus ex machina in their lives; they handled their own destinies.

141. **(D)**

The key words here are "current usage." The original term was used for a device in the theater that was lowered from the top of the stage as if a god were entering the drama to manipulate the turn of events. In current usage, the term is found in criticism of all genres for one who turns around imminent disaster.

142. **(C)**

The title and brief description should reveal the author. If you are not familiar with the work, the comparison with Faulkner and Kafka would immediately cancel choices (B) and (E). Then think of the body of work of (A) and (C) and fit the title into that body, or think of how they might resemble Faulkner and Kafka.

143. **(E)**

Some of the choices can be eliminated immediately if you do not recognize the work from the description. (C) is full of coarse mishaps and (D) has disembowelings and floggings, but never resurrection. (B) is more magical with Gulliver in the land of the giants, but as with the magic quality of (A), real life prevails and we do sympathize with the victims.

144. **(B)**

If you have identified the work correctly, you will recall Pangloss' statement. If unsure, identify the other choices: McCawber (A) is in *David Copperfield*, the narrator (C) is in *Slaughterhouse-Five*, Lambert Strether (D) is in *The Ambassadors*, and Uriah Heep (E) is in *David Copperfield*.

145. **(D)**

You may not recognize Emerson's work *Nature*, but the New England Transcendentalists had a certain turn of phrase that identifies them with the basic elements of their belief. In this passage, the notion of an extra sense, an inspiration from outside the body, links immediately to transcendentalism. The premise does not apply to the other choices.

146. **(D)**

William James wrote a number of brilliant essays but is best remembered for his work on pragmatism. The passage delineates some part of his philosophy and the word "pragmatically" is the key word here. Like that of his brother Henry, William James' prose is convoluted, the sentences longer than the modern norm—another key to identification.

147. **(A)**
The Transcendentalists were criticized for their withdrawal from society and seemingly effete approach to life. This is Emerson's defense, stressing the fact that he does not criticize progress or technology; he is not a "back to nature" hermit. But he does add the proviso that technology comes from an outside source that transcends the work of man.

148. **(B)**
You should recognize Gonzalo's ideal commonwealth from *The Tempest*. He is garrulous and not particularly smart, but wise enough to know when to cheer up the king and when to leave him alone. The utopia he describes is ridiculed by the other courtiers, but it does have some good points, without advocating an ideal communism.

149. **(D)**
Most Shakespeare texts explicate this passage clearly. If you do not know the passage, slip in each of the possibilities with close regard to the rest of the paradoxes, i.e., "tilth" may sound close to taxes—certainly Gonzalo does not want these, but the word means land cultivation. He is not against streams but against boundaries (bourn).

150. **(A)**
From context, gather the gist of the passage. Gonzalo may simply mean harvest (B) or fodder (E), but in this utopia, the crops would be abundant. In (D) you may be confused with the French word *poisson* meaning fish, but it does not fit the utopia context, nor does the similar sounding name poison (C), which no doubt Gonzalo would disallow on his island.

151. **(B)**
Gonzalo's utopia suggests that all the goodness and riches would be achieved without any effort on the part of the inhabitants (thus not an ideal communism), which counteracts the biblical teaching of man having to work for his living, from which developed the Protestant work ethic. None of the other choices are mentioned in the context of this passage.

152. **(B)**

Shakespeare read widely and borrowed extensively. He follows closely Montaigne's essay *Of the Cannibals* for Gonzalo's utopia. If you have identified *The Tempest* correctly, you can eliminate choices (A), (C), (D), and (E).

153. **(D)**

The general effect of the long sentence and the piling up of detail one after the other, separated only by the comma, is to create a breathlessness. (B) is a possibility, but the vigor and excitement is not the rambling of an old man, nor is there a haze over the writing (C), but rather an immediacy. The passage does not suggest waste (A) or sadness (E).

154. **(E)**

There is a rhetoric (B) here which is religious (D); there is celebration (C) and the whole effect is of someone reading aloud in an oratorical fashion (A). However, the specific oratory is the incantation of a psalm or prayer. If possible, read the passage aloud and the repetition of "for ever and ever (world) without end (Amen)" comes through very clearly.

155. **(D)**

The author looks back on those summers as if they would never end—the feeling one often has as a child. The other choices have some validity, but the point is the eternity of childhood summers captured by the incantation of a prayer. If you know the essay, the author returning to the same place with his son perpetuates the endless circle of time.

156. **(C)**

The key words are "background" and "design"; all the other details fill in the painting. Once the metaphor is established, return to line 1 and pick up the "fadeproof" idea, the lake in the painting's background never fading (a Keatsian notion). The photographs are not true pictures because they embellish. White's painting holds the truth within it.

157. **(C)**

Identify, first of all, the author of the piece. All the writers are capable of morbidity such as this, but here Dr. Lydgate refers to his trivial wife Rosamond who has destroyed his integrity in George Eliot's masterpiece *Middlemarch*. The allusion is to Keats's "Isabella or the Pot of Basil." If you know one of the works, the other will fall into place.

158. **(C)**
If you do not know the novel, the key words are "prison life." Analyze the other choices deliberating if those characters ever went to prison or experienced "rebirth." Without knowing the novel, think how the title alone suggests that the protagonist is punished, and the most famous of such protagonists is Raskolnikov.

159. **(D)**
Without knowing the novel or perhaps not recognizing the passage, read how the passage reveals that the man has been ill, but there is neither exultation at being raised from the dead as Lazarus experienced in the New Testament parable, nor a religious conversion. You need to know the parable and eliminate the choices that cannot be given from the text.

160. **(D)**
Strindberg's preface to *Miss Julie* holds a wealth of criticism on drama techniques as well as an insight into the playwright's methods. He criticizes the practice of writers simply pursuing stock characters and not attending to the range of human qualities. Even if you have not read the preface, the context will show the way the playwright thinks.

161. **(A)**
Stock characters produce stock phrases and Dickens has a full appreciation of how a stock character works. If you do not recognize the courting cry of Mr. Barkis, then analyze the other choices. None of the other works, despite their importance and possibility for stock characters, have produced a phrase that is instantly recognizable.

162. **(B)**
It is difficult to learn all the plots of the pilgrims' tales, but the main ones are worth studying closely. Some of the pilgrims have distinct personalities which Chaucer plays on and develops along with the tales. Read closely the description here and analyze which pilgrim tells which tale and which ones have a certain irony behind their story.

163. **(C)**
The Pardoner's story outrages the pilgrims because he has just revealed how he dupes country folk into believing pigs' bones are the relics of Christ, and makes a fortune out of duplicity. Yet his story's conclusion warns against

avarice, stressing the fact that "money is the root of all evil." The other tales are fun but without this depth of irony.

164.   **(B)**
Literary meals are very important, bringing together characters, or functioning as prologues to climaxes, disasters, or simply as celebrations. Here Mrs. Ramsey serves her beautiful stew with her family and friends gathered around her, each character revealing his or her thoughts. The wistful style of the passage distinguishes it from the other choices.

165.   **(C)**
If you do not know the epic poem *Le Morte D'Arthur* and the story of King Arthur bidding Sir Bedivere three times to throw away the sword, then recall the legend. Eliminate Gawain talking to his horse (B), and misplaced characters (E). Sir Lancelot (D) did not carry Excalibur. Sir Galahad (A) died before King Arthur upon beholding the Grail.

166.   **(D)**
Mystical materials such as samite are crucial to legends and epics. Think of Penelope's and the Lady of Shalott's webs. If you do not know the word, eliminate the heavy armor (A) and the heraldic devices (E)—illustrations show the material as pure and soft without decoration, glistening as silk does, especially inset with gold and silver.

167.   **(E)**
It is helpful to know the poem but the choices can be narrowed from thinking again of the legend, which often remains in our consciousness from childhood. Eliminate (A) and (B)—King Arthur goes to neither place. Eliminate (C) as no battleground is mentioned in the poetry here. Eliminate (D) as Bedivere outlives King Arthur.

168.   **(E)**
Tennyson followed closely the work of Malory's *Le Morte D'Arthur*, planning eventually to write twelve books for an "Arthurian Epic." If you do not know the poet's achievement here, eliminate Wordsworth (A) and Yeats (C), who did not work on this legend, and John Gardner (D), who adapted the legend of Beowulf into a novel, *Grendel*.

169. **(E)**

The vowel shift in the fifteenth century changed stressed vowels upward and changed the highest vowels to diphthongs. The diphthong in modern English "how" was pronounced by Chaucer like the high-back vowel in modern English "who." In addition, the high-front vowel in modern English, "be," was pronounced by Chaucer like the middle-front vowel of modern English "bay."

170. **(C)**

The character that Chaucer describes in this passage is the Monk. Medieval monks lived in cloisters, labored with their hands in raising their own food, and studied and copied theological and other texts. In contrast, the Parson (A) lived and worked among the people, the Pardoner (B) and Friar (E) traveled from place to place, and the Clerk (D) was a scholar who studied and wrote, but who would not have worked with his hands.

171. **(A)**

The object of the satire in the passage is the traditional topic of hypocrisy. Chaucer exposes the gap between what a monk is supposed to be, ideally, and what this monk actually is in practice. The passage is not anti-intellectual (B), because Chaucer implies that the monk ought to be in the monastery studying. The passage is not anti-religious (C) because, in ridiculing hypocrisy Chaucer reaffirms traditional religious values. Chaucer wrote prior to the Reformation and, therefore, was not expressing an explicitly Protestant view (D). As for Lollardism (E), Chaucer is not, at least in this passage, explicitly addressing the dispute concerning the publication of an English Bible or other issue of importance to Wycliff. The subject of the satire in this particular passage is more literary and traditional than that. It is part of a classical literary tradition satirizing hypocrisy in general.

172. **(C)**

A simile is an explicit comparison using the words *like* or *as*. In this poem, "like a raisin," "like a sore," "like rotten meat," "like a syrupy sweet," and "like a heavy load" are all similes. This device is the organizing principle of the poem. Antithesis (A) is the juxtaposition of opposites. Irony (B) is meaning one thing while saying the opposite, as in "What a nice day!" when it is raining. Personification (D) is a character representing an abstraction. Understatement (E) is a form of emphasis that implies more by saying less, as in "He wasn't a bad fighter," for someone who defeats every opponent. None of these other rhetorical devices are used in the poem.

173. (E)

On the face of it, the poem might be about Freudian dream theory (A) or adolescent frustration (B). There is no obvious way of determining what sort of dream is implied in the first line. There seems no particular reason, however, to read the poem as referring to pollution (C) or the transience of love (D). To read this as a statement about racism requires knowledge that the poet, Langston Hughes, is one of the foremost black poets of American literature and that Hughes often wrote on the topic of racism.

174. (B)

The phrase is from Tennyson's *In Memoriam A.H.H.* The phrase reflects the Victorian concern with a changing view of nature, particularly the effect of the writings of Charles Darwin. Nature is not a peaceful subject of contemplation as in the poetry of Wordsworth (A). On the other hand, although "tooth and claw" is a figure of speech, it is not a symbol as it might be in the poetry of Blake (C), Yeats (D), or Eliot (E). Tennyson refers to the literal violence of nature.

175. (B)

The repetitions and the use of the second person pronoun suggest the language of ordinary conversation. Thus, they are colloquial. They are questions of style, not grammar. They do not reflect one way or the other on literacy (A), the ability to read and write. Both literate and illiterate speakers use a colloquial style in conversation. They are not characteristic features of a particular dialect (C), either geographic, ethnic, or socio-economic. The author is affirming the ideas being expressed, not ridiculing them. Thus, there is no irony (D). They are not specifically for emphasis (E). The language suggests a conversation in which the economic conditions are being discussed.

176. (A)

The passage refers to the economic depression of the 1930s, during which farmers in Oklahoma and elsewhere lost their land and moved to California looking for work. The plight of the farmer was not a theme of literature describing periods (B) and (C). The socialist tone of the text dates it beyond periods (D) and (E).

177. (C)

The passage reveals the influence of Marx. Specifically, it implies economic determinism, that human behavior is the product of economic factors and class conflict, that an individual's point of view depends on his place in the economic system. Thoreau (A) was a liberal individualist and anti-slavery moralist. He was interested in economic factors mainly in so far as he could be as independent as possible from them. Rousseau (B) believed that human nature was corrupted by civilization and was concerned with protecting the individual from the tyranny of the majority. He was not particularly concerned with economic factors. Freud (D) developed the theory of the unconscious and was concerned with psychology, not economics. Mill (E) was a nineteenth-century liberal particularly concerned with the rights of the individual.

178. **(C)**
The context is Malory's fifteenth-century romance, *Le Morte D'Arthur*. The passage is from the description of the death of King Arthur near the end of the work. In context, then, it is a perfectly straightforward tragic and heroic passage from a medieval romance. It is not an example of irony (A) because there is no gap between what is said and what is meant. It is not mock epic (B) because it deals with an heroic past, not with everyday contemporary events. It is not estates satire (D) because it does not ridicule representatives of various classes and professions. Finally, it is not a parody of medieval literature (E), but rather it is the genuine item.

179. **(A)**
Auden is referring to the myth of Daedalus. In the myth, Daedalus and his son, Icarus, escape from Crete by attaching feathers to their arms with wax. With the feathers, they are able to fly. Not heeding his father's warning, Icarus flies too near the sun, the wax melts, and he falls into the sea and drowns. Joyce refers to the myth by naming the central character in his semi-autobiographical novel Stephen Dedalus. Shaw's *Man and Superman* (B) is based on the story of Don Juan. Shaw's *Pygmalion* (C) uses the Greek myth of the sculptor whose work of art comes alive for the title. O'Neill's *Mourning Becomes Electra* (D) is a modern adaptation of the *Oresteia*. Chaucer's "The Knight's Tale" (E) includes references to classical gods and goddesses. None of these works, however, refers to the myth of Daedalus.

180. **(C)**
Auden uses examples of famous paintings to show how great artists portrayed heroic events. He finds that great artists juxtaposed tragic suffering with the indifference of the immediate context. In this case, the ploughman is busy with his work and is indifferent to the fate of Icarus. The point is not that the ploughman lacks education (A). It is his indifference, not his lack of knowledge, that determines his reaction. The image of Icarus falling from the sky may or may not be universal (B). In some respects, he does fit the pattern

of the hero who reaches beyond human limitations (D). These are not, however, questions that concern Auden in this particular poem. Nor does he concern himself with the relative happiness of the ploughman in contrast to Icarus (E). The theme is the apparent insignificance of heroic action in its immediate context.

181. **(B)**
The term "courtly love" refers to the medieval tradition of a knight's worship of a lady, expressed in feudal and religious metaphors. A good example would be the relationship depicted in Chaucer's romance, *Troylus and Criseyde*. In *Beowulf* (A), women are not the object of worship or of literary cults. In Shakespeare's *Henry IV Part 2* (C), the focus is on the relationship between Hal and Falstaff, not courtly love, although there is some parody of romance in the scenes involving Falstaff and Doll Tearsheet. It is a minor element and the relationship is the opposite of "courtly." Milton's *Paradise Lost* (D) deals with the relationship between the sexes before and after the fall. The approach is theological, but not medieval. Pope's "The Rape of the Lock" (E) ridicules the behavior of both sexes in contemporary society.

182. **(D)**
Allegory is an extended metaphorical narrative with characters that are personifications. Spenser's work is allegorical throughout. Chaucer's "The Reeve's Tale" (A) is a fabliau, a short, humorous, "realistic" story about a student's tricking a miller and sleeping with his wife and daughter. The characters are not personifications and the narrative is not an extended metaphor. Shakespeare's *Richard II* (B) uses metaphor and symbolism throughout, but as figures of speech. The story itself is based on historical events. Milton's *Samson Agonistes* (C) is based on the biblical story of Samson, with parallels to Milton's own blindness. Wycherley's *The Country-Wife* (E) is a Restoration comedy satirizing contemporary society. Although characters in the other works might be said to personify certain virtues and vices, only in "The Faerie Queene" is the narrative metaphorical throughout in a consistent and systematic fashion.

183. **(B)**
The verse is iambic tetrameter. Each line consists of eight syllables alternating unstressed and stressed. Each pair of syllables constitutes a foot. The pattern of unstressed syllable followed by stressed syllable is an iamb. Since there are four of these in each line, it is iambic tetrameter. If there were ten syllables in each line, making five iambs, it would be iambic pentameter (A). If the poem had meter, but lacked rhyme, it would be blank verse (C). A line with twelve syllables, typically iambic hexameter, would be an Alexandrine

(D). Alliterative poetry (E) has a varying number of syllables in each line, but typically has four stressed syllables with a repetition of the initial sound in the first three of these.

184. **(A)**

The stanza is from "A Valediction: Forbidding Mourning" by John Donne. The unusual and original comparison of the separated souls to beaten gold is typical of seventeenth-century metaphysical poetry in general, and of Donne's poetry in particular. Chaucer (C) writes in Middle English typically in iambic pentameter and uses proverbs more than similes. He tends also to write narrative rather than lyric poetry. Ben Jonson (D), a contemporary of Donne's, wrote in a plainer, more straightforward neoclassical style. Both Keats (B) and Tennyson (E), as is typical of nineteenth-century poets, use more nature imagery and focus more on evoking moods and feelings. This particular detachment, analyzing a psychological situation from a theological point of view, is particularly typical of Donne.

185. **(C)**

In the first two lines, Shakespeare uses a phrase from the marriage service. In this context "impediments" refers to legal restrictions that might keep the marriage from taking place, such as, for example, a previous marriage that is still in effect. The word *impediment* can have other meanings [a barrier (A), a barricade (B), a stammer (E)], but none of these are relevant to this poem. The meaning here is determined by the metaphor ("marriage of true minds") and the reference to the marriage service.

186. **(A)**

In this context, "mark" refers to a manmade aid to navigation. A typical example from the Elizabethan period would be a pile of stones onshore by which one could determine one's position at sea. Although "mark" could have numerous other meanings, the navigational metaphor is continued throughout the quatrain.

187. **(B)**

Shakespeare wrote his sonnets in the 1590s. Thus, they are dated at the end of the sixteenth century. The fifteenth century (A) is still, for the most part, the Middle Ages in England. Shakespeare was not born yet and no one was writing sonnets in English. Shakespeare lived on into the seventeenth century (C) and continued to write plays, but not sonnets. During the eighteenth century (D), the neoclassical period, sonnet writing went out of style altogether. The Romantic poets of the nineteenth century (E) wrote sonnets, but they tended to write about nature and they did not use the complicated metaphors characteristic of Renaissance poetry.

188. **(B)**

"Art for art's sake" was the aesthetic philosophy of Oscar Wilde. It is typical of modern art generally, except when a particular philosophy, such as Freudianism or Marxism, dominates the art. The others, Plato, Eliot, Pope, and Horace, all embrace some degree of didacticism. Plato (A) argued in *The Republic* that the arts must serve a moral purpose or be excluded from society. Eliot (C) believed that art should be subordinate to religion. Horace (E) articulated the classical belief that art must "teach and delight." Pope (D) followed Horace in his neoclassicism.

189. **(D)**

The passage is an example of an Elizabethan soliloquy, a speech delivered by a character alone on the stage, talking to the audience. In this case it is Edmund from Shakespeare's *King Lear*. Browning's monologues (A) are poems in which a character, not the poet himself, speaks throughout. An eclogue (B) is a pastoral poem in which the poet speaks through the voice of a shepherd, or often through a dialogue between two shepherds. In the Anglo-Saxon elegies (C), "The Seafarer" and "The Wanderer," a speaking voice bewails the loss of comrades and the transience of all things. In a mock-epic invocation (E) the poet uses the formulas of epic style for comic effect.

190. **(C)**

Edmund argues in this soliloquy that the rights of inheritance are imposed by artificial and unnatural customs. He opposes nature to custom. According to nature, he is just as much his father's son as is his legitimate brother Edgar. In taking nature as his goddess, Edmund is justifying his plot to get rid of his brother and claim the inheritance for himself.

191. **(A)**

The speaker is Machiavellian in that he plots immoral political action for his own well being and without regard for moral considerations. An anti-hero (B) is a somewhat comic figure who has a heroic role but lacks heroic stature. Bloom in Joyce's *Ulysses* would be an example. A foil (C) is a character who sets off the heroic character by being more practical. An example would be Emilia (to Desdemona) in Shakespeare's *Othello*. A personification (D) is a character who represents an abstraction, like Good Deeds in *Everyman*. The protagonist

(E) is the hero or heroine of a drama or narrative, the character who is trying to accomplish something or who takes a stand for moral values. An example would be Antigone in Sophocles' *Antigone*.

192. **(B)**

These lines from Shakespeare's Sonnet 130 could best be classified as anti-Petrarchan. The term indicates a reversal of the Petrarchan conventions. Petrarch perfected the rhetoric of the love sonnet, especially a repertoire of comparisons for describing his beloved Laura. These particular metaphors and other rhetorical devices were much imitated by Renaissance poets, DuBellay and Ronsard in France, Wyatt and Spenser in England, among others. Wyatt's sonnets are in effect translations of Petrarch's into English. The comparisons typically praise the physical and spiritual perfections of the woman. What Shakespeare does is to reverse this convention: he calls attention to the absurdity of the comparisons. The sonnet is not Petrarchan (A) because it denies rather than reaffirms the tradition. It is not Romantic (C), as that would suggest a sonnet about nature. It is not mock epic (D), that would be a poem in which the rhetorical formulas of the epic, an invocation, heroic epithets, epic similes, and so on, are applied to everyday, trivial, contemporary events. It is not surreal (E): this term applies to modern poetry and art in which imagery is juxtaposed in a way to suggest the irrational and the subconscious. Shakespeare's reversal of the Petrarchan conventions is a rational, self-conscious display of wit.

193. **(C)**

The literary work that would best illustrate this definition of the Baroque would be Milton's *Paradise Lost*. Milton wrote the poem in the middle of the seventeenth century at the end of the English Renaissance. The focus on religious subject matter is typically Baroque. The magnificence of Milton's ornate rhetoric is also typically Baroque. Chaucer's *The Canterbury Tales* (A) is a late medieval work. Although there is religious subject matter, the style is plainer and more straightforward. It is less ornate and there is less emphasis on intense religious emotion. Ben Jonson's *Volpone* (B) is an example of Renaissance neoclassicism. It is moral, but not particularly theological. It is didactic, but provokes laughter and reflection rather than intense religious emotion. Pope's *An Essay on Man* (D) is a continuation of neoclassicism into the eighteenth century. It is to some extent a reaction against the Baroque in its balanced couplets, its rational consideration of philosophical questions, and its Deist theology. Wordsworth's *The Prelude* (E) is a Romantic text describing the cultivation of an aesthetic sensitivity to nature through childhood experiences. Although intensity of emotion is evoked, the subject matter is more psychological than theological and the style is relatively plain.

194. **(B)**

Melville uses a limited third-person point of view to create a gap between what we know and what is actually happening in the narrative. By limiting the reader's view of events to that of Captain Delano, Melville leads us through an experience of misunderstanding and recognition. We share in Captain Delano's observations and intuitions and we share his uncertainty. We actively participate with Captain Delano in trying to make sense out of the observations. In the end we are forced to reevaluate our own assumptions. This gap between what is actually happening and what we are aware of is a form of irony.

195. **(C)**

In these lines from Shakespeare's *Hamlet*, Polonius is giving advice to his son before Laertes returns to France. Polonius is somewhat pedantic and comic. Thus, there is an element of irony in having these truisms mouthed by a foolish character.

196. **(B)**

Blank verse is typical of Elizabethan drama. Blank verse is poetry with meter (specifically iambic pentameter), but without rhyme. Shakespeare uses it particularly in heroic, upper-class scenes. For comic, lower-class scenes, he typically uses prose. Free verse (A) is poetry without rhyme but without meter as well. There are no examples of alliteration (C, consecutive words beginning with the same letter or sound) in the passages. (D) and (E) are different types of rhymed verse.

197. **(E)**

"Conceit" in the first line refers to metaphor. The word is related to *concept* and originally meant *idea*. As used in the Renaissance with regard to poetry, it refers to a fanciful or witty idea or expression. In these lines from "An Essay on Criticism," Pope is referring disparagingly to the densely metaphorical style of seventeenth-century poetry. He particularly objects to the originality and oddness of the comparisons. This meaning of "conceit" is now archaic. The modern sense of the word, *a high opinion of oneself*, had a separate development from the same original meaning of *idea*.

198.   **(C)**
   The poetry that Pope is referring to and that he dislikes is often classified as metaphysical. The term designates a body of seventeenth-century poetry characterized by a densely metaphorical style. The metaphors themselves are often strikingly original. The term "metaphysical" refers to the theological and religious concerns that form the typical subject matter of this poetry.

199.   **(D)**
   Wordsworth's theme in this poem is that the experiences of the child determine the sensibilities of the adult. In particular, he felt that his love of nature was formed in childhood. (A), (B), and (C) refer to actual parent-child relationships, while Wordsworth is writing about them metaphorically in this poem.

200.   **(A)**
   By "natural piety," Wordsworth means the love and appreciation of nature. Wordsworth does not express specific theological concerns. He refers to a literal rainbow, not a symbolic one (B). He relates to nature directly, not as a means to an end (C). He does not characterize nature as mechanical (D), and he does not worship gods and goddesses (E).

201.   **(B)**
   The line is spoken by Satan in Milton's *Paradise Lost*, I, 263. It summarizes Satan's point of view, his pride, his rebellion, his ambition, and his role as tyrant among the fallen angels. It is, of course, not Milton's point of view (A), but rather a point of view created by Milton for a principal character in his epic poem. Dr. Faustus (C), the hero of Marlowe's tragedy, sells his soul to the devil, but he expresses no desire to "reign in hell." In return for selling his soul, he wants to satisfy his ambitions and desires in this life here on the earth before he dies. Machiavelli (D) was a diplomat of the Florentine Republic. He supported the republic through his work as a diplomat. After the downfall of the republic, he wrote *The Prince*, describing the actions required of a tyrant in order to keep control of a city seized illegitimately. Machiavelli was one of the first to describe what rulers actually did rather than what they were supposed to do. This so offended many people that Machiavelli became associated with evil. He, however, was a practical diplomat with no apparent interest in theology. Shakespeare's Othello (E) is a tragic hero consumed by jealousy. He is concerned with the faithfulness of his wife, not with the hereafter.

202.   **(B)**

The refrain is from Poe's poem "The Raven." Although the line is famous enough that most readers would immediately recognize it as Poe, it would be possible to eliminate (C) and (D) pretty readily, since the language is a bit too contemporary for these authors.

203.   **(D)**

This sonnet conforms more to Italian models than to those of his predecessors, Shakespeare and Spenser. (B) and (E) do not refer to variations of the sonnet form.

204.   **(D)**

The author retains the iambic pentameter and 14 lines requirements. The others are characteristics of this sonnet, and characteristic also of some Italian forms. The last two lines do not rhyme, which eliminates answer (A). The rhyme scheme of the octet is closed *(abba)*, eliminating answer (B). The author does not make a sharp distinction between the first eight lines and the final six (D), and as stated in the previous answer, the sonnet adheres to the Italian form (E).

205.   **(B)**

As mentioned in the previous answers, this sonnet differs in form from those written by Spenser (A) and Shakespeare (C). Although this is a form of Italian sonnet, Petrarch (D) wrote his sonnets in Italian and Latin. Wyatt (E) introduced the sonnet form to English poetry but often used irregular rhyme in his own sonnets.

206.   **(C)**

Manuductio is a work by the American cleric, Cotton Mather. *Areopagitica* (A) was written in defense of a free press, while (D) is a companion poem to *L'Allegro*. (B) and (E) are, along with *Paradise Lost*, Milton's last great works.

207.   **(C)**

"Assassination" (line 2) would imply the killing of a powerful leader eliminating (D) and (E). Brutus did not exhibit great reservations until after Caesar's death (A). The constant references to time and the worry about the speaker's own fate favors choosing *Macbeth* over *Hamlet* (B).

208. (D)

"Raw-boned" indicates a hollow-cheeked and gaunt appearance. "Penury," of course, is still indicative of poverty. The relation is clear: poverty brings on starvation—"did never dine." (B) is an alternate meaning for "pine" that does not fit in the context of the poem.

209. (D)

The lines are from Spenser's "The Faerie Queene." The language resembles modern English too closely to be mistaken for Chaucer (B). Marlowe (A) is best known for his dramas, written in blank verse. Sidney (C) wrote chiefly sonnets and pastoral romances, while Campion (E) is famous for his lyrical poetry.

210. (C)

In order to answer questions of this type, it is necessary to know some background information about each of the authors if the works themselves are unfamiliar. John Woolman was an eighteenth-century Quaker leader who was perhaps best known for, besides his *Journal*, his anti-slavery treatises.

211. (A)

The other four writers actually lived about a hundred years after the time of the Massachusetts Bay Colony, so these can be eliminated even if one is not aware who the leader of the Colony was.

212. (E)

Edwards is the only one on this list who had belonged to the clergy.

213. (C)

Harriet Jacobs' *Incidents in the Life of a Slave Girl* (1861) illustrates the particular horrors slavery held for black women. Behn's (A) and Stowe's (B) works are powerful portrayals of slavery, but the authors were not slaves themselves. Hurston's (D) book is actually a collection of folklore taken while traveling through Florida.

214. (D)

In this passage from *Mr. Edwards and the Spider*, Robert Lowell alludes to the text for Edward's sermon *Sinners in the Hands of an Angry God*. Edwards was known for his fiery calls for religious discipline, and his striking descriptions of hell often had congregations weeping or trembling in fear.

215. **(A)**
John Skelton's verse consists of short, rhymed lines of varying length. It is unconventional, "tumbling," and undignified, suited to his satirical purposes and apparently intended to offend the sensibilities of his learned peers.

216. **(B)**
Malory's *Le Morte D'Arthur* (A), Dryden's (C) opera libretto *King Arthur*, Tennyson's (D) *Idylls of the King*, and Twain's (E) *A Connecticut Yankee in King Arthur's Court* all make use of Arthurian legend. Milton contemplated an epic dealing with Arthur, but did not write one.

217. **(D)**
Passage (A) features a speaker that does not match the voice of James' narrators. (E) has a non-fictional tone, and (B) and (C) are perhaps not the best choices to those familiar with the recognizable style of James.

218. **(C)**
Peacock (A) and Eliot (B) wrote poetry long after the Puritan movement had ceased. Dryden (D) had defended his Protestantism in a poem, while Wycherley (E) lost his patronage when he married a Puritan woman.

219. **(B)**
Douglass is the author of the most famous of the slave narratives, which are autobiographical accounts of the experiences of black American slaves. Douglass was not a fiction writer, but his incredible oratorical and journalistic gifts culminated in the writing of his life's story.

220. **(B)**
The actual Tamburlaine was a fourteenth-century Mongol king; the play is a dramatic adaptation of the king's exploits.

221. **(B)**
Spenser's Sonnet 75 (from his sonnet sequence *Amoretti*) expresses an ancient and traditional theme—that poetry is capable of bestowing immortality (his verse will "eternize" her "vertues").

222. **(C)**
The Spenserian sonnet, a variant of the English sonnet, links each quatrain to the next by a continuing rhyme: *abab bcbc cdcd ee*. The fourteen-

line poem should be recognized as a sonnet [answers (D) and (E) can be eliminated]. Even if Spenser is not recognized as the author of the poem, the rhyme scheme is different than those of (A) and (B).

223. **(E)**
The second line, "Of princes, shall outlive this powerful rhyme," reveals the theme of the sonnet.

224. **(D)**
These are the opening lines from the medieval popular ballad, "Sir Patrick Spens." *Beowulf* (A) and *Sir Gawain and the Green Knight* (B), like most Old English works which survive, are marked by very strong alliteration in their lines. (E) is actually a prose work.

225. **(C)**
The stanza is from Marlowe's "The Passionate Shepherd to His Love." The last line of the excerpt is a famous one and should be readily recognized as Marlowe.

226. **(C)**
These two stanzas are from "A Valediction: Forbidding Mourning." Donne's use of metaphysics differs from Howard's use of blank verse (A) or Campion's lyricism (B). Milton (D) is more famous for his treatment of cosmic themes, whereas Shakespeare (E) is better known for writing sonnets.

227. **(B)**
These lines are from Wheatley's "On Being Brought from Africa to America." Wheatley is widely considered to be the first significant African-American poet.

228. **(B)**
These lines from *Paradise Lost* are spoken by Satan as he bids farewell to Heaven and enters Hell. The cosmic theme of the lines might be an immediate clue as to their author.

229. **(C)**
This stanza is from Lowell's *The Biglow Papers*, presented as the poetry of a young New England Yankee farmer who protests the spread of slavery.

Taylor (A) wrote on several religious themes; Freneau (B) was a satirist; Douglass (D) was not a poet; and Brooks (E) is a modern writer.

230. **(C)**
    This is the opening stanza from No. 286 (*The Poems of Emily Dickinson*, 3 vols., ed. T. Johnson, 1955). Dickinson's style can be identified by her short lines and the conceit of capitalization, which she often employed.

Practice Test 2

We have left the spaces below for you to record your scores on this Practice Test. Please refer to the Scoring section in the front of this book for how to compute your raw score and convert it into a scaled score. By comparing your scores on each Practice Test, you will be better able to mark your progress.

Raw Score   _____

Scaled Score   _____

GRE LITERATURE
IN ENGLISH

PRACTICE TEST 2

DIRECTIONS: Choose the best answer for each question and mark the letter of your selection on the corresponding answer sheet. Answer sheets can be found in the back of this book.

Questions 1 – 3 refer to the following excerpts.

1.   Which refers to Donne?

2.   Which refers to Wordsworth?

3.   Which refers to Swift?

(A)   As for his works in verse and prose,
       I own myself no judge of those;
       Nor can I tell what critics thought 'im:
       But this I know, all people bought 'em,
       As with a moral view designed
       To cure the vices of mankind.

(B)   With____, whose muse on dromedary trots,
       Wreathe iron pokers into truelove knots;
       Rhyme's sturdy cripple, fancy's maze and clue,
       Wit's forge and fire-blast, meaning's press and screw.

(C) Standing aloof in giant ignorance,
     Of thee I hear and of the Cyclades,
     As one who sits ashore and longs perchance
     To visit dolphin-coral in deep seas.
     So thou wast blind!—but then the veil was rent;
     For Jove uncurtained Heaven to let thee live,
     And Neptune made for thee a spumy tent,
     And Pan made sing for thee his forest-hive;...

(D) In honored poverty thy voice did weave
     Songs consecrate to truth and liberty,—
     Deserting these, thou leavest me to grieve,
     Thus having been, that thou should cease to be.

(E) Sheeplike, unsociable reptilian, two
     hell-divers splattered squawking on the water,
     loons devolving to a monochrome.
     You honored nature,
     helpless, elemental creature.
     The black stump of your hand
     just touched the waters under the earth
     and left them quickened with your name... .

---

4.   Her work "represents a romanticism *in extremis,* made public with grotesque clarity. Her poetry has been praised as a supreme example of the confessional mode in modern literature and disparaged as the "longest suicide note ever written." The subject of some of it is her parents, who are treated unsympathetically ("Daddy, daddy, you bastard, I'm through"). She wrote an autobiographical novel about personality distintegration, and committed suicide.

This passage describes

(A) Virginia Woolf.   (D) Sylvia Plath.

(B) Elizabeth Bishop.   (E) Adrienne Rich.

(C) Anne Sexton.

Questions 5 – 6 refer to the following poems.

    (A)   "Dover Beach"

    (B)   "Lines Composed a Few Miles Above Tintern Abbey"

    (C)   "La Belle Dame sans Merci"

    (D)   "Break, Break, Break"

    (E)   "To the Virgins, to Make Much of Time"

5.   Which one contains the following lines?

    And we are here as on a darkling plain
    Swept with confused alarms of struggle and flight
    Where ignorant armies clash by night.

6.   Which one is a carpe diem poem?

7.   The phrase "graveyard school" designates a group of eighteenth-century British poets who wrote long poems on death and immortality. The works of all of the following are associated with the graveyard school EXCEPT

    (A)   Thomas Parnell.   (D)   James Thompson.

    (B)   Robert Blair.   (E)   Thomas Gray.

    (C)   Edward Young.

8.   All of the following are sonnet sequences EXCEPT

    (A)   Sidney's *Astrophel and Stella.*

    (B)   Spencer's *Amoretti.*

    (C)   Tennyson's *In Memoriam A.H.H.*

    (D)   D. G. Rossetti's *House of Life.*

    (E)   William Ellery Leonard's *Two Lives.*

Questions 9 – 10 refer to the following selection.

> A shudder in the loins engenders there
> The broken wall, the burning roof and tower
> And Agamemnon dead.
>
> Being so caught up,
> So mastered by the brute blood of the air,   5
> Did she put on his knowledge with his power
> Before the indifferent beak could let her drop?

9. Agamemnon was

   (A) killed in battle in the Trojan War.

   (B) killed by Circe while accompanying Odysseus home from the Tro-jan War.

   (C) murdered by his son Orestes.

   (D) murdered by his wife Clytemnestra.

   (E) pierced by an arrow shot by Artemis.

10. "His" (line 6) refers to

   (A) Agamemnon.   (D) Apollo.

   (B) Priam.   (E) Zeus.

   (C) Orestes.

Questions 11 – 13 refer to the following excerpts.

11. Which is spoken by Shaw's Barbara?

12. Which is spoken by Wilde's Lady Bracknell?

13. Which is spoken by Congreve's Millamant?

(A)   Come to dinner when I please, dine in my dressing-room when I'm out of humor, without giving a reason. To have my closet inviolate; to be sole empress of my teatable, which you must never presume to approach without first asking leave. And lastly, wherever I am, you shall always knock at the door before you come in. These articles subscribed, if I continue to endure you a little longer, I may by degrees dwindle into a wife.

(B)   What business have you, miss, with *preference* and *aversion*? They don't become a young woman; and you ought to know, that as both always wear off, 'tis safest in matrimony to begin with a little *aversion*. I am sure I hated your poor dear uncle before marriage as if he'd been a black-amoor—and yet, miss, you are sensible what a wife I made! and when it pleased heav'n to release me from him, 'tis unknown what tears I shed!

(C)   I don't believe in that anymore. I believe that, before all else, I'm a human being, no less than you—or anyway, I ought to try to become one. I know the majority thinks you're right, Torvald, and plenty of books agree with you, too. But I can't go on believing what the majority says, or what's written in books. I have to think over these things myself and try to understand them.

(D)   I should have given you up and married the man who accepted it. After all, my dear old mother has more sense than any of you. I felt like her when I saw this place—felt that I must have it—that never, never, never could I let it go; only she thought it was the houses and the kitchen ranges and the linen and china, when it was really all the human souls to be saved; not weak souls in starved bodies, sobbing with gratitude for a scrap of bread and treacle, but fullfed, quarrel-some, snobbish, uppish creatures, all standing on their little rights and dignities, and thinking that my father ought to be greatly obliged to them for making so much money for him—and so he ought. That is where salvation is really wanted...I have got rid of the bribe of heaven.

(E)   I confess I feel somewhat bewildered by what you have just told me. To be born, or at any rate bred, in a handbag, whether it had handles or not, seems to me to display a contempt for the ordinary decencies of family life that remind me of the worst excesses of the French Revolution. And I presume you know what that unfortunate movement led to? As for the particular locality in which the handbag was found, a cloakroom at a railway station might serve to conceal a social indiscretion—has probably, indeed, been used for that purpose before now—but it could hardly be regarded as an assured basis for a recognized position in good society.

Questions 14 – 16

ROSALIND   Well, in her person I say I will not have you.
ORLANDO   Then in mine own person I die.
ROSALIND   No, faith, die by attorney. The poor world is almost six thousand years old, and in all this time there was not any man died in his own person, videlicet, in a love-cause. Troilus had his brains dash'd out with a Grecian club; yet he did what he could to die before, and he is one of the patterns of love. Leander he would have liv'd many a fair year, though Hero had turn'd nun, if it had not been for a hot midsummer night; for, good youth, he went but forth to wash him in the Hellespont and being taken with the cramp was drown'd; and the foolish chroniclers of that age found it was "Hero of Sestos."

14.   In line 1 of Rosalind's speech, "by attorney" means

    (A) of natural causes.   (D) by someone else's hand.

    (B) of old age.   (E) in a courtroom.

    (C) by proxy.

15.   Rosalind's account of Leander's death

    (A) is more accurate than that given by historians of Leander's day.

    (B) is intended to undercut romantic idealism.

    (C) is an exception to the general point she is making, the "exception that proves the rule."

    (D) outlines a pattern of chivalric behavior that she wishes Orlando to emulate.

    (E) is intended to reinforce Orlando's current mode of behavior.

16.   These lines are from

    (A) *As You Like It.*   (D) *Much Ado about Nothing.*

    (B) *Every Man in his Humour.*   (E) *The Rivals.*

    (C) *The Way of the World.*

Questions 17 – 19 refer to the following passage.

The poet is the sayer, the namer, and represents beauty. He is a sovereign and stands on the centre. For the world is not painted or adorned, but is from the beginning beautiful; and God has not made some beautiful things, but Beauty is the creator of the universe...

For poetry was all written before time was, and whenever we are so finely organized that we can penetrate into that region where the air is music, we hear those primordial warblings and attempt to write them down, but we lose ever and anon a word or a verse and substitute something of our own, and thus mis-write the poem. The men of more delicate ear write down these cadences more faithfully, and these transcripts, though imperfect, become the songs of the nations. For nature is as truly beautiful as it is good, or as it is reasonable, and must as much appear as it must be done, or be known.

17. The author of this passage is a spokesman of

    (A) naturalism.   (D) realism.

    (B) aestheticism.   (E) surrealism.

    (C) transcendentalism.

18. The second paragraph contains ideas associated with

    (A) optimism.   (D) nihilism.

    (B) materialism.   (E) existentialism.

    (C) utilitarianism.

19. The author of this passage is also the author of

    (A) "The Raven."   (D) *Self-Reliance.*

    (B) *Walden.*   (E) *Biographia Literaria.*

    (C) *On Liberty.*

Questions 20 – 24 refer to the following selection.

> But Lord Crist, whan that it remembreth me
> Upon my youthe and on my jolitee,
> It tikleth me aboute myn herte roote —
> Unto this day it dooth myn herte boote
> That I have had my world as in my time.   5
> But age, allas, that al wol envenime,
> Hath me biraft my beautee and my pith —
> Lat go, farewel, the devel go therwith!
>
> The flour is goon, ther is namore to telle:
> The bren as I best can now moste I selle;   10
> But it to be right merye wol I fonde.

20. What is the meaning of "envenime" in line 6?

(A) Enlighten   (D) Poison

(B) Perfect   (E) Delight

(C) Envy

21. In the metaphor in lines 9 and 10, what is compared to what?

(A) The speaker's body to the seed husk of cereal grain

(B) The speaker's beauty to faded flowers

(C) The speaker's body to cereal grain ready for harvesting

(D) The speaker's beauty to flour that has gone bad

(E) The speaker's body to flowers that are now difficult to sell

22. Which of the following best expresses the speaker's attitude toward past experience? The speaker

(A) tries not to think about the past.

(B) would like to do a number of things differently if given the chance.

(C) feels pleasure in recalling good times past.

(D) feels guilt for some previous flings.

(E) regrets numerous missed opportunities.

23.   The speaker might best be described as

(A)   a romantic.

(D)   a Pollyanna.

(B)   a misanthrope.

(E)   a pragmatist.

(C)   an idealist.

24.   The speaker is

(A)   Alison in "The Miller's Tale."

(B)   the Prioress.

(C)   the Wife of Bath.

(D)   the Pardoner.

(E)   Griselda in "The Clerk's Tale."

Questions 25 – 29 refer to the following selection.

His adherence to general nature has exposed him to the censure of criticks, who form their judgments upon narrower principles. Dennis and Rhymer think his Romans not sufficiently Roman; and Voltaire censures his kings as not completely royal. Dennis is offended, that Menenius, a senator of Rome, should play the buffoon; and Voltaire perhaps thinks decency violated when the Danish Usurper is represented as a drunkard. But our poet always makes nature predominate over accident; and if he preserves the essential character, is not very careful of distinctions superinduced and adventitious. His story requires Romans or kings, but he thinks only on men. He knew that Rome, like every other city, had men of all dispositions; and wanting a buffoon, he went into the senate-house for that which the senate-house would certainly have afforded him. He was inclined to shew an usurper and a murderer not only odious but despicable, he therefore added drunkenness to his other qualities, knowing that kings love wine like other men, and that wine exerts its natural power upon kings. These are the petty cavils of petty minds; a poet overlooks the casual distinction of country and condition, as a painter, satisfied with the figure, neglects the drapery.

25. The writer under discussion is

    (A) Sophocles.   (D) Dryden.

    (B) Milton.   (E) Spencer.

    (C) Shakespeare.

26. "Superinduced and adventitious" means

    (A) additional and chance, not inherent.

    (B) superficial and hazardous, not certain.

    (C) careless and unnatural, not innate.

    (D) unclear and indefinite, not carefully considered.

    (E) basic and essential, not accidental.

27. Which of the following best describes the writer's use of Dennis, Rhymer, and Voltaire in this passage?

    (A) He agrees with most of their criticism, but says it derives from narrower principles than he is using in this essay.

    (B) He finds greater merit in Voltaire's criticism than in that of Rhymer and Dennis.

    (C) He admires all three as critics, but respectfully differs with them on these matters.

    (D) He finds greater merit in the criticism of Rhymer and Dennis than in Voltaire's.

    (E) He believes the criticism of all three is trivial and misguided.

28. Which of the following best expresses the critical principle on which the author's specific arguments are based?

    (A) The poet, like the painter, must not neglect finishing touches, the "drapery" that particularizes the individual.

    (B) The poet must be aware of cultural differences and changing fashions in order to portray them accurately.

(C) The poet should focus his efforts on the accurate representation of universal truths and characteristics, on general nature common to all ages and places.

(D) The poet is a product of his own time and place, is best acquainted with it, and must therefore depict its unique characteristics in order to leave an accurate account for future generations.

(E) Particular manners and eccentricities best define human individuality; hence, the poet should concentrate on a just representation of these.

29.   The author of this passage is

(A) Sidney.   (D) Poe.

(B) Johnson.   (E) Ruskin.

(C) Shelley.

Questions 30 – 31 refer to the following excerpts.

30.   Which is the "I" of Poe's *The Cask of Amontillado*?

31.   Which is the "I" of Eudora Welty's *Why I Live at the P.O.*?

(A)   My family are naturally the main people in China Grove, and if they prefer to vanish from the face of the earth, for all the mail they get or the mail they write, why, I'm not going to open my mouth. Some of the folks here in town are taking up for me and some turned against me. I know which is which. There are always people who will quit buying stamps just to get on the right side of Pappa-Daddy.

But here I am, and here I'll stay. I want the world to know I'm happy.

And if Stella-Rondo should come to me this minute, on bended knees, and *attempt* to explain the incidents of her life with Mr. Whitaker, I'd simply put my fingers in both my ears and refuse to listen.

(B)   In walks these three girls in nothing but bathing suits. I'm in the third checkout slot, with my back to the door, so I don't see them until they're over by the bread. The one that caught my eye first was the one in the plaid green two-piece. She was a chunky kid, with a good tan and a sweet broad soft-looking can with those two crescents of white just under it, where the sun never seems to hit, at the top of the backs of her legs. I stood there with my hand on a box of HiHo crackers trying to remember if I rang it up or not. I ring it up again and the customer starts giving me hell. She's one of these cash-register-watchers, a witch about fifty with rouge on her cheekbones, and no eye brows, and I know it made her day to trip me up. She'd been watching cash registers for fifty years and probably never seen a mistake before.

(C)   I kept on creeping just the same, but I looked at him over my shoulder.

           "I've got out at last," said I, "in spite of you and Jane. And I've pulled off most of the paper, so you can't put me back!"

           Now why should that man have fainted? But he did, and right across my path by the wall, so that I had to creep over him every time!

(D)   No answer still. I thrust a torch through the remaining aperture and let it fall within. There came forth in return only a jingling of the bells. My heart grew sick—on account of the dampness of the catacombs. I hastened to make an end of my labor. I forced the last stone into its position; I plastered it up. Against the new masonry I re-erected the old rampart of bones. For the half a century no mortal has disturbed them. *In pace requiescat!*

(E)   I lingered before her stall, though I knew my stay was useless, to make my interest in her wares seem the more real. Then I turned away slowly and walked down the middle of the bazaar. I allowed the two pennies to fall against the sixpence in my pocket. I heard a voice call from one end of the gallery that the light was out. The upper part of the hall was now completely dark.

           Gazing up into the darkness I saw myself as a creature driven and derided by vanity; and my eyes burned with anguish and anger.

Questions 32 – 34 refer to the following excerpts.

32.   Which is spoken by Jaques?

33.   Which is spoken by Falstaff?

34.   Which is spoken by Caliban?

(A)   Slanders, sir; for the satirical rogue says here that old men have grey beards, that their faces are wrinkled, their eyes purging thick amber and plum-tree gum, and that they have a plentiful lack of wit, together with most weak hams. All which, sir, though I most power-fully and potently believe, yet I hold it not honesty to have it thus set down, for yourself, sir, shall grow old as I am, if like a crab you could go backward.

(B)   All the world's a stage,
And all the men and women merely players.
They have their exits and their entrances,
And one man in his time plays many parts,
His acts being seven ages. At first the infant,
Mewling and puking in the nurse's arms …
                                        Last scene of all,
That ends this strange eventful history,
Is second childishness and mere oblivion,
Sans teeth, sans eyes, sans taste, sans every thing.

(C)   Our revels now are ended. These our actors,
As I foretold you, were all spirits and
Are melted into air, into thin air;
And, like the baseless fabric of this vision,
The cloud-capp'd tow'rs, the gorgeous palaces,
The solemn temples, the great globe itself,
Yea, all which it inherit, shall dissolve
And, like this insubstantial pageant faded,
Leave not a rack behind. We are such stuff
As dreams are made on, and our little life
Is rounded with a sleep.

(D)   You taught me language, and my profit on 't
Is, I know how to curse. The red plague rid you
For learning me your language!

(E)   I'll starve ere I'll rob a foot further. An 'twere not as good a deed as drink to turn true man and to leave these rogues, I am the veriest varlet that ever chew'd with a tooth. Eight yards of uneven ground is threescore and ten miles afoot with me, and the stony-hearted villains know it well enough. A plague upon it when thieves cannot be true one to another!

---

35.   All of the following are pastoral elegies EXCEPT

(A) Milton's "Lycidas."

(B) Johnson's *The Vanity of Human Wishes*.

(C) the November eclogue of Spencer's *Shepheardes Calendar*.

(D) Shelley's "Adonais."

(E) Arnold's "Thyrsis."

Questions 36 – 38 refer to the following dialogue.

DORIMANT   You were talking of play, madam. Pray, what may be your stint?

HARRIET   A little harmless discourse in public walks, or at most an appointment in a box, barefaced, at the playhouse: you are for masks and private meetings, where women engage for all they are worth, I hear.

DORIMANT   I have been used to deep play, but I can make one at small game when I like my gamester well.

HARRIET   And be so unconcerned you'll ha' no pleasure in't.

DORIMANT   When there is a considerable sum to be won, the hope of drawing people in makes every trifle considerable.

36.   In this exchange, meaning is conveyed through

(A) classical allusions.   (D) direct statement.

(B) invective.   (E) dramatic irony.

(C) an extended metaphor.

37. Which of the following best captures the meaning of Dorimant's second speech?

    (A) Although he prefers to gamble for large sums, he can be content playing for lower stakes if the game is sufficiently interesting.

    (B) Although he has been accustomed to sexual conquest, he can settle for less if he likes his partner well enough.

    (C) He is competent at all kinds of games, whether serious or frivolous.

    (D) Although he prefers serious games, he is willing to play less serious ones if he likes his partner well enough.

    (E) He prefers many sexual partners, but can be content with one if she is sufficiently interesting.

38. The dialogue is characteristic of

    (A) Elizabethan comedy of humours.

    (B) heroic drama.

    (C) Restoration comedy.

    (D) eighteenth-century sentimental comedy.

    (E) theater of the absurd.

Questions 39 – 42 refer to the following poem.

We shall not always plant while others reap
The golden increment of bursting fruit,
Not always countenance, abject and mute,
That lesser men should hold their brothers cheap;
Not everlastingly while others sleep   5
Shall we beguile their limbs with mellow flute,
Not always bend to some more subtle brute;
We were not made eternally to weep.

The night whose sable breast relieves the stark
White stars is no less lovely being dark,   10
And there are buds that cannot bloom at all
In light, but crumple, piteous, and fall;

So in the dark we hide the heart that bleeds,
And wait, and tend our agonizing seeds.

39. The poem differs in form from the usual pattern of a Petrarchan sonnet in that

    (A) a shift in the thought process occurs at the beginning of line 9.

    (B) it contains an octave and a sestet rather than three quatrains and a couplet.

    (C) it contains more than five rhymes.

    (D) the sestet contains three couplets.

    (E) the octave contains eight lines.

40. Which of the following most accurately states the burden of the octave?

    (A) It protests the elevation of inferior men to high public office while more able men go unrecognized.

    (B) It predicts that the oppressed will not forever be oppressed.

    (C) It expresses a desire for the redistribution of wealth.

    (D) It is a plea for violent revolution.

    (E) It predicts that the abolition of slavery will be followed by years of more subtle oppression.

41. Which of the following most accurately expresses the idea contained in lines 9 and 10?

    (A) The armies of darkness will eventually overwhelm the armies of light.

    (B) The darkness of night threatens to obliterate starlight.

    (C) The night would be lovelier without stars.

    (D) The white stars are lovely in spite of the darkness of night.

    (E) Black is beautiful.

42. Countée Cullen, the author of this poem, was one of the more notable writers of the

    (A) Harlem Renaissance.

    (B) poetic movement known as Imagism.

    (C) Aesthetic Movement.

    (D) *fin de siécle.*

    (E) Age of Sensibility.

Questions 43 – 45 refer to the following excerpts.

43. Which was written by Henry Fielding?

44. Which was written by D. H. Lawrence?

45. Which was written by E. M. Forster?

(A)   But if you pick up a novel, you realize immediately that infinity is just a handle to this self-same jug of a body of mine; while as for knowing, if I find my finger in the fire, I know that fire burns, with a knowledge so emphatic and vital, it leaves Nirvana merely a conjecture. Oh, yes, my body, me alive, *knows*, and knows intensely. And as for the sum of all knowledge, it can't be anything more than an accumulation of all the things I know in the body, and you, dear reader, know in the body.

(B)   Now a comic Romance is a comic Epic-Poem in Prose; differing from Comedy, as the serious Epic from Tragedy: its Action being more extended and comprehensive; containing a much larger Circle of Incidents, and introducing a greater Variety of Characters. It differs from the serious Romance in its Fable and Action, in this; that as in the one these are grave and solemn, so in the other they are light and ridiculous: it differs in its Characters, by introducing Persons of inferiour Rank, and consequently of inferiour Manners, whereas the grave Romance, sets the highest before us; lastly in its Sentiments and Diction; by preserving the Ludicrous instead of the Sublime.

(C)   There is one point at which the moral sense and the artistic sense lie very near together; that is in the light of the very obvious truth that the deepest quality of a work of art will always be the quality of the mind of the producer. In proportion as that intelligence is fine will the novel, the picture, the statue partake of the substance of beauty and truth. To be constituted of such elements is, to my vision, to have purpose enough. No good novel will ever proceed from a superficial mind; that seems to me an axiom which, for the artist in fiction, will cover all needful moral ground: if the youthful aspirant take it to heart it will illuminate for him many of the mysteries of "purpose."

(D)   Fiction—if it at all aspires to be art—appeals to temperament. And in truth it must be, like painting, like music, like all art, the appeal of one temperament to all the other innumerable temperaments whose subtle and resistless power endows passing events with their true meaning, and creates the moral, the emotional atmosphere of the place and time. Such an appeal, to be effective, must be an impression conveyed through the senses; and, in fact, it cannot be made in any other way, because temperament, whether individual or collective, is not amenable to persuasion. All art, therefore, appeals primarily to the senses, and the artistic aim when expressing itself in written words must also make its appeal through the senses, if its high desire is to reach the secret spring of responsive emotions.

(E)   Yes, oh, dear, yes—the novel tells a story. That is the fundamental aspect without which it could not exist. That is the highest factor common to all novels, and I wish that it was not so, that it could be something different—melody, or perception of truth, not this low atavistic form.

Questions 46 – 48 refer to the following passage.

"Ah yes, a new journal might be worth trying. There was one advertised in the *Times Literary Supplement* a little while ago. Paton or some such name the editor fellow was called. You might have a go at him, now that it doesn't seem as if any of the more established reviews have got room for your... effort. Let's see now; what's the exact title you've given it?"

Dixon looked out of the window at the fields wheeling past, bright green after a wet April. It wasn't the double-exposure effect of the last half minute's talk that had dumbfounded him, for such incidents formed the staple material of Welch colloquies; it was the prospect of reciting the title of the article he'd written. It was a perfect title, in that it crystallised the article's niggling mindlessness, its funereal parade of yawn-enforcing facts, the pseudo-light it threw upon non-problems. Dixon had read, or begun to read, dozens like it, but his own seemed worse than most in its air of being convinced of its own usefulness and significance. "In considering this strangely neglected topic," it began. This what neglected topic? This strangely what topic? This strangely neglected what? His thinking all this without having defiled and set fire to the typescript only made him appear to himself as more of a hypocrite and fool. "Let's see," he echoed Welch in a pretended effort of memory: "Oh yes; *The economic influence of the developments in shipbuilding techniques, 1450 to 1485.* After all, that's what it's ..."

46. This passage satirizes

    (A) pedantic government reports.

    (B) yellow journalism.

    (C) writers who stoop to plagiarism.

    (D) trivial academic scholarship.

    (E) historians.

47. Which of the following best describes the narrative technique used in this excerpt?

    (A) The author uses Dixon as a kind of narrator, though in the third person; events are filtered through Dixon's consciousness by means of an inside view.

    (B) The author uses omniscient third-person narration; events are seen from the points of view of both Welch and Dixon, although we learn more about Dixon.

    (C) The author uses an objective point of view, neither commenting on nor judging events.

    (D) The author maximizes distance between Dixon and the reader, thereby reducing our sympathy for Dixon.

(E) The author uses first-person narration in which the narrator is a primary agent in the action.

48. The author of this passage is

(A) Jack Kerouac.   (D) Kingsley Amis.

(B) Woody Allen.   (E) Ken Kesey.

(C) Joyce Cary.

---

49. One of the chief tenets of Aestheticism (or the "Aesthetic Movement") is that

(A) any work of art is essentially utilitarian and that its "reality" must be defined by reference to objects outside the work.

(B) art is the highest value among man's works because it is self-sufficient and has no aim other than its own perfection.

(C) art increases in value in direct proportion to the degree to which it reflects current and redeeming social values.

(D) art will achieve perfection when artists pay equal attention to beauty and utility.

(E) organic form is superior to artifice because the former refers to the real world whereas the latter does not.

50.   In a universe deprived of illusions and light, man feels an alien. His is an irremediable exile ... This divorce between man and his life, the actor and his setting, truly constitutes the feeling of Absurdity.

Works influenced by this outlook have been written by

(A) Chekhov and Tolstoy.   (D) Turgenev and Lermontov.

(B) Ibsen and Silone.   (E) Doctorow and Malamud.

(C) Camus and Ionesco.

51. The term "negative capability" was introduced by

    (A) Dryden.   (D) Keats.

    (B) Coleridge.   (E) Hazlitt.

    (C) Johnson.

52. We real cool. We
    Left school. We

    Lurk late. We
    Strike straight. We

    Sing sin. We
    Thin gin. We

    Jazz June. We
    Die soon.

    The author is

    (A) Countée Cullen.   (D) Richard Wilbur.

    (B) Langston Hughes.   (E) Joyce Carol Oates.

    (C) Gwendolyn Brooks.

Questions 53 – 63. For each of the following passages, identify the author or the work. Base your decision on the content and style of each passage.

53. From hence, ye Beauties, undeceiv'd
    Know, one false step is ne'er retriev'd,
        And be with caution bold.
    Not all that tempts your wand'ring eyes
    And heedless hearts, is lawful prize;
        Nor all, that glitters, gold.

    (A) Sir Walter Raleigh   (D) Thomas Gray

    (B) Richard Lovelace   (E) William Blake

    (C) Jonathan Swift

54.   "And what in the world, my dear, did you mean by it?"—that sound, as at the touch of a spring, rang out as the first effect of Fanny's speech. It broke upon the two women's absorption with a sharpness almost equal to the smash of the crystal, for the door of the room had been opened by the Prince without their taking heed. He had apparently had time, moreover, to catch the conclusion of Fanny's act; his eyes attached themselves, through the large space allowing just there, as happened, a free view, to the shining fragments at this lady's feet. His question had been addressed to his wife, but he moved his eyes immediately afterwards to those of her visitor, whose own then held them in a manner of which neither party had been capable, doubtless, for mute penetration, since the hour spent by him in Cadogan Place on the eve of his marriage and the afternoon of Charlotte's reappearance. Something now again became possible for these communicants, under the intensity of their pressure, something that took up that tale and that might have been a redemption of pledges then exchanged.

(A) Jane Austen   (D) W. M. Thackeray

(B) Edith Wharton   (E) Henry James

(C) George Eliot

55.   [He] believed in the green light, the orgiastic future that year by year recedes before us. It eluded us then, but that's no matter—tomorrow we will run faster, stretch out our arms farther ... And one fine morning—

    So we beat on, boats against the current, borne back ceaselessly into the past.

(A) Melville   (D) Faulkner

(B) Dreiser   (E) Porter

(C) Fitzgerald

56.   I reason, Earth is short—
       And Anguish—absolute—
       And many hurt,
       But, what of that? ...

I reason, that in Heaven—
Somehow, it will be even—
Some new Equation, given—
But, what of that?

(A) Emily Dickinson   (D) Wallace Stevens

(B) Walt Whitman   (E) Dorothy Parker

(C) Ezra Pound

57. In Dublin a week later, that would be September 19th, Neary minus his whiskers was recognized by a former pupil called Wylie, in the General Post Office contemplating from behind the statue of Cuchulainn. Neary had bared his head, as though the holy ground meant something to him. Suddenly he flung aside his hat, sprang forward, seized the dying hero by the thighs and began to dash his head against his buttocks, such as they are.

(A) Jonathan Swift   (D) Samuel Beckett

(B) James Joyce   (E) J. P. Donleavy

(C) Dylan Thomas

58. She tried to go on with her letter, reminding herself that she was only an elderly woman who had got up too early in the morning and journeyed too far, that the despair creeping over her was merely her despair, her personal weakness, and that even if she got a sunstroke and went mad the rest of the world would go on. But suddenly, at the edge of her mind, Religion appeared, poor little talkative Christianity, and she knew that all its divine words from "Let there be Light" to "It is finished" only amounted to "boum." Then she was terrified over an area larger than usual; the universe, never comprehensible to her intellect, offered no repose to her soul, the mood of the last two months took definite form at last, and she realized that she didn't want to write to her children, didn't want to communicate with anyone, not even with God.

(A) D. H. Lawrence   (D) Virginia Woolf

(B) Joseph Conrad   (E) Graham Greene

(C) E. M. Forster

59. No matter: she was not happy, and never had been. Why was life so unsatisfying? Why did everything she leaned on instantly crumble into dust? ... But if somewhere there existed a strong, handsome man with a valorous, passionate and refined nature, a poet's soul in the form of an angel, a lyre with strings of bronze intoning elegiac nuptial songs to the heavens, why was it not possible that she might meet him some day? No, it would never happen! Besides, nothing was worth seeking—everything was a lie! Each smile hid a yawn of boredom, each joy a curse, each pleasure its own disgust; and the sweetest kisses only left on one's lips a hopeless longing for a higher ecstasy.

      (A) Zola   (D) Maupassant

      (B) Proust   (E) Anatole France

      (C) Flaubert

60. If you really want to hear about it, the first thing you'll really want to know is where I was born, and what my lousy childhood was like, and how my parents were occupied and all before they had me, and all that David Copperfield kind of crap.

      (A) Cheever's *The Wapshot Chronicle*

      (B) Salinger's *The Catcher in the Rye*

      (C) Roth's *Goodbye, Columbus*

      (D) Amis' *Lucky Jim*

      (E) Bellow's *Herzog*

61. O impotence of mind in body strong!
    But what is strength without a double share
    Of wisdom? Vast, unwieldy, burdensome,
    Proudly secure, yet liable to fall
    By weakest subtleties; not made to rule,
    But to subserve where wisdom bears command.
    God, when he gave me strength, to show withal,
    How slight the gift was, hung it in my hair.

      (A) *Everyman*   (D) *Samson Agonistes*

      (B) *Doctor Faustus*   (E) *All for Love*

      (C) *King Lear*

62. "No one who had ever seen [X] in her infancy would have supposed her born to be an heroine. Her situation in life, the character of her father and mother, her own person and disposition, were all equally against her."

These sentences are the first in

(A) *Emma.*

(D) *Mansfield Park.*

(B) *Pride and Prejudice.*

(E) *Northanger Abbey.*

(C) *Sense and Sensibility.*

63.   A central theme in many of his novels is man's struggle against the neutral force that rules the universe, a force that is indifferent to man's suffering. This theme is frequently joined to an examination of life's ironies and love's disappointments. One of his novels deals with an intelligent and sensitive girl of humble origins driven to murder and hence to death by hanging by a series of bitterly ironic circumstances and events. Another chronicles the destruction of a villager whose intellectual ambitions are thwarted by his sensuality and by circumstances.

This passage describes

(A) D. H. Lawrence.

(D) Evelyn Waugh.

(B) Thomas Hardy.

(E) Charles Dickens.

(C) Joseph Conrad.

Questions 64 – 66 refer to the following poem.

Where's Héloise, the learned nun,
    For whose sake Abeillard, I ween,
Lost manhood and put priesthood on?
    (From Love he won such dule and teen!)
    And where, I pray you, is the queen   5
Who willed that Buridan should steer
    Sewed in a sack's mouth down the Seine?
But where are the snows of yesteryear?

64.   This poem is structured around

(A) incremental repetition.

(B)   mock heroic conventions.

(C)   the "loathly lady"/beautiful princess motif.

(D)   the *carpe diem* motif.

(E)   the *ubi sunt* motif.

65.   Line 3 refers to the fact that Pierre Abelard

(A)   became a monk in order to avoid corrupting Héloise, who was a nun.

(B)   gave up a promising career at court because he was in love with Héloise, whom he could never marry.

(C)   turned from the masculine pursuits of knighthood, such as warfare, to the less vigorous pursuits of theology after falling in love.

(D)   became a monk after Héloise's uncle had him emasculated.

(E)   became a priest after falling in love with Héloise because he wanted to be as spiritually similar to her as possible.

66.   The poem's poignancy derives largely from the author's awareness of

(A)   the transitory, almost illusory, nature of all earthly beauty.

(B)   the futility of political intrigue.

(C)   the foolishness of theological quarrels.

(D)   the problem of evil in the world.

(E)   endless cycles of death and renewal.

Questions 67 – 69 refer to the following stanzas.

About suffering they were never wrong,
The Old Masters: how well they understood
Its human position; how it takes place
While someone else is eating or opening a window or just walking dully along;
How, when the aged are reverently, passionately waiting   5
For the miraculous birth, there always must be

Children who did not specially want it to happen, skating
On a pond at the edge of the wood:
They never forgot
That even the dreadful martyrdom must run its course   10
Anyhow in a corner, some untidy spot
Where the dogs go on with their doggy life and the torturer's horse
Scratches its innocent behind on a tree.

In Brueghel's *Icarus*, for instance: how everything turns away
Quite leisurely from the disaster; the plowman may   15
Have heard the splash, the forsaken cry,
But for him it was not an important failure; the sun shone
As it had to on the white legs disappearing into the green
Water; and the expensive delicate ship that must have seen
Something amazing, a boy falling out of the sky,   20
Had somewhere to get to and sailed calmly on.

67. Which of the following best describes the relationship of the second stanza to the first?

(A) The second stanza continues the development of the general idea advanced in stanza one.

(B) The second stanza proposes a general idea based on the specific examples in stanza one.

(C) The second stanza provides a specific example of the general idea advanced in stanza one.

(D) The second stanza proposes a general idea that contrasts with the general idea advanced in stanza one.

(E) The second stanza uses a specific instance to contradict the general idea advanced in stanza one.

68. What do the children in the first stanza have in common with the plowman in the second stanza?

(A) Both refuse to take responsibility for their actions.

(B) Both believe they are powerless to influence human history.

(C) They are used as examples of one of man's greatest strengths—the ability to carry on in the face of disaster.

(D) Both are indifferent to extraordinary events.

(E) Both would like to take part in the world around them, but realize the futility of any action they might take.

69. Auden uses dogs and a horse (line 12) chiefly to illustrate

(A) obliviousness to suffering.

(B) man's superior rationality in comparison to the animal world.

(C) the moral superiority of animals to man because of the former's greater innocence.

(D) the untidiness of nature.

(E) the necessity of suffering in daily life.

Questions 70 – 71 refer to the following lines.

My mistress' eyes are nothing like the sun;
Coral is far more red than her lips' red:
If snow be white, why then her breasts are dun;
If hairs be white, black wires grow on her head.

70. In these lines, the author is satirizing the use of which of the following by other Elizabethan sonneteers?

(A) Hackneyed Petrarchan conceits

(B) Encomia

(C) Rhymed quatrains

(D) Obscure metaphysical conceits

(E) Love as the subject of sonnets

71. The author of these lines is

(A) Wyatt.

(B) Sidney.

(C) Raleigh.

(D) Marlowe.

(E) Shakespeare.

Questions 72 – 73 refer to the following passage.

> ... a kind of discordia concors; a combination of dissimilar images, or discovery of occult resemblances in things apparently unlike ....The most heterogeneous ideas are yoked by violence together; nature and art are ransacked for illustrations, comparisons, and allusions ... but the reader commonly thinks his improvement dearly bought, and, though he sometimes admires, is seldom pleased.

72.   The author is discussing

(A) the pathetic fallacy.   (D) heroic drama.

(B) Renaissance pastoral poetry.   (E) Hudibrastic poetry.

(C) metaphysical wit.

73.   The author of this passage is

(A) Swift.   (D) Dryden.

(B) Pope.   (E) Johnson.

(C) Addison.

---

74.   He lived amidst th' untrodden ways,
To Rydal Lake that lead,
A bard whom there were none to praise,
And very few to read.

These lines parody the first stanza of a poem by

(A) Herrick.   (D) Arnold.

(B) Pope.   (E) Yeats.

(C) Wordsworth.

Questions 75 – 76 refer to the following passage.

I intend to let Lady Danvers see no farther of my papers, than to her own angry letter to her brother; for I would not have her see my reflections upon it; and she'll know, down to that place, all that's necessary for her curiosity, as to my sufferings, and the stratagems used against me, and the honest part I have been enabled to act: And I hope, when she has read them all, she will be quite reconciled: for she will see it is all God Almighty's doings; and that a gentleman of his parts and knowledge was not to be drawn in by such a poor young body as me…

And so, with my humble duty to you both, and my dear Mr. B____'s kind remembrance, I rest

Your ever-dutiful and gratefully happy Daughter.

75. The excerpt is from

(A) a picaresque novel.

(B) a novella.

(C) a Gothic novel.

(D) an epistolary novel.

(E) an historical novel.

76. The author of this passage is

(A) Defoe.

(B) Richardson.

(C) Fielding.

(D) Smollett.

(E) Sterne.

77. "Widsith" deals with the life of

(A) a Celtic king.

(B) an Anglo-Saxon scop.

(C) an Arthurian knight.

(D) an early Christian missionary.

(E) a Norman courtier.

78.   "Courage is the instrument by which the hero realizes himself. 'Fate often saves an undoomed man when his courage is good,' says ____ in his account of his swimming match: that is, if Fate has not entirely doomed a man in advance, courage is the quality that can perhaps influence Fate against its natural tendency to doom him now.... Doom, of course, ultimately claims him, but not until he has fulfilled to its limits the pagan ideal of a heroic life."

Which of the following correctly completes the second sentence?

(A) Cuchulainn   (D) Beowulf

(B) Odysseus   (E) Achilles

(C) Hrothgar

79.   Serious over my cereals I broke one breakfast my fast
With something-to-read searching retinas retained by print on a packet;
Sprung rhythm sprang, and I found (the mind fact-mining at last)
An influence Father-[X]-fathered on the copy-writing racket

These lines parody the style of (the"X" in line 4)

(A) Robinson Jeffers.   (D) Gerard Manley Hopkins.

(B) Hilda Doolittle.   (E) Hart Crane.

(C) Edna St. Vincent Millay.

80.   Gramercy, Good Deeds! Now may I true friends see.
They have forsaken me every one—
I loved them better than my Good Deeds alone.
Knowledge, will you forsake me also?

These lines are from

(A) *The Knight of the Burning Pestle.*

(B) *Everyman.*

(C) "The Faerie Queene."

(D) *The Brome Play of Abraham and Isaac.*

(E) *Volpone.*

Questions 81 – 83 refer to the following excerpts.

81.   Which is by William Blake?

82.   Which is by James Baldwin?

83.   Which is by Oscar Wilde?

(A)   So no wonder that in certain cities of America, in New York of course, and New Orleans, in Chicago and San Francisco and Los Angeles, in such American cities as Paris and Mexico, D.F., this particular part of a generation was attracted to what the Negro had to offer. In such places as Greenwich Village, a menage-a-trois was completed—the bohemian and the juvenile delinquent came face-to-face with the Negro, and the hipster was a fact in American life. If marijuana was the wedding ring, the child was the language of Hip for its argot gave expression to the abstract states of feeling which all could share, at least all who were Hip.

(B)   The day of my father's funeral had also been my nineteenth birthday. As we drove him to the graveyard, the spoils of injustice, anarchy, discontent, and hatred were all around us. It seemed to me that God himself had devised, to mark my father's end, the most sustained and brutally dissonant of codas. And it seemed to me, too, that the violence which rose all about us as my father left the world had been devised as a corrective for the pride of his eldest son. I had declined to believe in that apocalypse which had been central to my father's vision; very well, life seemed to be saying, here is something that will certainly pass for an apocalypse until the real thing comes along.

(C)   The Last Judgment is an Overwhelming of Bad Art & Science. Mental Things are alone Real; what is Called Corporeal Nobody Knows of its dwelling Place; it is in Fallacy & its Existence an Imposture. Where is the Existence Out of Mind or Thought? Where is it but in the Mind of a Fool?... "What," it will be Questioned, "When the Sun rises do you not see a round Disk of fire somewhat like a Guinea?" O no no, I see an Innumerable company of the Heavenly host crying "Holy Holy Holy is the Lord God Almighty." I question not my Corporeal or Vegetative Eye any more than I would Question a Window concerning a Sight. I look thro it & not with it.

(D)   I am not sure when the word "Gothic" was first generically applied to the architecture of the North; but I presume that whatever the date of its original usage, it was intended to imply reproach, and express the barbaric character of the nations among whom that architecture arose. It never implied that they were literally of Gothic lineage, far less that their architecture had been originally invented by the Goths themselves; but it did imply that they and their buildings together exhibited a degree of sternness and rudeness, which, in contradistinction to the character of Southern and Eastern nations, appeared like a perpetual reflection of the contrast between the Goth and the Roman in their first encounter.

(E)   It is the spectator, and not life, that art really mirrors. Diversity of opinion about a work of art shows that the work is new, complex, and vital. When critics disagree the artist is in accord with himself. We can forgive a man for making a useful thing as long as he does not admire it. The only excuse for making a useless thing is that one admires it intensely. All art is quite useless.

Questions 84 – 88 refer to the following stanzas.

If all the world and love were young,
And truth in every shepherd's tongue,
These pretty pleasures might me move
To live with thee and be thy love.

Time drives the flocks from field to fold   5
When rivers rage and rocks grow cold,
And Philomel becometh dumb;
The rest complains of cares to come.

The flowers do fade, and wanton fields
To wayward winter reckoning yields;   10
A honey tongue, a heart of gall,
Is fancy's spring, but sorrow's fall.

84.   These lines are from a poem ("The Nymph's Reply to the Shepherd") by ____, in reply to a poem ("The Passionate Shepherd to His Love") by ____. Which of the following correctly completes the preceding sentence?

(A) Shakespeare ... Surrey

(B) Raleigh ... Marlowe

(C) Marvell ... Spenser

(D) Waller ... Lovelace

(E) Jonson ... Herrick

85. The nymph asserts that the idyllic world portrayed by the shepherd is

(A) unrealistic, ignoring changes that come with the passage of time, harsh aspects of pastoral life, and such things as the need to provide for old age.

(B) no longer viable because time has brought about societal and economic changes that make pastoral life virtually impossible.

(C) tempting and possible, but not sufficiently enticing because she does not trust this shepherd.

(D) not appealing because such a pastoral life leads ultimately to a rustication and regret that she does not intend to experience.

(E) acceptable to the young, but not to her because she is no longer young.

86. Philomel (line 7) was

(A) the goddess of the fields and hence of fertility.

(B) a minor deity associated with rural locations and sometimes associated with pastoral poetry.

(C) turned into a nightingale or swallow but unable to sing because she betrayed her mate.

(D) a country girl who was abandoned by her lover after having been seduced by him.

(E) a maiden whose tongue was cut out by her sister's husband so she could not reveal that he raped her.

87. Which of the following best expresses the idea contained in lines 11 and 12?

    (A) Spring is a time of plenty, but fall is a time of want.

    (B) Submitting to fancy's sweet talk will eventually lead to remorse or bitterness.

    (C) We may think spring is a time of happiness, but experience teaches us it contains an equal portion of sorrow.

    (D) Spring fills the heart with thoughts of love and the ability to express them, but they eventually fade.

    (E) Although fancy rules the heart, sorrow follows a fall from virtue.

88. Another response to "The Passionate Shepherd to His Love" entitled "The Bait" was written by

    (A) John Skelton.   (D) George Herbert.

    (B) Michael Drayton.   (E) Sir John Suckling.

    (C) John Donne.

Questions 89 – 91 refer to the following poem.

When I heard the learn'd astronomer
When the proofs, the figures, were ranged in columns before me,
When I was shown the charts and diagrams, to add, divide, and measure them,
When I sitting heard the astronomer where he lectured with much applause in the
    lecture-room,
How soon unaccountable I became tired and sick,   5
Till rising and gliding out I wander'd off by myself,
In the mystical moist night-air, and from time to time,
Look'd up in perfect silence at the stars.

89. All of the following oppositions or contrasts are present in the poem EXCEPT

    (A) applause/silence.

    (B) scientific analysis/mysticism.

(C) mathematical certainty/error.

(D) light/dark.

(E) group/individual.

90. Which of the following words has more than one meaning in context?

(A) Figures (line 2)

(B) Measure (line 3)

(C) Applause (line 4)

(D) Mystical (line 7)

(E) Perfect (line 8)

91. The author of the poem is

(A) Emerson.

(B) James Russell Lowell.

(C) Sandburg.

(D) Whitman.

(E) Frost.

Questions 92 – 95 refer to the following passage.

Men are but children of a larger growth;
Our appetites as apt to change as theirs,
And full as craving too, and full as vain;
And yet the soul, shut up in her dark room,
Viewing so clear abroad, at home sees nothing;   5
But, like a mole in earth, busy and blind,
Works all her folly up, and casts it outward
To the world's open view: thus I discovered,
And blamed the love of ruined Antony;
Yet wish that I were he, to be so ruined.   10

92. "Her" in line 7 refers to

(A) Cleopatra.

(B) soul.

(C) mole.

(D) lust or passion.

(E) appetite.

93. Dolabella has "discovered" Antony's love primarily because

    (A) he has used stealth to observe Antony in the latter's unguarded moments.

    (B) he has observed Antony in two perspectives, from afar and up close.

    (C) he has had the advantage of viewing him from "abroad," which has given him the emotional detachment necessary for objective analysis.

    (D) Antony's increasing vanity has aroused Dolabella's suspicions.

    (E) Antony's "soul" has revealed it to him.

94. Dolabella's attitude toward Antony can best be described as one of

    (A) unqualified admiration.

    (B) compassionate understanding.

    (C) bitter disillusionment.

    (D) moral condemnation.

    (E) self-congratulatory superiority.

95. This passage is from

    (A) Shakespeare's *Antony and Cleopatra*.

    (B) Shakespeare's *Julius Caesar*.

    (C) Samuel Daniel's *Cleopatra*.

    (D) Dryden's *All for Love*.

    (E) Shaw's *Caesar and Cleopatra*.

Questions 96 – 101 refer to the following poem.

Cou'd our first Father, at his toilsome Plough,
Thorns in his Path, and Labour on his Brow,
Cloath'd only in a rude, unpolish'd Skin;
Cou'd he, a vain, fantastick Nymph have seen,
In all her Airs, in all her Antick Graces;   5

Her various Fashions, and more various Faces;
How had it pos'd that Skill, which late Assign'd
Just Appellations to each sev'ral Kind,
A right Idea of the Sight to frame,
T' have guest from what new Element she came,   10
T' have hit the wavering Form, or giv'n this Thing a Name.

96. "Father" in line 1 refers to

(A) God.   (D) Satan.

(B) time.   (E) George Washington.

(C) Adam.

97. "Pos'd" in line 7 means

(A) perplexed.   (D) undermined.

(B) possessed.   (E) contradicted.

(C) positioned.

98. The tone of the poem can best be described as

(A) nostalgic.   (D) prayerful.

(B) angry.   (E) jocose.

(C) solemn.

99. "Frame" (line 9) is closest in meaning to

(A) recall.   (D) enclose.

(B) analyze.   (E) devise falsely.

(C) formulate.

100. "Skill" (line 7) refers to the ability to

(A) solve puzzles from slight clues.

(B) interpret the ways of God to man.

(C) recognize the presence of incorporeal beings.

(D) deduce valid conclusions from premises.

(E) name things appropriately.

101. "Thing" in the last line refers to

(A) Skill.   (D) Nymph.

(B) Appellation.   (E) Idea.

(C) Element.

Questions 102 – 103 refer to the following descriptions.

102. Which describes John Ford's *'Tis Pity She's a Whore?*

103. Which describes Tennessee Williams' *A Streetcar Named Desire?*

(A)   Militant in its pride in the middle-class, this prose tragedy recounts the downfall and eventual execution of a naive apprentice who is seduced by a more experienced woman who leads him to embezzle from his employer and finally to murder his uncle to satisfy her greed. The play is overtly didactic; its author defined the end of tragedy as "the exciting of the passions in order to the correcting such of them as are criminal, either in their nature, or through their excess."

(B)   This play deals with a statesman and saint whose individualism, spirituality, and wit help him preserve his "ada mantine sense of his own self" while struggling with political forces that ultimately destroy him. His refusal to compromise costs him his life, but establishes him as a man of strong character and integrity. The author uses the device of the Common Man to address the audience directly and to comment on the action of the play.

(C)   This play deals with the incestuous love of brother and sister (Giovanni and Annabella). The pregnant Annabella marries one of her suitors, but refuses to name her lover after her pregnancy is discovered. Giovanni eventually stabs Annabella to forestall her husband's vengeance after the latter learns the identity of Annabella's lover. The husband and Giovanni are both killed in the final scene of the play. Like other plays by the same author, this work is marked by its powerful portrayal of melancholy and despair.

(D)   This expressionist play deals with the perversion of human strength by technological progress. Its protagonist, a stupid and brutal stoker on a transatlantic liner, is a study in dehumanization, literally subservient to machines. His growing discontent and ineffectual rebellion end when he is crushed to death by a beast he has liberated in a zoo. The author's work has been criticized for its social pleading, but praised for its depiction of the suffering of common men and for its probing of the psychology of alienation.

(E)   This play's heroine has "always depended on the kindness of strangers." Horrified by the contrast between her idealized vision of life at their former family estate and the squalid surroundings of her sister's home and her brother-in-law's crudity, she relies on liquor and self-delusions about her age, beauty, and former suitors in trying to cope with an uncongenial present. She is eventually raped by her brother-in-law and committed to a mental institution. The author's plays include a number of then-controversial subjects, such as castration, drug addiction, homosexuality, nymphomania, and cannibalism.

Questions 104 – 106 refer to the following poem.

A doll in the doll-maker's house
Looks at the cradle and bawls:
"That is an insult to us."
But the oldest of all the dolls,
Who had seen, being kept for show,   5
Generations of his sort,
Out-screams the whole shelf: "Although
There's not a man can report
Evil of this place,
The man and the woman bring   10
Hither, to our disgrace,
A noisy and filthy thing."
Hearing him groan and stretch
The doll-maker's wife is aware
Her husband has heard the wretch   15
And crouched by the arm of his chair,
She murmurs into his ear,
Head upon shoulder leant:
"My dear, my dear, O dear,
It was an accident."   20

104. The oldest doll's objections metaphorically point primarily to a contrast between

   (A) good and evil.

   (B) life and art.

   (C) happiness and sorrow.

   (D) permanence and impermanence.

   (E) single life and married life.

105. The doll-maker can best be seen as a metaphor for

   (A) the destructive effects of time on all men's lives.

   (B) the vanity of all earthly striving.

   (C) the artist who must live in the real world but create idealized objects.

   (D) the henpecked husband.

   (E) man's essential loneliness and isolation.

106. The author of this poem also wrote

   (A) "Ah, Are You Digging on My Grave?"

   (B) "Sailing to Byzantium."

   (C) "Ode to the West Wind."

   (D) "Fern Hill."

   (E) *The British Museum Reading Room.*

Questions 107 – 109 refer to the following passage.

> As though to breathe were life! Life piled on life
> Were all too little, and of one to me
> Little remains; but every hour is saved
> From that eternal silence, something more,
> A bringer of new things; and vile it were
> For some three suns to store and hoard myself …

> This is my son, mine own Telemachus,
> To whom I leave the scepter and the isle—
> Well-loved of me, discerning to fulfill
> This labor, by slow prudence to make mild
> A rugged people, and through soft degrees
> Subdue them to the useful and the good.
> Most blameless is he, centered in the sphere
> Of common duties, decent not to fail
> In offices of tenderness, and pay
> Meet adoration to my household gods,
> When I am gone. He works his work, I mine.

107. Which of the following best describes the portrait of Telemachus that emerges? He is

    (A) an ambitious man anxious for his father's throne.

    (B) a hypocrite.

    (C) a virtuous, dutiful, loving son and strong leader of men.

    (D) a potential tyrant who will abuse his authority.

    (E) an able administrator but unexciting man.

108. The speaker expresses

    (A) fear of death.

    (B) a desire for additional experience.

    (C) a belief in immortality.

    (D) a need for solitary meditation.

    (E) a desire for death.

109. The author of this passage is

    (A) Coleridge.   (D) Browning.

    (B) Keats.   (E) Arnold.

    (C) Tennyson.

110. Which is the "I" of Cather's *My Antonia*?

(A)   I had only to close my eyes to hear the rumbling of the wagons in the dark, and to be again overcome by that obliterating strangeness. The feelings of that night were so near that I could reach out and touch them with my hand. I had the sense of coming home to myself, and of having found out what a little circle man's experience is. For [her] and for me, this had been the road of Destiny; had taken us to those early accidents of fortune which predetermined for us all that we can ever be. Now I understood that the same road was to bring us together again. Whatever we had missed, we possessed together the precious, the incommunicable past.

(B)   Something quite remote from anything the builders intended has come out of their work, and out of the fierce little human tragedy in which I played; something none of us thought about at the time: a small red flame—a beaten-copper lamp of deplorable design, relit before the beaten-copper doors of a tabernacle; the flame which the old knights saw from their tombs, which they saw put out; that flame burns again for other soldiers, far from home, farther, in heart, than Acre or Jerusalem. It could not have been lit but for the builders and the tragedians, and there I found it this morning, burning anew among the old stones.

(C)   It must be observ'd, that when the old Wretch, my Brother (Husband) was dead, I then freely gave my Husband an Account of all that Affair, and of this Cousin, as I had call'd him before, being my own Son by that mistaken unhappy Match: He was perfectly easy in the Account, and told me he should have been as easy if the old Man, as we call'd him, had been alive; for, said he, it was no Fault of yours, nor of his; it was a Mistake impossible to be prevented; he only reproach'd him with desiring me to conceal it, and to live with him as a Wife, after I knew that he was my Brother, that, he said, was a vile part.

(D)   I planned my death carefully; unlike my life, which meandered along from one thing to another, despite my feeble attempts to control it. My life had a tendency to spread, to get flabby, to scroll and festoon like the frame of a baroque mirror, which came from following the line of least resistance. I wanted my death, by contrast, to be neat and simple, understated, even a little severe, like a Quaker church or the basic black dress with a single strand of pearls much praised by fashion magazines when I was fifteen…. At first I thought I'd managed it.

(E)   In the beginning of the last chapter, I inform'd you exactly *when* I was born;—but I did not inform you, *how*. No; that particular was reserved entirely for a chapter by itself;—besides, Sir, as you and I are in a manner perfect strangers to each other, it would not have been proper to have let you into too many circumstances relating to myself all at once.—You must have a little patience. I have undertaken, you see, to write not only my life, but my opinions also; hoping and expecting that your knowledge of my character, and of what kind of a mortal I am, by the one, would give you a better relish for the other.

Questions 111 – 112 refer to the following stanza.

> I on my horse, and Love on me doth try
>   Our horsemanships, while by strange work I prove
>   A horseman to my horse, a horse to Love;
>   And now man's wrongs in me, poor beast, descry.

111.   The poet's portrayal of "Love" in this stanza is an example of

(A) personification.   (D) apostrophe.

(B) metonymy.   (E) dead metaphor.

(C) synecdoche.

112.   "Horsemanships" in line 2 is plural because

(A) love rides the speaker while the speaker rides his horse.

(B) the speaker has committed more than one wrong.

(C) love exercises many forms of control over the speaker.

(D) love controls him better than he controls love.

(E) love appears in many forms.

Questions 113 – 114 refer to the following passage.

"I didn't want to kill!" Bigger shouted. "But what I killed for, I *am*! It must've been pretty deep in me to make me kill! I must have felt it awful hard to murder… .What I killed for must've been good! Bigger's voice was full of frenzied anguish. "It must have been good. When a man kills, it's for something… I didn't know I was really alive in this world until I felt things hard enough to kill for 'em… .It's the truth, Mr. Max. I can say it now, 'cause I'm going to die. I know what I'm saying real good and I know how it sounds. But I'm all right. I feel all right when I look at it that way…."

113.	The preceding passage best supports which of the following statements?

(A)	Bigger is an embodiment of the chief tenets of existentialist philosophy.

(B)	Bigger has achieved self-identity through violence.

(C)	Like Iago, Bigger is driven by motive, but there is also an inexplicable reality behind his rational exterior.

(D)	Ultimately, Bigger ends where he began, understanding little of the world around him and even less of himself.

(E)	Bigger now realizes that his acts have been impulsive and, therefore, meaningless.

114.	The passage is from

(A)	James Baldwin's *Another Country*.

(B)	Ralph Ellison's *Invisible Man*.

(C)	Norman Mailer's *The Armies of the Night*.

(D)	Richard Wright's *Native Son*.

(E)	James Dickey's *Deliverance*.

Questions 115 – 116 refer to the following poems.

(A)	"Do Not Go Gentle Into That Good Night"

(B)	"Ode: Intimations of Immortality"

(C)	"Endymion"

(D)	"Porphyria's Lover"

(E)	"Ozymandias"

115. Which is a dramatic monologue?

116. Which is a villanelle?

Questions 117 – 119 refer to the following passage.

     [His] mother had charged him to return with his shield or upon it. Or perchance he was some Achilles, who had nourished his wrath apart, and had now come to avenge or rescue his Patroclus. He saw this unequal combat from afar,—for the blacks were nearly twice the size of the red,— he drew near with rapid pace till he stood on his guard within half an inch of the combatants; then, watching his opportunity, he sprang upon the black warrior, and commenced his operations near the root of his right fore leg, leaving the foe to select among his own members; and so there were three united for life, as if a new kind of attraction had been invented which put all other locks and cements to shame. I should not have wondered by this time to find that they had their respective musical bands stationed on some eminent chip, and playing their national airs the while, to excite the slow and cheer the dying combatants. I was myself excited somewhat even as if they had been men. The more you think of it, the less the difference.

117. The combatants are

(A) Greeks.

(B) Americans.

(C) French.

(D) dogs.

(E) ants.

118. Patroclus was

(A) the husband of Helen of Troy.

(B) the king of Troy.

(C) once Achilles' friend, but killed Achilles after the two quarreled.

(D) Achilles' friend, killed in the Trojan War.

(E) Achilles' son.

119. The author of this passage is

    (A) Benjamin Franklin.   (D) Henry David Thoreau.

    (B) Washington Irving.   (E) Oliver Wendell Holmes.

    (C) Nathaniel Hawthorne.

Questions 120 – 121 refer to the following passage.

[He] had been a subordinate clerk in the Dead Letter Office at Washington, from which he had been suddenly removed by a change in the administration. When I think over this rumour, hardly can I express the emotions which seize me. Dead letters! does it not sound like dead men? … Sometimes from out the folded paper the pale clerk takes a ring—the finger it was meant for, perhaps, moulders in the grave, a bank-note sent in swiftest charity—he whom it would relieve, nor eats nor hungers any more; pardon for those who died despairing; hope for those who died unhoping; good tidings for those who died stifled by unrelieved calamities. On errands of life, these letters speed to death.

120. Dead letters serve as a metaphor for

    (A) government inefficiency.

    (B) the protagonist's existence.

    (C) governmental indifference to the suffering of its citizens.

    (D) man's inhumanity to man.

    (E) the protagonist's family.

121. The author of the previous passage is also the author of

    (A) *Benito Cereno*.

    (B) *The Red Badge of Courage*.

    (C) *Ethan Frome*.

    (D) *The Fall of the House of Usher*.

    (E) *The House of the Seven Gables*.

Questions 122 – 123 refer to the following excerpt.

O our Scots nobles were richt laith
    To weet their cork-heeled shoon
But lang owre a' the play were played
    Their hats they swam aboon.

O lang, lang may their ladies sit,   5
Wi' their fans into their hand,
Or e'er they see Sir Patrick Spens
Come sailing the land.

122. Which of the following best expresses the meaning of lines 3 and 4? The Scots nobles

(A) drowned.

(B) refused to go.

(C) changed their minds in the middle of the voyage.

(D) mutinied.

(E) jumped overboard and swam to shore.

123. This excerpt is from

(A) a sixteenth-century broadside ballad.

(B) a mock epic.

(C) a Middle English lyric.

(D) a medieval popular ballad.

(E) a seventeenth-century elegy.

124. The _____ was a medieval form: a short comic or satiric tale in verse that deals realistically with middle-class or lower-class characters and that revels in the obscene and ribald.

Which one of the following correctly completes the definition above?

(A) parable   (D) allegory

(B) beast fable   (E) exemplum

(C) fabliau

125.   The British had possessed the country so completely. Their withdrawal was so irrevocable. And to me even after many months something of fantasy remained attached to all the reminders of their presence. I had grown up in a British colony and it might have been expected that much would have been familiar to me. But England was at least as many-faceted as India. England, as it expressed itself in Trinidad, was not the England I had lived in; and neither of these countries could be related to the England that was the source of so much that I now saw about me.

The author of this passage is

(A) E. M. Forster.   (D) Nadine Gordimer.

(B) Rudyard Kipling.   (E) Doris Lessing.

(C) V. S. Naipaul.

Questions 126 – 128 refer to the following passage.

     That was when people had begun to feel really sorry for her. People in our town, remembering how old lady Wyatt, her great-aunt, had gone completely crazy at last, believed that the Griersons held themselves a little too high for what they really were. None of the young men were quite good enough for Miss Emily and such. We had long thought of them as a tableau, Miss Emily a slender figure in white in the background, her father a spraddled silhouette in the foreground, his back to her and clutching a horsewhip, the two of them framed by the back-flung front door. So when she got to be thirty and was still single, we were not pleased exactly, but vindicated; even with insanity in the family she wouldn't have turned down all of her chances if they had really materialized.

126.   The attitude of the townspeople toward Miss Emily is best described as one of

(A) disdain tempered by understanding.

(B) compassion mixed with self-congratulation.

(C) condescension and moral superiority.

(D) obsequiousness combined with self-righteousness.

(E) pity tinged with envy.

127. The tableau chiefly suggests

(A) that Miss Emily was an abused child.

(B) the social pretentiousness of Emily's family.

(C) the domineering and overly protective nature of Emily's father.

(D) Miss Emily's purity and her father's stern morality.

(E) that the Griersons successfully protected themselves from the ravages of passing time.

128. The author of this passage is

(A) Katherine Anne Porter.

(B) Stephen Crane.

(C) Eudora Welty.

(D) Flannery O'Connor.

(E) William Faulkner.

129.   The soote season, that bud and bloom forth brings,
With green hath clad the hill and eke the vale;
The nightingale with feathers new she sings;
The turtle to her make hath told her tale.
Summer is come, for every spray now springs;
The hart hath hung his old head on the pale;
The buck in brake his winter coat he flings,
The fishes float with new repairéd scale;
The adder all her slough away she slings,
The swift swallow pursueth the fliés small;
The busy bee her honey now she mings.
Winter is worn, that was the flowers' bale.
And thus I see among these pleasant things,
Each care decays, and yet my sorrow springs.

This sonnet, like those of many other Renaissance poets, draws its inspiration from the poetry of

(A) Sappho.

(B) Ovid.

(C) Tasso.

(D) Petrarch.

(E) Homer.

Questions 130 – 132 refer to the following passage.

Margaret greeted her lord with peculiar tenderness on the morrow. Mature as he was, she might yet be able to help him to the building of the rainbow bridge that should connect the prose in us with the passion. Without it we are meaningless fragments, half monks, half beasts, unconnected arches that have never joined into a man. With it love is born, and alights on the highest curve, glowing against the grey, sober against the fire. Happy the man who sees from either aspect the glory of these outspread wings. The roads of his soul lie clear, and he and his friends shall find easy going.

It was hard going in the roads of Mr. Wilcox's soul. From boyhood on he had neglected them. "I am not a man who bothers about my own inside," Outwardly he was cheerful, reliable, and brave; but within, all had reverted to chaos, ruled so far as it was ruled at all, by an incomplete asceticism. Whether as a boy, husband, widower, he had always the sneaking belief that bodily passion is bad, a belief that is desirable only when held passionately. Religion had confirmed him. The words that were read aloud on Sunday to him and to other respectable men were the words that had once kindled the souls of St. Catherine and St. Francis into a white-hot hatred of the carnal. He could not be as the saint and love the Infinite with a seraphic ardour, but he could be a little ashamed of loving a wife.

130. In the first paragraph, "prose" can best be said to be associated with

(A) monks and beasts.

(B) monks and grey.

(C) passion and fire.

(D) grey and fire.

(E) beasts and grey.

131. According to the narrator, Mr. Wilcox's greatest fault is

    (A) the chaotic nature of his inner life.

    (B) an inadequate education.

    (C) his lack of religious convictions.

    (D) his willingness to marry without loving his wife.

    (E) his occasional lapses from cheerfulness, reliability, and courage.

132. Which of the following statements best expresses the narrator's attitude toward carnality?

    (A) Sexual desire is incompatible with marital love.

    (B) Sexual desire necessarily leads to guilt or shame.

    (C) If man cannot attain a "white-hot hatred of the carnal," he should at least strive for an incomplete asceticism.

    (D) Absolute hatred of sexual desire is preferable to an incomplete asceticism.

    (E) Spiritual wholeness is possible only when bodily passion is suppressed.

Questions 133 – 136 refer to the following passages.

133. Which describes Aristophanes' *Lysistrata*?

134. Which describes Sophocles' *Antigone*?

135. Which describes Molière's *Tartuffe*?

136. Which describes Euripides' *Medea*?

    (A)   Forced to choose between loyalty to family and loyalty to a new king, who is also her uncle, the heroine chooses the former and duty to what she calls the laws of the gods rather than the laws of the state.

    (B)   This play satirizes both religious hypocrisy and fraudulence, and also makes fun of the obsessive fanaticism and gullibility of those who allow themselves to be victimized by the greedy and self-serving.

(C)   The heroine decides to leave her husband and to achieve self-realization after she discovers that his position in society is more important to him than her love and their mutual respect.

(D)   This play asks its audience to make love not war. The women of the play try to bring an end to a war that threatens their city by refusing to have sexual relations with their men as long as the latter continue the war.

(E)   Deserted by her husband for another woman, the protagonist seeks revenge by killing their two children and the "other woman."

Questions 137 – 139 refer to the following selection.

This is the excellent foppery of the world, that when
    we are sick in fortune—
often the surfeits of our own behavior—we make
    guilty of our disasters the sun,
the moon, and stars, as if we were villains on
    necessity, fools by heavenly
compulsion, knaves, thieves, and treachers
    by spherical predominance, drunkards,
liars, and adulterers by an enforc'd obedience   5
    of planetary influence, and all that
we are evil in, by a divine thrusting on. An
    admirable evasion of whoremaster
man, to lay his goatish disposition on the charge
    of a star! My father compounded
with my mother under the Dragon's Tail, and my
    nativity was under Ursa Major, so that
it follows I am rought and lecherous. Fut, I should
    have been that I am, had the
maidenliest star in the firmament twinkled on my   10
    bastardizing.

137.   "Foppery" (line 1) can best be understood to mean

(A) finery.

(B) appearance.

(C) habit.

(D) condition.

(E) foolishness.

138.   "Goatish" (line 7) means

(A)   sluggish.   (D)   fickle.

(B)   irrational.   (E)   irresponsible.

(C)   lecherous.

139.   Which of the following statements is LEAST accurate? The speaker

(A)   believes man shapes his own character.

(B)   believes man tries to blame his mistakes on something other than himself.

(C)   has little or no belief in Providence.

(D)   believes in astrological determinism.

(E)   believes that man's misfortunes are often the result of his own excessive behavior.

Questions 140 – 144 refer to the following poem.

I am poor brother Lippo, by your leave!
You need not clap your torches to my face.
Zooks, what's to blame? you think you see a monk!
What 't is past midnight, and you go the rounds,
And here you catch me at an alley's end   5
Where sportive ladies leave their doors ajar?
The Carmine's my cloister: hunt it up,
Do,—harry out, if you must show your zeal,
Whatever rat, there, haps on his wrong hole,
And nip each softling of a wee white mouse,   10
Weke, weke, that's crept to keep him company!
Aha, you know your betters! Then, you'll take
Your hand away that's fiddling on my throat,
And please to know me likewise. Who am I?
Why, one, sir, who is lodging with a friend   15
Three streets off—he's a certain ... how d' ye call?
Master— a ... Cosimo of the Medici,
I' the house that caps the corner. Boh! you were best!
Remember and tell me, the day you're hanged,

How you affected such a gullet's-gripe!   20
But you, sir, it concerns you that your knaves
Pick up a manner nor discredit you: ...

140. The poem is set in

(A) medieval Rome.

(B) early Renaissance Florence.

(C) medieval Spain.

(D) early Renaissance Naples.

(E) nineteenth-century Milan.

141. The opening scene takes place after midnight in an area

(A) infested by rats.

(B) adjacent to the Carmelite cloister where Lippo Lippi lives.

(C) in the city's main business district.

(D) in front of the Medici palace.

(E) that contains houses of prostitution.

142. To whom is Lippo Lippi speaking when he says "Boh! you were best?"

(A) The policeman (or watchman) who handled him most roughly

(B) The most aggressive of the ruffians or thieves who have accosted him

(C) The officer in charge of the police patrol

(D) The leader of the ruffians

(E) The respectable-looking friend who has rescued him

143. What causes the men who have stopped him to treat him more gently?

(A) They feel compassion for his situation.

(B) The effectiveness of his rhetorical self-defense

(C) The arrival of his friend

(D) His mention of his connection to the Medici

(E) He has embarrassed them by stressing his weakness and their greatly superior strength.

144. To whom is Lippo Lippi speaking in line 21 ("But you, sir")?

(A) The policeman who handled him most roughly

(B) The most aggressive of the ruffians

(C) The officer in charge of the police patrol

(D) The leader of the ruffians

(E) The respectable-looking friend who has rescued him

Questions 145 – 147 refer to the following poem.

Shall I compare thee to a summer's day?
Thou art more lovely and more temperate:
Rough winds do shake the darling buds of May,
And summer's lease hath all too short a date;
Sometime too hot the eye of heaven shines,   5
And often is his gold complexion dimm'd;
And every fair from fair sometimes declines,
By chance or nature's changing course untrimm'd:
But thy eternal summer shall not fade
Nor lose possession of that fair thou ow'st;   10
Nor shall Death brag thou wand'rest in his shade,
When in eternal lines to time thou grow'st;
So long as men can breathe or eyes can see,
So long lives this, and this gives life to thee.

145. According to the speaker, death will be unable to "brag thou wand'rest in his shade" because

(A) the beloved is like summer, which returns each year.

(B) the beloved is like summer, which is sunny, not shady.

(C) death releases the beloved into eternal life.

(D) the beloved, partaking of the earth's natural cycles, will be remembered each summer.

(E) the beloved derives life from this poem for as long as it is read.

146. The greatest shift in thought process in the poem occurs at the beginning of line

(A) 3.   (D) 11.

(B) 5.   (E) 13.

(C) 9.

147. The primary theme of the poem is

(A) the permanence of poetry.

(B) the beauty of the beloved.

(C) the disappointments of summer.

(D) the unreliability of nature.

(E) the impermanence of love.

Questions 148 – 149 refer to the following passage.

Proud of their weakness, however, they must always be protected, guarded from care, and all the rough toils that dignify the mind.—If this be the fiat of fate, if they will make themselves insignificant and contemptible, sweetly to waste "life away," let them not expect to be valued when their beauty fades, for it is the fate of the fairest flowers to be admired and pulled to pieces by the careless hand that plucked them. In how many ways do I wish, from the purest benevolence, to impress this truth on my sex; yet I fear that they will not listen to a truth that dear bought experience has brought home to many an agitated bosom, nor willingly resign the privileges of rank and sex for the privileges of humanity, to which those have no claim who do not discharge its duties.

148. Which of the following statements best expresses the "truth" the author wishes to impress upon her sex?

(A) Women must subordinate household pursuits to careers to achieve full humanity.

(B) Women must preserve their beauty as long as possible because they lose their power when it fades.

(C) Men are the natural antagonists of women; hence, women must substitute reasoned judgment for naive trust.

(D) To achieve full humanity, women must be willing to give up the arbitrary power of beauty.

(E) Women face more natural obstacles than men; hence, they must not allow socially-conditioned roles to add to those obstacles.

149. The author of this passage is

(A) Lady Mary Wortley Montagu.

(B) Mary Wollstonecraft.

(C) Mary Shelley.

(D) Kate Chopin.

(E) Virginia Woolf.

Questions 150–151. Identify the author of each of the following passages. Base your decision on the content and style of each passage.

150. ... but we must remain firm in our conviction that hymns to the gods and praises of famous men are the only poetry which ought to be admitted into our State. For if you go beyond this and allow the honeyed muse to enter, either in epic or lyric verse, not law and the reason of mankind, which by common consent have ever been deemed best, but pleasure and pain will be the rulers in our State.

(A) Plato

(B) Aristotle

(C) Horace

(D) Quintilian

(E) Boethius

151. The best means would be, my friend, to gain, first of all, clear knowledge and appreciation of the true sublime. The enterprise is, however, an arduous one. For the judgment of style is the last and crowning fruit of long experience. None the less, if I must speak in the way of precept, it is not impossible perhaps to acquire discrimination in these matters by attention to some such hints as those which follow.

    (A) Quintilian

    (B) Longinus

    (C) Demetrius

    (D) Cicero

    (E) Dionysius of Halicarnassus

152. We may divide characters into flat and _____.

    Complete the critic's description of character:

    (A) profound

    (B) deep

    (C) square

    (D) round

    (E) stretched

153. The violence of breaking down the door seemed to fill this room with pervading dust. A thin acrid pall as of the tomb seemed to lie everywhere upon the room decked and furnished as for a bridal.

    The room is

    (A) Miss Emily's in *A Rose for Emily*.

    (B) Miss Haversham's in *Great Expectations*.

    (C) Isabel's in *A Portrait of a Lady*.

    (D) Mrs. Mallard's in *The Story of an Hour*.

    (E) Bertha Rochester's in *Jane Eyre*.

154. Ancient _____ embodied for Yeats the union and subsequent transfigura-
    tion, through art, of the body and the holy idea.

    Which of the following completes the passage?

    (A) Rome   (D) Egypt

    (B) Greece   (E) India

    (C) Byzantium

155. Which of the following wrote a revenge tragedy?

    (A) Ben Jonson   (D) Farquhar

    (B) Webster   (E) Goldsmith

    (C) John Gay

156. Which modern novel incorporates within it a Jacobean revenge tragedy?

    (A) *The Waterfall*

    (B) *One Hundred Years of Solitude*

    (C) *The Crying of Lot 49*

    (D) *Jalousie*

    (E) *The Name of the Rose*

157. "I was taught to think, and I was willing to believe, that genius was not a
    bawd, that virtue was not a mask, that liberty was not a name, that love had
    its seat in the human heart. Now I would care little if these words were
    struck out of the dictionary, or if I had never heard them. They are become
    to my ears a mockery and a dream."

    The "I" in the passage above is

    (A) Dashiel Hammett.   (D) Franz Kafka.

    (B) T. S. Eliot.   (E) R. L. Stevenson.

    (C) William Hazlitt.

158. He had, to a morbid excess, that desire to rise which is vulgarly called ambition, but no wish for the esteem or the love of his species; only the hard wish to succeed—not shine nor serve—succeed, that he might have the right to despise a world which galled his self-conceit.

The writer referred to here is

(A) Walt Whitman.   (D) Edgar Allan Poe.

(B) Ezra Pound.   (E) Ernest Hemingway.

(C) Ralph Waldo Emerson.

159. From which poem is the following lover's message?

Dear fatal name! rest ever unrevealed,
Nor pass these lips in holy silence sealed.
Hide it, my heart, within that close disguise,
Where mixed with God's, his loved idea lies.

(A) "Epistle to Miss Blount"   (D) "To a Lady"

(B) "Eloisa to Abelard"   (E) "The Rape of the Lock"

(C) "Essay on Man"

Questions 160 – 161 refer to the following passage.

Let us make an image of the soul, an ideal image of the soul, like the composite creations of ancient mythology, such as the Chimera or Scylla or Cerberus; and there are many others to which two or more different natures are said to grow into one.

160. The writer's central admission is that

(A) the soul does not exist without man's suppositions.

(B) ideal images are composites of different natures.

(C) mythical figures never existed.

(D) images take on a life of their own after one imagines them.

(E) concepts of the soul can best be found in ancient mythology.

161. The writer's reference point may best be described as

    (A) Platonic.
    (B) Aristotelian.
    (C) Christian.
    (D) gnostic.
    (E) organic.

Questions 162 – 164 refer to the following excerpt.

There comes Emerson first, whose rich words, every one,
Are like gold nails in temples to hang trophies on,
Whose prose is grand verse, while his verse, the Lord knows,
Is some of it pr–No, 'tis not even prose;

I'm speaking of metres; some poems have welled
From those rare depths of should that have ne'er been excelled;
They're not epics, but that doesn't matter a pin,
In creating, the only hard thing's to begin:

162. The reference to "nails in temples" in the second line is an allusion to

    (A) the New Testament.
    (B) Greek fable.
    (C) the Seven Cities of Cibola.
    (D) the Old Testament.
    (E) Milton's *Lysistrata*.

163. This excerpt is similar to

    (A) an elegy.
    (B) a paean.
    (C) a contemporanium.
    (D) an encomium.
    (E) a satire.

164. This poem was written by

    (A) Henry David Thoreau.
    (B) William Cullen Bryant.
    (C) James Russell Lowell.
    (D) Walt Whitman.
    (E) John Greenleaf Whittier.

Questions 165 – 166 refer to the following excerpt.

> If you will aid me in this enterprise,
> Then draw your weapons and be resolute;
> If not, depart. Here will Benvolio die,
> But_____'s death shall quit my infamy.

165.   This quote is properly completed with the name

(A)   Macbeth.

(B)   Romeo.

(C)   Faustus.

(D)   Martino.

(E)   Carolus.

166.   The excerpt was written by

(A)   Ben Jonson.

(B)   Christopher Marlowe.

(C)   William Shakespeare.

(D)   Thomas Campion.

(E)   Robert Herrick.

Questions 167 – 168 refer to the following poem.

> in Just-
> spring   when the world is mud-
> luscious the little
> lame balloonman
> whistles   far   and wee
>
> and eddieand bill come
> running from marbles and
> piracies and it's
> spring
>
> when the world is puddle-wonderful
> the queer
> old balloonman whistles
> far   and   wee
> and bettyandisabel come dancing

from hop-scotch and jump-rope and

it's
spring
and
     the
         goat-footed

balloonMan   whistles
far
and
wee

167. The versification of the poem would be best classified as

(A) iambic pentameter.   (D) sprung rhythm.

(B) blank verse.   (E) free verse.

(C) ballad stanza.

168. The tone is best described as

(A) elegiac.   (D) whimsical.

(B) sarcastic.   (E) devotional.

(C) laudatory.

---

169. In which excerpt is the "I" character Huckleberry Finn?

(A)   Downstairs we came out through the first-floor dining-room to the street. A waiter went for a taxi. It was hot and bright. Up the street was a little square with trees and grass where there were taxis parked. A taxi came up the street, the waiter hanging out at the side. I tipped him and told the driver where to drive, and got in beside Brett. The driver started up the street. I settled back. Brett moved closer to me. We sat close against each other. I put my arm around her and she rested against me comfortably. It was very hot and bright, and the houses looked sharply white. We turned out onto the Gran Via.

(B)   Through the fence, between the curling flower spaces, I could see them hitting. They were coming toward where the flag was and I went along the fence. Luster was hunting in the grass by the flower tree. They took the flag out, and they were hitting. Then they put the flag back and they went to the table, and he hit and the other hit. Then they went on, and I went along the fence. Luster came away from the flower tree and we went along the fence and they stopped and we stopped and I looked through the fence while Luster was hunting in the grass.

(C)   Well, I got a good going-over in the morning, from old Miss Watson, on account of my clothes; but the widow she didn't scold, but only cleaned off the grease and clay and looked so sorry that I thought I would behave a while if I could. Then Miss Watson she took me in the closet and prayed but nothing come of it.

(D)   The tower, I should have said, was square; and in every corner the step was made of a great stone of a different shape, to join the flights. Well, I had come close to one of these turns, when, feeling forward as usual, my hand slipped upon an edge and found nothing but emptiness beyond it. The stair had been carried no higher; to set a stranger mounting it in the darkness was to send him straight to his death;...

(E)   For a long time I used to go to bed early. Sometimes, when I had put out my candle, my eyes would close so quickly that I had not even time to say "I'm going to sleep." And half an hour later the thought that it was time to go to sleep would awaken me; I would try to put away the book which, I imagined, was still in my hands, and to blow out the light; I had been thinking all the time, while I was asleep, of what I had just been reading, but my thoughts had run into a channel of their own, until I myself seemed actually to have become the subject of my book: a church, a quartet, the rivalry between Francois I and Charles V. This impression would persist for some moments after I was awake; it did not disturb my mind, but it lay like scales upon my eyes and prevented them from registering the fact that the candle was no longer burning.

170. Hog Butcher for the World,
      Tool Maker, Stacker of Wheat,
      Player with Railroads and the Nation's Freight Handler;
      Stormy, husky, brawling,
      City of the Big Shoulders:

      Identify the above city.

      (A) Athens   (D) Paris

      (B) Chicago   (E) London

      (C) New York

171. The fog comes
      on little cat feet.
      It sits looking
      over harbor and city
      on silent haunches
      and then moves on.

      Identify the author of the above descriptive passage.

      (A) Charles Dickens   (D) Robert Frost

      (B) Ernest Hemingway   (E) Carl Sandburg

      (C) T. S. Eliot

172. "The excursus upon the origin of Odysseus' scar is not basically different from
      the many passages in which a newly introduced character, or even a newly
      appearing object or implement, though it be in the thick of battle, is described
      as to its nature and origin."
            — Auerbach, *Mimesis*

      Although the above statement refers to Homer's *Odyssey*, the idea, if
      applied to English literature, could best be illustrated with examples
      from

      (A) Shakespeare's *King Lear*.

      (B) Spenser's "The Faerie Queene."

(C) Chaucer's "The Miller's Tale."

(D) *Sir Gawain and the Green Knight.*

(E) *Beowulf.*

173. "Neo-classicism is characterized by clarity of statement, by objectivity, reason and tolerance in attitude, and by balance and symmetry in form."

Which of the following would best illustrate this definition?

(A) Blake's "Jerusalem"

(B) Pope's "Essay on Criticism"

(C) Donne's "The Ecstasy"

(D) Smart's "A Song to David"

(E) Traherne's "Wonder"

174. By contrast, a Greek temple or even a Romanesque abbey is a completed whole, and in both the observer's eye eventually can come to rest. The appeal of the Gothic lies in the very restlessness that prevents this sense of completion. The observer is caught and swept up in the general stream of movement and from the initial impulse gets the desire to continue it. The completion, however, can only be in the imagination, since there were, in fact, no finished cathedrals.
— William Fleming, *Arts and Ideas*

Which of the following literary works comes closest to illustrating the structural aesthetic ascribed in the above passage to the Gothic cathedral?

(A) Dante's *The Divine Comedy*

(B) Chaucer's *The Canterbury Tales*

(C) Milton's *Paradise Lost*

(D) Boccaccio's *The Decameron*

(E) Shakespeare's *Hamlet*

175. Roland Barthes is associated with which school of criticism?

    (A) Formalism

    (B) Reader-response criticism

    (C) Psychoanalytical criticism

    (D) The New Criticism

    (E) Deconstruction

176.   The measure is <u>English</u> Heroic Verse without Rime, as that of <u>Homer</u> in <u>Greek</u>, and of <u>Virgil</u> in <u>Latin</u>; Rime being no necessary Adjunct or true Ornament of Poem or good Verse, in longer Works especially, but the Invention of a barbarous Age, to set off wretched matter and lame Meter; grac't indeed since by the use of some famous modern Poets, carried away by Custom, but much to their own vexation, hindrance, and constraint to express many things otherwise, and for the most part worse than else they would have exprest them.

In the above passage

    (A) Milton defends his use of blank verse in *Paradise Lost*.

    (B) Marlowe defends his use of blank verse in *Tamburlaine Part I*.

    (C) Ezra Pound defends his use of free verse in *The Cantos*.

    (D) John Dryden discusses his translation of Virgil's *Aeneid*.

    (E) Edmund Spenser discusses versification in "The Faerie Queene."

Questions 177 – 178 refer to the following selection.

> Batter my heart, three-personed God; for you
> As yet but knock, breathe, shine, and seek to mend;
> That I may rise, and stand, o'erthrow me, and bend
> Your force, to break, blow, burn, and make me new.
> I, like an usurped town, to another due,
> Labor to admit you, but Oh, to no end,
> Reason your viceroy in me, me should defend,

5

But is captived, and proves weak or untrue.
Yet dearly I love you, and would be loved fain,
But am betrothed unto your enemy: 10
Divorce me, untie, or break that knot again,
Take me to you, imprison me, for I
Except you enthral me, never shall be free,
Nor ever chaste, except you ravish me.

177. The best paraphrase of the second quatrain (lines 5-8) would be

(A) If I acted rationally, I would do what is right, but my mind is overpowered by evil motives.

(B) I am in love with another woman, but I am not willing to admit it.

(C) If the government were more rational in its policies, ordinary citizens wouldn't become traitors.

(D) Religion is one of the principal causes of conflict in the world.

(E) This town, London, is now controlled by the Puritans.

178. The "enemy" in line 10 is

(A) Satan.

(B) Spain, a country with which England was at war.

(C) the Anglican Church.

(D) the poet's rival.

(E) the poet's wife.

179.   "What is honor? A word. What is that word honor? Air—a trim reckoning! Who hath it? He that dies a Wednesday. Doth he feel it? No. Doth he hear it? No. 'Tis insensible then? Yea, to the dead. But will it not live with the living? No. Why? Detraction will not suffer it. Therefore I'll none of it. Honor is a mere scutcheon—and so ends my catechism."

The philosophical position that Falstaff assumes in the above speech might best be classified as

(A) stoicism.

(D) neo-Platonism.

(B) the Donatist heresy.

(E) nominalism.

(C) Calvinism.

180. For a theory of tragedy as the "catharsis" of emotions, one should read

(A) Sidney, *Defence of Poesie.*

(B) Tolstoy, *What Is Art?*

(C) Aristotle, *Poetics.*

(D) Freud, *The Psychopathology of Everyday Life.*

(E) A. C. Bradley, *Shakespearean Tragedy.*

181. In Jane Austen's *Sense and Sensibility*, "sense" refers to

(A) any one of the faculties of perception, sight, hearing, taste, smell, feeling, as the basis for empirical knowledge.

(B) sensuousness.

(C) sensuality.

(D) a practical and reasonable regard for one's own self-interest.

(E) aesthetic appreciation transcending moral conventions.

182. "Beauty is truth, truth beauty,"—that is all
Ye know on earth, and all ye need to know.

Critics have disagreed as to exactly what "ye" refers to in the poem. Which of the following are possible solutions?

(A) Either the nightingale or the poet

(B) Either the nightingale or humanity

(C) Either the urn or humanity

(D) Either the rose or the woman the poet loves

(E) Either the rose or humanity

183. An alternation of heroic and comic scenes is typical of the drama of which of the following playwrights?

(A) Sophocles

(B) Racine

(C) Shakespeare

(D) Dryden

(E) Congreve

184. Shakespeare wrote *Macbeth* in response to

(A) the ascension to the throne of England of James I.

(B) the death of Elizabeth I.

(C) the execution of Charles I.

(D) the defeat of the Spanish Armada.

(E) the execution of Mary, Queen of Scots.

185. Which of the following works could best be characterized as existentialist?

(A) Tolstoy's *War and Peace*

(B) Milton's *Paradise Lost*

(C) Sartre's *No Exit*

(D) Dante's *The Divine Comedy*

(E) Marlowe's *Doctor Faustus*

186. If it were done when 'tis done, then 'twere well
It was done quickly: if the assassination
Could trammel up the consequence, and catch
With his surcease success; that but this blow
Might be the be-all and the end-all here,   5
We'd jump the life to come.

In the above context, "success" (line 4) means

(A) victory.

(B) wealth.

(C) fame.

(D) the act or process of becoming entitled as a legal beneficiary to the property of a deceased person.

(E) any result or outcome.

187. The Sea of Faith
Was once, too, at the full, and round earth's shore
Lay like folds of a bright girdle furled.
But now I only hear
Its melancholy, long, withdrawing roar,
Retreating, to the breath
Of the night-wind, down the vast edges drear
And naked shingles of the world.

The author compares a withdrawing wave of the ocean to

(A) a general loss of religious faith.

(B) his personal loss of religious faith.

(C) a loss of trust between himself and someone he loves.

(D) a loss of self-confidence, of faith in himself.

(E) a general decrease in patriotism.

188. There was never a sound beside the wood but one,
And that was my long scythe whispering to the ground.
What was it it whispered? I knew not well myself;
Perhaps it was something about the heat of the sun,
Something, perhaps about the lack of sound —
And that was why it whispered and did not speak.
It was no dream of the gift of idle hours,
Or easy gold at the hand of fay or elf:
Anything more than the truth would have seemed too weak
To the earnest love that laid the swale in rows,

Not without feeble-pointed spikes of flowers
(Pale orchises), and scared a bright green snake.
The fact is the sweetest dream that labor knows,
My long scythe whispered and left the hay to make.

Which of the following best summarizes the author's concern?

(A) The secrets of nature surround us and can be revealed to anyone who will take time out and listen.

(B) One benefit of physical labor can be psychic revelation.

(C) Humans must work hard at discovering the truth; it will not come to the passive observer.

(D) The secrets of life are hinted at, yet never quite revealed.

(E) Mankind's role on Earth is to labor; to know anything beyond this is impossible.

189. The conventional divisions of pastoral elegy include each of the following EXCEPT

(A) invocation of the muse.

(B) an admonition to Death.

(C) an expression of grief.

(D) a digression, usually about the church.

(E) an admission that everyone is mortal.

Questions 190 – 193 refer to the following poem.

If I can stop one Heart from breaking
I shall not live in vain
If I can ease one Life the Aching
Or cool one Pain
Or help one fainting Robin
Unto his Nest again
I shall not live in Vain.

190. The most important characteristic of the poetry demonstrated here is the tendency toward

    (A) an emphasis on nature.

    (B) didacticism.

    (C) empathy with the greater world.

    (D) reclusiveness.

    (E) lament for lost love.

191. The poet's use of capital first letters (exclusive of the first words of each line and "I") may be accounted for by

    (A) the poet's love of hidden puzzles.

    (B) personification of concepts.

    (C) remnant eighteenth-century convention.

    (D) the random quality of free verse.

    (E) thematic emphasis.

192. The philanthropic tone is related to the traditions of

    (A) the eighteenth-century Enlightenment.

    (B) American Free Thinking.

    (C) Hobbesian materialism.

    (D) evangelical messianism.

    (E) late Puritan literary climate.

193. The author of the poem above is

    (A) Walt Whitman.   (D) Ogden Nash.

    (B) Edna St. Vincent Millay.   (E) Carl Sandburg.

    (C) Emily Dickinson.

194.   My heart leaps up when I behold
        A rainbow in the sky:
        So it was when my life began;
        So is it now I am a man;
        So be it when I shall grow old,
        Or let me die!
        The Child is the father of the Man;
        And I could wish my days to be
        Bound each to each by natural piety.

This poem illustrates a style and theme best termed

(A) Johnsonian.   (D) Wordsworthian.

(B) euphemistic.   (E) Dickinsonian.

(C) Freudian.

195.   Some artists, whether by theoretical knowledge or by long practice,
        can represent things by imitating their shapes and colours, and others do
        so by the use of the voice; in the arts I have spoken of the imitation as
        produced by means of rhythm, language, and music, these being used
        either separately or in combination.

The author describes artists in

(A) a predominantly Expressionistic mode.

(B) an Aristotelian ideal.

(C) a prevailing Pindaric attitude.

(D) a basically Impressionistic pattern.

(E) an Atomistic code.

196. Which of the following is an example of interior monologue?

(A)   I knew it. I knew if I came to this dinner, I'd draw something like
        this baby on my left. They've been saving him up for me for weeks.
        Now we've simply got to have him—his sister was so sweet to us in

London: we can stick him next to Mrs. Parker—she talks enough for two.

(B)   Up until I learned my lesson in a very bitter way, I never had more than one friend at a time, and my friendships, though ardent, were short.

(C)   An extraordinary thing happened today. I got up rather late, and when Marva brought my boots, I asked her for the time. Hearing that ten had struck quite a while before, I dressed in a hurry.

(D)   Well, I want to tell you, Mrs. Babbitt, and I know Mrs. Schmaltz heartily agrees with me, that we've never enjoyed a dinner more— that was some of the finest fried chicken I ever tasted in my life—and it certainly is a mighty great pleasure to be able to just have this quiet evening with you and George.

(E)   I know what is being said about me and you can take my side or theirs, that's your own business. It's my word against Eunice's and Olivia Ann's, and it should be plain enough to anyone with two good eyes which one of us has their wits about them.

Questions 197 – 199 refer to the following passage.

Indentured long to logic and the gown.
Lean as a rake the horse on which he sat,
And he himself was anything but fat,
But rather wore a hollow look and sad.
Threadbare the little outercoat he had,   5
For he was still to get a benefice
And thoughts of worldly office were not his.

197.   The character being described by Chaucer is

(A) the Monk.   (D) the Student.

(B) the Friar.   (E) the Pardoner.

(C) the Parson.

198. In line 6, the "benefice" is

    (A) a position in the church.

    (B) worldly gain.

    (C) scholarly advancement.

    (D) secular employment.

    (E) an inheritance.

199. Chaucer here draws a parallel between

    (A) the appearance of the subject and his chances for worldly success.

    (B) the appearance of the horse and the subject's ambitions.

    (C) the enslaved nature of both subject and horse.

    (D) the appearance of the subject and the appearance of the horse.

    (E) the quality of the subject's clothes and the quality of his thought.

---

200.   Wordsworth calls Voltaire dull, and surely the production of these (referring to a brief quoted passage above) un-Voltairian lines must have been imposed on him as a judgement. One can hear them being quoted at a Social Science Congress; one can call up the whole scene. A great room in one of our dismal provincial towns; dusty air and jaded afternoon daylight; benches full of men with bald heads and women in spectacles; an orator lifting up his face from a manuscript written within and without to declaim these lines of Wordsworth; and in the soul of any poor child of nature who may have wandered in thither, an unutterable sense of lamentation, and mourning, and woe!

The writer of this passage criticizes Wordsworth's poetry because of its

    (A) un-Voltairian lines.

    (B) scientific system of thought.

    (C) overdone lamentations.

    (D) popular appeal.

    (E) provincial quality.

Questions 201 – 202 refer to the following passage.

> I have been assured by a very knowing American of my acquaintance in London, that a young healthy child well nursed is at a year old a most delicious, nourishing, and wholesome food, whether stewed, roasted, baked, or boiled; and I make no doubt that it will equally serve in a fricassee or a ragout.

201. The tone of this passage may best be described as

    (A) factual description.

    (B) playful.

    (C) sarcastically outrageous.

    (D) comedically inventive.

    (E) cynical.

202. The reference to "a very knowing American" in this passage

    (A) reflects the belief that Americans are uncivilized.

    (B) underscores the preposterous nature of the author's proposition.

    (C) points out the paternalistic nature of colonialism.

    (D) is meant to be a statement of fact only.

    (E) offers a citation from someone more experienced in what the author proposes.

203. Whoever thinks a faultless piece to see,
Thinks what ne'er was, nor is, noe e'er shall be.
In every work regard the writer's end,
Since none can compass more than they intend;
And if the means be just, the conduct true,
Applause, in spite of trivial faults, is due.

The poet believes that it is more important for the critic to

(A) consider the technical merits of a piece than to criticize its message.

(B) consider the purpose of the piece than to look for flaws in the execution.

(C) consider the effect on the readership than to the impression made on the critic.

(D) consider any "trivial faults" as a natural adjunct of great works.

(E) consider the limitations of the writer when examining any technical flaws.

204. Let us just for the moment feel the pulses of Ulysses and of Miss Dorothy Richardson and M. Marcel Proust, on the earnest side of Briareus; on the other, the throb of The Shiek and Mr. Zane Grey, and, if you will, Mr. Robert Chambers and the rest. Is Ulysses in his cradle? Oh, dear! What a grey face! And Pointed Roofs, are they a gay little toy for nice little girls? Alas! You can hear the death-rattle in their throats. They can hear it themselves. They are listening to it with acute interest, trying to discover whether the intervals are minor thirds or major fourths. Which is rather infantile, really.

The author is criticizing most of all the

(A) melodramatic quality of contemporary authors.

(B) pointless attention to meaningless novelistic detail.

(C) trivial nature of the popular novel.

(D) self-consciousness of the serious novel.

(E) lack of quality in contemporary literature.

Questions 205 – 206 refer to the following poem.

It is not growing like a tree
In bulk, doth make man better be;
Or standing long an oak, three hundred year,
To fall a log at last, dry, bald, and sere:
A lily of a day
Is fairer far, in May,

Although it fall and die that night;
It was the plant and flower of light.
In small proportions we just beauties see,
And in short measures life may perfect be.

205. Which of the following is the closest restatement of the poem's central theme?

   (A) It is not the end that matters, but the means.

   (B) Fame and success are not as important as appreciating beauty.

   (C) It is how you live your life that matters, not whether you succeed.

   (D) The appreciation of nature and the understanding of truth are one and the same.

   (E) Perfection may be found in the small things of nature.

206. This poem is written in

   (A) the Pindaric mode.

   (B) the Petrarchan spirit.

   (C) the form of an Elizabethan Sonnet.

   (D) Adoration form.

   (E) the spirit of the Grands Rhetoriqueurs.

---

207. Love Virtue; she alone is free;
She can teach ye how to climb
Higher than the sphery chime:
Or, if Virtue feeble were,
Heaven itself would stoop to her.

This poem expresses

   (A) the Platonic Ideal.   (D) the Deistic Ideal.

   (B) the Puritan Ideal.   (E) the Renaissance Ideal.

   (C) the Zoroastrian Ideal.

Questions 208 – 209 refer to the following poem.

I found a dimpled spider, fat and white,
On a white heal-all, holding up a moth
Like a white piece of rigid satin cloth—
Assorted characters of death and blight
Mixed ready to begin the morning right,
Like the ingredients of a witches' broth—
A snow-drop spider, a flower like a froth,
And dead wings carried like a paper kite.

What had that flower to do with being white,
The wayside blue and innocent heal-all?
What brought the kindred spider to that height,
Then steered the white moth thither in the night?
What but design of darkness to appall?—
If design govern in a thing so small.

208. The first stanza of this poem is noted for

(A) personification.

(B) its detailed description of living forms.

(C) its attempt to compare natural objects to those of human use.

(D) the emergence of "death imagery" from the description of beautiful natural objects.

(E) its use of color in relating varied natural forms.

209. The answer posed in the last two lines of the second stanza might best be termed

(A) conditional.

(B) facetious.

(C) a question hidden within an answer.

(D) rhetorical.

(E) inquisitory.

Questions 210 – 211 refer to the following passage.

> One of the facts that might come to light in this process is our tendency to insist, when we praise a poet, upon those aspects of his work in which he least resembles anyone else. In these aspects or parts of his work we pretend to find what is individual, what is the peculiar essence of the man. We dwell with satisfaction upon the poet's difference from his predecessors, especially his immediate predecessors; we endeavour to find something that can be isolated in order to be enjoyed.

210. The "process" (line 1) to which the author of this passage is referring is

  (A) evaluating the relationship of a writer to the tradition that precedes him/her.

  (B) making an evaluation based on only the material itself.

  (C) criticizing within the limitations of the current literary period.

  (D) evaluating the personal relationship of a poet and the work.

  (E) criticizing the individual parts, not the poem itself as a whole.

211. The author most likely goes on to suggest that

  (A) looking at the individuality of an author is futile.

  (B) recognizing his individuality as part of a great tradition is beneficial.

  (C) appreciating a writer's spontaneity is what the contemporary reader calls for.

  (D) a mature writer will exhibit true individuality.

  (E) we should take little satisfaction in criticizing the writer.

212.   What I must do is all that concerns me, not what the people think. This rule, equally arduous in actual and in intellectual life, may serve for the whole distinction between greatness and meanness.

This may be seen as a statement of

(A)   the Renaissance.

(B)   the Nonconformist movement.

(C)   the Age of Enlightenment.

(D)   the Golden Age of New England.

(E)   the Beat Era.

213.   "When my love swears that she is made of truth,
I do believe her, though I know she lies."

These lines from Shakespeare's Sonnet 138 are examples of

(A)   synecdoche.   (D)   paradox.

(B)   ellipsis.   (E)   prosody.

(C)   pararhyme.

Questions 214 – 215 refer to the following passage.

Let me not, however, lose the historian in the man, nor suffer the doting recollections of age to overcome me, while dwelling with fond garrulity on the virtuous days of the patriarchs—on those sweet days of simplicity and ease, which never more will dawn on the lovely Island of Manna-hata.

214.   This passage is meant to reinforce the idea that

(A)   the author is fond of relating past times.

(B)   the author is quick to admit to his prejudices.

(C)   the author dislikes verbosity.

(D)   the author has struggled to retain his subjectivity.

(E)   the author is nostalgic about his lovely island.

215.   This passage is from

(A)   Cooper's *The Pioneers*.

(B)   Irving's *History of New York*.

(C)   Whitman's *Manna-hata*.

(D)   Coleridge's *Biographia Literaria*.

(E)   Hawthorne's *My Kinsman, Major Molineux*.

---

216.   If ever mortal "wreaked his thoughts upon expression," it was Shelley. If ever poet sang – as a bird sings – earnestly – impulsively – with utter abandonment – to himself – that poet was the author of "The Sensitive Plant." Of art – beyond that which is instinctive with genius – he either had little or disdained all.

The author of this passage is

(A)   Keats   (D)   Poe

(B)   Sheridan   (E)   Trilling

(C)   Faulkner

Questions 217 – 220 refer to the following passage.

Blow, winds, and crack your cheeks! rage! blow!
You cataracts and hurricanes, spout
Till you have drenched our steeples, drowned the cocks!
You sulphurous and thought-executing fires,
Vaunt-couriers to oak-cleaving thunderbolts,   5
Singe my white head! And thou, all-shaking thunder,
Smite flat the thick rotundity o' the world!
Crack nature's molds, all germens spill at one,
That make ungrateful man!

217. The speaker is addressing

    (A) winds.   (D) Caliban.

    (B) Macduff.   (E) King Lear.

    (C) wild nature.

218. In context, "germens" (line 8) refers to

    (A) the disease that afflicts man.

    (B) the seeds of discontent.

    (C) the origin of ingratitude.

    (D) future mankind.

    (E) storm-driven rains.

219. The verbs in this passage can best be characterized as

    (A) descriptive.   (D) action.

    (B) intransitive.   (E) helping.

    (C) Anglo-Saxon.

220. The speaker is

    (A) Lady Macbeth.   (D) Satan.

    (B) King Lear.   (E) Richard III.

    (C) Paulina.

221. Both *Lucky Jim* and *Catch-22* make use of

    (A) unreliable narrators.   (D) epistolary techniques.

    (B) naturalist conventions.   (E) first-person narration.

    (C) an anti-hero.

222. All of the following are associated with *The Dial* (Boston 1840-1844) EXCEPT

    (A) Ralph Waldo Emerson.   (D) Henry David Thoreau.

    (B) Margaret Fuller.   (E) Nathaniel Hawthorne.

    (C) Jones Very.

223. All of the following form part of the frontier tradition in American literature EXCEPT

    (A) Sarah Orne Jewett.   (D) Caroline Kirkland.

    (B) Artemus Ward.   (E) Hamlin Garland.

    (C) Bret Harte.

224. The "Melmoth" in Oscar Wilde's adopted name (Sebastian Melmoth) is taken from a romance by

    (A) Nathaniel Hawthorne.   (D) Charles Robert Maturin.

    (B) Robert Montgomery Bird. (E) Ann Radcliffe.

    (C) John Bunyan.

225. In his poem "Pied Beauty," _____ employed the prosodic technique known as _____.

    (A) William Wordsworth ... zeugma.

    (B) William Carlos Williams ... imagism.

    (C) Gerard Manley Hopkins ... sprung rhythm.

    (D) Dylan Thomas ... alliteration.

    (E) Thomas Hardy ... caesura.

226. In the play *The Tempest*, Prospero's first adversary is the island's original inhabitant, _____ .

    (A) Cranimor

    (B) Caliban

    (C) Romero

    (D) Miranda

    (E) Ferdinand

227. Ineluctable modality of the visible: at least that if no more, thought through my eyes. Signatures of all things I am here to read, seaspawn and seawrack, the nearing tide, that rusty boot. Snotgreen, bluesilver, rust: colored signs. Limits of the diaphane.

    The above passage suggests which variety of narrative?

    (A) Second-person

    (B) First person

    (C) Omniscient third-person

    (D) Limited third-person

    (E) Internal monologue

228.   *The Tempest* rehearses arguments that Europe is prevalent in the early-Modern period to the European presence in the New World, a presence represented in the play by Prospero. Consider the argument the Europeans were a civilizing force, necessitated to some degree by the unruly and unholy indigenous inhabitants, for whom the character of Caliban, Prospero's slave on the exotic island to which he has been exiled, becomes a figure. And yet Shakespeare complicates this argument by presenting Caliban's forceful and eloquent refusal to accept Prospero's discourse of legitimization: "This island's mine by Sycorax my mother / which thou tak'st from me." While the play does not seem explicitly to challenge Prospero's right to rule the island, it reveals some of the potential counter arguments to the nascent imperialism of early-Modern Europe.

    The above statement about William Shakespeare's *The Tempest* is an example of which of the following schools of literary criticism?

    (A) Deconstruction

    (B) New Criticism

    (C) Postcolonialism

    (D) Psychoanalysis

    (E) Marxism

229.   While fundamentally about the law, this novel in a wider sense deals with possible responses to social inequity. Its purpose is didactic, as seen in its concerns with reforming the Chancery, the necessity of relieving the neglected and poorer classes, and the urgency of recognizing first hand local impoverishment that requires real material assistance, as opposed to a vague notion of a charity that sends moral aphorisms to far flung lands.

The novel being described in the passage above is

(A)   Thomas Hardy's *Jude the Obscure*

(B)   Henry Fielding's *Tom Jones*

(C)   D. H. Lawrence's *Sons and Lovers*

(D)   Jane Austen's *Emma*

(E)   Charles Dickens' *Bleak House*

230.   O senseless strivings of the mortal round!
          how worthless is that exercise of reason
          that makes you beat your wings into the ground!
       One man was giving himself to law, and one
          to aphorisms; one sought sinecures,
          and one to rule by force or sly persuasion;
       One planned his business, one his robberies;
          one, tangled in the pleasure of the flesh,
          wore himself out, and one lounged at his ease;
       While I, of all such vanities relieved
          and high in Heaven with my Beatrice,
          arose to glory, gloriously received.

The poetry above is excerpted from

(A)   Homer's *Odyssey*   (D)   Dante's *Divine Comedy*

(B)   Boccaccio's *Decameron*   (E)   *Beowulf*

(C)   Milton's *Paradise Lost*

GRE LITERATURE IN ENGLISH

Practice Test 2
Answer Key

1.	(B)	26.	(A)	51.	(D)	76.	(B)
2.	(D)	27.	(E)	52.	(C)	77.	(B)
3.	(A)	28.	(C)	53.	(D)	78.	(D)
4.	(D)	29.	(B)	54.	(E)	79.	(D)
5.	(A)	30.	(D)	55.	(C)	80.	(B)
6.	(E)	31.	(A)	56.	(A)	81.	(C)
7.	(D)	32.	(B)	57.	(D)	82.	(B)
8.	(C)	33.	(E)	58.	(C)	83.	(E)
9.	(D)	34.	(D)	59.	(C)	84.	(B)
10.	(E)	35.	(B)	60.	(B)	85.	(A)
11.	(D)	36.	(C)	61.	(D)	86.	(E)
12.	(E)	37.	(B)	62.	(E)	87.	(B)
13.	(A)	38.	(C)	63.	(B)	88.	(C)
14.	(C)	39.	(D)	64.	(E)	89.	(C)
15.	(B)	40.	(B)	65.	(D)	90.	(E)
16.	(A)	41.	(E)	66.	(A)	91.	(D)
17.	(C)	42.	(A)	67.	(C)	92.	(B)
18.	(A)	43.	(B)	68.	(D)	93.	(E)
19.	(D)	44.	(A)	69.	(A)	94.	(B)
20.	(D)	45.	(E)	70.	(A)	95.	(D)
21.	(A)	46.	(D)	71.	(E)	96.	(C)
22.	(C)	47.	(A)	72.	(C)	97.	(A)
23.	(E)	48.	(D)	73.	(E)	98.	(E)
24.	(C)	49.	(B)	74.	(C)	99.	(C)
25.	(C)	50.	(C)	75.	(D)	100.	(E)

101.	(D)	136.	(E)	171.	(E)	206.	(A)
102.	(C)	137.	(E)	172.	(E)	207.	(B)
103.	(E)	138.	(C)	173.	(B)	208.	(C)
104.	(B)	139.	(D)	174.	(B)	209.	(D)
105.	(C)	140.	(B)	175.	(E)	210.	(A)
106.	(B)	141.	(E)	176.	(A)	211.	(B)
107.	(E)	142.	(A)	177.	(A)	212.	(D)
108.	(B)	143.	(D)	178.	(A)	213.	(D)
109.	(C)	144.	(C)	179.	(E)	214.	(D)
110.	(A)	145.	(E)	180.	(C)	215.	(B)
111.	(A)	146.	(C)	181.	(D)	216.	(D)
112.	(A)	147.	(A)	182.	(C)	217.	(A)
113.	(B)	148.	(D)	183.	(C)	218.	(C)
114.	(D)	149.	(B)	184.	(A)	219.	(D)
115.	(D)	150.	(A)	185.	(C)	220.	(B)
116.	(A)	151.	(B)	186.	(E)	221.	(C)
117.	(E)	152.	(D)	187.	(A)	222.	(E)
118.	(D)	153.	(A)	188.	(C)	223.	(A)
119.	(D)	154.	(C)	189.	(B)	224.	(D)
120.	(B)	155.	(B)	190.	(B)	225.	(C)
121.	(A)	156.	(C)	191.	(C)	226.	(B)
122.	(A)	157.	(C)	192.	(E)	227.	(E)
123.	(D)	158.	(D)	193.	(C)	228.	(C)
124.	(C)	159.	(B)	194.	(D)	229.	(E)
125.	(C)	160.	(B)	195.	(B)	230.	(D)
126.	(B)	161.	(A)	196.	(A)		
127.	(C)	162.	(D)	197.	(D)		
128.	(E)	163.	(B)	198.	(A)		
129.	(D)	164.	(C)	199.	(D)		
130.	(B)	165.	(C)	200.	(B)		
131.	(A)	166.	(B)	201.	(C)		
132.	(D)	167.	(E)	202.	(B)		
133.	(D)	168.	(D)	203.	(B)		
134.	(A)	169.	(C)	204.	(B)		
135.	(B)	170.	(B)	205.	(E)		

GRE LITERATURE IN ENGLISH

Detailed Explanations of Answers

1.   **(B)**
    This is Coleridge's four-line poem, "On Donne's Poetry." Donne had not been popular during the eighteenth century. Coleridge's terse commentary reveals his admiration, albeit qualified, for Donne's mastery of the metaphysical style.

2.   **(D)**
    This is from Shelley's "To Wordsworth," in which Shelley expresses his disillusionment with Wordsworth's abandonment of the liberal social causes that he formerly supported in his poetry.

3.   **(A)**
    This is Swift's comment on himself in "Verses on the Death of Dr. Swift," which he says he wrote in order to correct man's folly.

4.   **(D)**
    In order to answer this question, it is necessary to be somewhat familiar with the backgrounds of the authors. Plath's autobiographical novel, *The Bell Jar*, relates experiences from her early adult life, including a period of intense psychiatric therapy. "Daddy, daddy, you bastard, I'm through" is from a poem entitled "Daddy," one of several that expose the attitudes and personalities of her German father and Austrian mother. Although Woolf (A) did commit suicide, her relationship with her parents is not an issue in her works. Sexton (C) also explored similar themes in her poetry, but did not write an autobiographical novel.

5.   **(A)**

These are concluding lines from Matthew Arnold's "Dover Beach," in which the poet contrasts pleasing appearances (of both world and sea) with harsher realities.

6.   **(E)**

Herrick's poem, like many others that have a "seize the day" motif, emphasizes that life is short and time is fleeting in urging the pursuit of present pleasure.

7.   **(D)**

Parnell's "Night-Piece on Death" (A), Blair's "The Grave" (B), Young's "Night-Thoughts" (C), and Gray's "Elegy Written in a Country Churchyard" (E) are all associated with the graveyard school. Parnell is an early exemplar or forerunner; Gray's "Elegy" is the most famous poem produced by the group; and the poems of Blair and Young are perhaps most typical of the graveyard school.

8.   **(C)**

A sonnet is a poem consisting of fourteen lines, three quatrains and a couplet. The poems in *In Memoriam* form a sequence, but they are not sonnets. Rather, Tennyson's poem consists of quatrains.

9.   **(D)**

The excerpt is from the Yeats poem "Leda and the Swan." Agamemnon was murdered by his wife Clytemnestra and her lover Aegisthus upon his return from Troy; his murder was later avenged by his son Orestes.

10.   **(E)**

In Greek mythology, Zeus visited Leda in the form of a swan. The offspring of their union were Helen and Clytemnestra.

11.   **(D)**

When dealing with questions of this type, do not despair if you are not sure about the speaker of the passage. You may be able to discern who the author of the passage is by thinking of the character archetypes associated with that author. This passage is from Shaw's *Major Barbara*. Barbara has turned from the Salvation Army to the saving of another order of souls.

12.   **(E)**
This is Lady Bracknell's reaction, in *The Importance of Being Earnest*, to the news that Jack's first home was a handbag in a railroad station. The satiric portrayal of the upper class in the passage is an easily recognizable trait of Wilde's works.

13.   **(A)**
This is from the "marriage contract" scene in Congreve's *The Way of the World*, in which Millamant establishes conditions of her marriage to Mirabel. Her demands underscore the desire of heroines in the Restoration comedy of manners to maintain independence and individuality after marriage.

14.   **(C)**
Rosalind urges Orlando to hire someone else to die in his place rather than die himself from unrequited love. In the world's history, Rosalind says, no man has ever died for love.

15.   **(B)**
Rosalind's account of Leander's death is highly anti-romantic; in her account, Leander drowned from a cramp after going to cool off on a hot summer evening in the Hellespont, not while swimming across it to visit Hero, as other accounts claim.

16.   **(A)**
The dialogue is from Shakespeare's *As You Like It*, set in the Forest of Arden.

17.   **(C)**
The passage reflects such transcendental notions as the presence of truths that are beyond the reach of man's limited senses, the usefulness of intuition as a guide to universal truth, and nature as an image in which the divine can be perceived.

18.   **(A)**
Emerson's belief that God is all-loving and all-pervading underlies his assertions that nature is "beautiful" and "good" in the second paragraph. Materialism (B) and nihilism (D) are antithetical to Emerson's ideas, while existentialism (E) focuses on the individual. Utilitarianism (C) is a reason-based method of thinking and does not fit the passage.

19.   **(D)**

This excerpt is from Emerson's *The Poet* (1844). He wrote *Self-Reliance*, his celebration of individualism, somewhat earlier. Emerson is perhaps the leading spokesman of transcendentalism in America. Be careful not to choose Thoreau, even though the tone of the passage is similar to *Walden* (B), this passage is clearly not from Thoreau's other famous essay, *Resistance to Civil Government*.

20.   **(D)**

The word's meaning can be determined from its similarity to the word "venom." Age poisons all, including the speaker, whose beauty has been taken from her by the passage of time.

21.   **(A)**

Her "pith" has been taken by age; the flour is gone, leaving her only the "bran," the seed husk, which she will now sell as best she can.

22.   **(C)**

Unto this day, she says, it makes her heart glad that she had her fling earlier in life. When she thinks about her "youthe" and "jolitee," it does her "herte boote" (heart good).

23.   **(E)**

Although she is not happy about losing her beauty, she accepts the ravages of time, realistically appraises what she has left (and what its value might be if marketed properly), and is determined to make the most of what she has.

24.   **(C)**

The Wife of Bath gives this account of herself in the prologue to her tale in Chaucer's *The Canterbury Tales*. Choice (D) can be eliminated because the speaker is clearly feminine, but "The Wife of Bath's Tale" is perhaps the best known of the Canterbury Tales, and should be recognized by the reader.

25.   **(C)**

A general critical precept underlying the essay is the author's belief that "nothing can please many, and please long, but just representations of general nature." Shakespeare has pleased many and pleased long; the reason, according to the author, is that Shakespeare is the preeminent painter of general nature. Milton (B) and Spenser (E) did not write tales based on historical figures, while the reference to a European prince eliminates Sophocles (A).

26. **(A)**

Shakespeare is always careful to preserve the essential characteristics of men, the author says, but is less careful with additional and chance distinctions (that is, characteristics that are accidental, deriving merely from social position or place of abode, as opposed to those that derive from nature and are inherent). This is less a criticism of Shakespeare than an assertion that he gave more attention to what is important than to what is unimportant.

27. **(E)**

Since this author is dismissive of all three critics, (E) is the only correct choice. All concentrate on "accident" rather than "nature"; hence, they focus on the unimportant at the expense of the significant. Consequently, the author says their objections are "the petty cavils of petty minds."

28. **(C)**

Since the differences between men are "casual," Shakespeare rightly focuses on the universal rather than the specific. Like the artist who "neglects the drapery," Shakespeare ignores the inessentials of nationality and custom.

29. **(B)**

The passage is from Johnson's preface to his edition (in eight volumes) of Shakespeare's plays. *The Preface to Shakespeare* has been praised highly; a later Shakespearean editor called it "perhaps the finest composition in our language."

30. **(D)**

The dark, damp setting of the passage immediately identifies its author as Poe. Poe's narrator, Montresor, finishes building a tomb containing his living "friend," Fortunato, in the catacombs under Montresor's residence. Montresor lures Fortunato there on the pretext of looking at a cask of amontillado, but then chains him to a wall inside a vault.

31. **(A)**

The passage reflects the youthful determination and distinctive voice of Welty's narrator, who moves to the post office to "get even" with her family.

32.   **(B)**

Ironically, while this passage has found its way into our popular speech, its origin is definitely less well-known. This is Jaques' melancholy portrait of the stages of man's life in *As You Like It*.

33.   **(E)**

The portly Falstaff complains of having to walk any distance, and vows to give up theft if thieves cannot be true to one another. The passage is from *Henry IV, Part I*.

34.   **(D)**

The angry tone of the passage is a clue as to its speaker. This is Caliban's reply to Miranda, who has tried to "civilize" the savage by, among other things, teaching him speech in *The Tempest*.

35.   **(B)**

An elegy is a formal and sustained poetic lament for the dead. The pastoral elegy is a species of the elegy that represents both the mourner and the one he mourns as shepherds. The pastoral elegy developed elaborate conventions, including an invocation of the muses, nature joining in the mourning for the dead shepherd, a procession of appropriate mourners, a closing consolation, and so forth. Johnson's poem is a meditation on, as the title makes clear, the futility of ambition that leads to discontent; it is not a pastoral elegy.

36.   **(C)**

This exchange between the hero and heroine of Sir George Etherege's *The Man of Mode* is typical of many such exchanges in the Restoration comedy of manners. Its meaning depends on the audience's recognition of the speakers' use of an extended metaphor, which is sometimes similar to metaphysical wit. The two seem to be speaking of one thing, but the meaning refers to something else. In this instance Dorimant and Harriet appear to be talking about gaming; in fact, Harriet lets Dorimant know that she will engage in innocent diversions but will not submit to him sexually. Each tests the other to see what the terms and conditions of their relationship might be.

37.   **(B)**

Dorimant lets Harriet know that he can be content with less than sexual conquest (the meaning depends on a pun in "deep play") if he likes his partner well enough; implicit in his remark is the notion that he *does* like Harriet well enough.

38.   **(C)**
       The exchange is characteristic of the wit present in the battle of the sexes in the Restoration comedy of manners. Such exchanges are based on extended conceits, often with sexual undertones. One of the yardsticks by which a character's "worth" is measured in Restoration comedy is the ability to handle language, which is a reflection of social grace, intellect, and the ability to manipulate others. The most admirable use language as a form of power, rather than being controlled by language. Wit in this sense is not a primary virtue in the other choices offered (for example, the language of heroic drama is noted for bombast; that of sentimental comedy avoids sexual innuendo).

39.   **(D)**
       The sonnet adheres to Petrarchan form in the octave (rhyming *abbaabba*), but differs from it in the sestet by introducing couplets rather than the usual rhyme scheme (*cdecde* or some variant, such as *cdccdc*). In other ways it adheres to the conventions of the Petrarchan sonnet—a shift of thought occurs at the beginning of the sestet, and it contains no more than five rhymes.

40.   **(B)**
       Countée Cullen, an African-American poet, predicts that the oppressed will not always be oppressed, will not always plant what others reap, and will not always "beguile" the limbs of the oppressor "with mellow flute" while the oppressor sleeps. The oppressed, he says, were not made to weep eternally.

41.   **(E)**
       The night is "no less lovely" for being black; in fact, the blackness of the night "relieves the stark white stars," giving them a loveliness they would not have without blackness.

42.   **(A)**
       The Harlem Renaissance denotes a period of literary achievement in the 1920s in Harlem, a section of upper Manhattan. Other writers of the period include Langston Hughes and Jean Toomer.

43.   **(B)**
    In order to answer questions of this type, it is important to consider the author's attitudes toward literature if one is not immediately familiar with these non-fiction passages. This is Fielding's definition of the comic romance, as distinct from comedy and from the serious romance, in his preface to *Joseph Andrews*. Since (B) is the only passage that seems to have a somewhat dated use of language and tone, the early eighteenth-century author Fielding might be a good choice here.

44.   **(A)**
    This is from Lawrence's *Why the Novel Matters*. The passage reflects Lawrence's belief that one "knows" only through the body and his assertion that the novelist understands this, while parsons, philosophers, and scientists may not. It is interesting to note the use of fire as a symbol, which is heavily employed by Lawrence in his fictional works as well.

45.   **(E)**
    In *Aspects of the Novel*, Forster says that although all novels tell stories, story-telling is not the novelist's greatest achievement. Forster differentiates between the "form" of the novel and its "content," the story within the novel. The passage reflects the distinction between the two aspects of the novel.

46.   **(D)**
    Dixon pokes fun at mindless, insignificant academic scholarship; aware of the limited value of such work, he persists in order to keep his university teaching position.

47.   **(A)**
    Although the novel is related in third-person narration, events are seen through Dixon's eyes. It is his perspective on other characters and action that shapes the reader's responses. Although Dixon evokes considerable laughter at his own expense, he is treated sympathetically by the author.

48.   **(D)**
    The passage is from Kingsley Amis' comic novel, *Lucky Jim*. Jack Kerouac (A) is best known for his autobiographical work *On The Road*. Woody Allen (B) is an excellent satiric writer, but his humor often delves into the absurd. Cary (C) and Kesey (E) are satirists as well, but their more famous works attack different targets than Amis' work.

49. **(B)**

The Aesthetic Movement was a European phenomenon of the latter nineteenth century. Its rallying cry became "art for art's sake." The references of (A), (C), and (D) to "utility" as well as the relationship of art to "social value," are antithetical to the concept of aesthetics. The concept espoused in tenet (E) decries art as a pale imitation of nature.

50. **(C)**

The passage is from *The Myth of Sisyphus*, by the existentialist writer Albert Camus. Eugene Ionesco is a leading writer of the drama of the absurd. Chekhov and Turgenev have a much more sympathetic attitude towards their characters, which would eliminate (A) and (D). Ibsen (B) is known for his psychological realism, while Doctorow (E) was also known for his use of realistic characters as a commentary on society.

51. **(D)**

The term was used by Keats to describe the objective, impersonal aspect of Shakespeare and has subsequently been used to denote an artist's ability to avoid expressing his own personality in his work.

52. **(C)**

This is Gwendolyn Brooks' poem "We Real Cool," subtitled *The Pool Players. Seven at the Golden Shovel*. Brooks has spent most of her life in the Chicago area. She is the first African-American writer to win a Pulitzer Prize. Cullen (A), Hughes (B), and Wilbur (D) did not utilize short lines to the extent that Brooks is known for, and Oates (E) is a prose writer.

53. **(D)**

This is the concluding stanza of Thomas Gray's comic (sometimes called mock-heroic) poem, "Ode on the Death of a Favourite Cat, Drowned in a Tub of Gold Fishes." Raleigh (A), Lovelace (B) and Blake (E) are not known for comical poetry, and Swift (D) was a satirist.

54. **(E)**

The passage, in typical Jamesian style, is from *The Golden Bowl*. The scene occurs immediately after Fanny Assingham has broken the golden bowl. The husband and wife are Amerigo (the Prince) and Maggie.

55.   **(C)**

These are the concluding lines of Fitzgerald's *The Great Gatsby*. The "he" is Gatsby, whose pursuit of a vision destroys him; the passage emphasizes the influence of the past on man's attempts to shape the future. Although the lines are famous enough to be almost immediately recognizable, the styles of Melville (A) and Dreiser (B) are nowhere near as compact as the style in the passage, and can be readily eliminated.

56.   **(A)**

The lines given are two of the three stanzas from Dickinson's "I reason, Earth is short," reflecting the style and thematic concerns of much of her poetry. Whitman's (B) poetry is more flowing and earthly, and Parker (E) is known for her humorous style.

57.   **(D)**

This passage is from Beckett's novel *Murphy*, which deals with Murphy's humorous and tragic search for self. The author draws on Gaelic legend in Murphy's quest for self-identity. The work is written in Beckett's highly individual style and is set in both Dublin and London. Although Beckett is often more famous for his plays, the passage is not representative of Swift's (A) satire, Joyce's (B) stream-of-consciousness, Thomas' (C) imagery, or Donleavy's (E) sardonic wit.

58.   **(C)**

The passage is from E. M. Forster's *A Passage to India*. It relates the aftermath of Mrs. Moore's nihilistic experience in the Marabar caves, an experience that undermines her "grip on life." This passage contradicts the epiphanies usually enjoyed by Lawrence's (A) characters. Conrad's (B) examination of the human condition usually involves man's cruelty to his fellow man. The works of Woolf (D) and Greene (E) are often pessimistic but do not descend into nihilism.

59.   **(C)**

This passage is from Flaubert's *Madame Bovary*. The passage reflects Emma's disillusionment as well as her persistent romantic illusions. Maupassant (D) and France (E) often utilized writing as social commentary, while Zola (A) employed a more scientific method in his character studies. Proust (B) wrote his most famous works in first-person interior monologue.

60.   **(B)**
This is the vivid, vernacular narrative voice of Holden Caulfield at the beginning of Salinger's *The Catcher in the Rye*. (D) is a satirical work about life in academia, and (A) concerns itself with the lives of a family rather than an individual. (E) is narrated by a character older than the one in the passage.

61.   **(D)**
The passage is from Milton's *Samson Agonistes*. Samson is reflecting on the relative importance of his gift of strength from God. The last line alludes to the fact that the seat of Samson's strength is his hair, which Delilah has cut, thereby depriving him of his strength.

62.   **(E)**
Jane Austen's patronizing description is of Catherine Morland, the heroine of *Northanger Abbey*. Plain and unimpressive, Catherine only gradually wins our admiration. The female protagonist in (A) is described as a privileged child. Answers (B), (C) and (D) open with more general comments about families.

63.   **(B)**
The two novels alluded to are Hardy's *Tess of the D'Urbervilles* and *Jude the Obscure*. Lawrence (A) did not believe in a "neutral force," but in the tension generated by two opposing forces. In Conrad's (C) works, people struggle against man's own inhumanity and the suffering people cause to each other. Waugh (D) is known for his satires and society tales, and while Dickens (E) did explore some of the themes listed, the plot outlines do not match his works.

64.   **(E)**
A number of poems from the Middle Ages are concerned with beauty that must die. An important element of these poems is the *ubi sunt* motif, from the Latin sentence, *"Ubi sunt qui ante nos fuerunt?"* ("Where are they who before us were?"). This stanza is the second in Francois Villon's "The Ballad of Dead Ladies"; the *ubi sunt* motif is stated directly in the last line ("Where are the snows of yesteryear?").

65.   **(D)**
Héloise and Abelard are famous lovers whose relationship has been the subject of many literary works. Abelard was a scholastic philosopher and theologian; Héloise was his student. They were secretly married to avoid

hindering Abelard's advancement in the church. After Héloise's uncle took revenge, Abelard became a monk and Héloise a nun. Abelard lived from 1079 to 1142.

66.   **(A)**
All of the beautiful ladies of the past are dead, gone like the snows of yesteryear. Medieval poems like Villon's combine an appreciation for the world's beauty with an awareness of the transitory nature of that beauty, which is nearly illusory when viewed against the background of eternity. In asking the *ubi sunt* question, the poet calls to mind life's splendor, but the grim and inevitable answer poignantly reminds the reader how short-lived that splendor is.

67.   **(C)**
Everything turning away from Icarus' fall in stanza two provides a specific example of the general idea (indifference to suffering or to the extraordinary) advanced in stanza one; similarly, Brueghel's painting is a specific instance of Auden's generalization about the Old Masters' understanding the human position of suffering. Because there is a concrete example in the second stanza, answers (A) and (B) can be eliminated. Furthermore, the use of "for instance" in line 14 indicates that the idea in the second stanza does not contradict the previous stanza, thus eliminating answers (D) and (E).

68.   **(D)**
The children are indifferent to the miraculous birth and the plowman is indifferent to the fall of Icarus. The children and the plowman never consciously refuse to take part in the world around them, so answers (A) and (E) can be eliminated. Answer (C) is clearly incorrect because no strength of character is shown by anyone in the poem save Icarus, and answer (B) is irrelevant.

69.   **(A)**
The dogs and horse are oblivious to suffering; we might think that the world should take notice of something as dreadful as martyrdom, but, in fact, daily life continues unaffected. Answers (B) and (C) are incorrect because the animals' behavior is similar to that of humans in the poem, so neither animals nor humans are shown to be morally superior. Answers (D) and (E) refer to themes that are not explored in the poem.

70.   **(A)**
    While novel and effective in Petrarch, the types of figures used by him became tired and conventional in love poems written by his imitators. Shakespeare satirizes some of the standard objects used for similes by Elizabethan sonneteers in this sonnet. Encomia (B), or works that pay tribute to heroes, are not discussed here, and the excerpt *is* a rhymed quatrain (C). There is nothing about the excerpt that suggests obscure conceits are being satirized (D), and the lines are directed more towards the cliches of love rather than the subject of love (E).

71.   **(E)**
    This is a stanza from Shakespeare's Sonnet 130. Wyatt (A) is credited with introducing the sonnet form into English poetry, while Sidney (B), as a predecessor to Shakespeare, utilized the sonnet form before it became a cliche to do so. Raleigh (C) and Marlowe (D) did not employ the sonnet form in their writing.

72.   **(C)**
    This is Johnson's unsympathetic description of metaphysical wit in his *Life of Cowley*. While the pathetic fallacy (A) involves the assigning of personal emotions to inanimate objects, no "discordia" occurs. "A combination of dissimilar images" is not a characteristic of pastoral poetry (B) or heroic drama (D). The passage does not seem to describe the mock heroism of Hudibrastic poetry (E).

73.   **(E)**
    The passage is from Johnson's *Life of Cowley*. The forceful tone of the passage suggests Johnson, whereas one might expect a slightly more humorous or satiric piece from Swift (A) or Pope (B). Addison (C) and Dryden (D) were also critics, but their poetry has better survived to the present day.

74.   **(C)**
    It parodies Wordsworth's "She Dwelt Among the Untrodden Ways." Wordsworth's early style was marked by invocations of nature and gentle rhythms, which were innovative for their time and very influential for future romantic writers and poets.

75.   **(D)**

The excerpt is an example of an epistolary novel, that is, a novel which consists of a series of letters. This is an excerpt from one of the heroine's letters to her parents, filled with her usual self-justifications in discussing her behavior toward "Mr. B." and others. (A) involves a hero's quest; (C) is a famous eighteenth-century genre, which usually involves a plot with a female protagonist and a dark setting.

76.   **(B)**

The excerpt is from Richardson's *Pamela*. All of Samuel Richardson's novels were written in epistolary form and promoted virtue. Defoe (A) displayed a similar tone in his writing but did not utilize the epistolary form. Fielding (C), Smollett (D), and Sterne (E) were all humorists who satirized the form and content made famous by Richardson.

77.   **(B)**

The seventh-century English poem deals with an Anglo-Saxon court poet named Widsith. The scop's functions are somewhat similar to those of the poet laureate of later times.

78.   **(D)**

Beowulf explores this statement by its hero. He uses his strength to test fate, and extends courage to its outer limits. Fate ultimately controls men's lives, but it can be influenced by heroism, as Beowulf's life illustrates.

79.   **(D)**

This stanza is from Anthony Brode's "Breakfast with Gerard Manley Hopkins," in which he parodies Hopkins' sprung rhythm. Jeffers (A) was known for his reworking of classicism; Doolittle (B) often wrote in free verse; Millay (C) is known for her sonnets; and Crane (E) was more famous for his imagery than his use of rhyme.

80.   **(B)**

Everyman is the best surviving example of a medieval morality play. The play is an allegory that dramatizes the moral struggle of all Christians and teaches that man can take with him from this world only what he has given and nothing that he has received. In this play, the allegorical significance of each actor is defined by his name (Knowledge, Beauty, Strength, Good Deeds, and so on).

81. **(C)**

This excerpt is from Blake's *A Vision of the Last Judgement* and deals with the relationship between imaginative vision and the corporeal eye. Reality is defined in relation to the visionary (mental), not in relation to corporeal being.

82. **(B)**

This excerpt is from the beginning of Baldwin's *Notes of a Native Son* and deals with the death of Baldwin's father.

83. **(E)**

This is from the preface to *The Picture of Dorian Gray*, and contains Wilde's characteristically witty remarks about the uselessness of art.

84. **(B)**

Raleigh's response is a critique of the pastoral form utilized by Marlowe. (D) and (E) are unlikely responses since the poets who replied lived *before* the poets who supposedly wrote the original poem. Surrey (A) introduced the sonnet to England but not pastoral poetry.

85. **(A)**

The nymph's reply denies the accuracy of the shepherd's portrait of an idyllic rustic existence in a land of plenty and eternal spring. Her reply emphasizes changes that come with the passage of time, the harshness of winter, and the need to be aware of and to plan for such conditions.

86. **(E)**

In Greek mythology, after Philomela was raped and her tongue cut out by her brother-in-law, she was turned into a swallow (in some accounts, a nightingale; "Philomel" is the allusive name often given to the nightingale in English poetry). The nymph's mention of Philomel draws attention to the brutal aspects of love, in contrast to the romantic vision of the shepherd.

87. **(B)**

"Honey tongue" is associated with "fancy's spring," and "heart of gall" is associated with "sorrow's fall." Listening to fancy's sweet talk in the spring will later result in bitterness or remorse ("gall"). Since the use of "spring" here is symbolic, answers (A), (C), and (D), which refer to spring as a period of time, are incorrect. (E) is simply a non sequitur.

88.   **(C)**
Although this is a difficult question to determine if one does not know who wrote the poem, Skelton (A) lived before Marlowe's time, and (D) and (E) were not contemporaries of Marlowe.

89.   **(C)**
The lecture is associated with applause, scientific analysis, light, and crowds, in contrast to the speaker's solitary contemplation of the stars, associated with silence, mysticism, darkness, and individuality. A contrast between mathematical certainty and error is not present in the poem; while mathematical certainty might be associated with the astronomer's lecture, the speaker would not associate "error" with his silent contemplation of the heavens.

90.   **(E)**
"Perfect" is used in the sense of "complete" silence, but also suggests perfection (the welcome silence that allows for wonder after the noise of the lecture-hall).

91.   **(D)**
Whitman's "When I Heard the Learn'd Astronomer" implicitly celebrates nature's mystical qualities and the individual's solitary communion with nature. The use of free verse and the praise of nature are characteristic of Whitman.

92.   **(B)**
The soul, like a mole, casts its folly out of its tunnel for all the world to see. The soul may be perceptive in viewing others, but fails to see its own folly. (A) and (D) are not referred to in the passage, and appetite (E) is a reference to the desires of men in the previous line. Mole (C) is used in a simile for the soul, but is not used in place of the soul itself.

93.   **(E)**
"Thus I discovered" continues the analogy of the soul and the mole. Antony's soul has revealed its folly to plain view, and Dolabella has seen it. (A) is a conclusion that may be drawn if the passage is read too literally. (B) and (C) are based upon a misreading of the word "abroad." There is nothing in the passage to suggest that Dolabella's suspicions were aroused by Antony's vanity (D).

94. **(B)**

Although Dolabella once blamed Antony's love for Cleopatra, he now wishes he were Antony "to be so ruined" (that is, he knows that Antony's love has ruined him, but understands, even approves of, the reasons Antony persists in his ruin).

95. **(D)**

The passage is from Dryden's *All for Love*, written in conscious imitation of Shakespeare's style. Although it might be easy to mistake the work for a Shakespearean play, none of the other four plays has a character named Dolabella.

96. **(C)**

This short, humorous poem, "Adam Pos'd," is by Anne Finch, Countess of Winchilsea. Finch imagines that Adam would have had difficulty identifying and naming a vain, affected eighteenth-century coquette, having seen nothing like her in the natural world. "Father" refers to Adam. The toiling of the "Father" on the field would probably eliminate choices (A) and (D), while the poem's antiquated language indicates that it predates the time of Washington (E). Time (B) does not possess the skill of naming as described in the second stanza.

97. **(A)**

The nymph's appearance would have perplexed Adam's ability to identify and name things. Choices (B), (C), and (E) do not make sense in the context of the line. Choice (D) fits in the line, but the language indicates that the "Father" would be confused, not rendered powerless.

98. **(E)**

The poem makes fun of the affected behavior and appearance of the coquette. Although the poem does make use of biblical figures, there are no invocations to God (D), and the tone is certainly not solemn (C) or angry (B).

99. **(C)**

Adam would have difficulty formulating the right idea of what he is seeing. (A) does not make sense because he has never seen such a thing, and (B) is inaccurate because Adam seeks to define the person before him, not merely examine the person. (D) is too literal an interpretation of the word "frame," and (E) is not the proper definition of the word in this context.

100. **(E)**
The reference is to Genesis 2:19-20, Adam's naming of species. If we have already concluded that the speaker is Adam, then the only other possible choice could be (B), and there is no reference to this skill in the poem.

101. **(D)**
The wavering form, the "Thing," is the Nymph of line 4. (A), (B), and (E) do not make sense in the context of the poem, while Element (C) refers to the possible origin of this Thing, rather than the Thing itself.

102. **(C)**
Ford's play was published in 1633. Passages (D) and (E) clearly make references to themes and objects that are too contemporary for Ford.

103. **(E)**
Williams' masterpiece is frequently produced. The line from the heroine is a well-recognized line; also, Williams was known for dealing with controversial themes.

104. **(B)**
The lifeless perfection of the dolls (they are not "filthy") contrasts with the filth and the noise of a real, living human child. Both are small and human in form, but the dolls are the product of art. The lines "There's not a man can report/Evil of this place" eliminates choice (A). There is no example of happiness (C) to contrast with the sad man and woman. There is a differentiation between immortal art and life, but the distinction is not made in the manner suggested by choice (D), and (E) is a non sequitur.

105. **(C)**
The poem gives us a glimpse of two different realms, art and life, both "inhabited" by the doll-maker. Both make demands on the artist as art comes into conflict with the real world.

106. **(B)**
Yeats is the author of both "The Dolls" and "Sailing to Byzantium." The jarring final line of this poem might remind one of another Yeats poem, "The Second Coming."

107. **(E)**

Unlike his father, Telemachus has the patience and prudence to rule "a rugged people" effectively, but he also lacks Ulysses' heroism and sense of adventure. Answers (A) and (D) might be accurate descriptions but are not borne out by Ulysses' words. (B) and (C) are traps if the irony of the passage is not detected.

108. **(B)**

The elderly Ulysses plans to set sail in search of additional experience for its own sake and to test further his will. He cannot be content merely "to breathe," and plans to use fully the little time left to him. The speaker clearly neither fears death (A) or desires it (E). His mention of "eternal silence" indicates he does not believe in immortality (C), and there is no indication that he is anxious for solitude (D).

109. **(C)**

The passage is from Tennyson's dramatic monologue, "Ulysses." Coleridge (A) was not known for utilizing mythology, while Keats (B) and Arnold (E) utilize a more introspective tone. Although the use of dramatic monologue is similar to Browning (D), he preferred to use Renaissance settings.

110. **(A)**

Jim Burden, Cather's narrator, returns to the scene of his and Antonia's childhood in Nebraska at the end of the novel; the passage stresses the extent to which life's early circumstances and experiences shape adult destinies. Passages (C) and (E) can be eliminated readily because the language of these passages does not match that of the twentieth-century author.

111. **(A)**

In these lines from a sonnet by Sidney, love is personified (i.e., an abstraction given human attributes). Metonymy (B) is a technique in which a concept is identified by a readily recognizable word, while synecdoche (C) is the use of a part to represent a whole. Apostrophe (D) is a technique where one addresses a person who is either dead or absent. A dead metaphor (E) is a metaphor that, through constant use, has lost its original meaning and become a standard phrase in English.

112.   **(A)**

If the speaker rides his horse, he in turn is ridden by love ("a horse to Love"), which controls him as completely as he controls his horse. The relationship is not properly expressed by any of the other choices.

113.   **(B)**

Bigger asserts his identity ("I am") only after committing murder and defines his identity through acts of violence. Unlike Max, who attempts to "explain" Bigger in terms of class struggle, Bigger attaches individual (not class) meaning to his acts. He does not see himself as a sociological phenomenon or an illustration of communist doctrine, but as someone who has been awakened to a sense of self only after exercising personal control of others, however violent.

114.   **(D)**

The passage is from the conclusion of *Native Son*. (A) deals with a man coming to terms with his homosexuality. Ralph Ellison's novel (B) is written in the first person. (C) is non-fiction. (E) ends with the protagonist hiding the fact that he has murdered someone.

115.   **(D)**

Browning's "Porphyria's Lover" is a dramatic monologue delivered by a deranged speaker who has strangled Porphyria, whose only crime has been acts of kindness to the speaker. The speaker in a dramatic monologue is a character other than the poet, eliminating (A), (B), and (E), and the focus of the work is some sort of secret about the speaker unwittingly revealed to the reader, which eliminates choice (C).

116.   **(A)**

The villanelle consists of five tercets and a quatrain, all on two rhymes; it also systematically repeats the first and third lines of the first tercet. Thomas' poem is surprising for its depth of emotion conveyed in such an elaborate, self-conscious stanzaic form.

117.   **(E)**

The author is describing a battle between red and black ants in his woodpile; he unflatteringly compares man's militaristic tendencies or behavior to the behavior of the ants. Although the author makes reference to Greek heroes, the participants in the fight are clearly not human [eliminate choices

(A), (B), and (C)], and ants are perhaps a better reflection of man's behavior in society than dogs (D).

118. **(D)**
Patroclus, Achilles' friend, was killed in the Trojan War while Achilles sulked. The latter then returns to battle to avenge Patroclus' death. Since Achilles fought the Trojans, choices (A) and (B) can be easily eliminated, as can (C) if one is aware that Paris slew Achilles.

119. **(D)**
The passage is from *Walden*. The philosophical, introspective piece is not similar to the tone of Irving (B) or Hawthorne (C). The passage does not exhibit the economic wit of Franklin (A) or the fervor of Holmes (E).

120. **(B)**
As the narrator says, dead letters sound like "dead men," especially Bartleby, whose hopeless and ineffectual life has been a kind of death-in-life. The references to government in this passage are secondary, thus eliminating answers (A) and (C). The introspective tone of the piece eliminates answers (D) and (E).

121. **(A)**
Melville wrote *Benito Cereno* as well as *Bartleby, the Scrivener*. The narrator does have a voice that resembles some of Poe's characters (D), but the setting of the tale does not match.

122. **(A)**
Lines 3 and 4 tell us that long before this action was completed, their hats swam above them (that is, the men drowned). Action (B), (C), or (D) would not result in their hats being in the water, and action (E) does not make sense in the context of the poem.

123. **(D)**
The excerpt is from one of the best of the medieval popular ballads, "Sir Patrick Spens." The language is not so far removed from our present-day tongue as Middle English (C); a broadside ballad (A) is more limited to the description of events; and elegies (E) usually focus on the death of one important figure.

124.   **(C)**

The fabliau was popular in France in the twelfth and thirteenth centuries and in England during the fourteenth century. Chaucer's "The Miller's Tale" is a fabliau. Parables (A), beast fables (B), allegories (D) and exempla (E) are variants of short, didactic tales.

125.   **(C)**

Naipaul grew up in Trinidad, but visited India, the country his family had left two generations earlier. E. M. Forster (A), Kipling (B), and Lessing (E) all wrote about the relationship of England to its colonies, with various degrees of sympathy to those colonies, but usually from the perspective of the English. Gordimer (D) focused on life in South Africa.

126.   **(B)**

The townspeople felt sorry for Miss Emily (the narrator consistently displays a compassionate understanding of her position in society), but their compassion is tempered by self-congratulation about being right that she had not received numerous marriage proposals (that is, they feel vindicated in their belief that "the Griersons held themselves a little too high for what they really were").

127.   **(C)**

The horse-whip is to drive away Miss Emily's suitors while Miss Emily stands behind him; she is thus both protected and dominated by her father. The reader can discern that the horsewhip is used on Emily's suitors because the next sentence concerns Emily's marital status [eliminate answer (A)]. Although the narrator does find Emily's family pretentious (B), the tableau does not suggest that. Answers (D) and (E) cannot be inferred from the information in the passage.

128.   **(E)**

The story is Faulkner's *A Rose for Emily*. This passage does not contain the sympathy for female characters that Porter (A) and Welty (C) usually display, nor does it contain the comically grotesque behavior evident in many of O'Connor's (D) works.

129.   **(D)**

This poem is Surrey's adaptation of a Petrarchan sonnet, to which it owes its subject matter. Unrequited love is a common subject in poems imitative of Petrarch.

130. **(B)**

The narrator urges the building of a rainbow bridge that connects the two sides of man's being, his "prosaic" half and his "passionate" half, in order to achieve wholeness. If man consists only of "prose," he becomes a monk and is "grey"; if he consists only of "passion," he becomes a "beast," an uncontrolled fire. When the two are connected, man achieves wholeness as opposed to complete self-denial or unbridled lust. The narrator associates "passion" with "beasts" and "fire," while associating "prose" with "monks" and "grey."

131. **(A)**

The narrator says that Mr. Wilcox, while appearing reliable and brave on the outside, has never examined his inner life—his motives, beliefs, feelings. Having failed to engage in self-examination and self-criticism, his attitudes toward such matters as personal relations and sexual desire are muddled.

132. **(D)**

Although the narrator argues for the wholeness that comes from connecting passion (including sexual desire) with prose, he also asserts that the absolute rejection of carnality is preferable to Mr. Wilcox's incomplete asceticism, which leads him to be ashamed of loving his wife. One can say that the narrator most admires the man who successfully builds a rainbow bridge and is thus complete, but one can also admire the Saints' complete rejection of carnality because it is based on absolute conviction, whereas Mr. Wilcox's view of sexual desire lacks conviction and prevents him from achieving fully satisfying personal relationships. The narrator believes that sexual desire is fully compatible with marital love, need not be guilt-ridden, and is an important part of spiritual wholeness.

133. **(D)**

Aristophanes' play addressed actual conditions. War with Sparta threatened the fabric of Athenian life. Aristophanes' comic solution might have had as good a chance as any other to stop the war.

134. **(A)**

Creon had only recently been crowned, so Antigone's refusal to abide by his decree forbidding the burial of one of her brothers constitutes a challenge, from his point of view, to his authority. He sees the conflict as one between duty to family and duty to state, with the latter taking priority. Antigone broadens the terms of the conflict, appealing to the laws of the gods, which require burial of the dead and which take priority over the laws of the state.

135. **(B)**

Tartuffe is one of the best-known works of the French neoclassical theater. It relies on satire, brilliant dialogue and characterization, and the ingenuity of its plot to achieve its effects.

136. **(E)**

Euripedes' material is drawn from Greek mythology, but reshaped to underscore the contrast between Medea's powerful character and the relatively weak Jason. The play is especially remarkable for its characterization of Medea, whose acts repel and whose strength and sense of betrayal attract audiences.

137. **(E)**

The speaker is Edmund in *King Lear*. Edmund says that men blame the sun, the moon, and the stars when things go wrong, when in fact man's disasters result from his own character and behavior. This tendency to claim that we cannot control what we are or what we do, to claim that we are what we are because of some external influence or necessity, is "the excellent foppery" (foolishness) of the world, designed to avoid responsibility for the consequences of one's own action.

138. **(C)**

Edmund says that he would have been lecherous regardless of the constellations in ascendance at his birth. The term "whoremaster" in the same line is a clue as to the meaning of "goatish."

139. **(D)**

Edmund has no belief in the influence of the stars, sun, and moon on man's life and character. While statement (D) is probably inaccurate, Edmund is not making direct references to astrology in his speech, although he is using similar terms to describe Providence.

140. **(B)**

Robert Browning's poem "Fra Lippo Lippi" is set at the beginning of the Renaissance in Italy, at a time when medieval attitudes were beginning to give way to a greater appreciation of earthly pleasures. Lippo Lippi was a Florentine painter and friar, who lived from 1406 to 1469; the Medici were a powerful banking family and virtual rulers of Florence.

141. (E)

Lippo Lippi is caught in an alley where "sportive ladies" (i.e., prostitutes) leave their doors ajar (to welcome business). Statements (A), (B), and (E) are all supported in the passage. Choices (A) and (B) are based upon misinterpretations of Lippi's use of words, and answers (C) and (D) are based upon the literal interpretation of Lippi's description of this "place of business."

142. (A)

After the grip on his throat has been relaxed, Lippo Lippi says to the policeman who had held him by the throat that he was "best" (i.e., most thorough in carrying out his role). From the term "you go the rounds" (line 4), it can be determined that Lippi is speaking to a policeman of some kind, which eliminates choices (B), (D), and (E). (C) can be eliminated because Lippi makes specific reference to the officer in charge later.

143. (D)

Lippo Lippi's patron was extremely influential; hence, Lippo Lippi's mention of his connection with the Medici causes the police to treat him with greater deference.

144. (C)

Lippo Lippi suggests to the officer in charge of the patrol that he must be concerned about the manner in which his subordinates behave because their behavior will reflect on him. It can be deduced that Lippi is talking to a policeman.

145. (E)

"This," in line 14, refers to this poem, and it is this poem that gives life to the beloved as long as the poem survives and is read. The beloved's "eternal summer" will fade, when that eternal summer is conceived in physical terms, because time destroys all youth and beauty, but the beloved's eternal summer has been preserved in this poem and is, thus, no longer subject to the ravages of time.

146. (C)

The first two quatrains compare the beloved to a summer's day, emphasizing the imperfection and changeability of summer. Line 9 introduces the chief thought of the poem that will be developed through line 14—the notion that the beloved's beauty can triumph over time by being captured in poetry.

The first eight lines emphasize impermanence; the last six emphasize permanence. The final couplet completes the thought begun in line 9.

147. **(A)**
Although the sonnet appears at the beginning to be an elaborate compliment that compares the beloved favorably to a summer's day, it uses that comparison to make a larger point about the permanence of poetry, one vehicle that allows man to triumph over death and time. The poem moves steadily from the beauty of the beloved to a stronger preoccupation with the power of poetry.

148. **(D)**
The author argues that women who depend entirely on beauty for power must expect to lose their power when beauty fades. Hence, full humanity must result from such things as independent reasoning. The author is not advocating abolishing the roles of daughters, wives, and mothers, but rather building different foundations for those roles.

149. **(B)**
The passage is from Mary Wollstonecraft's *A Vindication of the Rights of Women*. Lady Montagu (A) is known for her letters on traveling in Turkey. Mary Shelley (C) is best known for *Frankenstein*, which has a male narrator. Chopin (D) and Woolf (E) are too contemporary to be considered as authors of this piece.

150. **(A)**
The passage is from Plato's *Republic*, in which he disallows epic and lyric poetry a place in his Utopian state. Aristotle (B) is better known for his analysis of drama, rather than poetry. Horace (C) was a lyric poet. Quintilian (D) wrote about the practice of oratory, while Boethius (E) wrote about logic and ethics.

151. **(B)**
The passage is from Longinus' *On the Sublime*, the source of much later discussion of the sublime in the arts, especially in the eighteenth century.

152. **(D)**
A famous criticism from *Aspects of the Novel*, well worth studying, together with Forster's comments on story, plot ("The King died" is a story... "The Queen then died of grief" is a plot), and time structure. He divides famous

literary characters into "flat and round" and shows how they function within their particular novel structure.

153. **(A)**

If you do not know this climactic scene in Faulkner's short story, eliminate the others. Chopin's Mrs. Mallard (D) comes down from her room to die. Mr. Rochester opens Bertha Rochester's cell (E) to show Jane Eyre and the wedding guests the "bride" he is forced to live with; Miss Haversham's whole house (B) is a tomb; and Isabel Archer (C) looks into the tiny room that symbolizes her husband's world.

154. **(C)**

For a number of poets, Byzantium embodies the Golden Age, civilization and richness. Yeats elaborated one stage further and endowed it with a holiness which, as the comment suggests, makes for a transfiguration of the body's spirituality and physicality. Think of the options and poems associated with them—Byzantium is the only choice.

155. **(B)**

John Webster is most famous for *The Duchess of Malfi*, perhaps the darkest of all the Jacobean revenge tragedies. If you do not know the playwright, think of the plays in the body of work of the other choices. All of them are renowned for their light comedies, particularly Gay (C) and Farquhar (D), both of whom have had plays turned into operas.

156. **(C)**

Thomas Pynchon deftly manipulates a Jacobean revenge plot within his own plot of the Trystero. If you do not know the novel, think of the other choices and analyze if the authors use the other genre. (D) and (E) might be possibilities, but those works deal with the darkness of a man's possessiveness of his wife and a "detective story" within a monastery.

157. **(C)**

This passage is from *On the Pleasure of Hating*, 1821. A fine critical intellect at work here should be a clue, as well as a hatred for hypocrisy. The language is too anachronistic for the more contemporary voices of Hammett (A) and Kafka (D). The vitriol in this passage does not match Eliot (B). Although Stevenson (E) wrote critical essays, he is better known for his adventure novels.

158. **(D)**

This is from Poe's obituary in the *New York Tribune*, 1849. Poe was known as morbid even in his own time. What is less well known to contemporary readers was his professional life: important editorships won and lost, and power in literary circles wielded, at times, in a formative and forceful manner.

159. **(B)**

In reference to the tragic love affair, "fatal" here is an important clue. The "Epistle to Miss Blount" (A) is told by a detached voice. Works (C) and (D) adopt a more general philosophical tone, and (E) is a mock epic poem.

160. **(B)**

This is the author's central point. The supposition is that an ideal image of the soul can be constructed. Mythological figures are used for comparison in this passage, but mythology is not a central point of the passage [eliminating choices (C) and (E)].

161. **(A)**

This is from Plato's *The Beast and the God in Man*. Implicit here is that reality and the ideal differ significantly, since reality is a vague reflection of the ideal—a key Platonic point. Aristotle (B) viewed the soul as a mechanism by which all senses and experiences were tied together. Christianity (C) and Gnosticism (D) separate the earthly from the spiritual completely.

162. **(D)**

This is a reference to Ecclesiastes XII—referring to the "words of the wise." The word "temple" might lead to the wrong choice of answer (B), while answer (C) is a trap for those who fixate on the use of the word "gold."

163. **(B)**

A paean is a choral song in honor of a great person. Elegies (A) and encomia (D) also praise figures, but serve as eulogies to the departed person. There is nothing in the passage that suggests a satiric (E) tone.

164. **(C)**

This is an excerpt from Lowell's A *Fable for Critics*, published in 1848, which was written in praise of various authors. Thoreau's (A) pieces are more contemplative. Bryant (B) and Whitman (D) often wrote works praising nature, rather than specific people. Whittier (E) often described pastoral scenes in his poetry.

165. **(C)**
Although the use of the name "Benvolio" might cause one to immediately think of (B), this is a trap. (A) refers to another Shakespeare play, and (D) and (E) are other characters from the play *Doctor Faustus*.

166. **(B)**
This passage is from Marlowe's *Doctor Faustus*, IV, iii. Since these questions are somewhat connected, (C) seems to be the obvious choice. Jonson (A) is better known for his comedies, while Campion (D) and Herrick (E) were poets rather than dramatists.

167. **(E)**
Iambic pentameter (A) would require lines of ten syllables with alternating unstressed and stressed syllables. Blank verse (B) would be iambic pentameter without rhyme. A ballad stanza (C) would be a quatrain rhyming *abcb*. Sprung rhythm (D) is a somewhat eccentric meter devised by Hopkins, basically iambic pentameter with numerous substitutions creating longer and irregular lines. Since the poem has neither meter nor rhyme, it is best classified as free verse.

168. **(D)**
An elegiac tone (A) would express sorrow at the death of a loved one or with respect to some other profound loss. The emphasis would be on the transience of worldly things. A sarcastic tone (B) would be typical of satire. One might expect sarcasm if the poet were ridiculing politicians, pedants, quacks, hypocrites or other traditional targets of satire. A laudatory tone (C) would be appropriate to a poem praising the deeds or virtues of exemplary individuals, those who have exhibited great courage in war or in other stressful situations. A devotional tone (E) would be appropriate to a religious poem in which the poet expresses personal religious feeling or relates religious experiences. This poem is not theological or patriotic or satirical. It is not about death. The tone is rather playful, which is appropriate for a very positive statement about children and spring. It is, thus, best described as whimsical.

169. **(C)**
The speaking voice of Mark Twain's hero, Huckleberry Finn, is characterized by colloquial diction and syntax. The themes of "good behavior,"

discipline, and religion are also typical. Huck resists the civilizing influences of Miss Watson and the widow. The author implies that if Huck is to be influenced at all, it will be more through the positive and gentle approach of the widow than through the more rigid approach of Miss Watson. Through his own voice, Huck reveals himself to be a character of genuine and spontaneous virtue, a nature neither refined nor corrupted by civilization.

170. **(B)**
These are the opening lines of Carl Sandburg's "Chicago." He celebrates the modern city's energy, industry, and productivity. It is a very positive statement about the city. He sees it as a center of life and creativity. The poem is full of the concrete imagery typical of modern poetry. Sandburg uses colloquial diction and free verse.

171. **(E)**
The comparison of fog to a cat is by Carl Sandburg. The poem is typical of Sandburg's free-verse style and of his celebration of urban imagery. Dickens (A) and Hemingway (B) are known for their prose, not their poetry. Sandburg's use of urban imagery differs from Eliot's (C) view of urban life, and Frost (D) utilizes more pastoral images.

172. **(E)**
In this passage, Auerbach discusses a feature of epic style: the tendency to identify every character, every object even, in terms of history, both its past history and its future destiny. The same stylistic feature can be found in the English epic *Beowulf.* As in the *Odyssey*, characters are introduced in terms of their family lineage. Digressions explain the origin of a sword of the destiny of a mead hall. As in the *Odyssey*, there is a continual opening up of the story and no attempt to create suspense by withholding information concerning the ultimate fate of anyone. In contrast, in *Sir Gawain and the Green Knight* (D), a romance from the fourteenth century, meaning is determined not by history, but by symbolism, by imbuing characters and objects with a special significance, symbolic colors like red and green, symbolic plants like the holly, and symbolic images like the five-pointed star. In Chaucer's "The Miller's Tale" (C), characters are described in terms of their nature, but not in terms of history. Meaning in the fabliau depends to a large extent on the implicit contrast with the serious romance genre, the juxtaposition with the "The Knight's Tale." In Spenser's Renaissance allegory, "The Faerie Queene" (B), symbolism becomes, if anything, more self-conscious, more complex. As for Shakespeare (A), although he often uses history for subject matter, the dramas have a

classical balance of symbolism and realism. In none of these other works is there the continual insistence on history, the continual digression or epithet that ties each character and object into the web of time. This feature is characteristic of the epic.

173. **(B)**
Pope's "Essay on Criticism" best illustrates this definition of neoclassicism. Donne's "The Ecstasy" (C) is characterized by metaphorical density and complexity of statement rather than by clarity of statement. Blake's "Jerusalem" (A) is characterized by a complex personal symbolism, rather than clarity of statement. Smart's "A Song to David" (D) and Traherne's "Wonder" (E) both express intense personal religious emotion, not objectivity and reason. Blake's and Smart's poems have long lines of varying lengths, not balance and symmetry of form.

174. **(B)**
Among the works of literature listed, the one that comes closest to illustrating the aesthetic ascribed to the Gothic cathedral is *The Canterbury Tales* by Chaucer. Like the cathedral, Chaucer's collection of tales is an unfinished work. It has a beginning and an end, but it is unfinished from within. In this way it points, like the cathedral, beyond itself from the finite to the infinite. This idea is expressed in the other works, but in *The Canterbury Tales*, Chaucer expresses the idea through the structure of the work.

175. **(E)**
Roland Barthes is a major figure in deconstructionism. This school of criticism traces its philosophical origins back to the linguistic theories of Saussure. In particular, deconstruction applies to literary criticism, the linguistic notion that the meaning of a word depends in part on the implied contrast between the word and other words that might be used in its place.

176. **(A)**
The passage is from a prefatory note to Milton's *Paradise Lost*. The note is entitled "Verse." In the note, Milton justifies his use of blank verse in the epic with the argument that Greek and Latin poets did not use rhyme.

177. **(A)**
The poem is organized around a sequence of metaphors. The metaphor in the second quatrain compares the poet to a town that is governed by

usurping power. The rightful governor is God. As his representative, God has given the poet reason. The poet's reason, however, has not proved strong enough or loyal enough to defend the poet against evil. Thus, the best paraphrase is that the poet's mind is "overpowered by evil motives." The particular evil is not specified. It is not necessarily adultery or love with another woman (B). The political references in the poem are all part of the metaphor (C). The poet is not referring to political policies, or to London (E) or any other town. The poet expresses his need for God's help, not any dissatisfaction with organized religion (D) or any concern over religion as a cause of conflict.

178.   **(A)**

In the sestet, the poet continues with a metaphor comparing himself to a bride about to marry someone she does not love, someone referred to as "your enemy" in line 10. Since, from the first line on, the poem is addressed directly to God, "your" means "God's." Thus, the enemy is God's enemy, Satan, not the enemy of England in a war (B). The poet, John Donne, converted to the Anglican church and became a famous preacher. He would not have considered the Anglican church (C) to be God's enemy; in any case, the poem is not about conflicts between religions. It is not a poem about a rival poet (D). The marriage in the sestet is metaphorical and, thus, does not refer to the poet's literal marriage (E).

179.   **(E)**

The philosophical position could best be classified as nominalism, the view that abstract concepts are merely words and have no other existence. It is not stoicism (A), a classical philosophy that taught the patient endurance of suffering and bad fortune, and the cultivation of moral self-discipline. Stoicism is associated with Roman patriotism. Falstaff's lack of interest in honor is the antithesis of Roman stoicism. The Donatist heresy (B) is an early variant of Christianity, according to which offices performed by heretical or corrupt clergy were deemed invalid. According to orthodox theology, the spiritual condition of the clergy is irrelevant to the efficacy of the sacrament. In any case, it is not a question with which Falstaff is concerned. According to Calvinism (C), the religious teachings of John Calvin, salvation is predestined by God and not determined by good works. Falstaff is not concerned with such questions. Neo-Platonism (D) is a Renaissance variation of Plato's philosophy. While Plato taught that art was an imitation of an imitation, and thus a further step removed from the "reality" of ideal forms, neo-Platonists believed that art could mediate between ordinary experience and ideal forms. Falstaff's nominalism is directly opposed to any form of Platonism, since it denies reality to an abstraction.

180. **(C)**
The theory of tragedy as offering the audience a "catharsis" of emotions is presented by Aristotle in *Poetics*. Sidney in his *Defence of Poesie* (A) argues for the superiority of poetry over history and philosophy. He is not specifically concerned with drama. Tolstoy in *What Is Art?* (B) argues in favor of folk art, in favor of authenticity generally, and against the cultivation of highbrow art as a social affectation. He does not present a theory of tragedy per se. Freud (D) in *The Psychopathology of Everyday Life* is concerned with slips of the tongue and lapses of memory, not with theories of tragedy. Bradley in *Shakespearean Tragedy* (E) analyzes Shakespeare's plays, focusing particularly on characterization. He does not present a theory of tragedy based on catharsis.

181. **(D)**
Austen's title implies a balance between hard-headed reason and emotion. "Sensibility" refers to the refinement of emotional sensibility that was much in vogue at the time. Austen views its excesses as a form of foolish self-indulgence. She opposes it to "sense" which, thus, refers to "a practical and reasonable regard for one's own self-interest."

182. **(C)**
These are the final lines of Keats' "Ode on a Grecian Urn." The quotation marks imply that the final words are not spoken by the urn. If they are spoken by the poet to the urn, then "ye" refers to the urn and the final lines imply the urn's limitations. Elsewhere in the poem, however, the urn is referred to as "thou," the singular second person pronoun. Why should the poet shift from singular to plural or from informal to formal in addressing the urn? If the words are spoken either by the urn to humanity or by the poet to his readers, then the lines have a very different meaning. The lines then imply that the urn's message is the only truth we can know or need to know. The nightingale figures, of course, in Keats' "Ode to a Nightingale," not this poem. Here the subject referred to by "ye" is either the urn or humanity, not a nightingale, a rose, or a woman, none of which are topics of the ode.

183. **(C)**
The alternation of heroic and comic scenes is typical of Elizabethan drama, and many examples can be found in the writings of William Shakespeare. Sophocles (A) was a fifth-century B.C. Athenian playwright. He wrote tragedies and did not include comic scenes in his plays. Congreve (E) wrote Restoration comedy and did not include serious or heroic scenes. Racine (B) wrote classic French tragedy and did not include comic scenes. Dryden (D)

followed the strict neoclassical format and did not mix comic and tragic material. Good examples from Shakespeare would be the alternation of tavern and court or battlefield scenes in *Henry IV, Parts One and Two*, the gravedigger scene in *Hamlet*, the porter scene in *Macbeth*, and the scene between the nurse and Mercutio in *Romeo and Juliet*.

184. **(A)**
The ascension of James I united the kingdoms of England and Scotland. Shakespeare shifted his attention from questions of Tudor legitimacy going back to fifteenth-century English politics, to matters of Scottish history. James based his claim to the Scottish throne back to Banquo and the opposition to the supposed usurper, Macbeth. In showing Macbeth as a villain, Shakespeare was supporting the new King of England. James also had an interest in witchcraft, making it a suitable topic for the play.

185. **(C)**
Of the works listed, the one that could best be characterized as existentialist would be Sartre's *No Exit*. According to existentialism, of which Sartre is a principal exponent, the material world exists without meaning, and the meaning is provided by individual human beings in their exercise of free choice and moral responsibility. The play *No Exit* is about an imaginary afterlife in which three people are stuck in a room forever together, an inescapable damnation. The imaginary afterlife contrasts with this life, in which, Sartre implies, one is always free to leave. The works by Milton (B), Dante (D), and Marlowe (E) would not be existentialist because, even though all three emphasize the importance of free choice, the meaning of every choice, its implications, are already determined according to theology: salvation or damnation in the afterlife. In contrast, Tolstoy's novel (A) supports a thesis of historical determinism that tends to minimize the importance of individual choice.

186. **(E)**
In the context, "success" means the result or outcome of the action. This is a meaning that was current for Shakespeare, but that now is archaic and no longer in use. The results that Macbeth is referring to would apparently be additional murders, the murder of Macbeth himself perhaps, in imitation of this murder. Macbeth worries that having once set the example, he and Lady Macbeth will become the next victims. He sees a contradiction between his plan to break the law in order to get power and his subsequent need to maintain law and order when he wants to keep power. This is one of the central themes of the play.

187. **(A)**

The comparison is between the withdrawing ocean wave and a general loss of religious faith. The passage does not convey the sense of personal change that the other four answers imply.

188. **(C)**

In "Mowing," Frost states that there was "never a sound beside the wood but one," and this was the sound of man laboring. His central question, however, is: "What did it whisper?"—in other words, what is the purpose of labor and what is his place in nature's universe? The laborer is sensitive enough to know that a "hidden message" exists (it is "whispered," he can guess at it, though he "knows not well"); this knowledge alone is what gives him his sense of purpose and place. Ultimate knowledge, however, resides in the hidden processes of nature (what and how the hay "makes"). He can only appreciate the mystery.

189. **(B)**

The pattern for most pastoral elegies on the Classical model (from Bion's the *Lament for Bion*) does not include any admonition to Death. Rather, there is a realization of grief and an inquiry into the causes of Death. This is an important difference in posture and speaks to these poets' belief in the place of man within the universe.

190. **(B)**

Dickinson's poetry is known for its need to instruct (didacticism). While she has empathy for the greater world (C), her notorious reclusiveness intervened. There is no pointed emphasis on nature (A). The poet does not seem to be lamenting (E) or reclusive (D) in this poem.

191. **(C)**

Writing in the middle of the nineteenth century, Dickinson, like many writers, employed remnant conventions—like the capitalization of important words. This often resulted in personification, but just as often it did not. Free verse (D) does not have rhyming lines, but the passage does.

192. **(E)**

Dickinson's biblical tone is derived from the sermons and hymns of the Amherst Church and the late Puritan literary climate that spawned her contemporaries Thoreau and Emerson. The tone does not match the rationalist ideas of (A) and (B), nor does the passage contain any materialist ideas (C).

193.   **(C)**
Emily Dickinson is the author. Whitman (A) has somewhat similar sentiments but does not use this conceit of capitalization. Nash (D) often employed unusual techniques for comic effect, and Sandburg (E) often wrote in free verse.

194.   **(D)**
Both the concentration on nature and an appreciation of the miraculous quality of the ordinary identify the sentiments in the poem as Romantic. It was written by Wordsworth in 1834. Johnson (A) and Dickinson (E) often wrote with a more didactic tone.

195.   **(B)**
The passage is taken from Chapter 1 of Aristotle's *On the Art of Poetry*, entitled "The Media of Poetic Imitation." Imitation of a more fixed "ideal" is characteristic of Aristotle's teacher, Plato. Expressionism (A) involves an attempt to concretely display abstract emotion in art. Pindar (C) is known for his lyrical odes. Impressionism (D) eschews imitation in favor of a capturing of spontaneity. Atomism (E) deals with the manner in which all items in the universe are related.

196.   **(A)**
This passage is from Dorothy Parker's *But the One On the Right*. In interior monologue, the speaker is thinking to himself—the reader only overhears the speaker's thoughts. Passages (D) and (E) are clearly dialogue, and while (B) and (C) are not overtly dialogue, they also do not offer the inner thoughts of the speaker.

197.   **(D)**
The Student is described by Chaucer. The "threadbare" coat is perhaps a clue to the correct answer, as is the line "Indentured long to logic and the gown."

198.   **(A)**
A "benefice" is a position in the church. Answers (B) and (E) are directly contradicted by the next line, "thoughts of worldly office were not his." Answers (C) and (D) are traps for more contemporary views on students.

199. **(D)**
Both the subject and the horse are "anything but fat." Answers (A) and (E) are in fact contradictory images, not parallel ones. There is no parallel drawn between the "enslaved" nature of the two (C), and answer (B) is simply a non sequitur.

200. **(B)**
The writer says just before the cited Wordsworth poem: "Finally, the 'scientific system of thought' in Wordsworth gives us at least such poetry as this, which the devout Wordsworthian accepts—." The writer refers to this when he speaks of the poem's imagined popularity at a "Social Science Congress."

201. **(C)**
The use of modifiers like "very" and "most" mocks any sincerity about the subject—especially one as outrageous as cannibalism. "Fricassee" and "ragout" are almost comic in their bizarre implications. Outright sadism for its own sake has rarely been the stock and trade of great writing, so we must assume this description has a greater purpose, even if we are not familiar with the author's writing.

202. **(B)**
A common belief that American colonials were less civilized than their English counterparts is used to underscore the author's preposterous suggestion that cannibalism is a way by which Irish overpopulation might be controlled. In fact, the author implies the opposite of (A) in order to sustain his sarcastic tone: he does not take seriously the belief that Americans are uncivilized. The proposition he is making should be taken in the same sarcastic vein.

203. **(B)**
"Regard the writer's end" is the controlling line of thought within the passage. Choices (D) and (E) are concerned with the discovery of flaws while the passage asks that "trivial faults" are weighed against the greater message of the writer's piece. Choices (A) and (C) cannot be inferred from the passage.

204. **(B)**
D. H. Lawrence in *Surgery for the Novel—Or a Bomb* claims that the serious novel is on its "death-bed": "It is self-consciousness picked into such fine bits that the bits are most of them invisible, and you have to go by smell."

Lawrence feels that modern writers are too busy striving for accuracy to notice the impact that their works are missing.

205. **(E)**
This passage is from Jonson's "Perfection in Small Things." Like the lily, human life is short. All things that seem permanent are, in reality, transitory. To strive for the "great" is futile. Perfection can be found in the fleeting moments of man and nature.

206. **(A)**
Jonson is also the author of "Ode on the Death of Sir H. Morison," considered a fine imitation of Pindar. (B), (C), and (D) are variants of sonnets in which love of another is its primary theme.

207. **(B)**
This passage is from the Puritan Milton's *Comus*. The Platonic Ideal (A) is based on the existence of a higher realm, of which this world is merely a pale imitation. Zoroastrianism (C) is a religion based in dualism, while Deism (D) is based on rational thinking. The Renaissance (E) involved a shift to humanistic thinking.

208. **(C)**
In comparing the spider to a person, the moth to human clothing, and the mixture to a witch's broth, the author here places the natural world he is describing within the human world of the reader's experience. None of the creatures described in the poem display distinctly human characteristics [eliminate (A)], and the description is secondary to comparison of the objects to those of human use [eliminate (B) and (D)]. There is no variety of color in the passage (E).

209. **(D)**
The answer is really rhetorical. The title of the poem is "Design," and throughout the two stanzas there can be little doubt that the poet is saying, "Of course, there is great design in nature: let me show it to you." Since the author is aware of the answer, answers (A), (C) and (E) can be eliminated. The tone of the last two lines is meant to comfort, so answer (B) can be eliminated as well.

210. (A)

The author is analyzing how new writers are evaluated in relationship to tradition. Since the first sentence refers to the comparison of a writer to his or her peers, the choices which describe isolated evaluations, (B), (D), and (E), can be eliminated. The process refers to finding something new about a work, not pigeon-holing the work into a set period (C).

211. (B)

The author of this passage counterposes what he has said by way of criticizing the critics with the comment that "if we approach a poet without this prejudice, we shall often find that not only the best, but the most individual parts of his work may be those in which the dead poets, his ancestors, assert their immortality most vigorously."

212. (D)

This is from Emerson. The concentration here on deed, rather than simply on nonconformity, is an indicator, as is its similarity to Thoreau. Since individuality by itself is not in fact a goal, choices (A) and (B) can be eliminated. The Age of Enlightenment (C) marked a newfound respect for science. The Beat Era (E) was marked by a dissatisfaction for contemporary society.

213. (D)

These lines, which at first appear impossible, appear on closer reading, valid—the essence of paradox. The question here: why believe a lie, especially when that lie is that the person swears she tells the truth? (A) is a technique in which a part is used to represent the whole. Ellipsis (B) is a poetic trope in which an understood word is omitted. Pararhyme (C) is a rhyme in which the consonant sounds are shared but the vowel sounds are not, while prosody (E) is the study of systems of versification.

214. (D)

In an artful series of clauses, the author lets the reader in on his thought process: to wit, although he is trying to be objective, he is obviously sentimentally remembering his island. Although statements (A) and (E) might be somewhat accurate, they fail to take into account the author's obvious struggle. Statements (B) and (C) are non sequiturs.

215. (B)

It is from Irving's *History of New York*. Cooper (A) is more known for his depictions of American frontier life. Coleridge (D) is a British artist, not American, and Hawthorne (E) utilized the themes of sin and atonement in most of his works. Whitman (C) often described the same region as in the passage, but is not known for writing prose.

216. **(D)**

It is from Poe's *Marginalia*. The tone of the passage does not match the controlled Romanticism of Keats (A). Sheridan (B) was a dramatist. Faulkner (C) was concerned about the accurate psychological portrayal of his characters. Trilling (E) was concerned with society's effect on the individual.

217. **(A)**

While it might at first seem as if (C) is the addressee, the speaker calls on the winds to "crack" the plans of nature. Winds are personified and appear to represent a greater primeval force than simply what is connoted today by "wind" as the movement of air.

218. **(C)**

The speaker is asking for that which creates "ingrateful" human beings to be destroyed. "Germens" is clearly meant here metaphorically to describe something intangible, which eliminates (A) and (E). Answers (B) and (D) are non sequiturs.

219. **(D)**

The verbs describe actions: Blow / rage / singe / smite / spill. Answers (B) and (E) are grammatically incorrect, while (A) and (C) are broad and inaccurate.

220. **(B)**

The speaker is King Lear. The use of the word "ungrateful" is perhaps the key clue here, as Lear suffers due to the ingratitude of his children.

221. **(C)**

Jim Dixon and Yossarian are examples of anti-heroes, that is, protagonists who do not act in the traditionally heroic sense. Neither novel has a first-person (E) narrator, and unreliable narrators (A) are first-person narrators as well. Both novels are satiric rather than naturalist (B), and neither uses the convention of communication through letters (D).

222. (E)
Emerson, Fuller, Very, and Thoreau all contributed to *The Dial*. Fuller was its first editor, Emerson its second. *The Dial* was a periodical that served as a mouthpiece for the New England Transcendentalists.

223. (A)
The frontier writers were known for their often humorous and colorful depictions of life in the developing West of the mid-19th century. Jewett is a "local-colorist," but her subject matter is Maine or New England.

224. (D)
Maturin's novel of terror and mystery is *Melmoth the Wanderer*. Although Ann Radcliffe (E) is the most famous novelist of the Gothic period, she did not write *Melmoth the Wanderer*. Hawthorne (A), Bird (B), and Bunyan (C) did not write in the Gothic tradition.

225. (C)
Gerard Manley Hopkins is generally considered to be the originator of sprung rhythm.

226. (B)
This question may be difficult because (D) and (E) are also characters in the play—Prospero's daughter and his future son-in-law, respectively. (C) is a corruption of the name Romeo, and (A) is included as a false-lead.

227. (E)
The passage, taken from James Joyce's *Ulysses*, seeks to capture and communicate the thoughts running through the mind of Stephen Dedalus. Joyce is generally held to be the first writer to use internal monologue throughout a novel.

228. (C)
The keywords "imperialism" and "indigenous" should clue the reader that the critic is writing about exploration and colonialism. The contest between an external "civilizing force" and a resisting native population described in the analysis of *The Tempest* should further indicate that the subject here is colonialism and the politics involved in justifying it. Postcolonial criticism seeks to recover the lost or suppressed voices of oppressed subjects; the insertion of a quotation from Caliban helps focus our attention on one such

voice. The other schools of criticism named are concerned more with contradictions and ambiguities internal to language [answers (A) and (B)], the interior development of subjects as gendered beings in response to trauma and loss (D), and the economic/class conflicts that are revealed by literature (E). While all of these are certainly relevant to Shakespeare and can be applied to *The Tempest,* none of their principles are systematically applied in this passage as are the basic tenets of postcolonial criticism.

229. **(E)**

The law is often a central concern with Dickens; this is nowhere more true than in *Bleak House,* in which an obscure lawsuit has embroiled the families of the central characters for years. The specific plot implied details that should remind readers of *Bleak House* are the mention of the Chancery and the critique of missionary work. *Bleak House*'s Mrs. Jellyby is a famous Dickens character, who neglects her own house and children while she invests her time and efforts in moralistic missionary projects that involve little or no true charity for African countries. Those unfamiliar with the novel itself should be able to recognize Dickens in this passage as well, in particular the reference to the novel's concern with the address of social inequality and reform. While all other authors are to varying degrees also interested in social issues, none is as explicitly committed to the cause of reform and relief to the poor and marginalized as is Dickens.

230. **(D)**

The terza rima rhyme scheme, made famous by Dante, should be an immediate tip-off that this is his work. A further clue comes in the name Beatrice, a central figure in the *Divine Comedy*. For those unfamiliar with the work, the time period of the poem can be identified by its rehearsal of several moral commonplaces from the medieval period, namely the critique of worldly matters when eternal life or damnation is at stake. The medieval time period and the religious nature of the excerpt and its particularly Christian cast should help readers eliminate Homer; similarly Beowulf's distinctive verse form and subject matter should disqualify it as a choice. Its concern with the theological makes *Decameron*, Boccaccio's celebrated work on mainly secular/social themes, an unfit choice. *Paradise Lost* might seem a viable answer because of the excerpt's discussion of heaven, but the verse style should immediately eliminate Milton as a choice: his epic is written in unrhymed iambic pentameter, or blank verse. Further, there is little use of the first person "I" in *Paradise Lost,* and never an "I" who is himself in heaven.

Practice Test 3

We have left the spaces below for you to record your scores on this Practice Test. Please refer to the Scoring section in the front of this book for how to compute your raw score and convert it into a scaled score. By comparing your scores on each Practice Test, you will be better able to mark your progress.

Raw Score   _____

Scaled Score   _____

GRE LITERATURE
IN ENGLISH

PRACTICE TEST 3

DIRECTIONS: Choose the best answer for each question and mark the letter of your selection on the corresponding answer sheet. Answer sheets can be found in the back of this book.

---

1. The basic tenet of Existentialism is that

 (A) nothing exists but what is imagined.

 (B) meaning is determined by the imagination.

 (C) existence is the significant fact, but it has no intrinsic meaning.

 (D) meaning is established by general agreement.

 (E) agreement as to significance is the only true existence.

2. "...handsome, clever, and rich, with a comfortable home and happy disposition seemed to unite some of the best blessings of existence; and had lived nearly twenty-one years in the world with very little to distress or vex her."

 The sentence completed above describes

 (A) Flaubert's Madame Bovary.

 (B) Austen's Emma.

(C)   Cather's Antonia.

(D)   Dickens' Agnes Wakefield.

(E)   Fitzgerald's Daisy.

Questions 3 – 5 refer to the following poem.

Ae Fond Kiss

Ae fond kiss, and then we sever!
Ae farewell, and then forever!
Deep in heart-wrung tears I'll pledge thee,
Warring sighs and groans I'll wage thee.
Who shall say that Fortune grieves him
While the star of hope she leaves him?
Me, nae cheerfu' twinkle lights me;
Dark despair around benights me.

I'll ne'er blame my partial fancy,
Nothing could resist my Nancy:
but to see her was to love her;
Love but her, and love forever.
Had we never lov'd sae kindly,
Had we never lov'd sae blindly,
Never met — or never parted —
We had ne'er been broken-hearted.

Fare thee weel, thou first and fairest!
Fare Thee weel, thou best and dearest!
Thine be ilka joy and treasure,
Peace, enjoyment, love, and pleasure!
Ae fond kiss, and then we sever;
Ae farewell, alas, forever!
Deep in heart-wrung tears I'll pledge thee,
Warring sighs and groans I'll wage thee!

3.   In the first stanza, the poet implies that

(A)   his love has left him a glimmer of hope that she will return to him.

(B)   his love gives him no hope that she will return to him.

(C)   their separation was unexpected.

(D) their separation was expected.

(E) their heartbreak was of little consequence.

4. Which of the following most closely restates the poet's view of his affair with Nancy?

(A) Their love was unavoidable, as was their heartbreak.

(B) They could have avoided falling in love, but once done, they could not have avoided the heartbreak.

(C) If it wasn't for his "partial fancy" he could have avoided both love and heartbreak.

(D) He holds himself to blame for falling in love with her.

(E) He holds Nancy to blame for their tragic affair.

5. This poem is written in

(A) Chaucerian English.   (D) Scots dialect.

(B) Spenserian English.   (E) Standard English.

(C) West Country dialect.

---

6. The school of poetry known as "Fleshly" is associated with

(A) Dickinson.   (D) Swinburne.

(B) Wordsworth.   (E) Wilde.

(C) Whitman.

Questions 7 – 9 refer to the following passages.

7. Which one of the following is from the *Declaration of Independence?*

8. Which one of the following is from *The Mayflower Compact?*

9. Which one of the following is from *The Republic?*

(A)   They in their humble address have freely declared that it is much on their hearts (if they may be permitted) to hold forth a lively experiment, that a most flourishing civil State may stand and best be maintained, and that among our English subjects, with a full liberty in religious concernments...

(B)   What reason, then, remains for preferring justice to the extreme of injustice, when common belief and the best authorities promise us the fulfillment of our desires in this life and the next, if only we conceal our ill-doing under a veneer of decent behaviour?

(C)   We have granted, moreover, to all free men of our kingdom, for us and our heirs forever, all the liberties written below to be had and holden by themselves and their heirs from us and our heirs.

(D)   We whose names are underwritten, the loyall subjects of our dread soveraigne Lord, King James, by ye grace of God, of Great Britaine, Franc, and Ireland king, defender of ye faith...

(E)   We have Petitioned for Redress in the most humble terms: Our repeated Petitions have been answered only by repeated injury. A Prince, whose character is thus marked by every act which may define a Tyrant, is unfit to be the ruler of a free people.

Questions 10 – 12 refer to the following passage.

> Build thee more stately mansions, O my soul,
> As the swift seasons roll: —
> Leave thy low-vaulted past.
> Let each new temple, nobler than the last,
> Shut thee from heaven with a dome more vast,
> Till thou at length art free,
> Leaving thine outgrown shell by life's unresting sea.

10.   The excerpt above expresses sentiments typical of the

(A)   Age of Enlightenment.

(B)   New England Renaissance.

(C)   *fin de siécle.*

(D)   Classic Revival.

(E)   Cavalier poets.

11.   The soul is compared here to

    (A) a molting shellfish.   (D) a church builder.

    (B) the ocean.   (E) a monastery.

    (C) a home builder.

12.   This poem was written by

    (A) Edgar Allan Poe.

    (B) Oliver Wendell Holmes.

    (C) John Greenleaf Whittier.

    (D) Henry Wadsworth Longfellow.

    (E) William Ellery Channing.

Questions 13 – 15 refer to the following passage.

> And Julia's voice was lost, except in sighs,
>   Until too late for useful conversation;
> The tears were gushing from her gentle eyes,
>   I wish, indeed, they had not had occasion;
> But who, alas, can love, and then be wise?
>   Not that remorse did not oppose temptation:
> A little still she strove, and much repented,
>   And whispering "I will ne'er consent" — consented.

13.   The tone of this stanza can best be described as

    (A) paenic.   (D) half-serious.

    (B) congratulatory.   (E) cynical.

    (C) oxymoronic.

14.   The poem is written in

    (A) trochaic pentameter.   (D) rhopalic verse.

    (B) ottava rima.   (E) rime riche.

    (C) versi sciolti.

15. The selection is taken from

    (A) *Childe Harold's Pilgrimage.*

    (B) "The Rape of the Lock."

    (C) *Don Juan.*

    (D) "Byzantium."

    (E) *Cynara.*

---

16. Ah, happy, happy boughs! that cannot shed
        Your leaves, nor ever bid the Spring adieu;
    And happy melodist, unwearied,
        Forever piping song forever new;
    More happy love! more happy, happy love!
        Forever warm and still to be enjoyed,
        Forever panting, and forever young;
    All breathing human passion far above,
        That leaves a heart high-sorrowful and cloyed,
        A burning forehead, and a parching tongue.

    This selection demonstrates craftsmanship similar to that of

    (A) Shakespeare.   (D) Wordsworth.

    (B) Rossetti.   (E) Milton.

    (C) Browning.

Questions 17 – 19 refer to the following poem.

    In Reading gaol by Reading town
        There is a pit of shame,
    And in it lies a wretched man
        Eaten by teeth of flame,
    In a burning winding-sheet he lies,
        And his grave has got no name.

    And there, till Christ call forth the dead,
        In silence let him lie:

No need to waste the foolish tear,
    Or heave the windy sigh:
The man had killed the thing he loved,
    And so he had to die.

And all men kill the thing they love,
    By all let this be heard,
Some do it with a bitter look,
    Some with a flattering word,
The coward does it with a kiss,
    The brave man with a sword!

17. The connection developed in this poem is one between

    (A) the murderer and the brave man.

    (B) the murderer's corpse and the objects of love.

    (C) the murderer and all men.

    (D) resurrection through Christ and insensitivity.

    (E) reading gaol and the pit of shame.

18. The author implies that brutalizing others

    (A) will cause physical death.

    (B) will cause spiritual death.

    (C) shows a brave man to be a coward.

    (D) is a result of Original Sin.

    (E) is a cause for being sent to Hell.

19. The poem was written by

    (A) Thomas Hardy.   (D) Wilfred Owen.

    (B) Vachel Lindsay.   (E) Oscar Wilde.

    (C) Samuel Taylor Coleridge.

20. The Beowulf utterances, "Wa–la–wa, Wa–la–wa," and the American Indian "Nyah–eh–wa, Nyah–eh–wa," are considered by poets to be

    (A) synecdoches.

    (B) pararhymes.

    (C) poesias lyricas.

    (D) parallel refrains.

    (E) tone-colors.

21. Which Alexander Pope work refers to "Belinda" as a pseudonym?

    (A) "Epistle to Miss Blount"

    (B) "Eloisa to Abelard"

    (C) "Essay on Man"

    (D) "To a Lady"

    (E) "The Rape of the Lock"

22.   I believe Shakespeare was not a whit more intelligible in his own day than he is now to an educated man, except for a few local allusions of no consequence. He is of no age — nor of any religion, or party, or profession. The body and substance of his works came out of the unfathomable depths of his own oceanic mind: his observation and reading, which was considerable, supplied him with the drapery of his figures.

    In this passage, S. T. Coleridge is answering the central question:

    (A) What was the origin of Shakespeare's drama?

    (B) What political alignment can we assign to Shakespeare?

    (C) Why are his plays difficult for the modern reader to understand?

    (D) Are Shakespeare's plays as comprehensible now as they were when they were written?

    (E) What role do local allusions play in understanding Shakespeare's plays?

Questions 23 – 25 refer to the following passage.

Cuddie, for shame, hold up thy heavye head,
And let us cast with what delight to chace,
And weary thys long lingring Phoebus race.

Whilome thou want the shepheards laddes to leade,
In rymes, in ridles, and in bydding base: 5
Now they in thee, and thou in sleepe art dead.

23.   The poet uses archaic language

      (A) out of homage to Chaucer.

      (B) to reinforce Classical allusions.

      (C) to ensure proper "ryme."

      (D) to reflect the language of the time at which he writes.

      (E) to reinforce the biblical nature of his story.

24.   Lines 2 and 3 may be paraphrased as:

      (A) Let us consider how much delight there is in winning.

      (B) Let us see how much good it is to run a race.

      (C) Let us see with what happiness Phoebus races.

      (D) Let us see how we may pass the day pleasantly.

      (E) Let us see how races help us rush the lingering day.

25.   This poem was written by

      (A) Geoffrey Chaucer.   (D) Christopher Marlowe.

      (B) Dante.   (E) Edmund Spenser.

      (C) Caedmon.

Questions 26 – 28 refer to the following poem.

      She that but little patience knew,
      From childhood on, had now so much
      A gray gull lost its fear and flew
      Down to her cell and there alit,
      And from her fingers ate its bit.

Did she in touching that lone wing
Recall the years before her mind
Became a bitter, an abstract thing,
Her thought some popular enmity:
Blind and leader of the blind
Drinking the foul ditch where they lie?

When long ago I saw her ride
Under Ben Bulben to the meet,
The beauty of her countryside
With all youth's lonely wildness stirred,
She seemed to have grown clean and sweet
Like any rock-bred, sea-borne bird:

Sea-borne, or balanced on the air
When first it sprang out of the nest
Upon some lofty rock to stare
Upon the cloudy canopy,
While under its storm-beaten breast
Cried out the hollows of the sea.

26. The "she" (line 1) in this poem is

    (A) the poet's daughter.   (D) a temptress.

    (B) a murderess.   (E) the poet's wife.

    (C) a political prisoner.

27. The poem contrasts the

    (A) woman before she became embittered, to the time afterward.

    (B) poet's idealization of the woman and her true nature.

    (C) "sea-borne" bird to the "gray gull."

    (D) "beauty of her countryside" to the "lofty rock."

    (E) "popular enmity" to the "little patience" of her youth.

28.   The poem was written by

(A) Wallace Stevens.   (D) William Yeats.

(B) Gertrude Stein.   (E) Robert Frost.

(C) John Keats.

Questions 29 – 30 refer to the following passage.

I fretted the other night at the hotel at the stranger who broke into my chamber after midnight, claiming to share it. But after his lamp had smoked the chamber full and I had turned round to the wall in despair, the man blew out his lamp, knelt down at his bedside, and made in low whisper a long earnest prayer. Then was the relation entirely changed between us. I fretted no more, but respected and liked him.

29.   Which of the following passages was also written by the author of the passage quoted above?

(A)   Yesterday I weeded out violets from the iris bed. The iris was being choked by thick bunches of roots, so much like fruit under the earth. I found one single very fragrant violet and some small autumn crocuses.

(B)   I had a couple of close ones during this show. On the way in, my platoon was evidently silhouetted against the night sky, and was fired on four times at a range of maybe 300 yards by an eighty-eight.

(C)   When summer opens, I see how fast it matures, and fear it will be short; but after the heats of July and August, I am reconciled, like one who has had his swing, to the cool of autumn. So will it be with the coming of death.

(D)   While taking my noon walk today, I had more morbid thoughts. What is it about death that bothers me so much? Probably the hours. Melnick says the soul is immortal and lives on after the body drops away, but if my soul exists without my body I am convinced all my clothes will be too loose-fitting.

(E)   As the least drop of wine tinges the whole goblet, so the least particle of truth colors our whole life. It is never isolated, or simply added as treasure to our stock. When any real progress is made, we unlearn and learn anew what we thought we knew before.

30.   The author of the initial passage quoted above is

   (A)   Henry David Thoreau.   (D)   Francis Parkman.

   (B)   Ralph Waldo Emerson.   (E)   William Byrd.

   (C)   Oliver Wendell Holmes.

Questions 31 – 33 refer to the following passage.

> But sires, by cause I am a burel man,
> At my biginning first I you beseeche
> Have me excused of my rude speeche.
> I lerned nevere retorike, certain:
> Thing that I speke it moot be bare and plain;   5

31.   The character speaking in this Chaucer tale is

   (A)   the Knight.   (D)   the Franklin.

   (B)   Chanticleer.   (E)   the Friar.

   (C)   the Miller.

32.   Which of the following has two syllables when the lines are properly read aloud?

   (A)   rude (line 3)   (D)   excused (line 3)

   (B)   moot (line 5)   (E)   speke (line 5)

   (C)   bare (line 5)

33.   The word "burel" (line 1) may best be interpreted as meaning

   (A)   slovenly.   (D)   sophisticated.

   (B)   pugnacious.   (E)   brutal.

   (C)   uneducated.

Questions 34 – 35 refer to the following.

PEREGRINE Sir, I am grieved I bring you worse disaster:
The gentleman you met at the port today,
That told you, he was newly arrived —
SIR POLITIC Ay, was. A fugitive punk?
PEREGRINE No sir, a spy set on you;
And he has made relation to the senate
That you professed to him to have a plot
To sell the state of Venice to the Turk.

34. The "gentleman" referred to here is

(A) Candide.

(D) Shylock.

(B) Corbaccio.

(E) Ernest.

(C) Peregrine.

35. The play from which this excerpt is drawn is entitled

(A) *The Duchess of Malfi.*

(D) *Rasselas.*

(B) *Volpone.*

(E) *The Secular Masque.*

(C) *Everyman.*

36. What's Hecuba to him, or he to Hecuba,
That he should weep for her? What would he do,
Had he the motive and the cue for passion
That I have? He would drown the stage with tears
And cleave the general ear with horrid speech;
Make mad the guilty and appal the free,
Confound the ignorant, and amaze indeed
The very faculties of eyes and ears.

The speaker is

(A) Coriolanus.

(D) Paulina.

(B) Miranda.

(E) Hamlet.

(C) Antony.

Questions 37–44. For each of the following passages, identify the author or the work. Base your decision on the content and style of each passage.

37. My worthy booksellers and friends, Messieurs Dilly in the Poultry, at whose hospitable and well-covered table I have seen a greater number of literary men than at any other, except that of Sir Joshua Reynolds, had invited me to meet Mr. Wilkes.

    (A) Pepys   (D) Franklin

    (B) Johnson   (E) Burke

    (C) Boswell

38. The commonwealth of learning is not at this time without master-builders, whose mighty designs in advancing the sciences will leave lasting monuments to the admiration of posterity: but every one must not hope to be a Boyle or a Sydenham; and in an age that produces such masters as the great Huygenius, and the incomparable Mr. Newton.

    (A) Pope   (D) Burke

    (B) Locke   (E) Smith

    (C) Ruskin

39. Everyone will be conscious of a likeness here to Wordsworth; and if Wordsworth did great things with this nobly plain manner, we must remember, what indeed he himself would always have been forward to acknowledge, that Burns used it before him.

    (A) Coleridge   (D) Newman

    (B) Goethe   (E) Arnold

    (C) Dryden

40. But we may agree to all this, and yet strongly dissent from the assumption that literature alone is competent to supply this knowledge. After having learnt all that Greek, Roman, and Eastern antiquity have thought and said, and all that modern literature has to tell us, it is not self-evident that we have laid a sufficiently broad and deep foundation...

    (A) Wilde's *The Critic as Artist*

    (B) Pater's *The Renaissance*

    (C) Arnold's *Preface to Poems*

    (D) Huxley's *Science and Culture*

    (E) Lawrence's *Etruscan Places*

41. What we mean by "aristocracy" is merely the richer part of the community, that live in the tallest houses, drive real carriages, (not "kerridges,") ked-glove their hands, and French-bonnet their ladies' heads, give parties where the persons who call them by the above title are not invited, and have a provokingly easy way of dressing...

    (A) Thoreau's *Walden*

    (B) Emerson's *Nature*

    (C) Hawthorne's *The Artist of the Beautiful*

    (D) Holmes' *Elsie Venner*

    (E) Wharton's *The Custom of the Country*

42. A more secret, sweet, and overpowering beauty appears to man when his heart and mind open to the sentiment of virtue. Then instantly he is instructed in what is above him. He learns that his being is without bound; that, to the good, to the perfect, he is born, low as he now lies in evil and weakness.

    (A) Thoreau   (D) Lincoln

    (B) Freneau   (E) Emerson

    (C) Poe

43. Good Heavens! What liberties have I been taking with one of the potentates of the earth, and the man on whose conduct more important consequences depend than on that of any other historical personage of the century!

    (A) Poe

    (B) E. B. White

    (C) Hawthorne

    (D) Jefferson

    (E) Emerson

44. I was first of all the kings who drew
    The knighthood-errant of this realm and all
    The realms together under me, their Head,
    In that fair Order of my Table Round

    (A) Tennyson

    (B) Mansfield

    (C) Poe

    (D) Marlowe

    (E) Arnold

Questions 45 – 46 refer to the following poem.

    Love_____ , she alone is free;
    She can teach ye how to climb
    Higher than the sphery chime:
    Or, if _____ feeble were,
    Heaven itself would stoop to her.

45. Which repeated word will complete the poem?

    (A) Comus

    (B) Venus

    (C) Beauty

    (D) Virtue

    (E) Truth

46. The author of this poem is

    (A) Pope.

    (B) Dryden.

    (C) Milton.

    (D) James Legge.

    (E) Jonson.

47.	Privat prayer, suche as men secreitlie offer onto God by thame selves, requyres no speciall place; althocht that Jesus Chryst commandeth when we pray to enter into out chamber, and to clois the dur, and sa to pray secretlie unto our Father.

The passage above is written in a dialect similar to that of

(A)	Chaucer.

(B)	Beowulf.

(C)	Grendel.

(D)	Burns.

(E)	Shakespeare.

48.	Whenever we read the obscene stories, the voluptuous debaucheries, the cruel and tortuous executions, the unrelenting vindictiveness, with which more than half (of it) is filled, it would be more consistent that we call it the work of a demon… It is a history of wickedness that has served to corrupt and brutalize mankind.

In this passage

(A)	Mencken is discussing Shakespeare's plays.

(B)	Poe is discussing Chaucer.

(C)	Shaw is discussing *The Book of the Dead.*

(D)	Paine is discussing the Bible.

(E)	Trilling is discussing *The Way of All Flesh.*

Questions 49 – 50 refer to the following descriptions.

49.	Which describes Thomas Hardy?

50.	Which describes Edgar Allan Poe?

(A)	His wild love for Jesus is mixed with perverse and poisonous hate of Jesus: his moral hostility to the devil is mixed with secret worship of the devil.

(B)   For though (he) consciously made the younger betrayer a plebian and an imposter, unconsciously, with the supreme justice of the artist, he made him the same as de Stancy, a true aristocrat, or as Fitzpiers, or Troy.

(C)   ... he chose to sentimentalise and glorify the most doggy sort of sex. Setting out to satirise the Forsytes, he glorifies the anti, who is one worse.

(D)   His Mr. Ashenden is also an elderly author, who becomes an agent in the British Secret Service during the War.

(E)   The absence of real central or impulsive being in himself leaves him inordinately, mechanically sensitive to sounds and effect, associations of sounds, associations of rhyme ...

Questions 51 – 53 refer to the following passages.

51.   Which of the following is a parody of Twain?

52.   Which of the following is a parody of Salinger?

53.   Which of the following is a parody of Camus?

(A)   Dear Scottish Lady, — Your problems are quite easily solved. The root cause of chronic sleep-walking is nervous tension, so please relax and above all avoid fretting about domestic matters.

(B)   But you know — I felt kinda sorry for the guy. I get like that sometimes — and when he spoke, I was damn near bawling. I really was.

(C)   As they walked on, she smelled good. She smells good, thought Perley. But that's all right, I add good. And when we get to Schrafft's, I'll order from the menu, which I like very much indeed.

(D)   I keep hoping for some dark horse to gallop over the horizon, eyes ablaze and mane slick as snake juice. I keep hoping, but I remember to say hello to the Senator when he nods my way. A body can't be too careful these days, and can't have too many friends.

(E)   Stayed in bed reading *The Ecstasy of Indifference* by Claude who plays on the left wing. Got half way through but couldn't be bothered to finish it.

Questions 54 – 55 refer to the following excerpts.

54.   Which "I" is T. S. Eliot?

55.   Which "I" is William Dean Howells?

(A)   I had fallen in love at first sight with the whole place — she herself was probably so used to it that she didn't know the impression it was capable of making on a stranger — and I had felt it really a case to risk something.

(B)   I say judged, not amputated, by them; not judged to be as good as, or worse or better than, the dead; and certainly not judged by the canons of dead critics.

(C)   I would beseech the literary critics of our country to disabuse themselves of the mischievous notion that they are essential to the progress of literature in the way critics have vainly imagined.

(D)   I can't help it, I'm crazy about thoroughbred horses. I've always been that way. When I was ten years old and saw I was going to be big and couldn't be a rider I was so sorry I nearly died.

(E)   But I liked to hear him talk — it made my work, when not interrupting it, less mechanical, less special.

Questions 56 – 58 refer to the following selection.

Unreal City,
Under the brown fog of a winter dawn,
A crowd flowed over London Bridge, so many,
I had not thought death had undone so many.
Sighs, short and infrequent, were exhaled,
And each man fixed his eyes before his feet.
Flowed up the hill and down King William Street ...

56. The description of the city is similar to one found in the writings of

    (A) Flaubert.

    (B) Dante.

    (C) Baudelaire.

    (D) Shakespeare.

    (E) Ovid.

57. The poet's reference to sighs is cited by him as derived from

    (A) "La Belle Dame Sans Merci."

    (B) *Faustus.*

    (C) *Don Juan.*

    (D) *The Inferno.*

    (E) *Prometheus Unbound.*

58. The author of the poem is

    (A) John Dos Passos.

    (B) Theodore Roethke.

    (C) T. S. Eliot.

    (D) Langston Hughes.

    (E) William Carlos Williams.

Questions 59 – 61 refer to the following excerpt.

> Vanity, saity the preacher, vanity!
> Draw round my bed: is Anselm keeping back?
> Nephews — sons mine … ah God, I know not! Well —
> She, men would have to be your mother once,
> Old Gandolf envied me, so fair she was!

59. The excerpt above is an example of

    (A) decalogue.

    (B) stream-of-consciousness.

    (C) discursive argument.

    (D) dramatic monologue.

    (E) expressive mode.

60. The first line is an allusion to

    (A) Shakespeare.   (D) The Old Testament.

    (B) Thackeray's *Vanity Fair.*   (E) *Pilgrim's Progress.*

    (C) Shelley's "Ozymandias."

61. The poem was written by

    (A) Christina Rossetti.   (D) Oscar Wilde.

    (B) Charles Swinburne.   (E) Matthew Arnold.

    (C) Robert Browning.

Questions 62 – 63 refer to the following speech.

> What is a man, if his chief good and market of his time be but to sleep and feed? A beast, no more. Sure he that made us with such large discourse, looking before and after, gave us not that capability and godlike reason to fust in us unused.

62. The speaker is arguing that

    (A) unconscious impulses destroy mankind's potential for greatness.

    (B) man can never be more than a beast who sleeps and feeds.

    (C) because of Original Sin, humans lost any potential to transcend their bestial natures.

    (D) God intended mankind to be more than mere beasts; our minds are proof of that.

    (E) money causes an obsession with physical gratification, causing people to ignore their higher mental faculties.

63. This speech was given by

    (A) Falstaff.   (D) Miranda.

    (B) Caesar.   (E) Beatrice.

    (C) Hamlet.

Questions 64 – 65 refer to the following passage.

> Come, seeling night, scarf up the tender eye of pitiful day; and
> with thy bloody and invisible hand cancel and tear to pieces that
> great bond which keeps me pale! — Light thickens; and the crow
> makes wing to rocky wood; good things of day begin to droop and
> drowse; whiles night's black agents to their prey do rouse.

64. The "prey" referred to in this passage are

  (A) night's hands.   (D) daylight's fading rays.

  (B) the birds of night.   (E) living creatures.

  (C) dreams.

65. The passage is taken from

  (A) *Measure for Measure.*   (D) *Macbeth.*

  (B) *Cymbeline.*   (E) *King Lear.*

  (C) *Henry V.*

---

66. BRUTUS   Fates, we will know your pleasures: that we shall die, we
                   know; 'tis but the time and drawing days out, that men stand
                   upon.

     CASSIUS   Why, he that cuts off twenty years of life, cuts off so many
                   years of fearing death.

     BRUTUS   Grant that, and then is death a benefit.

Brutus' sentiments are best paraphrased:

  (A) It is better to die young and brave than old and cowardly.

  (B) Only the old know that their death is certain.

  (C) A youth of twenty fears death more than an older man.

  (D) Cowards die many times before their deaths.

  (E) Death benefits those who have grown old in spirit.

67. For form is not a personal thing like style. It is impersonal like logic. And just as the school of _____ was logical in its expressions, so it seems the school of Flaubert is, as it were, logical in its aesthetic form.

    Which of the following correctly completes the quote?

    (A) Whitman   (D) Chaucer

    (B) Mallory   (E) T. S. Eliot

    (C) Pope

Questions 68 – 70 refer to the following poem.

As I went down the hill along the wall
There was a gate I had leaned at for the view
And had just turned from when I first saw you
As you came up the hill. We met. But all
We did that day was mingle great and small   5

Footprints in summer dust as if we drew
The figure of our being less than two
But more than one as yet. Your parasol
Pointed the decimal off with one deep thrust.
And all the time we talked you seemed to see   10

Something down there to smile at in the dust.
(Oh, it was without prejudice to me!)
Afterward I went past what you had passed
Before we met and you what I had passed.

68. The first eight lines are similar in rhyme scheme to

    (A) the Shakespearean sonnet.   (D) the Petrarchan sonnet.

    (B) the Spenserian sonnet.   (E) the Rossettian sonnet.

    (C) the Dantean sonnet.

69. "Less than two / But more than one as yet" (lines 7 and 8) refers to

    (A) the lovers' shadows in the dust.

    (B) the tracing of the parasol in the dust.

    (C) the time before the lovers' relationship broke apart.

    (D) the time before the two lovers had fully committed themselves to each other.

    (E) the time before they met.

70. This poem was written by

    (A) Vachel Lindsay.

    (B) Edna St. Vincent Millay.

    (C) Robert Frost.

    (D) Lord Byron.

    (E) Elizabeth Barrett Browning.

Questions 71 – 72 refer to the following.

MOTHER I know, dear, but don't say it's ridiculous, because the papers were full of it; I don't know about New York, but there was half a page about a man missing even longer than Larry, and he turned up from Burma.

CHRIS He couldn't have wanted to come home very badly, Mom.

MOTHER Don't be so smart.

CHRIS You can have a helluva time in Burma.

71. In the above exchange, Chris is

    (A) concerned with providing information.

    (B) concerned with ridiculing his mother's false beliefs.

    (C) using humor to bring his mother back to reality.

    (D) arguing for greater freedom for himself at home.

    (E) defending Larry's recent excuses for not returning.

72. This excerpt is from

    (A) *Tea and Sympathy.*

    (B) *The Rose Tattoo.*

    (C) *Incident at Vichy.*

    (D) *All My Sons.*

    (E) *The Caucasian Chalk Circle.*

---

73.   A lovere and a lusty bacheler,
       With lokkes crulle ans they were laid in presse.
       Of twenty yeer of age he was, I gesse.

    The character described above is

    (A) the Franklin.   (D) the Knight.

    (B) the Yeoman.   (E) the Monk.

    (C) the Squire.

Questions 74 – 77 refer to the following excerpt.

    Some guide the course of wandering orbs on high,
    Or roll the planets through the boundless sky.
    Some less refined, beneath the moon's pale light
    Pursue the stars that shoot athwart the night,
    Or suck the mists in grosser air below,
    Or dip their pinions in the painted bow,
    Or brew fierce tempests on the wintry main,
    Or o'er the glebe distill the kindly rain.

74. "Some" in the first line refers to

    (A) human professions.

    (B) the pantheon of gods.

    (C) the tasks assigned to the spheres.

(D) the links in the Great Chain of Being.

(E) nature's cycles.

75. The poet here uses the technique of

(A) discourse.   (D) extrapolation.

(B) specification.   (E) extirpation.

(C) cataloguing.

76. "Glebe" in the last line can best be interpreted as meaning

(A) faces of the people.   (D) cultivated fields.

(B) mountain crags.   (E) oceans' beaches.

(C) desert sands.

77. This excerpt is from

(A) Congreve's *Love for Love.*

(B) Bacon's *Novum Organum.*

(C) Pope's "The Rape of the Lock."

(D) Lovelace's "To Althea from Prison."

(E) Milton's *Paradise Lost.*

Questions 78 – 80 refer to the following passage.

The first of these characters has struck every observer, native and foreign. In place of the discordant local dialects of all the other major countries, including England, we have a general Volkssprache for the whole nation, and if it is conditioned at all it is only by minor differences in punctuation and vocabulary, and by the linguistic struggles of various groups of newcomers.

78. The "first character" that the author notes is

   (A) the tendency of American English to develop into different dialects.

   (B) the tendency for different American dialects to coalesce into one.

   (C) the general uniformity of American English throughout the country.

   (D) the tendency of immigrants to alter American pronunciation.

   (E) the general inability of scholars to identify Standard American English.

79. The author implies that

   (A) immigrants are a threat to the linguistic integrity of American English.

   (B) immigrants have no influence on the general accent.

   (C) immigrants have a minor influence on linguistic aspects.

   (D) immigrants have traditionally altered American speech.

   (E) only in spoken English do immigrants have an influence.

80. This passage was written by

   (A) H. L. Mencken.   (D) James Michener.

   (B) J. C. Furnas.   (E) William Safire.

   (C) T. S. Eliot.

Questions 81 – 82 refer to the following passage.

   Ye who listen with credulity to the whispers of fancy, and pursue with eagerness the phantoms of hope; who expect that age will perform the promises of youth, and that the deficiencies of the present day will be supplied by the morrow — attend to the history of Rasselas, prince of _____.

81. This opening paragraph suggests that the "history" the author is about to relate will be a

    (A) parable.

    (B) biblical allusion.

    (C) philosophical fable.

    (D) paradoxical *roman a clef.*

    (E) totological summary.

82. The passage was written by

    (A) William Congreve. (D) James Boswell.

    (B) Jonathan Swift. (E) Thomas Gray.

    (C) Samuel Johnson.

Questions 83 – 84 refer to the following passage.

  The poet of whose works I have undertaken the revision may now begin to assume the dignity of an ancient and claim the privilege of established fame and prescriptive veneration. He has long outlived his century, the term commonly fixed as the test of literary merit.

83. The poet the author is speaking of is

    (A) Christopher Marlowe. (D) Dante.

    (B) Geoffrey Chaucer. (E) Sir Walter Raleigh.

    (C) William Shakespeare.

84. The author of the passage is

    (A) William Wordsworth. (D) Samuel Johnson.

    (B) Thomas Gray. (E) Jonathan Swift.

    (C) Matthew Arnold.

85.   Adam walked round by the rick-yard, at present empty of ricks, to the little wooden gate leading into the garden — once the well-tended kitchen-garden of a manor house; now, but for the handsome brick wall with stone coping that ran along one side of it … a true farmhouse garden.

The author of this passage is

(A)   Jane Austen.   (D)   Thomas Hardy.

(B)   George Eliot.   (E)   Jack London.

(C)   Charles Dickens.

Questions 86 – 87 refer to the following passage.

Who cares whether Mr. Ruskin's views on Turner are sound or not? What does it matter? That mighty and majestic prose of his, so fervid and so fiery colored in its noble eloquence, so rich in its elaborate symphonic music, so sure and certain at its best, in subtle choice of word and epithet, is at least as great a work of art as any of those wonderful sunsets that bleach or rot on their corrupted canvases in England's Gallery …

86.   The author is arguing that

(A)   criticism is irrelevant to the purity of art.

(B)   criticism is independent to the quality of art.

(C)   criticism is equal with art as a form of art.

(D)   artists should not be bounded by what critics say about them.

(E)   critics should not be held to account for what they say about art.

87.   The author of this passage is

(A)   Matthew Arnold.   (D)   Oscar Wilde.

(B)   Henry Newman.   (E)   G.B. Shaw.

(C)   Walter Pater.

Questions 88 – 90 refer to the following poem.

Look in my face; my name is Might-have-been;
I am also called No-more, Too-late, Farewell;
Unto thine ear I hold the dead-sea-shell
Cast up thy Life's foam—fretted feet between;
Unto thine eyes the glass where that is seen
Which had Life's form and Love's, but by my spell
Is now a shaken shadow intolerable,
Of ultimate things unuttered the frail screen.
Mark me, how still I am! But should there dart
One moment through thy soul the soft surprise
Of that winged Peace which lulls the breath of sighs, —
Then shalt thou see me smile, and turn apart
Thy visage to mine ambush at thy heart
Sleepless with cold commemorative eyes.

88. One poetic device that is repeated throughout this poem is

   (A) personification.   (D) allegory.

   (B) assonance.   (E) onomatopoeia.

   (C) alliteration.

89. The poet is

   (A) appealing to his lover to be more attentive.

   (B) regretting a loss of love.

   (C) announcing his reluctance to proceed further with the affair.

   (D) explaining his wish for some response to his overtures of love.

   (E) appealing to his former lover for a resurrection of their romance.

90. The author of this poem is

   (A) Browning.   (D) Rossetti.

   (B) Tennyson.   (E) W. S. Gilbert.

   (C) Donne.

Questions 91 – 92 refer to the following poem.

> Have the elder races halted?
> Do they droop and end their lesson, wearied over there beyond the seas?
> We take up the task eternal, and the burden and the lesson,
> Pioneers! O pioneers!

91.   The "elder races" cited here refer to

(A) the ancient Greeks.

(B) the ancient Romans.

(C) the contemporary Europeans.

(D) pre-historic man.

(E) first-century Christians.

92.   This poem was written by

(A) John Greenleaf Whittier.   (D) Alfred Noyes.

(B) Ralph Waldo Emerson.   (E) Ellery Channing.

(C) Walt Whitman.

Questions 93 – 95 refer to the following passage.

> He had before served me a scurvy trick, which set the Queen laughing, although at the same time she were heartily vexed, and would have immediately cashiered him, if I had not been so generous as to intercede. Her Majesty had taken a marrow bone upon her plate, and after knocking out the marrow, placed the bone again in the dish, erect as it stood before; the dwarf watching his opportunity, while Glumdalclitch was gone to the sideboard …

93.   This passage is an account of

(A) a descent into Hades.

(B) a voyage to Brobdingnag.

(C) the arrival in Wonderland.

(D) an introduction to Utopia.

(E) an expedition in *Journey to the Center of the Earth.*

94.   "Cashiered" is best interpreted as meaning

(A) paid off.   (D) ridiculed.

(B) executed.   (E) rewarded.

(C) dismissed.

95.   The passage was written by

(A) Lewis Carroll.   (D) Jules Verne.

(B) Isaac Asimov.   (E) H. G. Wells.

(C) Jonathan Swift.

Questions 96 – 98 refer to the following poem.

Ever such is time, which takes in trust
Our youth, our joys, and all we have,
And pays us but with age and dust,
Who in the dark and silent grave
When we have wandered all our ways
Shuts up the story of our days,
And from which earth, and grave, and dust
The Lord shall raise me up, I trust.

96.   This poem is best described as

(A) an elegy.   (D) an epitaph.

(B) a pastoral.   (E) an encomium.

(C) a psalm.

97.   In this poem, three forces battle each other; they are

      (A) youth, time, and death.

      (B) trust, time, and the Lord.

      (C) joy, death, and dust.

      (D) youth, age, and death.

      (E) life, death, and the Lord.

98.   The poem was written by

      (A) Shakespeare.   (D) Lovelace.

      (B) Spenser.   (E) Daniel.

      (C) Raleigh.

---

99.   For no very intelligible reason, Mr. Lucas had hurried ahead of his party. He was perhaps reaching the age at which independence becomes valuable, because it is so soon to be lost. Tired of attention and consideration, he liked breaking away from the younger members, to ride by himself, and to dismount unassisted.

This passage is taken from

      (A) *The Road to Colonus.*

      (B) *To the Lighthouse.*

      (C) *Far From the Madding Crowd.*

      (D) *The Open Window.*

      (E) *The House of Mirth.*

Questions 100 – 101 refer to the following passage.

    And that's what you learn, when you're a novelist. And that's what you are very liable not to know, if you're a parson, or a philosopher, or a scientist, or a stupid person. If you're a parson, you talk about souls in heaven. If you're a novelist, you know that paradise is in the palm of your hand, and on the end of your nose, because both are alive; and alive, and man alive, which is more than you can say, for certain, of paradise.

100. The author of this passage has learned

    (A) that parsons are not qualified to talk about heaven.

    (B) that paradise is the realm of the philosopher.

    (C) that what you hold in your hand is all that is real.

    (D) that whatever else might be true, he himself is alive.

    (E) that stupidity and belief in paradise go hand in hand.

101. The author of this passage is also the author of

    (A) *The Mayor of Casterbridge.*

    (B) *To the Lighthouse.*

    (C) *The Great Gatsby.*

    (D) *Sons and Lovers.*

    (E) *To Your Scattered Bodies Go.*

---

102.   My family originated in a village in the mountains of Leon, where Nature was kinder to them than Fortune, although in those poor villages my father was reputed to be a rich man, and indeed, he would have been if he had been as skillful in preserving his estate as he was in spending it.

The character here describing his family's history is

    (A) David Copperfield.   (D) Don Quixote.

    (B) Huckleberry Finn.   (E) Jean Valjean.

    (C) Tess.

103.　　Levin laid his brother on his back, sat down beside him and, hardly daring to breathe, gazed at his face. The dying man lay with closed eyes but the muscles of his forehead twitched every now and then, as with one thinking deeply and intently.

This passage is from

(A) *The Cossacks.*

(B) *War and Peace.*

(C) *Anna Karenina.*

(D) *Fathers and Sons.*

(E) *Crime and Punishment.*

Questions 104 – 105 refer to the following passage.

　　"In contrast to Newton and Schopenhauer, your ancestor did not believe in a uniform, absolute time. He believed in an infinite series of times, in a growing, dizzying net of divergent, convergent and parallel times. This network of times which approached one another, forked, broke off, or were unaware of one another for centuries, embraces *all* possibilities of time. We do not exist in the majority of these times; in some you exist, and not I; in others, I, and not you; in others, both of us. In the present one, which a favorable fate has granted me, you have arrived at my house; in another, while crossing the garden, you found me dead; in still another, I utter these same words, but I am a mistake, a ghost."

　　"In every one," I pronounced, not without a tremble to my voice, "I am grateful to you and revere you for your re-creation of the garden of Ts'ui Pen."

　　"Not in all," he murmured with a smile. "Time forks perpetually toward innumerable futures. In one of them I am your enemy."

104.　The tone of the passage is

(A) threatening.

(B) gloomy.

(C) sarcastic.

(D) patronizing.

(E) instructive.

105. The author of this passage is

   (A) Jorge Luis Borges.   (D) Kurt Vonnegut.

   (B) John Barth.   (E) Margaret Atwood.

   (C) Samuel Beckett.

Questions 106 – 109 refer to the following excerpts.

106. Which is by Aldous Huxley?

107. Which is by Flannery O'Connor?

108. Which is by F. Scott Fitzgerald?

109. Which is by John Updike?

   (A)   The chairman spoke in Bulgarian, musically, at length. There was polite laughter. Nobody translated for Bech. The professorial type, his hair like a flazen toupee, jerked forward.

   (B)   The old woman and her daughter were sitting on their porch when Mr. Shiftlet came up their road for the first time. The old woman slid to the edge of her chair and leaned forward, shading her eyes from the piercing sunset with her hand.

   (C)   Inert, Sebastian abandoned himself to the tenderness which at ordinary times he would never allow her to express, and in the very act of self-abandonment found a certain isolation. Suddenly and irrelevantly, it came into his mind that this was one of the situations he had always looked forward to in his dream of a love affair with Mary Esdaile — or whatever other name one chose to give the dark-haired mistress of his imagination.

   (D)   As I watched him he adjusted himself a little, visibly. His hand took hold of hers, and as she said something low in his ear he turned toward her with a rush of emotion. I think that voice held him most, with its fluctuating, feverish warmth, because it couldn't be over-dreamed — that voice was a deathless song.

   (E)   Lem hesitated only long enough to take a firm purchase on his store teeth, then dashed into the path of the horses. With great strength and agility, he grasped their bridles and dragged them to a rearing halt, a few feet from the astounded and thoroughly frightened pair.

Questions 110 – 111 refer to the following passage.

There was something in his physiognomy extremely singular, and that cannot easily be defined. It bore the traces of many passions, which seemed to have fixed the features they no longer animated. An habitual gloom and severity prevailed over the deep lines of his countenance; and his eyes were so piercing that they seemed to penetrate, at a single glance, into the hearts of men, and to read their most secret thoughts; few persons could support their scrutiny or even endure to meet them twice.

110. This is a classic description of

   (A) the existential hero.   (D) the satanic hero.

   (B) the anti-hero.   (E) the psalmic hero.

   (C) the Byronic hero.

111. The passage quoted above was written by

   (A) Samuel Coleridge.   (D) Lord Byron.

   (B) Ann Radcliffe.   (E) Albert Camus.

   (C) Matthew Arnold.

Questions 112 – 114 refer to the following excerpt.

Let us begin and carry up this corpse,
   Singing together.
Leave we the common crofts, the vulgar thorpes
   Each in its tether
Sleeping safe on the bosom of the plain,   5
   Cared for till cock-crow:
Look out if yonder be not day again
   Rimming the rock-row!
That's the appropriate country: there, man's thought,
   Rarer, intenser,   10

Self-gathered for an outbreak, as it ought, Chafes in the censer.

112. "Thorpes" (line 3) might best be interpreted as meaning

    (A) corrals.

    (B) stagnant pools.

    (C) mountainsides.

    (D) villages.

    (E) citadels.

113. The tone of this poem is characterized by a contrast between

    (A) the life of the corpse bearers and the lifelessness of the corpse.

    (B) the low nature of the "common crofts" and the loftiness of the mountain tops.

    (C) the night of death and the dawning with the cock-crow.

    (D) intense idealistic thought and the realities of the earth.

    (E) the sleeping crofts and the outbreak of singing.

114. This excerpt was written by

    (A) Tennyson.

    (B) Coleridge.

    (C) Browning.

    (D) Christina Rossetti.

    (E) Shelley.

Questions 115 – 117 refer to the following.

PRINCE	Where shall we take a purse tomorrow, Jack?
FALSTAFF	Zounds, where thou wilt, lad; I'll make one; and I do not, call me villain and baffle me.
PRINCE	I see a good amendment of life in thee — from praying to purse-taking.
FALSTAFF	Why, Hal, 'tis my vocation, Hal; 'tis no sin for a man to labor in his vocation.
POINS	Now shall we know if Gadshill have set a match. O, if men were to be saved by merit, what hole in hell were hot enough for him? This is the most omnipotent villain that ever cried "stand" to a true man.

115. "Baffle" in the second speech can best be interpreted as meaning

    (A) confound.

    (B) command.

    (C) reprimand.

    (D) disgrace.

    (E) beat.

116. The characters are planning

    (A) to enter a monastery.

    (B) to change their lives dramatically.

    (C) to call a meeting of their fellows.

    (D) to commit a robbery.

    (E) to appoint a new leader.

117. "Zounds" can best be interpreted as meaning

    (A) Go!

    (B) By God!

    (C) A swoon take me!

    (D) Jesus' wounds!

    (E) I am astonished!

Questions 118 – 119 refer to the following passage.

Rather than love, than money, than fame, give me truth. I sat at a table where were rich food and wine in abundance, and obsequious attendance, but sincerity and truth were not; and I went away hungry from the inhospitable board. The hospitality was as cold as the ices. I thought there was no need of ice to freeze them.

118. The reference to "ices" (line 4) refers to

    (A) the lack of hospitality and the indifference to truth.

    (B) the dessert and the ice needed to keep it cold.

    (C) the lack of hospitality, the dessert, and the ice needed to keep it cold.

(D) the cold pursuit of truth and the lack of hospitality.

(E) the weather from which the author is escaping and the lack of hospitality.

119. This passage was written by

(A) Emerson.   (D) Thoreau.

(B) Melville.   (E) Channing.

(C) Whitman.

---

120.   To conclude, then, there is no occupation concerned with the management of social affairs which belongs either to woman or to man, as such. Natural gifts are to be found here and there in both creatures alike; and every occupation is open to both, so far as their natures are concerned, though woman is for all purposes the weaker.

The writer is arguing here for

(A) the equality of women.

(B) the inequality of women to men.

(C) the equality of women in occupations.

(D) the equality of women in the management of social affairs.

(E) the inequality of the nature of women to that of men.

Questions 121 – 123 refer to the following excerpt.

The Sea of Faith
Was once, too, at the full and round earth's shore
Lay like the folds of a bright girdle furled.
But now I only hear
Its melancholy long, withdrawing roar,   5
Retreating, to the breath
Of the night wind, down the vast edges drear
And naked shingles of the world.

121. The reference to the "folds of a bright girdle furled" (line 3) compares the sea to

    (A) folds of bright clothing.   (D) loose flesh.

    (B) a pennant.   (E) an encompassing shore.

    (C) an undergarment.

122. The poet's tone and imagery attempts to imitate

    (A) the ebbing of the tide.

    (B) the lapping of the waves at high tide.

    (C) a full, pounding tide.

    (D) a neap tide.

    (E) a red tide.

123. The author of this poem is

    (A) Charles Swinburne.   (D) Matthew Arnold.

    (B) John Keats.   (E) Alfred Tennyson.

    (C) Percy Shelley.

Questions 124 – 126 refer to the following excerpt.

_____	(Dropping his familiarity and speaking with freezing politeness) If our conversation is to continue, Louka, you will please remember that a gentleman does not discuss the conduct of the lady he is engaged to with her maid.
LOUKA	It's so hard to know what a gentleman considers right. I thought from your trying to kiss me that you had given up being so particular.

124. The unidentified speaker is

    (A) Volpone.   (D) Sergius.

    (B) Candide.   (E) Hyperion.

    (C) Mercutio.

125. The comic force of this interchange hinges on the use of the word

    (A) "gentleman."   (D) "right."

    (B) "particular."   (E) "conduct."

    (C) "maid."

126. The play from which this excerpt is taken is

    (A) *She Stoops to Conquer.*

    (B) *Measure for Measure.*

    (C) *Arms and the Man.*

    (D) *The Comedy of Errors.*

    (E) *Sunday in The Park With George.*

---

127. _____ had a syncophantish, but a sincere admiration of the genius, erudition and virtue of Ursa-Major, and in recording the noble growlings of the Great Bear, thought not of his own Scotch snivel.

    The quote above concerns a biography written by

    (A) Ben Johnson.   (D) James Boswell.

    (B) Ben Franklin.   (E) Edward Fitzgerald.

    (C) John Milton.

Questions 128 – 129. For each of the following passages, identify the author of the work. Base your decision on the content and style of each passage.

128. It is only by the exercise of reason that man can discover God. Take away that reason and he would be incapable of understanding anything; and, in this case, it would be just as consistent to read even in a book called the Bible to a horse as to a man. How then is it that those people pretend to reject reason?

    (A) John Locke

    (B) Bertrand Russell

    (C) Benjamin Franklin

    (D) Thomas Paine

    (E) John Stuart Mill

129. Far other, however, was the truly fashionable gentleman of those days — his dress, which served for both morning and evening, street and drawing-room, was a linsey-woolsey coat, made, perhaps, by the fair hands of the mistress of his affections...

    (A) Washington Irving

    (B) Samuel Clemens

    (C) Stephen Crane

    (D) Bret Harte

    (E) Hart Crane

Questions 130 – 131 refer to the following excerpt.

Wha for Scotland's king and law
Freedom's sword will strongly draw,
Freeman stand, or freeman fa',
    Let him follow me!

By Oppression's woes and pains,
By your sons in servile chains,
We will drain our dearest veins,
    But they shall be free!

Lay the proud usurpers low!
Tyrants fall in every foe!
Liberty's in every blow!
    Let us do or die!

130. The poet imagines that these words were spoken by

    (A) Robert Emmett.   (D) Robert Bruce.

    (B) Macduff.   (E) Athelred.

    (C) Edward II.

131. The excerpt might best be termed

    (A) a rallying cry to the speaker's troops.

    (B) a response in defiance of a challenge.

    (C) a soliloquy by a doomed soldier.

    (D) a rebel leader's appeal to desert.

    (E) an appeal to the populace for soldiers.

Questions 132 – 135 refer to the following excerpt.

> Yet once more, O ye laurels, and once more
> Ye myrtles brown, with ivy never sere,
> I come to pluck your berries harsh and crude,
> And with forced fingers rude,
> Shatter your leaves before the mellowing year.   5
> Bitter constraint and sad occasion dear,
> Compels me to disturb your season due;
> For_____ is dead, dead ere his prime,
> Young_____, and hath not left his peer.

132. This excerpt might best be described as a(n)

    (A) dramatic dialogue.   (D) epic.

    (B) elegy.   (E) colloquy.

    (C) monody.

133. The use of the word "crude" in the third line indicates that

    (A) the speaker will be rough as he harvests the berries.

(B)   the berries are of low quality.

(C)   the words which the poet sings are primitive ones.

(D)   the berries are not yet ripe.

(E)   there are bitter truths he will reveal.

134.   The repeated name which best completes this excerpt is

(A)   Angelica.   (D)   Lycidas.

(B)   Valentine.   (E)   Prometheus.

(C)   Lysistrata.

135.   The author of this poem is

(A)   William Shakespeare.   (D)   John Milton.

(B)   John Donne.   (E)   Alexander Pope.

(C)   John Dryden.

Questions 136 – 137 refer to the following excerpt.

> Hear me recreant!
> On thine allegiance, hear me!
> Since thou hast sought to make us break our vow,
> Which we durst never yet, and with strained pride
> To come between our sentence and our power,
> Which nor our nature nor our place can bear,
> Our potency made good, take thy reward.
> Five days we do allot thee, or provision.
> To shield thee from diseases of the world;
> And on the sixth to turn thy hated back
> Upon our kingdom: if, on the tenth day following,
> Thy banished trunk be found in our dominions,
> The moment is thy death. Away! by Jupiter,
> This shall not be revoked.

136. The most appropriate contextual interpretation of the word "recreant" (line 1) is

    (A) one who commits evil deeds.

    (B) one who does not do his duty.

    (C) one who has recreated the truth to his own liking.

    (D) a blackguard.

    (E) a traitor.

137. This excerpt is from

    (A) *Julius Caesar.*   (D) *King Lear.*

    (B) *Romeo and Juliet.*   (E) *Much Ado About Nothing.*

    (C) *Richard II.*

Questions 138 – 140 refer to the following excerpt.

> When that rich soul which to her heaven is gone,
> Whom all do celebrate who know they have one
> (for who is sure he hath a soul, unless
> It see, and judge, and follow worthiness,
> And by deeds praise it? He who doth not this,   5
> May lodge an inmate soul, but 'tis not his);
> When that queen ended here her progress time,
> And, as to her standing house, to heaven did climb,
> Where, loath to make the saints attend her long,
> She's now a part both of the choir and song   10

138. Line 9 indicates that the subject of the poem

    (A) was always considerate.

    (B) was always in a hurry.

    (C) never received the attention she deserved.

    (D) lived an eventful life.

    (E) died early.

139. The poem might best be described as

    (A) an invocation to the Muse.   (D) an epigram.

    (B) a declaration of love.   (E) an encomium.

    (C) a commemorative.

140. The poem was written by

    (A) John Donne.   (D) John Milton.

    (B) John Dryden.   (E) Sir Francis Bacon.

    (C) Ben Jonson.

---

141.   "The object of the imitation is not only a complete action but such as stir up pity and fear, and this is best achieved when the events are unexpectedly interconnected. This, more than what happens accidentally and by chance, will arouse wonder."
        —Aristotle, *Poetics*

On the basis of the above observation, Aristotle might be expected to object most strongly to which of the following?

    (A) Hardy's *The Return of the Native*.

    (B) Shakespeare's *Macbeth*.

    (C) Steinbeck's *The Grapes of Wrath*.

    (D) O'Neill's *Long Day's Journey into Night*.

    (E) Ibsen's *The Wild Duck*.

142.   "The concentration of attention upon matter-of-fact is the supremacy of the desert. Any approach to such triumph bestows on learning a fugitive, and a cloistered virtue, ..."
        —Alfred North Whitehead, *Modes of Thought*

In the above passage, Whitehead borrows a phrase from

    (A) Mill's *On Liberty*.

    (B) Milton's *Areopagitica*.

(C) Thoreau's *Civil Disobedience.*

(D) Aristotle's *Ethics.*

(E) Rousseau's *The Social Contract.*

Questions 143 – 145 refer to the following passage.

He answered, "I don't know how to sing; for that was the reason I left the entertainment and came out to this place, because I couldn't sing." The other who talked to him replied, "All the same, you shall sing for me." "What must I sing?" he asked. "Sing the beginning of created things!" said the other. Hereupon he at once began to sing verses which he had never heard before, to the praise of God the creator.
— Bede, *Historia Ecclesiastica Gentis Anglorum*

143. The singer in the above passage is

   (A) Beowulf.   (D) Chaucer.

   (B) Sir Gawain.   (E) Dante.

   (C) Caedmon.

144. The versification of the song is

   (A) alliterative.   (D) free verse.

   (B) iambic pentameter.   (E) heroic couplets.

   (C) ballad stanza.

145. The passage itself could best be classified as an example of

   (A) epic simile.   (D) mock epic.

   (B) comic relief.   (E) dream vision.

   (C) classical allusion.

Questions 146 – 147 refer to the following poem.

THE LAKE ISLE

O God, O Venus, O Mercury, patron of thieves,
Give me in due time, I beseech you, a little tobacco-shop
With the little bright boxes
      piled up neatly upon the shelves
And the loose fragrant cavendish
      and the shag,
And the bright Virginia
      loose under the bright glass cases,
And a pair of scales not too greasy,
And the whores dropping in for a word or two in passing,
For a flip word, and to tidy their hair a bit.

O God, O Venus, O Mercury, patron of thieves,
Lend me a little tobacco-shop,
      or install me in any profession
Save this damned profession of writing,
      where one needs one's brains all the time.

146. The title of the poem refers to

    (A) the place where the poem was written.

    (B) the birth of Venus.

    (C) a poem by W. B. Yeats.

    (D) a brand of tobacco.

    (E) the place where the poet would like to go on vacation.

147. The poem might be classified as

    (A) Petrarchan.   (D) anti-Romantic.

    (B) Romantic.   (E) pre-Raphaelite.

    (C) anti-Petrarchan.

Questions 148 – 149 refer to the following passage.

> The end then of learning is to repair the ruins of our first parents by regaining to know God aright and out of that knowledge to love Him, to imitate Him, to be like Him, ...

148. The passage is from

    (A) St. Augustine's *The City of God.*

    (B) More's *Utopia.*

    (C) Mill's *On Liberty.*

    (D) Dewey's *Experience and Education.*

    (E) Milton's *On Education.*

149. The metaphor "repair the ruins" depends for its meaning on

    (A) Freud's theory of the Oedipal Complex.

    (B) the etymology of "ruin" which is derived from Latin "ruo, ruere," meaning "to fall."

    (C) knowledge about archaeological sites.

    (D) reference to the tearing down of medieval churches by Protestants during the Reformation.

    (E) reference to Greek and Roman temples.

---

150.   Sailor, can you hear
The Pequod's sea wings, beating landward, fall
Headlong and break on our Atlantic wall
Off 'Sconset, where the yawing S-boats splash
The bellbuoy, ...
      —Robert Lowell, *The Quaker Graveyard in Nantucket*

In the above lines, Lowell alludes to

(A) the biblical story of Jonah.   (D) Melville's *Moby Dick*.

(B) Homer's *Odyssey*.   (E) Shakespeare's *The Tempest*.

(C) Sinbad.

151. Which of the following plays by Eugene O'Neill is based on the myth of Hippolytus?

(A) *Mourning Becomes Electra*   (D) *Desire Under the Elms*

(B) *Moon for the Misbegotten*   (E) *The Emperor Jones*

(C) *Strange Interlude*

152.   Now, as there is an infinity of possible universes in the ideas of God, and as only one of them can exist, there must be a sufficient reason for the choice of God, which determines him to select one rather than another.

And this reason can be found in the fitness, or in the degrees of perfection that these worlds contain, each possible world having a right to claim existence in proportion to the measure of perfection which it possesses.

The idea expressed above is most directly ridiculed in

(A) Aristophanes' *The Clouds*.

(B) Swift's *Gulliver's Travels*.

(C) Voltaire's *Candide*.

(D) Molière's *Tartuffe*.

(E) Oscar Wilde's *The Importance of Being Earnest*.

153. Which of the following poets did NOT write sonnets?

(A) Robert Frost   (D) John Donne

(B) Edna St. Vincent Millay   (E) Alexander Pope

(C) John Milton

Questions 154 – 156 refer to the following poem.

> The world is too much with us; late and soon,
> Getting and spending, we lay waste our powers:
> Little we see in Nature that is ours;
> We have given our hearts away, a sordid boon!
> This Sea that bares her bosom to the moon;
> The winds that will be howling at all hours,
> And are up-gathered now like sleeping flowers;
> For this, for everything, we are out of tune;
> It moves us not. — Great God! I'd rather be
> A Pagan suckled in a creed outworn;
> So might I, standing on this pleasant lea,
> Have glimpses that would make me less forlorn;
> Have sight of Proteus rising from the sea;
> Or hear old Triton blow his wreathed horn.

154. The poem can best be classified as

(A) Petrarchan.

(B) anti-Petrarchan.

(C) deist.

(D) pantheist.

(E) satirical.

155. An understanding of the last two lines is helped most by the knowledge that

(A) the adjective "protean," meaning "variable," is derived from "Proteus."

(B) the prefix "tri-" means "three."

(C) the prefix "pro-" means "for."

(D) Proteus and Triton are sea gods from classical mythology.

(E) Menelaus tells about an encounter with Proteus in Homer's *Odyssey*.

156. Human sacrifice is a theme in

   (A) *Oedipus Rex* by Sophocles.

   (B) *Antigone* by Sophocles.

   (C) *The Eumenides* by Aeschylus.

   (D) *Iphigenia in Aulis* by Euripides.

   (E) *The Dead* by James Joyce.

Questions 157 – 158 refer to the following poem.

> Let observation, with extensive view,
> Survey mankind, from China to Peru;
> Remark each anxious toil, each eager strife,
> And watch the busy scenes of crowded life;
> Then say how hope and fear, desire and hate,   5
> O'erspread with snares the clouded maze of fate,
> Where wav'ring man, betrayed by vent'rous pride
> To tread the dreary paths without a guide,
> As treach'rous phantoms in the mist delude,
> Shuns fancied ills, or chases airy good.   10
> How rarely reason guides the stubborn choice,
> Rules the bold hand, or prompts the suppliant voice;
> How nations sink, by darling schemes oppressed,
> When vengeance listens to the fool's request.
> — from Dr. Samuel Johnson, *The Vanity of Human Wishes*

157. Which of the following statements best summarizes the theme that Johnson expresses in these fourteen lines?

   (A) Because human beings are governed by pride instead of reason, they create many problems for themselves.

   (B) Placing too much faith in human reason leads to tragedy.

   (C) Most of the problems that humanity faces are the result of archaic social institutions and outmoded customs.

(D) In China and Peru, human progress is being held back by religious superstition, while, by implication, England is moving ahead economically because it is governed rationally.

(E) Although there are many problems in the world, through education and technological progress, we will be able to find solutions for these problems.

158. The break in line 10 between "ills" and "or" is referred to as

(A) enjambment.

(B) a troche.

(C) elision.

(D) ellipsis.

(E) a caesura.

Questions 159 – 161 refer to the following selection.

The scene harks back to the fabliaux in its superficial features, but it is more broadly meaningful than any scene in that literature. In the context of the *Prologue's* doctrinal material, we behold not only a magnificently natural creature in domestic squabble; she is also the embodiment of experience ripping out the pages of the book of authority, and of militant feminism fetching traditional masculine domination a healthy blow on the cheek. The symbolism of her position could not have been made secure without the naturalistic style whereby Chaucer creates and then protects it.
— Charles Muscatine, *Chaucer and the French Tradition*

159. The character referred to above is

(A) Criseyde in *Troylus and Criseyde.*

(B) Alison in "The Miller's Tale."

(C) Emelye in "The Knight's Tale."

(D) May in "The Merchant's Tale."

(E) The Wife of Bath.

160. For an example of a fabliau that illustrates the point Muscatine makes in the first sentence, one might refer to

    (A) "The Pardoner's Tale."   (D) "The Monk's Tale."

    (B) "The Nun's Priest's Tale."   (E) "The Knight's Tale."

    (C) "The Reeve's Tale."

161. The most rigorous defense of the unities of time, place, and action is to be found in

    (A) Antonin Artaud's *The Theater and its Double.*

    (B) Dr. Samuel Johnson's *Preface to Shakespeare.*

    (C) Dryden's *An Essay of Dramatic Poesy.*

    (D) T. S. Eliot's *Tradition and the Individual Talent.*

    (E) Sir Philip Sidney's *The Defense of Poesie.*

Questions 162 – 163 refer to the following poem.

> Much have I travell'd in the realms of gold,
> And many goodly states and kingdoms seen;
> Round many western islands have I been
> Which bards in fealty to Apollo hold,
> Oft of one wide expanse had I been told   5
> That deep-brow'd Homer ruled as his demesne;
> Yet did I never breathe its pure serene
> Till I heard Chapman speak out loud and bold:
> Then felt I like some watcher of the skies
> When a new planet swims into his ken;   10
> Or like stout Cortez when with eagle eyes
> He star'd at the Pacific — and all his men
> Look'd at each other with a wild surmise —
> Silent, upon a peak in Darien.

162. The words "fealty" (line 4) and "demesne" (line 6) establish a metaphor derived from

    (A) Ancient Greek city states.

    (B) Plato's *Republic.*

    (C) Aristotle's *Politics.*

    (D) medieval feudalism.

    (E) Rousseau's *The Social Contract.*

163. In line 11, Keats apparently misidentifies the discoverer of the Pacific Ocean. An error of this sort is an example of

    (A) the intentional fallacy.　　(D) poetic justice.

    (B) the pathetic fallacy.　　(E) Romantic irony.

    (C) poetic license.

Questions 164 – 165 refer to the following excerpts.

164. Which excerpt is by Robert Frost?

165. Which excerpt is by Jonathan Edwards?

    (A) I found a dimpled spider, fat and white,
    On a white heal-all, holding up a moth
    Like a white piece of satin cloth —
    Assorted characters of death and blight...

    (B)　　There is a spider, too, in the bathroom, of uncertain lineage, bulbous at the abdomen and drab, whose six-inch mess of web works, works somehow, works miraculously, to keep her alive and me amazed. The web is in a corner behind the toilet, connecting tile wall to tile wall. The house is new, the bathroom immaculate, save for the spider, her web, and the sixteen or so corpses she's tossed to the floor.

    (C)　　The person of Pope is well known not to have been formed by the nices model. He has, in his account of the "Little Club," compared himself to a spider...

(D)   The God that holds you over the pit of hell, much as one holds a spider, or some loathsome insect, over the fire, abhors you and is dreadfully provoked...

(E)   Blasted with sighs, and surrounded with tears,
Hither I come to seek the spring,
And at mine eyes, and at mine ears,
Receive such balms as else cure everything;
But oh, self-traitor, I do bring
The spider love, which transubstantiates all, ...

---

166.   In the plan and cross section of Chartres cathedral the number 3 is all-pervasive. There are the triple entrance portals. The facade rises in three steps from the level of the doorways, through the intermediate story, to the rising towers intended to elevate the thoughts of the worshipers and direct their aspirations heavenward. In the interior there are the three corresponding levels, beginning with the nave arcade, the triforium gallery, and the windowed clerestory.
    — William Fleming, *Arts and Ideas*

Which of the following literary works exhibits a number symbolism in its structure most nearly similar to that described above in the architecture of Chartres cathedral?

(A)   Dante's *Divine Comedy*

(B)   Chaucer's *The Canterbury Tales*

(C)   Milton's *Paradise Lost*

(D)   *Beowulf*

(E)   Boccaccio's *The Decameron*

167.   The corrupt world is the final clue to the meaning of the Fool. He is not of tragic scope. He affirms the dignity of man neither as animal nor angelic reason. Nor has he the ennobling weakness of compassion. He remains a figure of pathos because he is so helpless — helplessly immobilized by a handy-dandy of opposites neither of which he can choose. Nor will he admit of any third ground, the possibility that knavishness might not

be an ultimate, that wisdom might be redeemable, that society might be capable of re-birth. He does not survive his own grim laughter, and disappears for that reason.
— Danby, *The Fool and Handy-Dandy.*

The author of the passage discusses a problem of interpretation in

(A) Chaucer's "The Miller's Tale."

(B) Marlowe's *The Jew of Malta.*

(C) Jonson's *Volpone.*

(D) Shakespeare's *King Lear.*

(E) Webster's *The Duchess of Malfi.*

168. In *The Divine Comedy*, Dante is guided through Hell by

(A) St. Augustine.

(B) St. Jerome.

(C) Beatrice.

(D) Ovid.

(E) Virgil.

169. "One of those writers, of whom there are not a great many in any literature, who have discovered a new way of writing, valid not only for themselves but for others. I should place him... as one of those rare writers who have brought their language up to date."
— T. S. Eliot

In the above passage Eliot is referring to

(A) Mark Twain.

(B) James Joyce.

(C) William Shakespeare.

(D) Geoffrey Chaucer

(E) Edmund Spenser.

170. Which of the following poets reported seeing, as a child, a tree full of angels?

    (A) Geoffrey Chaucer   (D) William Blake

    (B) William Shakespeare   (E) William Wordsworth

    (C) John Milton

Questions 171 – 173 refer to the following poem.

> When my love swears that she is made of truth
> I do believe her, though I know she lies,
> That she might think me some untutored youth,
> Unlearned in the world's false subtleties.
> Thus vainly thinking that she thinks me young.   5
> Although she knows my days are past the best,
> Simply I credit her false-speaking tongue;
> On both sides thus is simple truth suppressed.
> But wherefore says she not she is unjust?
> And wherefore say not I that I am old?   10
> O, love's best habit is in seeming trust,
> And age in love loves not to have years told.
> Therefore I lie with her and she with me,
> And in our faults by lies we flattered be.

171. An editor's footnote to line 13 reads: 13 *lie with* i.e. lie to (with *double entendre*). The footnote implies

    (A) that line 13 contains a misprint and that "with" was probably originally "to."

    (B) that the meaning of "lie with" has changed and that what the poet originally meant is closer to what we would mean today by "lie to."

    (C) that the poet is using the phrase metaphorically, not literally.

    (D) that "lie with" is a pun with intentional ambiguity.

    (E) that the poet was being intentionally obscure.

172. In order for the rhythm of line 4 to be consistent with the metrical pattern in the rest of the poem

    (A) "Unlearned" must be read as three syllables.

    (B) the silent "e" at the end of "false" must be pronounced.

    (C) "subtleties" must be pronounced as two syllables.

    (D) "subtleties" must be pronounced as four syllables.

    (E) the words "in the" must be counted as one unstressed syllable.

173. Which of the following features is essential in classifying this poem as a sonnet?

    (A) It ends with a rhymed couplet.

    (B) It is about erotic love.

    (C) The first twelve lines are divided into three quatrains.

    (D) The tone of the poem is witty and ironic.

    (E) The poem has fourteen lines.

---

174. Which of the following is a satire of religious hypocrisy?

    (A) Molière's *Tartuffe*

    (B) Jonson's *Volpone*

    (C) Wycherley's *The Country-Wife*

    (D) Aristophanes' *The Clouds*

    (E) Sheridan's *The Rivals*

175. For a view of the human condition as totally absurd, one should read

    (A) Tolstoy.   (D) Dante.

    (B) Zola.   (E) Virgil.

    (C) Kafka.

176. Which of the following is an example of a masque?

 (A) Ben Jonson's *Volpone*

 (B) *Everyman*

 (C) Milton's *Comus*

 (D) Shakespeare's *As You Like It*

 (E) Congreve's *The Way of the World*

177.　　"... and then I asked him with my eyes to ask again yes and then he asked me would I yes to say yes my mountain flower and first I put my arms around him yes and drew him down to me so he could feel my breasts all perfume yes and his heart going like mad and yes I said yes I will Yes"

The speaker in the above passage is

 (A) Emma Bovary.

 (B) Anna Karenina.

 (C) Catherine Earnshaw.

 (D) Molly Bloom.

 (E) Becky Sharp.

Questions 178 – 179 refer to the following passage.

```
Avenge O Lord thy slaughter'd Saints, whose bones
    Lie sacatter'd on the Alpin mountains cold,
    Ev'n them who kept thy truth so pure of old
    When all our Fathers worship't Stocks and Stones,
Forget not: in thy book record their groanes            5
    Who were thy Sheep and in their antient Fold
    Slayn by the bloody Piemontese that roll'd
    Mother with Infant down the Rocks. Their moans
The Vales redoubl'd to the Hills, and they
    To Heav'n. Their martyr'd blood and ashes sow    10
    O're all th'Italian fields where still doth sway
The triple Tyrant: that from these may grow
    A hunder'd-fold, who having learnt thy way
    Early may fly the Babylonian wo.
```

178. The "slaughter'd Saints" in line 1 are

    (A) Protestants massacred by Catholics.

    (B) Catholics massacred by Protestants.

    (C) Christians massacred by Moslems.

    (D) Christians massacred by Romans.

    (E) innocent civilians killed in the Napoleonic Wars.

179. Lines 8–10, "Their moans/ The Vales redoubl'd to the Hills, and they/ To Heav'n," illustrates

    (A) irony.   (D) enjambment.

    (B) synesthesia.   (E) sprung rhythm.

    (C) litotes.

---

180.   "He was small in stature, with a furrowed visage, which, as yet, could hardly be termed aged. There was a remarkable intelligence in his features, as of a person who had so cultivated his mental part, that it could not fail to mould the physical to itself and become manifest by unmistakable tokens."

These two sentences describe

    (A) Roger Chillingworth in *The Scarlet Letter*.

    (B) Roderick Usher in *Fall of the House of Usher*.

    (C) Natty Bumpo in *Last of the Mohicans*.

    (D) Jack Potter in *The Bride Comes to Yellow Sky*.

    (E) Giovanni in *Rappacini's Daughter*.

181.   "He lay down on a wide bunk that stretched across the end of the room. In the other end, cracker boxes were made to serve as furniture. They were grouped about the fireplace. A picture from an illustrated weekly was upon the log walls, and three rifles were paralleled on pegs. Equipments

hung on handy projections, and some tin dishes lay upon a small pile of firewood."

The writing style of this passage is most characteristic of American

(A) Naturalism.

(D) Romanticism.

(B) Sentimentalism.

(E) Modernism.

(C) Rodomontadism.

Questions 182 – 183 refer to the following passage.

<pre>
      Of man's first disobedience, and the fruit
      Of that forbidden tree, whose mortal taste
      Brought death into the world, and all our woe,
      With loss of Eden, till one greater Man
      Restore us, and regain the blissful seat,   5
      Sing, Heavenly Muse, that on the secret top
      Of Oreb, or of Sinai, didst inspire
      That shepherd, who first taught the chosen seed
      In the beginning how the Heavens and Earth
      Rose out of Chaos; or if Sion hill   10
      Delight thee more, and Siloa's brook that flowed
      Fast by the oracle of God, I thence
      Invoke thy aid to my adventurous song,
      That with no middle flight intends to soar
      Above the Aonian mount, while it pursues   15
      Things unattempted yet in prose of rhyme.
</pre>

182. The governing verb in this opening sentence is

(A) "restore."

(D) "sing."

(B) "taught."

(E) "invoke."

(C) "delight."

183. The style of this passage can best be described as

(A) blank verse.

(D) Spenserian.

(B) free verse.

(E) syncretic.

(C) iambic tetrameter.

---

184. Whenever I find myself growing grim about the mouth;
whenever it is a damp, drizzly November in my soul;
whenever I find myself involuntarily pausing before coffin
warehouses and bringing up the rear of every funeral I meet;
and especially whenever my hypos get such an upper hand of
me, that it requires a strong moral principle to prevent me
from deliberately stepping into the street, and methodically
knocking people's hats off — then I account it high time
_____.

The passage is completed with the words

(A) "...pause and consider my condition."

(B) "...get to the sea as soon as I can."

(C) "...light out for the Territories."

(D) "...consider the words of Cato."

(E) "...return to the roots I was raised from."

Questions 185 – 186 refer to the following poem.

If the autumn would
End!! If the sweet season,
The late light in the tall trees would
End! If the fragrance, the odor of
Fallen apples, dust on the road,
Water somewhere near, the scent of
Water touching me; if this would end
I could endure the absence in the night,
The hands beyond the reach of hands, the name
Called out and never answered with my name:

The image seen but never seen with sight.
I could endure this all
If autumn ended and the cold light came.

185. An underlying contrast is presented between

    (A) images of light and of darkness.

    (B) images of coolness and of warmth.

    (C) expressions of life and of death.

    (D) sensations of contact and of loss.

    (E) impressions of fall and of winter.

186. The poet implies that

    (A) death would be preferable to his present state.

    (B) he would be more comfortable if he could not experience the everday sensations of life.

    (C) knowing more about the absent person's fate would alleviate his guilt.

    (D) only a return of his absent companion can bring happiness.

    (E) only the passage of time can heal his grief.

---

187. I met the Bishop on the road
    And much said he and I.
    "Those breasts are flat and fallen now,
    Those veins must soon be dry;
    Live in a heavenly mansion,
    Not in some foul sty."

    "Fair and foul are near of kin,
    And fair needs foul," I cried.
    "My friends are gone, but that's a truth
    Nor grave nor bed denied,
    Learned in bodily lowliness
    And in the heart's pride."

"A woman can be proud and stiff
When on love intent;
But love has pitched his mansion in
The place of excrement;
For nothing can be sole or whole
That has not been rent."

The author indicates a belief in all of the following EXCEPT

(A) the paradox that wisdom may reside with fools and beggars.

(B) the presentation and resolution of opposites.

(C) the lack of understanding by representatives of orthodoxy.

(D) the recognition of the destructive potential of self-indulgence.

(E) the necessity of familiarity with suffering.

Questions 188 – 189 refer to the following excerpts.

188. Which is a parody of Albert Camus?

189. Which is a parody of Willa Cather?

(A)   By chance, blew up Perpigan Airport killing 3,000 people including my mother. It was a gloriously sunny day and if it hadn't been for the fact of stepping over the mutilated bodies the walk back to the boat would have been quite agreeable. I whistled to myself, thinking about the way I moved my tongue to vary the notes, and my benign disinterest stretched on to the limbless corpses that were strewn over the runway.

(B)   I took a pull from the bottle. The whiskey was good. It burned my mouth and felt good and warm going down my esophagus and into my stomach. From there it was digested, and went to my kidneys and my bladder and into my intestines, and was good.

(C)   I was just thinking around in my sad backyard, looking at those little drab careless starshaped clumps of crabgrass and beautiful chunks of some old bicycle crying out without words of the American Noon and half a newspaper with an ad about lotion for people with dry skins and dry souls, when my mother opened our frantic banging screen door and shouted, "Gogi Himmelman's here."

(D)   I dropped off a Burlington train at Sweet Water one afternoon last fall to call on Marian Forrester. It was a lovely day. October stained the hills with quiet gold and russet, and scarlet as violent as the blood spilled not far away so many years ago along the banks of the Little Big Horn.

(E)   The room was hot. Glancing round, Guy sensed that all eight of his companions were strangers to each other as well as to himself. Why had he, and they, come? What was his Lordship's motive in inviting this heterogeneous assembly to Motley Hall today?

---

190. In which of the following excerpts is the "I" Thomas Hardy's Jude?

(A)   I have heard that in violent fevers, men, all ignorance, have talked in ancient tongues; and that when the mystery is probed, it turns out always that in their wholly forgotten childhood those ancient tongues had been really spoken in their hearing by some lofty scholars.

(B)   I mean from henceforth to lead a life of extreme seclusion; you must not be surprised, nor must you doubt my friendship, if my door is closed to you. You must suffer me to go my own dark way. I have brought on myself a punishment and a danger that I cannot name.

(C)   I am to blame — more than you think. I was quite aware that you did not suspect till within the last meeting or two what I was feeling about you. I admit that our meeting as strangers prevented a sense of relationship, and that it was a sort of subterfuge to avail myself of you. But don't you think I deserve a little consideration for concealing my wrong, very wrong, sentiments, since I couldn't help having them?

(D)   I am a stranger, and have been a wanderer, sorely against my will. I have met with grievous mishaps by sea and land, and have been long held in bonds among the heathen-folk.

(E)   At first I'd a sor o' feeling come across me now and then, as if you might be changed into the gold again; for some times, turn my head which way I would, I seemed to see the gold, and I thought I should be glad if I could feel it.

191. Stick your patent name on a signboard
     brother — all over — going west — young man
     Tintex — Japalac — Certain-teed Overalls ads
     and land sakes! under the new playbill ripped
     in the guaranteed corner — see Bert Williams what?
     Minstrels when you steal a chicken just
     save me the wing, for if it isn't
     Erie it ain't for miles around a
     Mazda — and the telegraphic night coming on Thomas

     The language of this poem is an example of

     (A) stream-of-consciousness.   (D) free association.

     (B) free-form.   (E) the New York School.

     (C) beat poetry.

Questions 192 – 193 refer to the following passage.

   Had (he) written his own life, in conformity with the opinion which
he has given, that every man's life may be best written by himself; had he
employed in the preservation of his own history, that clearness of narration
and elegance of language in which he has embalmed so many eminent
persons, the world would probably have had the most perfect example of
biography that was ever exhibited.

192. Consistent with the author's established attitude toward his subject, it is
     most likely that he will attribute the subject's failure to write an autobi-
     ography to

     (A) his uneventful life.

     (B) his inexperience in biographical forms.

     (C) his lack of diligence.

     (D) his belief that no one would be really interested.

     (E) his egocentricity.

193. The author of this passage is referring to

    (A) Benjamin Franklin.   (D) Samuel Johnson.

    (B) Izaak Walton.   (E) William Shakespeare.

    (C) John Milton.

Questions 194 – 195 refer to the following excerpt.

> Meanwhile the South, rising with dabbled
>   wings,
> A sable cloud athwart the welkin flings,
> That swilled more liquor than it could contain,
> And, like a drunkard, gives it up again.

194. The governing device in this excerpt is

    (A) a parallelism between the South and a bird-like creature.

    (B) a metaphor between a drunk cloud and a drunkard.

    (C) an allusion to revolution in nature.

    (D) a simile, in the last line.

    (E) a paradox in the inability of natural objects to become drunk.

195. This excerpt most closely resembles a famous passage in

    (A) *Paradise Lost.*

    (B) "The Love Song of J. Alfred Prufrock."

    (C) "The Tiger."

    (D) "The Rape of the Lock."

    (E) "Stopping by Woods on a Snowy Evening."

Questions 196 – 197 refer to the following passage.

Now she was absolutely alone. Her father had long been dead, and his armchair lay in the attic, covered with dust and lame of one leg. She got thinner and plainer, and when people met her in the street they did not look at her as they used to, and did not smile to her; evidently her best years were over and left behind, and now a new sort of life had begun for her, which did not bear thinking about. In the evening Olenka sat in the porch, and heard the band playing and the fireworks popping in the Tivoli, but now the sound stirred no response. She looked into her yard without interest, thought of nothing, wished for nothing, and afterwards, when night came on she went to bed and dreamed of her empty yard. She ate and drank as it were unwillingly.

And what was worst of all, she had no opinons of any sort. She saw the objects about her and understood what she saw, but could not form any opinion about them, and did not know what to talk about. And how awful it is not to have any opinions! One sees a bottle, for instance, or the rain, or a peasant driving in his cart, but what the bottle is for, or the rain, or the peasant, and what is the meaning of it, one can't say, and could not even for a thousand roubles. When she had Kukin, or Pustovalov, or the veterinary surgeon, Olenka could explain everything, and give her opinion about anything you like, but now there was the same emptiness in her brain and in her heart as there was in her yard outside. And it was as harsh and as bitter as wormwood in the mouth.

196. What is the author's attitude toward Olenka?

(A) Sarcastic

(D) Sympathetic

(B) Patronizing

(E) Bitter

(C) Contemptuous

197. What does Chekhov imply about opinions?

(A) There is no difference between intuitive understanding and the ability to express one's ideas.

(B) Opinions are often nothing more than a thoughtless repetition of other people.

(C) Social oppression is often a cause of alienation from life and from knowledge.

(D) One must contemplate "meaningful" ideas in order to formulate any kind of valid opinion.

(E) Contact with people often causes a loss of understanding of self.

Questions 198 – 199 refer to the following passage.

For, while he fascinated many, there were not a few who distrusted him. He was very nearly blackballed at a West End club of which his birth and social position fully entitled him to become a member, and it was said that on one occasion, when he was brought by a friend into the smoking-room of the Churchill, the Duke of Berwick and another gentleman got up in a market manner and went out. Curious stories became current about him after he had passed his twenty-fifth year. It was rumoured that he had been seen brawling with foreign sailors in a low den in the distant parts of Whitechapel, and that he consorted with thieves and coiners and knew the mysteries of their trade. His extraordinary absences became notorious, and, when he used to reappear again in society, men would whisper to each other in corners, or pass him with a sneer, or look at him with cold searching eyes, as though they were determined to discover his secret.

198. The individual described above is being criticized by his contemporaries for

(A) committing immoral acts.

(B) not observing the behavioral codes of his birthright.

(C) being a hypocrite.

(D) engaging in social behavior with the underclasses.

(E) attempting to engage with both classes at the same time.

199. In its fascination with "secret lives," the author of this passage is reflecting

(A) the emerging study of psychology at the beginning of the twentieth century.

(B) the rebellion against Victorian restraints through an interest in "novel experiences" during the English Decadence of the 1890s.

(C) the possibility of multiple personalities as explored in the 1930s and 1940s.

(D) the study of the nature of evil popular in the early to mid-1800s.

(E) the disillusionment with the upper classes as a result of the Industrial Revolution in the mid-1800s.

Questions 200 – 204 refer to the following stanzas.

Lullay, lullay, litel child, why weepestou so sore?
Needes most thou weepe, it was y-yarked thee
    yore
Evere to live in sorwe, and siken everemore,
As thine eldren dide er this, whil they alives wore.
Lullay, lullay, litel child, child, lullay, lullow,   5
Into uncouth world ycomen so art thou.

Beestes and thise fowles, the fishes in the flood,
and eech sheef alives, ymaked of boon and blood,
Whan they cometh to the world they dooth hemself some
good —
Al but the wrecche brol that is of Adames   10
    blood.
Lullay, lullay, litel child, to care art thou bimet:
Thous noost nat this worldes wilde bifore thee is yset.

200. "Wrecche brol" in line 10 is best understood as meaning

(A) unhappy brood.

(B) miserable composure.

(C) rich broth (of Adam's blood).

(D) wretched brat.

(E) wrenching misery.

201. Though the content of this stanza may seem inappropriate, it represents a

    (A) love lyric.

    (B) love complaint.

    (C) signature tune.

    (D) lullaby.

    (E) Heatho-Bardic Lay.

202. According to this selection, humans differ from animals in that

    (A) only humans can find Christian salvation.

    (B) only humans can truly experience high and low points in life.

    (C) only humans are predestined to suffer.

    (D) both animals and humans live in sorrow.

    (E) animals are biblically proscribed to serve humans.

203. "As thine eldren dide er this, whil they alives wore," (line 4) might be paraphrased:

    (A) Your ancestors suffered this way too.

    (B) Suffering is the oldest thing in the world.

    (C) You will suffer more as you get older.

    (D) Parents suffer most because they witness their children's pain.

    (E) Your children will suffer just like you.

204. The implication is that the speaker is not surprised at the "litel child's" crying because

    (A) that is a natural reaction to pain, much as in the animal kingdom.

    (B) that is what the child's ancestors have had to do since the days of Adam.

    (C) that is the condition of humankind because of Original Sin.

(D) children are trusting by nature, and do not understand the vagaries of life.

(E) all Christians are "pilgrims" in an "uncouth world."

---

205.   When the friend shows his inmost heart to his friend… then deem me a monster, for the symbol beneath which I have lived and die! I look around me, and lo! on every visage a Black Veil.

The "black veil" is a metaphor for

(A) the inevitability of death.

(B) the "veil" that separates one person from another.

(C) the need to separate oneself from the sin of one's neighbors.

(D) the evil that lurked in the speaker's heart.

(E) the stained soul from Original Sin.

Questions 206 – 207 refer to the following stanza.

When a deed is done for Freedom, through the broad earth's aching breast
Runs a thrill of joy prophetic, trembling on from east to west,
And the slave, where'er he cowers, feels the soul within him climb
Of a century bursts full-blossomed on the thorny stem of Time.

206.   The crisis which this first stanza of a long poem addresses is

(A) the Civil War.   (D) the Annexation of Texas.

(B) the First World War.   (E) the Barbary Piracy.

(C) the War of 1812.

207.   The stanza is governed by

(A) awkward use of metaphor.

(B) personification of geography.

(C) didacticism.

(D) biblical reference.

(E) grammatical parallelism.

Questions 208 – 209 refer to the following passage.

(Her) career has covered less ground, for she began far above Main Street. What she tried to do at the start was to imitate the superficial sophistication of Edith Wharton and Henry James — a deceptive thing, apparently realistic in essence, but actually as conventional as table manners or the professional buffooneries of a fashionable rector. She had extraordinary skill as a writer, and so her imitation was scarcely to be distinguished from the original, but in the course of time she began to be aware of its hollowness. Then she turned to first-hand representation — to pictures of the people she actually knew.

208. The author of this passage states

(A) that the writer was satisfied with imitation early in her career.

(B) that the writer was inept at imitating the writing styles of others.

(C) that the writer switched from imitation to first-hand representation.

(D) that all of her attempts at imitation were really first-hand representation.

(E) that she was too daring early in her career.

209. This quote refers to

(A) Edith Wharton.

(B) Gertrude Stein.

(C) Virginia Woolf.

(D) Willa Cather.

(E) Marjorie Kinnan Rawlings.

Questions 210 – 213 refer to the following poem.

Tears, idle tears, I know not what they mean,
Tears from the depth of some divine despair
Rise in the heart, and gather to the eyes,
In looking on the happy Autumn-fields,
And thinking of the days that are no more.

Fresh as the first beam glittering on a sail,
That brings our friends up from the underworld,
Sad as the last which reddens over one
That sinks with all we love below the verge;
So sad, so fresh, the days that are no more.

Ah, sad and strange as in dark summer dawns
The earliest pipe of half-awaken'd birds
To dying ears, when unto dying eyes
The casement slowly grows a glimmering square;
So sad, so strange, the days that are no more.

Dear as remember'd kisses after death,
And sweet as those by hopeless fancy feign'd
On lips that are for others; deep as love,
Deep as first love, and wild with all regret;
O Death in Life, the days that are no more.

210.   The poem may be classified as

(A)   a prolonged metaphor.   (D)   a lengthened parallelism.

(B)   a Frottola.   (E)   an allegory.

(C)   an extended simile.

211.   To the poet, "Death in Life" could best be described as a result of

(A)   having lived too long.

(B)   having regretted too much.

(C)   having most of life's intense emotions in the past.

(D)   not being capable of experiencing intense emotion.

(E)   enveloping loneliness.

212. The poet's philosophical response to life is similar to

    (A) Poe's.
    (B) Swinburne's.
    (C) Rossetti's.
    (D) Coleridge's.
    (E) Wordsworth's.

213. The poem is written in

    (A) mimetic verse.
    (B) elegiac verse.
    (C) accentual verse.
    (D) free verse.
    (E) blank verse.

Questions 214 – 215 refer to the following poem.

> O, I have bought the mansion of a love,
> But not possess'd it, and, though I am sold,
> Not yet enjoy'd: so tedious is this day
> As in the night before some festival
> To an impatient child that hath new robes   5
> And may not wear them.

214. "Mansion of a love" is a metaphor for

    (A) an emotional commitment.
    (B) an engagement.
    (C) a marriage.
    (D) an extramarital affair.
    (E) a reawakening of love.

215. In lines 2 and 3, the speaker

    (A) compares herself to a slave.

    (B) refers to herself as a woman with a fine dowry.

    (C) says she has not enjoyed the relationship thus far.

    (D) compares herself to a commodity that can bring pleasure.

    (E) refers to herself as an emotion waiting.

216.　FAUSTUS　　　　　Why, dost thou think that Faustus shall be damned?
　　　MEPHISTOPHELES　Ay, of necessity, for here's the scroll
　　　　　　　　　　　In which thou hast given thy soul to Lucifer.
　　　FAUSTUS　　　　　Ay, and body too; but what of that?
　　　　　　　　　　　Thinkst thou that Faustus is so fond to imagine
　　　　　　　　　　　That after this life there is any pain?
　　　　　　　　　　　No, these are trifles and mere old wives' tales.

Faustus implies that

(A) affection blinds a person to pain.

(B) affection cannot guard against pain in the afterlife.

(C) he does not believe there is an afterlife at all.

(D) he does not believe that the afterlife is painful.

(E) selling one's soul to the Devil is the most painful thing a person can do.

217.　The caged bird sings
　　　With a fearful trill
　　　Of things unknown
　　　But longed for still
　　　And his tune is heard
　　　On the distant hill
　　　For the caged bird
　　　Sings of freedom.

The above excerpt is from Maya Angelou's *I Know Why the Caged Bird Sings*. The caged bird most likely represents what?

(A) Psychological imprisonment

(B) Literal imprisonment

(C) A bird in a cage

(D) Social and racial oppression

(E) (A), (B), and (D)

218.   In *Atlas Shrugged,* I explain the philosophical, psychological and moral meaning of the men who value their own lives and of the men who don't. I show that the first are Prime Movers of mankind and that the second are metaphysical killers, working for an opportunity to become social ones.

In the above excerpt from the forward to her novel *We The Living*, Ayn Rand points to a persistent theme in her work that can best be described as

(A) altruism.

(B) egoism.

(C) epicurianism.

(D) decadence.

(E) naturalism.

Questions 219 – 221 refer to the following excerpt from Vonnegut's *Mother Night*.

About that Purgatory of mine in New York City: I was in it for fifteen years. I disappeared from Germany at the end of the Second World War. I reappeared, unrecognized, in Greenwich Village. There I rented a depressing attic apartment with rats squeaking and scrabbing in the walls. I continued to inhabit that attic until a month ago, when I was brought to Israel for trial.

There was a pleasant thing about my ratty attic: the back window of it overlooked a little private park, a little Eden formed by joined back yards. That Park, that Eden, was walled off from the streets by houses on all sides.

It was big enough for children to play hide-and-seek in.

I often heard a cry from that little Eden, a child's cry that never failed to make me stop and listen. It was the sweetly mournful cry that meant a game of hide-and-seek was over, that those still hiding were to come out of hiding and that it was time to go home.

The cry was this: "Olly-olly-ox-in-free."

And I, hiding from many people who might want to hurt or kill me, often longed for someone to give that cry for me, to end my endless game of hide and seek with a sweet and mournful "Olly-olly-ox-in-free."

219. The speaker in the passage is most likely a former

   (A) Nazi.

   (B) U. S. foot soldier.

   (C) Prisoner of war.

   (D) Marine.

   (E) Policeman.

220. The figures in the garden, "that Eden," represent what kind of longing for the speaker?

   (A) Material ambition

   (B) Sexual desire

   (C) A return to a state of innocence

   (D) Legal vindication

   (E) A redress of grievances

221. The prose style of the passage would best be characterized as

   (A) ornamental.

   (B) plain.

   (C) experimental.

   (D) epic.

   (E) derivative.

---

222.   At that moment when the world around him melted away, when he stood alone like a star in the heavens, he was overwhelmed by a feeling of icy despair, but he was more firmly himself than ever. That was the last shudder of his awakening, the last pains of birth. Immediately he moved on again, and began to walk quickly and impatiently, no longer homewards, no longer to his father, no longer looking backwards.

   Which of the choices below best describes the theme of this passage from Herman Hesse's novel *Siddhartha*?

   (A) The individual's struggle for autonomy

   (B) The search for meaning in community

   (C) The pain of childbirth

(D)   The quest to fight evil

(E)   The fear of the unknown

223.   The two young Guardians salute us, raising three fingers to the rims of their berets. Such tokens are accorded to us. They are supposed to show respect, because of the nature of our service.

        We produce our passes, from the zippered pockets in our wide sleeves, and they are inspected and stamped. One man goes into the right-hand pillbox, to punch our numbers into the Compuchek.

Based on this passage, what best describes the setting of Margaret Atwood's *The Handmaid's Tale*?

(A)   A court setting in the distant past

(B)   A futuristic, totalitarian-militaristic society

(C)   World War II

(D)   The American Civil War

(E)   The present

Questions 224 – 225 refer to the following passage

        Notwithstanding his generally realistic outlook and his practical bent, he is a moral idealist, far ahead of his age in his sense of human decency, and, at times, a mystic and a day-dreamer—or, more accurately, a night-dreamer—who is uncommonly sensitive to the presence of divine beauty in nature. He is, finally, the good Bad Boy whom Americans have always idolized in one form or another. And, though he is exposed to as much evil in human nature as young Goodman Brown had seen, Huck is saved from Brown's pessimistic gloom by his sense of humor and, what is more crucial, by his sense of humanity.

224.   The passage above best adheres to which school of literary theory?

(A)   Psychoanalytic theory

(B)   New Criticism

(C) Archetypal theory

(D) Historical-biographical theory

(E) Reader-response theory

225. The author of the passage is describing a novel written by _____ .

(A) Herman Melville

(B) Mark Twain

(C) Nathaniel Hawthorne

(D) Henry James

(E) John Steinbeck

Question 226 refers to a criticism of the following lines.

> Thy beauty shall no more be found,
> Nor, in they marble vault, shall sound
> My echoing song; then worms shall try
> That long preserved virginity,
> And your quaint honor turn to dust,
> And into ashes all my lust.

This statement, in even sharper contrast with the gentle cajolery of the first stanza, is brutal—even coarse—in its explicitness. The "marble vault" is a thinly disguised vaginal metaphor suggesting, perhaps, both rigor mortis and the fleshless pelvis of the skeleton. "My echoing song" and the sensual meanings of the lines following, are clear enough. From the eternal burning of a vegetable passion, in the face of reality, we see that all love must at last end in ashes—just as all chastity must end, the same as sexual profligacy, in dust.

226. The critical exploration of the stanza is best placed within which theoretical approach?

(A) Feminist theory

(B) Reader-response theory

(C) Deconstructionist theory

(D) Psychoanalytic theory

(E) Marxist theory

227. For the social hierarchy under God, the Romantics substituted an esthetic hierarchy, based on the prerogatives of the man of feeling, the immoralist, the artist, the confidence trickster. The Romantics could easily dismiss the Lord of Creation for a God of Love, Sympathetic Nature, or the Demon of the Absolute. Instead of Bunyan's plodding Christian earning his heavenly reward by imitating the life of Christ, they invoked a monstrous egoist who lavishly loved woman, knowledge, power, or freedom more than the world, and who, when frustrated, sought to impoverish it by his suicide.

This passage centers upon the narrative trope of _____.

(A) theme

(B) allegory

(C) bricolage

(D) symbol

(E) the unreliable narrator

228. During the daytime he did not want to show himself at the window, out of consideration for his parents, but he could not crawl very far around the few square yards of floor space he had, nor could he bear lying quietly at rest all during the night, while he was fast losing interest he had ever taken in food, so that for mere recreation he had formed the habit of crawling crisscross over the walls and ceiling. He especially enjoyed hanging suspended from the ceiling; it was much better than lying on the floor; one could breathe more freely; one's body swung and rocked lightly; and in the almost blissful absorption induced by this suspension it could happen to his surprise that he let go and fell plump on the floor.

From the following passage, it appears that "he" is

(A) an acrobat.

(B) a snake.

(C) loved by his family.

(D) confused.

(E) None of the above.

Questions 229 – 230 refer to the following passage.

Until next Sunday when we are walking through the flea market on Maxwell Street and *there!* Lying on the street next to some tool bits, and platform shoes with the heels all squashed, and a florescent green wicker wastebasket, and aluminum foil, and hubcaps, and a pink shag rug, and windshield wiper blades, and dusty mason jars, and a coffee can full of rusty nails. *There!* Where? Two Mattel boxes. One with the "Career Gal" ensemble, snappy black and white business suit, three-quarter-length sleeve jacket with kick-pleat skirt, red sleeveless shell, gloves, pumps, and matching hat included. The other, "Sweet Dreams," dreamy pink-and-white plaid nightgown and matching robe, lace-trimmed slippers, hair-brush and hand mirror included. How much? Please, please, please, please, please, please, please, until they say okay.

229. What are the items that the protagonists of this passage so desire?

(A) Platform shoes

(B) Rusty nails

(C) A business suit and skirt

(D) A pair of dolls

(E) A hair-brush and a hand mirror

230. From the tone of the passage, how do the protagonists appear to feel about the items they have described?

(A) Indifferent   (D) Pleased

(B) Annoyed   (E) Obsessed

(C) Saddened

GRE LITERATURE IN ENGLISH

Practice Test 3
Answer Key

1.	(C)	26.	(C)	51.	(D)	76.	(D)
2.	(B)	27.	(A)	52.	(B)	77.	(C)
3.	(B)	28.	(D)	53.	(E)	78.	(C)
4.	(A)	29.	(C)	54.	(B)	79.	(C)
5.	(D)	30.	(B)	55.	(C)	80.	(A)
6.	(D)	31.	(D)	56.	(C)	81.	(C)
7.	(E)	32.	(E)	57.	(D)	82.	(C)
8.	(D)	33.	(C)	58.	(C)	83.	(C)
9.	(B)	34.	(C)	59.	(D)	84.	(D)
10.	(B)	35.	(B)	60.	(D)	85.	(B)
11.	(A)	36.	(E)	61.	(C)	86.	(C)
12.	(B)	37.	(C)	62.	(D)	87.	(D)
13.	(D)	38.	(B)	63.	(C)	88.	(C)
14.	(B)	39.	(E)	64.	(E)	89.	(E)
15.	(C)	40.	(D)	65.	(D)	90.	(D)
16.	(D)	41.	(D)	66.	(D)	91.	(C)
17.	(C)	42.	(E)	67.	(C)	92.	(C)
18.	(B)	43.	(C)	68.	(D)	93.	(B)
19.	(E)	44.	(A)	69.	(D)	94.	(C)
20.	(D)	45.	(D)	70.	(C)	95.	(C)
21.	(E)	46.	(C)	71.	(C)	96.	(D)
22.	(D)	47.	(D)	72.	(D)	97.	(B)
23.	(A)	48.	(D)	73.	(C)	98.	(C)
24.	(D)	49.	(B)	74.	(C)	99.	(A)
25.	(E)	50.	(E)	75.	(C)	100.	(D)

101.	(D)	136.	(E)	171.	(D)	206.	(A)
102.	(D)	137.	(D)	172.	(A)	207.	(C)
103.	(C)	138.	(E)	173.	(E)	208.	(C)
104.	(E)	139.	(C)	174.	(A)	209.	(D)
105.	(A)	140.	(B)	175.	(C)	210.	(C)
106.	(C)	141.	(A)	176.	(C)	211.	(C)
107.	(B)	142.	(B)	177.	(D)	212.	(E)
108.	(D)	143.	(C)	178.	(A)	213.	(E)
109.	(A)	144.	(A)	179.	(D)	214.	(C)
110.	(C)	145.	(E)	180.	(A)	215.	(D)
111.	(B)	146.	(C)	181.	(A)	216.	(D)
112.	(D)	147.	(D)	182.	(D)	217.	(E)
113.	(D)	148.	(E)	183.	(A)	218.	(B)
114.	(C)	149.	(B)	184.	(B)	219.	(A)
115.	(D)	150.	(D)	185.	(D)	220.	(C)
116.	(D)	151.	(D)	186.	(C)	221.	(B)
117.	(D)	152.	(C)	187.	(D)	222.	(A)
118.	(D)	153.	(E)	188.	(A)	223.	(B)
119.	(D)	154.	(D)	189.	(D)	224.	(C)
120.	(D)	155.	(D)	190.	(C)	225.	(B)
121.	(A)	156.	(D)	191.	(D)	226.	(D)
122.	(A)	157.	(A)	192.	(C)	227.	(B)
123.	(D)	158.	(E)	193.	(D)	228.	(E)
124.	(D)	159.	(E)	194.	(D)	229.	(D)
125.	(D)	160.	(C)	195.	(B)	230.	(E)
126.	(C)	161.	(C)	196.	(D)		
127.	(D)	162.	(D)	197.	(B)		
128.	(A)	163.	(C)	198.	(B)		
129.	(A)	164.	(A)	199.	(B)		
130.	(D)	165.	(D)	200.	(D)		
131.	(A)	166.	(A)	201.	(D)		
132.	(C)	167.	(D)	202.	(C)		
133.	(D)	168.	(E)	203.	(A)		
134.	(D)	169.	(A)	204.	(C)		
135.	(D)	170.	(D)	205.	(B)		

GRE LITERATURE IN ENGLISH

Detailed Explanations of Answers

1. **(C)**
This is close to Sartre, and to his borrowing from Descartes: "I think, therefore, I exist." Meaning is determined by our actions, not from some intrinsic force. The other four answers can be eliminated because existence is not the most significant force in those tenets.

2. **(B)**
This sentence is from *Emma*. Austen's attention to domestic details is evident here. Flaubert's Emma Bovary (A) is not a privileged girl, and Cather (C) normally depicted the lives of immigrant families. The description does not suit a Dickensian character (D), and although Fitzgerald's Daisy (E) is also a sheltered girl, she is older than twenty-one.

3. **(B)**
The poet implies that she has NOT left him any hope, because "dark despair around benights me." Before this he states that no one would grieve as long as there was some hope—some star of light—but "nae cheerfu' twinkle lights" him at all.

4. **(A)**
The poet presents a somewhat unexpected and sympathetic view of their affair. He could not have avoided falling in love with Nancy, for "nothing could resist my Nancy," and he therefore does not blame himself (his "partial fancy"). The heartbreak was inevitable, or so is the implication.

5.   **(D)**
     The poem is written by Robert Burns, the popularizer of "the Guid Scots Tongue." It does not strain at archaism, as does Spenser's poetry (B), nor is its rhyme dependent on ancient Germanic pronunciations, as is Chaucer's (A).

6.   **(D)**
     This is from the title of an essay by Buchanan (1871) which criticized Swinburne, Morris, and Rossetti for praising each others' work as part of their "Mutual Admiration School." Swinburne, of course, had often been criticized for a decadent and pronounced attention to sensuality.

7.   **(E)**
     Note that "Petition for Redress" is a thematic clue. The reference to the Prince as a "Tyrant" is also a famous part of the *Declaration of Independence*.

8.   **(D)**
     The reign of James I is a clue to historical placement. The document, signed by all the male Pilgrims, was an agreement that they would abide by whatever decisions were made according to a majority vote.

9.   **(B)**
     The Greek love of Classical Argument is evident here in the phrasing. This is, of course, one of Plato's famous dialogues.

10. **(B)**
     The dedication to self-improvement and attention to the details of nature are typical elements in this period. The biblical syntax bespeaks the poet's Puritan progenitors. (A) was a period marked by the embracing of scientific thought, while period (C) was marked by disillusionment. There is nothing in the passage which suggests a return to Classical values (D). The Cavalier poets (E), such as Robert Herrick, reacted to the overwrought excesses of Romanticism.

11. **(A)**
     The soul is compared to a molting shellfish—as the living organism grows ever-larger vaults and domes with which to enclose its expanding flesh, and leaving the old shell behind on the sand. Answer (B) is used to represent the passage of time. (C) and (D) depend on literal interpretations of the first line.

While the word "temple" is used in the poem, it is not meant to represent the soul (E).

12. **(B)**

From "The Chambered Nautilus," this is a classic New England contemplation of the higher responses possible in human nature. This poem does not contain any of the dark imagery usually utilized by Poe (A). Whittier (C) often invokes pastoral images in his poetry. Longfellow (D) often celebrated physical accomplishments, while Channing (E), as founder of the Unitarian church, often wrote about the injustice of slavery.

13. **(D)**

The poet himself described it as "the half-serious rhyme." Qualifiers such as "not that" and "indeed" contribute to this tone, as does the rather clipped rhyme in this stanza. There is nothing to imply that Julia's "consent" indicated her victory [eliminate (A) and (B)], yet at the same time, the author finds Julia a bit naive [though (E) is still not the correct choice].

14. **(B)**

Ottava rima has 8 iambic lines rhyming *abababcc*. Although the poem consists of five-foot lines, trochaic pentameter (A) is a line with the stress on every first syllable on the foot, rather than on the second syllable (as with the iamb).

15. **(C)**

This passage is typical of Byron's interest in women, romance, and romantic conquest. The "tears gushing" is more evidence of the grand displays of emotion common in Byron's poetry.

16. **(D)**

This is from Keats' "Ode on a Grecian Urn." Keats' poetry is placed on a level with Wordsworth's in demonstrating the best Romantic craftsmanship. Shakespeare (A) and Milton (E) wrote in a different era than Keats. Rossetti (B) utilized supernatural imagery more than Keats did, while Browning's (C) occasional discordance separated him from his Victorian peers.

17. **(C)**

The basic connection developed in this poem is between the murderer and "all men." Just as the murderer had killed the thing he loved, so do all men, usually in much more subtle ways. Answer (A) connects the murderer's deeds with only some men, while (B), (D), and (E) describe connections that do not actually exist in the poem.

18.   **(B)**

Though the wretched man is eaten by "teeth of flame" in the "pit of shame," it is a spiritual Hell that is more likely to engulf the insensitive person while he and his victim are alive. "All men kill the thing they love," but the instruments of death range from "a sword" to "a flattering word."

19.   **(E)**

This is from "The Ballad of Reading Gaol." Wilde's exposure of hypocrisy differs from Hardy's (A) works, which are marked with a social determinism. Lindsay (B) usually wrote in a lyrical style. Coleridge (C) wrote in a purely Romantic mode, and Owen (D) is best known for his antiwar poetry.

20.   **(D)**

Based in tense emotion, they are considered to represent the most elemental lyrical nature of poetry, and, because of the repetition, they are considered refrains. Synecdoche (A) is a technique in which a part is used to represent the whole. Pararhyme (B) is a type of rhyme in which the consonant sounds match but the vowel sounds do not. Tone-color (E) is a general musical reference to the pitch of a sound made by a musical instrument or voice.

21.   **(E)**

While pseudonyms were standard, the satire "The Rape of the Lock" required special attention to anonymity. Pope utilizes the name Zephalinda to describe the main character in (A). Poems (C) and (D) utilize a variety of proper names, while (B) utilizes the two names in the title.

22.   **(D)**

This passage is from *Table Talk*. It is precisely because Coleridge believes Shakespeare's writings are not based in locale, political affiliation, or religious identification that he considers the Bard's works to have been equally understandable to both Shakespeare's educated contemporaries and the succeeding generations of readers.

23. **(A)**

In this poem, "the god of shepherds" is named Tityrus, really Chaucer, to whom he wishes to pay homage. (B), (C), and (E) need not be achieved by the use of archaic language, while the author did, in fact, live almost two centuries after Chaucer had died.

24. **(D)**

The god Phoebus is associated with the passage of the day—a clue here to the paraphrase. The other answers rely on a misinterpretation of the word "race" as a competition.

25. **(E)**

This passage is from the *Shepheardes Calendar*. Pastoral elements and archaisms [sometimes criticized as being forced—as opposed to Chaucer's poetry (A)] are strong indications. Translations of Dante (B) are rarely so obscure in syntax. Caedmon (C) in fact predated Chaucer, while Marlowe (D) often translated the works of ancient Latin poets.

26. **(C)**

This passage is from "On a Political Prisoner." The word "cell" in the first stanza is not the only clue. "Bitterness," an abundance of time, "popular enmity," and "blind and leader of the blind" all contrast with the freedom of the bird of her youth.

27. **(A)**

The poet's central question is whether the woman recalled the "years before her mind/ Became a bitter, an abstract thing." He wonders if the feeding bird has caused this recollection—as the poet remembers her.

28. **(D)**

Note the typical Yeatsian lyrical voyage between the exuberant expansiveness of nature (lofty rock/cloudy canopy), and the detailed particularness (ate its bit). Stevens (A) often wrote about the lack of spirituality of modern life, while Stein (B) wrote experimental prose. The jarring violence of the passage does not match the more introspective voices of Keats (C) and Frost (E).

29. **(C)**

Passages (A) and (B) are not as contemplative as the first passage. (D) starts in the same tone as the original, but continued reading reveals it to be a satire of the first passage. (E) does not utilize the first-person as the original, so (C) is the best choice.

30.   **(B)**

This passage is from his *Journal*. Remember that the author was a minister. This helps explain the moral tone and didactic nature, even of this diary entry. Thoreau (A) was contemplative, but also isolated. Holmes (C) wrote in a lighter tone than found in the initial passage. Parkman (D) and Byrd (E) were historical writers.

31.   **(D)**

Curiously, Chaucer's language, like the Franklin's, has been praised for its directness, its "bare and plain" talk. It is this characteristic, among others, that sets Chaucer aside from his more florid contemporaries. The Knight (A), the Friar (E), and Chanticleer (B) speak in a much less modest tone than the narrator of the passage, while the Miller (C) is not apologetic.

32.   **(E)**

It is pronounced, "spek-eh." Whereas the final *e* of a word is silent in Modern English, it was pronounced in Middle English in verse if it was necessary to give the line an extra unstressed syllable.

33.   **(C)**

It means uneducated—this is reinforced by the rest of the passage. The Franklin, although modest, speaks with an apolitical common sense that serves as a contrast to the more provocative tales.

34.   **(C)**

Although this might be a matter of simple recall, the non-Italian names (note "Venice") could be eliminated [(A), (D), and (E)]. One might also think of the convention in comedic plays of a character referring to him or herself in the third person to deceive another.

35.   **(B)**

The play is by Ben Jonson, 1606. The reference to Venice in the passage allows one to eliminate the answers in which an Italian setting cannot be inferred from the title [(C), (D), and (E)].

36. **(E)**
This is from *Hamlet,* Act II, scene ii. This is from Hamlet's famous soliloquy in which he attacks himself for lacking the courage to avenge his father's death, but ultimately decides to stage a play in order to determine whether Claudius is indeed guilty of the murder of Hamlet's father.

37. **(C)**
This is from *The Life of Samuel Johnson.* The detailed, accurate, almost note-taking quality should be a clue to the famous biographer's authorship. Pepys (A) kept detailed diaries but did not keep company with men of literature. The tone is a bit too lofty for Franklin (D) and although Burke (E) was a friend of Johnson and Boswell, he did not write about his time in Johnson's Literary Club.

38. **(B)**
This is from *An Essay Concerning Human Understanding.* The political and philosophical scope of the author's concerns should give a clue to its origin. The empiricist ideas do not match the philosophies of Pope (A), Ruskin (C), or Burke (D).

39. **(E)**
This is from *Wordsworth.* The eye of the literary critic is obviously at work. References locate the piece more precisely as to time. Dryden (C) preceded Wordsworth, while Coleridge (A) and Goethe (B) were contemporaries. John Newman (D) was a clergyman known for his oratory.

40. **(D)**
This is from Huxley's *Science and Culture.* The other four works promoted the idea of aesthetics and "art for art's sake," a phrase actually taken from Pater's work.

41. **(D)**
Social knowledge and critical commentary are emphasized in this short passage. These are qualities that make authorship by most of the other choices doubtful.

42. **(E)**
This is from *Divinity School Address.* Puritanical origin (evil and weak man) and New England Renaissance belief in the unbounded moral potential

of man should be clues here. Thoreau (A) spoke more of man's value to his fellow man rather than virtue, Freneau (B) is a satirist, while the tone of the passage does not match Poe (C) or Lincoln (D).

43.   **(C)**
While the exuberance at the beginning of the passage may seem out of character, the historical concern and concentration on individual psychology are characteristic of Hawthorne. E. B. White (B) and Emerson (E) wrote with a gentler tone than indicated in the passage. The narrator does seem to have an intensity that matches Poe (A), but Poe's narrators do not generally have an interest in historical figures.

44.   **(A)**
This is from "King Arthur's Order of Chivalry." Tennyson had a particular interest in knighthood and the "glorious" days of the Middle Ages. Mansfield (B), Poe (C), and Arnold (E) did not utilize the knights of King Arthur in their poetry, and Marlowe (D) is better known as a dramatist.

45.   **(D)**
Morality was seen as a guiding factor in seventeenth-century England—during which it was written, as indicated by the language of this poem. (C) and (E) are guiding principles of Romantic poetry.

46.   **(C)**
This is from *Comus*. Note the clean, short, almost epigramic tone. Pope (A) wrote in the Romantic era, while Dryden (B) and Jonson (E) are better known for their comedies.

47.   **(D)**
Though written two hundred years before, the passage shows obvious elements of Scots (althocht/dur, etc.). Pronunciation indicates the presence of the heavy "r." The passage is too anachronistic for Chaucer (A) and Shakespeare (E). Although the passage shares some characteristics with Old English [(B) and (C)], particularly the use of alliteration, there is the additional Scottish element to take in account.

48.   **(D)**
This is from *The Age of Reason*. The author means that there's something surprising in his viewpoint—even shocking. Paine, of course, was never one to

strive for popularity by advancing traditional views, and his "Unitarian" orientation toward rationality and against iconoclasm are evidenced in this passage.

49.   **(B)**

This is from Lawrence's *Thomas Hardy*. Hardy's ability to ennoble the common man is what impresses D. H. Lawrence here. The other passages do not describe Hardy's display of naturalism, in which all men can be destined for equal greatness.

50.   **(E)**

This is from Lawrence's *Edgar Allan Poe*. A look at Poe's poem "The Bells" is evidence of the descriptive accuracy of this passage. Passages (A) and (C) can be easily eliminated as they describe writers more moralistic and didactic than Poe, while (D) can be eliminated because it describes characters and settings not normally utilized by Poe.

51.   **(D)**

In Silverma's *Pro Malo Publico*, usage such as "a body" is a clue to the satirist attempt to imitate Clemens' style. The passage's humor, which tweaks the subject in a manner seemingly gentle to the subject but a bit more caustic to the reader, is also characteristic of Twain.

52.   **(B)**

This is from Hopkins' *The Grand Old Duke Of York*. It is an exceptionally comic exaggeration of Salinger's style—as is easily found in Holden Caulfield's casual and qualified speaking in *The Catcher In The Rye*.

53.   **(E)**

This is Pellman in *Diary of a Stranger*. The internal joke, while not characteristic of Camus, makes the piece illustrative of the stranger's cold indifference to the universe that surrounds him.

54.   **(B)**

This is from *Tradition and the Individual Talent*. Eliot, the precise critic, is seen in this small excerpt.

55. **(C)**

This is from *Criticism and Fiction*. The nineteenth-century writer did not feel awkward with "beseech," and his message to the first or second generation of American critics as they start "anew" also places the time.

56. **(C)**

In *Fleurs de Mal* the description is "Swarming city, city filled with dreams / Where the ghost in full daylight hails the passerby." Flaubert (A) was a prose writer rather than a poet, and the setting is modern compared to the times of Dante (B), Shakespeare (D), and Ovid (E).

57. **(D)**

It is from IV, 25–27: Heathen who uttered "sighs, which caused the eternal air to tremble." The general portrayal here of London as an "Unreal City" and the imagery, which suggests hell, are also clues.

58. **(C)**

It is from "The Waste Land," lines 60–65. While all of the writers were American-born, only Eliot resided in England for much of his adult life.

59. **(D)**

One person is speaking in a poetic form. The self-questioning emphasizes the monologic nature of the passage. Stream-of-consciousness (B) would include the senses perceived by the subject, and would not be transmitted through voice. Decalogue (A) is an alternative title for the Ten Commandments, and (C) and (E) imply a dialogue.

60. **(D)**

See Ecclesiastes i.2. Vanity is in fact an important theme in Shelley's poem (C), but no priest is alluded to in the poem. *Pilgrim's Progress* (E) is concerned with the search for salvation.

61. **(C)**

This is from "The Bishop Orders His Tomb at Saint Praxed's Church." Dramatic monologue is characteristic of many of Browning's finest works. The break from traditional Victorian poetry also placed Browning at odds occasionally with Rossetti (A) and Arnold (E). Swinburne (B) often shocked Victorian audiences with his celebration of physical love, while Wilde (D), of course, wrote in a satirical vein.

62.   **(D)**

Its main thrust is to reinforce the denial in the first sentence that man is not just a beast. (A), (B), and (C) contradict the meaning of the passage, and (E) is a non sequitur.

63.   **(C)**

This is from *Hamlet* IV.v. The Prince of Denmark wrestles with the meaning of life and the purpose of humanity in the famous play, even as the lofty thinker wrestles with his own base and murderous impulses. This passage is a good representation of the struggles Hamlet articulates in his soliloquies.

64.   **(E)**

The passage speaks of the coming of death (night). The agents of death prey on living creatures and kill them. (A) and (B) are objects that refer to night as well, while (C) and (D) are adversaries of night itself, rather than "night's black agents."

65.   **(D)**

In III.ii., Shakespeare's command of the language indicates a character's need to slough off mortal fears and call up courage to face difficult deeds. The dark imagery in this passage is also particularly representative of *Macbeth*, which explores the descent into evil.

66.   **(D)**

Cassius is playing the devil's advocate. Brutus and Cassius do not mean to imply that it is better to die young [(A) and (E)] but that fear of death often consumes one.

67.   **(C)**

This is from Lawrence's *Thomas Mann*. Pope, author of "Whatever is, is right," is considered the true believer in seventeenth-century logical methods. Whitman (A) and Eliot (E) utilize the aesthetic form as described to contrast with the method of Pope.

68.   **(D)**

The octave of the Petrarchan sonnet reads *abbaabba*. Two other famous forms of the sonnet are the Shakespearean sonnet (A), the first octave of which is rhymed *ababcdcd*, and the Spenserian sonnet (B) which utilizes the *ababbcbc* octet rhyme scheme.

69.   **(D)**

The traditional metaphor for marriage (or in contemporary parlance—commitment) is two people becoming one. The speaker is recalling their first meeting, remembering it as the first momentous step toward their union.

70.   **(C)**

This is from "Meeting and Passing." Hills, walls, and footprints, as well as the typical lilt of Frostian poetry, indicate its origin. The tone of the passage is more subdued than that of Byron (D) or Browning (E).

71.   **(C)**

Chris is frustrated by his mother's belief in the fantasy that Larry will be found alive. Chris is attacking what his mother says, not providing information on his own (A), but at the same time, his intent is not to ridicule (B).

72.   **(D)**

Domestic arguments symbolizing greater issues are typical of Miller's work. Here, in what Miller used as practice for his later *Death of a Salesman*, mother and son argue for possession of memories and over Chris' effort to marry Larry's old girlfriend, Annie.

73.   **(C)**

Chaucer describes the Squire by his age in the Prologue. The Knight (D) and the Monk (E) can be dismissed out of hand due to age and lack of bachelorhood, respectively, and the Franklin (A) is certainly not "lusty." The Yeoman (B) is typically recognized by his weapons and green apparel.

74.   **(C)**

The passage begins: "Ye know the spheres and various tasks assigned…" The items in the passage are the spheres' tasks. Answer (A) can be eliminated as the power being referred to is clearly not earthly. (E) can be discarded because it is not universal enough.

75.   **(C)**

More than just listing, cataloguing is generally employed to achieve a desired emotional effect. (A) is a general term for the form of a work rather than its content. The poet does not go into greater detail about the tasks [eliminate (B) and (D)].

76. **(D)**

Rain, to be "kindly," needs to fall on that which needs it, i.e., cultivated fields. (A) can be readily eliminated since the previous lines also refer to natural areas.

77. **(C)**

It is from Pope's "The Rape of the Lock." The violent acts of nature portrayed are consistent with the imagery used in the Romantic era [eliminate (B), (D), and (E)]. Congreve (A) was better known for his comedies.

78. **(C)**

These words taken from the preceding paragraph: "Volkssprache"—people's language—reinforces the point. As a contrast, the author points to Europe where the different languages within Europe are further splintered within each country.

79. **(C)**

Immigrants can "condition" American pronunciation and vocabulary. It is of interest that one of the prime conditionings is the addition of vocabulary (single words and expressions)—often associated with food from the countries of immigrant origin.

80. **(A)**

This passage is from *The American Language*. A particular interest of Mencken was the influence of immigrants (such as his own family's German background) on American English. Eliot (C) did not live in America for most of his adult life. Michener (D) is famous for his gargantuan novels on different regions in the world.

81. **(C)**

This is a type of fiction that was popularized and inspired by the *Arabian Nights*. Parables (A) often do not employ historical figures. A *roman a clef* (D) usually involves an allusion to a contemporary of the author, and the name does not seem biblical (B).

82. **(C)**

This passage is from *The History of Rasselas, Prince of Abyssinia*. The didactic nature of the piece points to Johnson, but also readily eliminates Congreve (A) who is better known for his comedies, and the satirical writer

Swift (B). Boswell (D) is best known for his biography on Johnson, while Gray (E) was a great influence on the poets of the Romantic era.

83.   **(C)**
This passage is from *The Preface to Shakespeare*. After half a millenium, debates on the greatness of Shakespeare—where they have ever existed—have now almost passed from the critical scene.

84.   **(D)**
Johnson wrote a century and a half after Shakespeare's death. Although the tone of the passage points to Johnson, if one is aware that the poet being talked about is Shakespeare, one can eliminate other answers based upon the time the passage was written.

85.   **(B)**
This is from *Adam Bede*, although the minute attention to domestic details is characteristic of Austen as well. The pastoral farm house does not match the city descriptions of Dickens (C) and Hardy (D), nor does it match the fierce Yukon settings of most of London's (E) work.

86.   **(C)**
Ruskin's prose, the author says, should be looked at as an art form itself. The author's commentary on views indicates that what is being examined is the criticism itself, not the artist ("Turner").

87.   **(D)**
In *The Critic as Artist*, Wilde uses a typical tone of chatty debate and forceful impressionistic language. Arnold (A) and Pater (C) are also known for their excellent literary criticism but were more concerned with the function of criticism, rather than criticism as a form of art.

88.   **(C)**
Prominent among the devices employed here is the repetition of initial sound: "foam-fretted feet" (line 4), "shaken shadow" (line 7), "soul the soft surprise" (line 10). The passage has many examples of repeating consonant sounds rather than vowel sounds (B), and the words have meaning, which eliminates answer (E).

89.   **(E)**

The poet's relationship has been called (presumably by his lover) "Nomore," but he does not accept this. He only looks for a sign of hope (a "dart through thy soul"), and then, he tells her, he will smile again. Answer (B) is a trap to the reader who pays attention to the more famous first four lines, but does not look to the meaning of the entire passage.

90.   **(D)**

This is from "A Superscription." Note especially Rossetti's fine use of metaphor. The display of traditional Romantic emotion does not match the sometimes jarring prose of Browning (A) or the idyllic Tennyson (B). W. S. Gilbert (E) is best known for the comic operas he wrote with Sir Arthur Sullivan.

91.   **(C)**

The poet, commenting on the new American mission, refers to the "Old World." The verse implies that the "elder races" have nothing left to explore, and that the new "pioneers" must take up the task now that there is uncharted space before them.

92.   **(C)**

In "Pioneers! O Pioneers!" free verse and patriotic theme, amplified by frequent use of exclamation marks, are clues to the origin. The celebratory tone does not match the contemplative Emerson (B), while Whittier (A) and Channing (E) are better known for their anti-slavery writings. Noyes (D) was a British poet.

93.   **(B)**

The proper name "Glumdalclitch" and the quasi-reportorial tone of the passage are clues to this tale of adventure. The mystical land is too earthly for Hades (A) and Wonderland (C), but too fantastic for (D) and (E).

94.   **(C)**

The dwarf, a seeming supplicant to the Queen, would have been dismissed; "cashiered" still retains most of its original meaning. Although (A) and (E) might seem similar in meaning, it can be derived from the passage that "cashiered" has a negative connotation.

95.　**(C)**

This passage is from *Gulliver's Travels*. As before, the passage seems a bit too serious to be written by Carroll (A), but too fantastic for science fiction [(B), (D), and (E)].

96.　**(D)**

In "The Author's Epitaph, Made by Himself," note the heavy beat, the morbid imagery, and the barely hopeful tone. The passage is more resigned in tone than (A) or (E), which are also pieces that lament the loss of a loved one.

97.　**(B)**

Time takes in trust (and delivers death); only the Lord can undo the process. Although death's important in this poem, it is not displayed as an active force, so the other four choices can be eliminated.

98.　**(C)**

The poem is supposed to have been written on the eve of his beheading in the Tower of London, although this has from time to time been contested. The resigned, subdued tone of the poem easily eliminates (A) and (B) as potential choices.

99.　**(A)**

This is by E. M. Forster. Note the enormous amount of "information" contained within the prose while, at the same time, the syntax remains tight. This is indicative of Forster and others of the early twentieth century.

100.　**(D)**

Immediately preceding this passage, the author said, "And whatever is me alive is me." Blood and bones are in his hand, and he can see that if he cuts his hand open—proof positive of life. The passage does not debate the existence of the spiritual, but rather is interested in the spiritual power that can be found in the corporeal body.

101.　**(D)**

This is from Lawrence's *Why the Novel Matters*. Lawrence's use of repetition "alive... alive... alive" and the nature of these repetitions mark this passage as uniquely his. Lawrence was a firm believer in the force that could be taken up within the human body, and disputed the idea that the earthly and spiritual are separate.

102.   **(D)**

This passage is from Cervantes. The haplessness described in the father is about to devolve upon the son. David Copperfield (A) was an orphan who had no knowledge of who his father is, and the language is more refined than that used by Huckleberry Finn (B). Tess (C) descended from an English royal family, while Jean Valjean (E) is the unfortunate protagonist of *Les Miserables*.

103.   **(C)**

Levin's response to an intensity of feeling is about to be tested—a favorite theme of the author. The manner in which death is directly confronted is also a feature of Tolstoy, who would approach the subject again in *The Death of Ivan Ilych*.

104.   **(E)**

Although the stream of time bears infinite tones, this passage has only one. The possibility of enmity exists, but the passage is mostly concerned with describing Ts'ui Pen's idea of time. It is clear in the passage that the speaker wishes to show a reality that the listener (and the audience) had never contemplated.

105.   **(A)**

This is from *The Garden of Forking Paths*. This passage does not become humorous or absurd, eliminating (B), (C), and (D). Atwood (E) is better known for the questioning of societal gender roles in her works.

106.   **(C)**

This is from *Time Must Have A Stop*. Note the analytic and precise description, indicative of a scientific mind at work. Huxley often expressed disillusionment through his characters.

107.   **(B)**

This is from *The Life You Save May Be Your Own*. The matronly woman often populates O'Connor's Southern Gothic stories.

108.   **(D)**

This is from *The Great Gatsby*. The lush description of Daisy's voice ("fluctuating, feverish," "deathless song") is a clue. The "rush of emotion" is also representative of the moments of true feeling that come through the boring activity of the society in which the characters live.

109. **(A)**

This is from *The Bulgarian Poetess*. Politeness and decorum (as would be found in a meeting) are a thin haze over more serious and tumultuous concerns of civilization. The short, but sharp description of the action is characteristic of Updike.

110. **(C)**

This is from *The Italian Villain*. The portraits of Lord Byron often included in anthologies are said by many to show these same features—the Byronic hero is as much based on the man as his work.

111. **(B)**

A reading of Radcliffe's passage while viewing Byron's portraits is a lesson in her descriptive powers. The use of terms such as "gloom and severity" also point to Radcliffe, since she also utilized a dark tone in her Gothic novels.

112. **(D)**

Villages, especially evident alongside "crofts" (small, farmed tracts of land). (B) and (C) can be readily eliminated as the poet is entering the realm of the uninhabitable, not leaving it. Citadels (E) are not typically "vulgar," and corrals (A) usually are the tethers, not in them.

113. **(D)**

It is the common nature of the details provided to contrast with the hint that the corpse belongs in a rare (also "thin" as air) atmosphere. The other four answers rely on a literal interpretation of the poem.

114. **(C)**

From "A Grammarian's Funeral," the passage demonstrates that Browning was a master of more lyrical forms as well as the free verse of his dramatic monologues. His jarring imagery also often deviated from the traditional images of his Victorian colleagues.

115. **(D)**

This refers to a method of disgrace for knights; to be hung upside down by the heels. Falstaff is promising that he will carry out the task that he and the Prince have planned.

116. **(D)**

The clues are "Gadshill," a notorious hill outside London where robberies took place; taking a purse; and the command "stand," as in "Stand and deliver! Your money or your life." Since Falstaff is morally moving away "from" the act of praying, (A) is incorrect. It seems that the action is going to be a private one, so (C) and (E) may also be eliminated.

117. **(D)**

It is also interpreted as "God's wounds!" As an exclamation, answer (B) is also similar in meaning, but (A), (C), and (E) have other connotations, so those three can be readily eliminated.

118. **(D)**

The play on the word "ices" is a triple entendre. "Ices" in the seventeenth century was dessert, a term used like today's "as cold as ice," and an obvious reference to a lack of hospitality.

119. **(D)**

This passage is from *Walden*. Note the diarist's attention to detail mixed with Thoreau's perhaps overly high expectations for his fellow man. Emerson (A) and Whitman (C) are far more tolerant of other people, while Melville's style (B) is very complex compared to the passage. Channing's work (E) is characterized by his proselytizing fervor.

120. **(D)**

The author is specific in the argument—not just in occupations, but in type. Although the last statement is a bit vague, it is not meant to imply that women are not equal in the general way answers (B) and (E) indicate.

121. **(A)**

Undergarments (C) and flesh (D) cannot be furled, a pennant is inconsistent with the ocean imagery, and the sea is already at the shore (E) so folds of bright clothing is the most logical answer.

122. **(A)**

The sea is retreating. It leaves behind "naked shingles"—the rocky shore. Emotionally, the retreating of the tide mirrors the manner in which the poet loses faith.

123. **(D)**

The excerpt is from "Dover Beach." The passage exhibits some of Arnold's conventions, namely, his philosophical despair and loneliness.

124. **(D)**

This is from Louka's oft-repeated retort to Sergius. Volpone (A) and Mercutio (C) can be eliminated since they are closer in character type to Louka than to Sergius.

125. **(D)**

The dramatic situation itself contributes to the comedy, but the word "right," coming as it does in response to a plausible—if hypocritical—statement by Sergius and before Louka's biting comment that she "thought… you had given up being so particular"—acts as a pivot point for the comic scene's full emotional delivery.

126. **(C)**

It is from G.B. Shaw's *Arms and the Man*. The dialogue does not resemble that of Shakespeare [(B) and (D)], while Goldsmith's play (A) has a female protagonist. (E) is a contemporary musical.

127. **(D)**

It is from John Wilson's *Noctes Ambrosianae*, 1822. This piece of vitriole refers to the Scottish Boswell's admiration for Samuel Johnson—The Great Bear. The passage is typical of the manner in which Boswell examines Johnson's contemporaries with a discerning eye.

128. **(A)**

The passage is from John Locke's *Essay on Human Understanding*, in which he propounds his theories of empiricism. The other four writers are also philosophers, but deal with more contemporary issues.

129. **(A)**

In *The Golden Reign of Wouter Van Twiller*, Irving, the social historian, knew how to manipulate precise descriptive terms (linsey-woolsey) and quaint modifiers (the fair hands of his mistress) to spin a tale of bygone days.

130. **(D)**

This is from the Battle of Bannockburn, 1314. Bruce is one of Scotland's greatest heroes—often recalled by Scots in the century following the Battle of Culloden. Bruce is known as the liberator of Scotland, and was Scotland's first king.

131. **(A)**

This is evident from the high rhetoric and sense of imminent bloodshed. The final cry to "do or die" is a final appeal. The call seems to immediately precede battle [eliminate (D) and (E)], and is certainly not negative in tone (C).

132. **(C)**

The poet himself subtitles it this way. Monody is a song sung in Greek drama by a single voice. While the passage is clearly not a dialogue (A) or an epic (D), this work does share many of the characteristics of an elegy (B), save the refrain.

133. **(D)**

This parallels the premature taking of life—the berries were plucked too early and the human life was taken before its time. (A) is a trap which relies on a modern interpretation of the word "crude."

134. **(D)**

The prematurely fallen hero here was really the poet's college friend, Edward King, who drowned in the Irish Sea in 1637. The name is apparently male [eliminate (A) and (C)], and Prometheus (E) was an immortal.

135. **(D)**

This is from "Lycidas," termed "probably the most perfect piece of pure literature in existence," by Arthur Machen in 1923. This poem, in addition to being a tribute to Milton's departed friend, finds him once again struggling with questions of existence.

136. **(E)**

If "miscreant" is "misbeliever," then "recreant" resembles "rebeliever," or someone who has turned on previous commitments. The idea of being a traitor is reinforced in the following lines, where the subject of the speech is accused of making the speaker "break [his] vow."

137. **(D)**

The royal "we," the unwillingness to reconsider the order, and the obsession with the nature of his power are indicative of King Lear.

138. **(E)**

"Attend" here means "await." Taken in context, it emphasizes her short time on earth. (A) and (B) are traps that rely on an overly literal interpretation of the line.

139. **(C)**

This was written to commemorate the death of Elizabeth Drury, a 14-year-old girl. (A), (B), and (D) are not used to commemorate the dead, while (E) is usually more of a lament than indicated in the passage.

140. **(B)**

This is from "An Anatomy of the World." The artful use of many rhymed couplets while avoiding monotony is indicative of Dryden's poetic genius.

141. **(A)**

Hardy, in *The Return of the Native*, constructs a tragic story based to a large extent on coincidental events. This stands in contrast to the plays by Shakespeare (B) and O'Neill (D), in which tragedy is determined more by character. It also stands in contrast with the novel by Steinbeck (C) and the play by Ibsen (E) in which tragedy is determined more by economic and social factors.

142. **(B)**

The phrase "cloistered virtue" is from Milton's *Areopagitica,* in which he argues against censorship because it deprives the public of the freedom and responsibility of choosing good over evil, a freedom that Milton felt to be necessary for true virtue. The notion of a "cloistered virtue" is thus, to Milton, a contradiction, since it implies ignorance of evil, and not the exercise of free choice. The essays by Mill (A) and Rousseau (E) are concerned with the rights of individuals and minorities in a democracy. Thoreau (C) argues for disobeying immoral laws, even in a democracy. Aristotle (D) establishes the basis of morality in moderation between evil extremes.

143.   **(C)**

Both Beowulf (A) and Sir Gawain (B) are characters in major medieval works. Beowulf fights Grendel, Grendel's mother, and a dragon. Sir Gawain seeks the Green Knight in order to fulfill a bargain with him. Neither Beowulf nor Gawain is known for his singing. Chaucer (D) and Dante (E) are major medieval authors. Dante wrote *The Divine Comedy*, Chaucer *The Canterbury Tales*. Again, neither was inspired to sing. The answer is Caedmon.

144.   **(A)**

Like other early Germanic and Anglo-Saxon poetry, Caedmon's hymn is alliterative. The tradition of iambic pentameter (B) in English does not start until the late Middle Ages, for example, Chaucer's *The Canterbury Tales*. Ballad stanza (C) is typical of the Scottish border ballads from the late medieval period. Free verse (D) is characteristic of twentieth-century poetry, and heroic couplets (E) are typical of eighteenth-century poetry.

145.   **(E)**

Like *The Dream of the Rood* and a number of other medieval works, the passage from Bede could be classified as a dream vision. Caedmon, after leaving the hall, falls asleep and is visited by an angel in a dream. When he wakes up, he returns and sings the songs as instructed by the angel. An epic simile (A) is an extended comparison, as found in Homer's *Iliad* and *Odyssey* and as imitated by Virgil in Latin or by Spenser or Milton in English. Comic relief (B) might best be illustrated by the interlude scenes in Marlowe's *Doctor Faustus* or other Elizabethan drama, when lower-class characters parody the activities of the heroic characters. Classical allusions (C) are references to Greek and Roman mythology, characteristic of Renaissance literature. A mock epic (D) is a work that imitates epic form while dealing with commonplace topics for humorous effect. An example would be Pope's "The Rape of the Lock."

146.   **(C)**

This poem by Ezra Pound is a parody of a poem by W. B. Yeats entitled "The Lake Isle of Innisfree." In his poem, Yeats remembers a little island in a lake near where he grew up and his dream of living there in a little cottage in imitation of Thoreau in *Walden*.

147.   **(D)**

In his parody of Yeats, Pound substitutes an urban and middle-class setting, a tobacco shop, for the island. He implies that Yeats' desire to run off to an island is a form of escapism. From Pound's point of view, poetry is not to be found by escaping into nature. Instead, it is a craft, an art, requiring hard work and discipline. In comparison, running a tobacco shop seems like an escape. The emphasis on art as craft rather than inspiration, the references to art as the subject matter, and the invocation of classical gods and goddesses are all features of Pound's classicism. In making fun of Yeats' desire to escape into nature, Pound is anti-Romantic.

148. **(E)**

The passage is from Milton's *On Education*. It is characteristic of Milton in that it provides a theological basis for his ideas about education. Humanity is alienated from God, and it is the aim of education to direct humanity back to God. Although St. Augustine (A) and More (B) would share similar views, their works are not specifically about education. Mill (C) addresses the limits on social control of individual freedom. His views are not theological and are not directly related to education. Dewey (D) writes about education, but not from a traditional theological viewpoint.

149. **(B)**

The use of "ruin" in this context is characteristic of Milton's style. The Latin root means "fall" and Milton's phrase, "the ruins of our first parents" becomes the "fall" in a theological sense, alienation from God as a result of the eating of the apple in the Garden of Eden. Milton frequently uses English words derived from Latin with the Latin meaning adding a second, usually literal, level to the text.

150. **(D)**

The Pequod is Ahab's ship on which he pursues the white whale in Melville's novel *Moby Dick*. The term "sailor" allows one to eliminate answers (A) and (E).

151. **(D)**

O'Neill used the myth of Hippolytus as the basis for *Desire Under the Elms*. In the myth, Phaedra falls in love with her stepson, is rejected by him, accuses him of trying to seduce her, and then commits suicide. Believing the false accusation, the husband, Theseus, curses his son, Hippolytus, resulting in the son's death. O'Neill modernized the story, placing it in rural New England in order to have classical tragedy in a modern, colloquial form.

152. **(C)**

The passage given is from Leibniz's *Monadology*. It sums up his belief that this world is "the best of all possible worlds." That view is expressly ridiculed in Voltaire's *Candide* in the character of Pangloss. *The Clouds* (A) is a satirical look at Socrates, (B) and (E) are satires of the respective societies in which the authors lived, and (D) is a satire of hypocrisy and religion.

153. **(E)**

Sonnet writing in England started in the Renaissance and continued through the first part of the seventeenth century. Both Donne (D) and Milton (C) wrote sonnets. The sonnet was associated with the densely metaphorical style of the Renaissance. After the Restoration, this style fell out of fashion and poets stopped writing sonnets. This hiatus lasted about 150 years until the Romantic period. Wordsworth and Keats wrote sonnets and the practice continued on into the first half of the twentieth century. Both Robert Frost (A) and Edna St. Vincent Millay (B) wrote sonnets. Thus, the poet who did *not* write sonnets was Alexander Pope, living in the eighteenth century when the form was out of fashion.

154. **(D)**

Insofar as the poem expresses a worship of nature, or at least a nostalgia for the worship of nature, it could be classified as pantheist. A Petrarchan poem (A) would be, for example, a typical Renaissance sonnet imitating the style of Petrarch. An anti-Petrarchan poem (B) would be one that parodied the Petrarchan style. A deist poem (C) would be one like Pope's "An Essay on Man," expressing a belief in God, but rejecting or ignoring other theological notions such as the fall, the trinity, and the redemption. A satirical poem (E) would be one ridiculing contemporary society. Wordsworth does criticize contemporary society, but with a serious, even somewhat desperate tone. It is not the playful or bitter ridicule of satire.

155. **(D)**

The important point in the last two lines is that Proteus and Triton are sea gods. Wordsworth conjectures that a pantheist religion would make possible a more intense enjoyment of nature. The modern meaning of "protean" (variable) derives from the ability of the sea god, Proteus, to change shape. This is illustrated in the account when Menelaus tells Telemachos of his encounter with Proteus. Wordsworth is not concerned here with the modern meaning of "protean" (A), the episode from the *Odyssey* (E), or with the meanings of the prefixes "pro" (C) and "tri" (B).

156. **(D)**

Human sacrifice is a theme in *Iphigenia in Aulis* by Euripides. In this play, Agamemnon sacrifices his daughter, Iphigenia, in order to propitiate Artemis and gain favorable winds for the Greek fleet setting sail for Troy. The murder of their daughter becomes an issue between Agamemnon and his wife, Clytemnestra, throughout the Mycenian legend. Revenge for the sacrifice is part of Clytemnestra's motivation in murdering Agamemnon when he returns from Troy. The other Greek plays [(A), (B), and (C)] deal with various forms of murder, death, and execution, but not with human sacrifice per se. *The Dead* (E) by James Joyce depicts contemporary life in modern Ireland and is the last story in his collection, *Dubliners*.

157. **(A)**

In these lines, Johnson sets pride in opposition to reason, and notes that it is by following pride that humanity creates many problems for itself. There is no indication that mankind ever uses too much reason (B). Johnson laments the infrequency with which humanity follows reason. These problems are the result, not of institutions and customs (C), but of human nature itself. The problems are not limited to China and Peru (D). The phrase "from China to Peru" implies that this condition is utterly universal and includes the whole world. There is no indication in this passage that humanity can change this condition through education or technology (E).

158. **(E)**

The correct term for the break is "caesura." The artful variation of this caesura is considered one of the important technical problems in the writing of eighteenth-century rhymed couplets. Enjambment (A) refers to the running of the syntactic unit beyond the end of the line, so that the sentence continues through the rhyme and on into the next line. A troche (B) is a metrical foot with two syllables, the first stressed and the second unstressed. An elision (C) is the omission of an unstressed vowel or syllable so that the line fits the meter. Ellipsis (D) is the omission of words or phrases that are understood or implied in context.

159. **(E)**

The reference is to the Wife of Bath. Muscatine refers to "The Wife of Bath's Prologue" in which the Wife of Bath presents a history of her five marriages and gives her views on the relationship between the sexes. In her fifth marriage, she ripped up her husband's book, which gave examples of wicked wives, and this lead to a fight between husband and wife. Muscatine sees these actions as symbolic of the conflict between experience and authority, between feminism and masculine domination.

160. **(C)**

"The Reeve's Tale" is an example of a fabliau. "The Pardoner's Tale" (A) consists of a sermon, the "spiel" used by the Pardoner to sell pardons, illustrated by a moral exemplum, the story of the three revelers who kill each other over the gold that they find. "The Nun's Priest's Tale" (B) is an animal fable. "The Monk's Tale" (D) is a series of "tragedies," each one an example of the fall of a great person. "The Knight's Tale" (E) is a romance.

161. **(C)**

A rigorous defense of the unities is to be found in Dryden's *An Essay of Dramatic Poesy*. Dryden is writing from a later seventeenth-century neoclassical point of view. Artaud's essay (A) is a somewhat incoherent manifesto of the theater of the absurd and has nothing to do with unities. Johnson (B) defends Shakespeare's violations of the unities of time and place and argues that they are artificial notions of no real importance in the drama. Neither Eliot (D) nor Sidney (E) are particularly concerned with drama or with dramatic unities.

162. **(D)**

"Fealty" and "demesne" are terms derived from medieval feudalism. "Fealty" is the loyalty pledge by a subject to a lord in the feudal system. "Demesne" refers to the land controlled by an individual within the feudal system. In this sonnet, the poet, John Keats, uses "fealty" to refer to the loyalty of the poet to his art as represented by Apollo, the Greek god of poetry, among other things. Keats uses "demesne" to refer to the poet's works. This metaphor of poetry as land is extended in the general metaphor of the poem, in which reading is discussed as a form of traveling and exploring.

163. **(C)**

Balboa, not Cortez, discovered the Pacific. This sort of error is referred to as poetic license, implying that it is a minor detail irrelevant to the overall effect of the poem. The intentional fallacy (A) occurs when the reader focuses on what an author supposedly meant to say rather than on what he actually did say. The pathetic fallacy (B) is the author's use of nature to heighten emotional intensity, as for example, a sudden thunderstorm during a murder scene. Poetic justice (D) refers to the rewarding of good and the punishing of bad characters in the outcome of a narrative. Romantic irony (E) is the undercutting of artistic illusion by the self-conscious intrusion of the artist revealing himself as creator. Examples would be Sterne's *Tristram Shandy* and Byron's *Don Juan*.

164. **(A)**

This is the opening quatrain from Robert Frost's sonnet, "Design." Features that are typical of Frost's style are the detailed observation of nature, the detached and ironic reflections on those observations, and the traditional meter and rhyme scheme.

165. **(D)**

The passage is from Jonathan Edwards' sermon *Sinners in the Hands of an Angry God*. Edwards was an eighteenth-century American Protestant theologian. He was part of an eighteenth-century religious revival known as the Great Awakening.

166. **(A)**

Of these works of literature, the one that makes the most elaborate use of number symbolism, especially of the number three, is Dante's *Divine Comedy*. The work is divided into three books: Hell, Purgatory, and Heaven. Each book consists of thirty-three cantos with one introductory canto to make an even hundred. The cantos are written in terza rima, three-line stanzas with an interlacing rhyme scheme: *aba bcb cdc*...etc.

167. **(D)**

In this passage, Danby discusses the character of the fool in Shakespeare's *King Lear*. In particular, Danby considers the disappearance of the fool from the play after Act III. He explains this disappearance in thematic terms.

168. **(E)**

Dante is guided through Hell by Virgil. In the Middle Ages, Virgil was considered to be the foremost of classical writers. The Greek language and Greek literature were not widely known in western Europe during the Middle Ages. Among Latin authors, Virgil was revered for his high seriousness and patriotism. His works were read as allegorized foreshadowings and prophesies of Christianity. Ovid's works (D) were perceived as less serious, more licentious, and he was more popular in the Renaissance. Beatrice (C) is the woman who inspires Dante and who guides him in Heaven. It is appropriate that his guide in Hell should be pre-Christian.

169. **(A)**
Eliot refers here to Mark Twain's use of colloquial language, the language of everyday conversation. Shakespeare used colloquial language, especially in comic scenes, but in this respect he was not really different from other Elizabethan dramatists. Both Chaucer (D) and Shakespeare (C) used language that was contemporary for their time, but it has since grown out of style. Spenser (E), on the other hand, used an archaic style. His language was just the opposite of "up-to-date." James Joyce (B) pioneered the style of stream-of-consciousness, but it was not the language itself that was unusual but the idea of presenting characterization through the free association of thoughts. Eliot's point, then, applies to Mark Twain because Twain bridged the gap between current style and what was considered in nineteenth-century America to be "literary" language. Mark Twain violated the notion of correct literary language by making literature out of ordinary language. Other writers had done this before, but in the nineteenth century it came as a shock to many readers. It was in this sense that he brought his language, that is to say, the accepted literary language, "up-to-date."

170. **(D)**
William Blake was a visionary poet. He reacted against the rationalism of the eighteenth century, especially against the influence of Newton and Locke. He stressed the importance of the imagination in shaping the human condition. In this he was similar to other Romantic poets. For Blake, however, the products of the imagination seemed as real, or even more real, than the material world. This was reflected in complicated personal symbolism of his poetry. He had a number of visions and he took them quite literally.

171. **(D)**
Double entendre is a phrase meaning "twofold meaning" or "pun." Thus, the editor implies that Shakespeare used the phrase "lie with" with the intention of creating ambiguity. The phrase can mean both "tell an untruth to" and "have sexual relations with." Both meanings make sense in the context.

172. **(A)**
The "-ed" in "unlearned" is pronounced as an unstressed syllable. In Elizabethan English, poets exercised an option either to pronounce "-ed" as a separate syllable or to elide the "e." The "e" is elided in "untutored" (line 3) and in "suppressed" (line 8). This is determined by the meter and with the rhyme with "best." In line 4, however, the unstressed syllable is needed for the meter.

The pronunciation was in transition and both forms were acceptable variations.

173. **(E)**
The standard definition of a sonnet requires that the poem have fourteen lines. Shakespeare's sonnets end with a couplet (A), but the Italian form with a sestet is typical. Petrarch's sonnets were about love (B), and this was the typical subject matter of the sonnet throughout the Renaissance. Other topics were possible, however. John Donne wrote sonnets about religion, William Wordsworth about nature. Shakespeare's sonnets have three quatrains (C) and then a couplet, but the Italian form has only two quatrains before the sestet. Wit and irony (D) are typical of much Renaissance poetry, especially seventeenth-century poetry. Wit and irony are not, however, essential to the genre. They are lacking, for example, in the sonnets of Romantic poets like Keats and Wordsworth.

174. **(A)**
Molière's *Tartuffe* is a satire of religious hypocrisy. Tartuffe himself is the hypocrite. The other plays are satirical, but they are not directed specifically at religious hypocrisy. Jonson's *Volpone* (B) is a satire of avarice. Wycherley's *The Country-Wife* (C) is a Restoration comedy satirizing adultery, marriage, and relations between the sexes. Aristophanes' *The Clouds* (D) is a Greek comedy satirizing Socrates, philosophy, and education. Sheridan's *The Rivals* (E) is a late eighteenth-century comedy about, like Wycherley's play, relations between the sexes.

175. **(C)**
Kafka, in works like *The Trial,* presents a view of the human condition as an absurd and meaningless predicament. All of the other authors wrote within the framework of cultural and philosophical assumptions that provided meaning to human experience. Virgil (E) viewed human experience from the perspective of Roman patriotism, and classical mythology and philosophy. Dante (D) viewed human experience from the point of view of medieval Christian theology. Tolstoy (A) viewed human experience from the point of view of historical determinism, and Zola (B) from the point of view of naturalism.

176. **(C)**
Ben Jonson wrote many masques, but *Volpone* (A) is not one of them. *Volpone* is a five-act satirical drama. Shakespeare included a masque as an entertainment in *The Tempest. As You Like It* (D), however, is a full-length

comedy. Congreve's *The Way of the World* (E) is a Restoration comedy, and *Everyman* (B) is a medieval morality play. The masque was a short play, usually including music and dance, written for private entertainment at a court or household and performed by members of the household, not a professional acting troupe. Milton's *Comus* is an example.

177. **(D)**

The speaker is Molly Bloom. These are the final words in the third and final section of Joyce's *Ulysses*. The section is an extended, unpunctuated, inner monologue representing Molly Bloom's stream-of-consciousness. This style distinguishes the text from the thoughts or expressions of any of the other heroines.

178. **(A)**

The subject of this sonnet by John Milton is the massacre of the Waldenses, a Protestant sect that had separated from the Catholic church in the twelfth century. They lived principally in the Alps, along the border between France and Italy.

179. **(D)**

The lines illustrate enjambment, the running over syntactically of a sentence from one line to the next without any pause of punctuation, and with the sentence, clause, or phrase ending in the middle of the next phrase. Thus there is enjambment in the first line of the poem in the relative clause "whose bones/Lie scattered..." which carries over from the first verse to the second. There is not enjambment, however, in the second verse since the relative clause comes to a close at the end of the verse: "...on the Alpine mounts cold..." Lines 8-10 do not illustrate irony (A), since Milton is not saying one thing and meaning something else. It is not synesthesia (B), which is the mixing of senses. It is not litotes (C), which is understatement. It is not sprung rhythm (E), since the meter is standard iambic pentameter.

180. **(A)**

The quote is taken from *The Scarlet Letter*, Chapter 1, and describes Roger Chillingworth. The sharp psychological descriptions of characters is a trademark of Hawthorne.

181. **(A)**

It has often been said of Stephen Crane (from whose writing the passage is taken) that he used the devices of Impressionism to produce Naturalistic novels, which are characterized by an attempt to be accurate as well as somewhat selective in the relation of otherwise commonplace details.

182. **(D)**

"Sing, Heavenly Muse" introduces the governing verb in the opening sentence. Urania, the muse of sacred poetry, is invoked to help the poet produce his great work: his "adventurous song" that intends to "soar" above the traditional home of the muses—"the Aonian mount, Mount Helicon."

183. **(A)**

Milton's passage is characterized by unrhymed iambic pentameter lines—blank verse. (B) is characterized by lack of rhyme *and* lack of meter. (C) refers to four-foot lines while this passage has five-foot lines. (D) is a type of rhyme pattern, and (E) refers to the manner in which the same word can fit two different linguistic patterns.

184. **(B)**

The passage is completed in this way. As Melville says in the sentences before, "I thought I would sail about a little and see the watery part of the world. It is a way I have of driving off the spleen, and regulating the circulation." Even not knowing this, it is obvious that the speaker desires escape from the familiar, which eliminates (E) and his restlessness dictates action as a response, eliminating (D) and (A). (C), of course, is taken from Twain's *Huckleberry Finn*.

185. **(D)**

In the first half of Archibald MacLeish's poem, sensations of smell, sight, and touch (apples, light, water) are presented; in the second, loss (hands reaching out, no verbal response, ghostly memories). What is presented is the frustration of a person much in contact with his physical world, but grieving terribly over some other person's absence.

186. **(C)**

The poem has a modest message, even though it deals with the wrenching problem of human loss. (A) and (D) are more extreme in their possibilities; the poet only metaphorically wishes he were dead; there does not seem any real hope that the absent one will return. (B) is more the secondary message of the poem: pain in the presence of pleasure is particularly frustrating. The passage of the seasons, however, does not seem to be what he is waiting for. The poet primarily longs for the "cold light" of truth; if he only knew the explanation for the absence, the "why" behind the other's departure or death, then he might be able to endure the guilt of his survival, able to experience the sensations of life.

187. **(D)**
Self-indulgence, rather than being ultimately destructive, can and does lead to a truer understanding of divine love ("For nothing can be sole or whole/ That has not been rent"). The wordplay on "sole" underscores this, as well as the statement that "love has pitched his mansion in/ The place of excrement."

188. **(A)**
The juxtaposition of violence and seeming indifference is the hallmark of much of Camus' writing. Here it is exaggerated to make the speaker seem like a particularly demented human monster.

189. **(D)**
The obvious American setting here, the arrival by train, and the attention to natural imagery, all are indications of this parody of one of America's best writers of life on the prairies.

190. **(C)**
There is a psychological intensity here that is characteristic of Hardy— a concentration on involved motive and conscience.

191. **(D)**
From psychoanalysis, free association involves the seemingly haphazard recollection of associated images, from which a pattern of concern may emerge.

192. **(C)**
The author states in the sentence following, "But although he at different times, in a desultory manner, committed to writing many particulars of the progress of his mind and fortunes, he never had persevering diligence enough to form them into a regular composition."

193. **(D)**

The passage is taken from Boswell's *Life of Samuel Johnson*. The man being described certainly exhibits some of Johnson's most famous characteristics, notably his strong opinions and his eloquence in defending those opinions.

194. **(D)**

This last line from Swift's "A Description of a City Shower" is a simile that compares the rain generated from the Southern clouds (in the previous lines), to the sickness of a drunkard. Similes are comparative devices that employ the word "like" or "as."

195. **(B)**

"When the evening is spread out against the sky/like a patient etherized upon a table" is from Eliot. Swift's simile has often been pointed to as the inspiration for Eliot's famous comparison.

196. **(D)**

Chekhov's concentration on Olenka's pitiful plight ("She was absolutely alone," "how awful it is not to have any opinions") indicates a sympathetic attitude. However, he does not make Olenka a noble martyr; rather she is a wretched creature doomed to derive meaning solely through her relationships with men. Chekhov is pitying, but he never respects her profound misery.

197. **(B)**

Clearly Olenka has an "understanding" of the world around her intuitively, but she is unable to formulate any opinion on her own. She has always been dependent on others for meaning—her father, Kukin, Pustovalov, or the veterinary surgeon. Chekhov does not imply that her social condition or her focus on the mundane is the cause of her inability to communicate. Rather, her isolation from the sources of her ideas has left her alone and opinionless.

198. **(B)**

The subject has violated the formal behavior required of his gentlemanly station. In the next paragraph, the author states: "For the canons of good society are, or should be, the same as the canons of art. Form is absolutely essential to it."

199. **(B)**

Considered a corruption of Pater's beliefs as stated in *The Renaissance*, this practice became popular in the 1890s, much to Pater's dismay. Pater was a leading critic at the time, a proponent of aesthetics and the phrase "art for art's sake."

200. **(D)**

"Of Adam's blood" is the important phrase here, indicating that the noun of which the poet speaks is a descendant and, being "wretched," could easily be followed by the description "brat"—an annoying child.

201. **(D)**

The rather depressing commentaries about the life the young child is embarking upon are actually common to lullabies ("Down will come baby, cradle and all," etc.). There is no touching the theme of love in this work, so (A) and (B) can be readily eliminated. A lay (E) has eight syllables in a line.

202. **(C)**

"Whan [animals] cometh to the world they dooth hemself some good/Al but the wrecche brol (wretched brat) of Adames blood." Man is destined to suffer because of Original Sin. The other four choices are basically non sequiturs.

203. **(A)**

Suffering is the legacy of Original Sin: we all sorrow in this world. The little child will soon find itself suffering "as thine eldren dide."

204. **(C)**

It is not that tradition or the conditions of the world dictate human misery, but that it is preordained because of Adam's Fall. The desire to make the child sleep, is so that the child may forget for a moment about its destined sorrow.

205. **(B)**

The speaker wears a literal black veil to symbolize the isolation we all endure. Only when someone "shows his inmost heart" to another will the speaker's belief become monstrous. Although a "black veil" seems to be a pretty obvious symbol for death, the fact that it is worn "on every visage" might convince one not to choose (A).

206. **(A)**
References to "slave" and "Freedom" are important markers from which to identify the event for which this poem served as a rallying cry.

207. **(C)**
The didactic nature of this poem is evident from the first stanza, and reflects the political involvement of its author, James Russell Lowell, in *The Present Crisis.* While some elements of the other choices exist in the selection, they are not consistent throughout, and, therefore, do not govern or control the stanza.

208. **(C)**
Mencken, here in this passage from *The Novel,* gives almost no judgmental statement—his attitude here is more the reporter. Thus, while the writer may have been aware of the hollowness of her original work, Mencken does not agree with her until the following paragraphs, wherein he praises *My Antonia* for its "accurate representation."

209. **(D)**
This quote refers to Willa Cather.

210. **(C)**
This is best classified as an extended simile, with "tears" being compared (using "as") to sails, dawn, and kisses. Note that the constant repetition of "as" makes (C) a better answer than (A).

211. **(C)**
The poet is certainly capable of experiencing intense emotion (witness the welling up of tears for no particular reason, which is the situation in the poem). Yet, he recalls not just the people, but more especially, the intense emotions of the past, most of which cannot be repeated (e.g., "first love").

212. **(E)**
The reader, even today, is moved by the pain of the poet and the suddenness with which it descended on him as he found himself reflecting on the intense emotions of the past (indeed, first there were tears, and then, recollection). In many ways this is similar to the singular "peak experience" typical of Wordsworth's Romantic philosophy.

213. **(E)**

It is characterized by unrhymed iambic pentameter—the medium of much reflective verse—especially in the nineteenth century. Accentual verse (C) is based on a fixed number of stressed syllables in a line, while free verse (D) has no rhyme but also has no fixed meter.

214. **(C)**

Juliet was married by Friar Laurence only two scenes before, but she has not seen Romeo since, nor consummated their new relationship.

215. **(D)**

This is particularly evident when taken in the context of the previous line, in which Juliet compares herself to a consumer. The last two lines of the passage indicate that Juliet wishes to "enjoy" her new possession.

216. **(D)**

Within the context of these lines, Faustus simply asks if Mephistopheles is so foolish as to think that Faustus imagines that there will be pain in the afterlife.

217. **(E)**

Maya Angelou is widely recognized as one of the most important poets of our time. Her career has been marked by particular attention to the condition of being black in America and coping with the historical legacy of slavery and racism. The poem is ambiguous but at the same time is clearly metaphorical, with its other-worldly description of a bird cage high on a hill, that consciously sings of "freedom." The metaphorical use of language, then, can help us eliminate choice (C). The figure of the bird can represent one who has imprisoned him- or herself from the social world at the same time as he or she longs to connect to the world (A), or it can more explicitly engage the literal imprisonment of men of color in America and the controversies of the high rate of incarceration among black men (B). The most likely answer is (D), an emphasis on the ways that racism and social inequality become restrictions of human development, a kind of cage that constricts real access to freedom but in which the mind can still find ways to articulate a desire for such freedom. While (D) then is most likely, (A) and (B) are not excluded, but (C) is clearly not appropriate given the language of the poem and the social concerns of the poet.

218.   **(B)**

Rand's work is known for its celebration of capitalism and its condemnation of collective forms of social organization. These themes are perhaps best seen in her most famous novels, *The Fountainhead* and the work in question, *Atlas Shrugged.* She is associated with a school of thought—objectivism—that is highly individualistic, and places an extreme emphasis on the drive for self-preservation and advancement as the energizing force of a progressive civilization. The excerpt equates those who put the needs of others before themselves—altruists, collectivists, communists—with murders, while celebrating the egoist who puts him- or herself and his or her own well-being first. The other choices are either the opposite of the theory expounded by Rand (A) or irrelevant to the passage (C), (D). Choice (E) represents a kind of writing that denies human agency in its fatalistic descriptions of the minute traumas of existence, and is inappropriate for Rand's emphasis on the "self-made" person.

219.   **(A)**

The historical clues of the passage should be unmistakable. The speaker has fled Germany after World War II, is in hiding in a remote apartment in a large city, and has been apprehended by Israeli authorities.

220.   **(C)**

The passage never touches on sexual themes, thus eliminating choice (B), and while the description of the squalor in which the speaker lives is vivid, he does not articulate a desire for material goods or a better standard of living (A). While the law is invoked in the reference to his arrest, he does not comment on whether or not this is unjust (D) and (E). By elimination, then we can identify the answer as (C). The return to the state of innocence can be positively identified by paying close attention to the speaker's longing to have his ordeal be over and to be released from the burden of his past—to be told that he, like the children in the game, can simply come out of hiding and go home. The image of children at play makes the scene powerfully evocative of a need to return to a less complicated time, a time before the speaker's involvement in the crimes for which he is being hunted. As a metaphor, Eden always carries connotations of the unfallen state of humanity, before corruption, before pain and guilt: all things from which the speaker seeks escape.

221.   **(B)**

The frequency of one line paragraphs and the absence of complicated diction makes (B) the correct answer choice. Answer (D) is not, strictly speaking, appropriate for prose, but even so the passage is bereft of a lofty or self-important tone. The words tend to be short and expressive, with very little elaborate or figurative language employed, making (A) incorrect. We cannot really judge whether this passage is derivative based on this small excerpt. With no obvious previous work being referenced, the conventionality and simplicity of the language makes (C) also incorrect.

222.   **(A)**

In this passage, we see many allusions to the singularity of the figure it describes: he is like a star and is distanced from the world that has "melted away." The lack of desire to return to "home" or a "father" helps us both eliminate answer (B) and identify answer (A) as correct. In the line "More firmly himself than ever," we can see the subject of the passage in the struggle of becoming and finding meaning in disconnection from one's surrounding environment. Choice (C) could only result from a very sloppy reading of the text that fails to recognize the reference to childbirth as figurative. Choices (D) and (E) are both plausible, but can be eliminated. As far as (D) is concerned, there is a lack of any specific mention of an evil that needs to be destroyed, and while the passage certainly invokes the fear of the subject at his new state, this seems to be quickly overcome, as he "impatiently" goes forward into the unknown, rather than returning to the familiar.

223.   **(B)**

The Handmaid's Tale is a futuristic allegory about the oppression of women and the dangers of fascism. The passage's attention to details that are foreign to present day readers marks it as set out of our time, eliminating choice (E), while the technological apparatuses depicted let us know that the setting could not be that of answers (A), (C), or (D). Answer (B) is suggested not only by the technology of the Compuchek, but also by the attention to the fascistic uniforms and titles of the "Guardians," and the grim picture of authority and surveillance that is suggested.

224.   **(C)**

Throughout the passage, the critic makes connections between the character discussed (Huck Finn) and the larger context of American civilization, instructing the reader as to what Huck represents in the American psyche.

225.   **(B)**

Although the critic refers to the title character of Hawthorne's short story *Young Goodman Brown*, a careful reading of the passage reveals that the third-person pronouns refer to "Huck," as in Huckleberry Finn, of Mark Twain's famous novel.

226. **(D)**
    In elucidating the poem's imagery in terms of sexuality and emotions, the critic is seeking to explore the poet's feelings and psychological state of mind.

227. **(B)**
    Allegory involves a narrative in which the characters, objects, actions, and themes represent more than their literal meanings. Allegory requires that these metaphors function in a coordinated fashion to create one or more alternate intentions. This distinguishes it from symbolism.

228. **(E)**
    Taken from Franz Kafka's *Metamorphosis,* this passage describes Gregor Samsa, who turns into a beetle. While there is every indication that the protagonist in this passage is not human, there is nothing to suggest that "he" is a snake.

229. **(D)**
    Although not actually named as such in the passage (taken from *Barbie-Q,* by Sandra Cisneros), the items in the Mattel boxes would naturally be accessories for dolls, quite possibly made for Barbie dolls. Note the setting of the passage: a flea market, instead of a hardware or department store.

230. **(E)**
    Considering the loving attention paid to the description of the items (compared, for example, to the other objects listed but not described), and the repetition of "please" at the end of the passage, the reader may reasonably deduce that the protagonists' feelings about the items border on the fanatical, as opposed to an indifferent (A), a negative [(B) or (C)], or a merely pleased (D) response.

GRE LITERATURE
IN ENGLISH

Practice Test 1
Answer Sheet

1. Ⓐ Ⓑ Ⓒ Ⓓ Ⓔ
2. Ⓐ Ⓑ Ⓒ Ⓓ Ⓔ
3. Ⓐ Ⓑ Ⓒ Ⓓ Ⓔ
4. Ⓐ Ⓑ Ⓒ Ⓓ Ⓔ
5. Ⓐ Ⓑ Ⓒ Ⓓ Ⓔ
6. Ⓐ Ⓑ Ⓒ Ⓓ Ⓔ
7. Ⓐ Ⓑ Ⓒ Ⓓ Ⓔ
8. Ⓐ Ⓑ Ⓒ Ⓓ Ⓔ
9. Ⓐ Ⓑ Ⓒ Ⓓ Ⓔ
10. Ⓐ Ⓑ Ⓒ Ⓓ Ⓔ
11. Ⓐ Ⓑ Ⓒ Ⓓ Ⓔ
12. Ⓐ Ⓑ Ⓒ Ⓓ Ⓔ
13. Ⓐ Ⓑ Ⓒ Ⓓ Ⓔ
14. Ⓐ Ⓑ Ⓒ Ⓓ Ⓔ
15. Ⓐ Ⓑ Ⓒ Ⓓ Ⓔ
16. Ⓐ Ⓑ Ⓒ Ⓓ Ⓔ
17. Ⓐ Ⓑ Ⓒ Ⓓ Ⓔ
18. Ⓐ Ⓑ Ⓒ Ⓓ Ⓔ
19. Ⓐ Ⓑ Ⓒ Ⓓ Ⓔ
20. Ⓐ Ⓑ Ⓒ Ⓓ Ⓔ
21. Ⓐ Ⓑ Ⓒ Ⓓ Ⓔ
22. Ⓐ Ⓑ Ⓒ Ⓓ Ⓔ
23. Ⓐ Ⓑ Ⓒ Ⓓ Ⓔ
24. Ⓐ Ⓑ Ⓒ Ⓓ Ⓔ
25. Ⓐ Ⓑ Ⓒ Ⓓ Ⓔ

26. Ⓐ Ⓑ Ⓒ Ⓓ Ⓔ
27. Ⓐ Ⓑ Ⓒ Ⓓ Ⓔ
28. Ⓐ Ⓑ Ⓒ Ⓓ Ⓔ
29. Ⓐ Ⓑ Ⓒ Ⓓ Ⓔ
30. Ⓐ Ⓑ Ⓒ Ⓓ Ⓔ
31. Ⓐ Ⓑ Ⓒ Ⓓ Ⓔ
32. Ⓐ Ⓑ Ⓒ Ⓓ Ⓔ
33. Ⓐ Ⓑ Ⓒ Ⓓ Ⓔ
34. Ⓐ Ⓑ Ⓒ Ⓓ Ⓔ
35. Ⓐ Ⓑ Ⓒ Ⓓ Ⓔ
36. Ⓐ Ⓑ Ⓒ Ⓓ Ⓔ
37. Ⓐ Ⓑ Ⓒ Ⓓ Ⓔ
38. Ⓐ Ⓑ Ⓒ Ⓓ Ⓔ
39. Ⓐ Ⓑ Ⓒ Ⓓ Ⓔ
40. Ⓐ Ⓑ Ⓒ Ⓓ Ⓔ
41. Ⓐ Ⓑ Ⓒ Ⓓ Ⓔ
42. Ⓐ Ⓑ Ⓒ Ⓓ Ⓔ
43. Ⓐ Ⓑ Ⓒ Ⓓ Ⓔ
44. Ⓐ Ⓑ Ⓒ Ⓓ Ⓔ
45. Ⓐ Ⓑ Ⓒ Ⓓ Ⓔ
46. Ⓐ Ⓑ Ⓒ Ⓓ Ⓔ
47. Ⓐ Ⓑ Ⓒ Ⓓ Ⓔ
48. Ⓐ Ⓑ Ⓒ Ⓓ Ⓔ
49. Ⓐ Ⓑ Ⓒ Ⓓ Ⓔ
50. Ⓐ Ⓑ Ⓒ Ⓓ Ⓔ

51. Ⓐ Ⓑ Ⓒ Ⓓ Ⓔ
52. Ⓐ Ⓑ Ⓒ Ⓓ Ⓔ
53. Ⓐ Ⓑ Ⓒ Ⓓ Ⓔ
54. Ⓐ Ⓑ Ⓒ Ⓓ Ⓔ
55. Ⓐ Ⓑ Ⓒ Ⓓ Ⓔ
56. Ⓐ Ⓑ Ⓒ Ⓓ Ⓔ
57. Ⓐ Ⓑ Ⓒ Ⓓ Ⓔ
58. Ⓐ Ⓑ Ⓒ Ⓓ Ⓔ
59. Ⓐ Ⓑ Ⓒ Ⓓ Ⓔ
60. Ⓐ Ⓑ Ⓒ Ⓓ Ⓔ
61. Ⓐ Ⓑ Ⓒ Ⓓ Ⓔ
62. Ⓐ Ⓑ Ⓒ Ⓓ Ⓔ
63. Ⓐ Ⓑ Ⓒ Ⓓ Ⓔ
64. Ⓐ Ⓑ Ⓒ Ⓓ Ⓔ
65. Ⓐ Ⓑ Ⓒ Ⓓ Ⓔ
66. Ⓐ Ⓑ Ⓒ Ⓓ Ⓔ
67. Ⓐ Ⓑ Ⓒ Ⓓ Ⓔ
68. Ⓐ Ⓑ Ⓒ Ⓓ Ⓔ
69. Ⓐ Ⓑ Ⓒ Ⓓ Ⓔ
70. Ⓐ Ⓑ Ⓒ Ⓓ Ⓔ
71. Ⓐ Ⓑ Ⓒ Ⓓ Ⓔ
72. Ⓐ Ⓑ Ⓒ Ⓓ Ⓔ
73. Ⓐ Ⓑ Ⓒ Ⓓ Ⓔ
74. Ⓐ Ⓑ Ⓒ Ⓓ Ⓔ
75. Ⓐ Ⓑ Ⓒ Ⓓ Ⓔ

76. Ⓐ Ⓑ Ⓒ Ⓓ Ⓔ	111. Ⓐ Ⓑ Ⓒ Ⓓ Ⓔ	146. Ⓐ Ⓑ Ⓒ Ⓓ Ⓔ
77. Ⓐ Ⓑ Ⓒ Ⓓ Ⓔ	112. Ⓐ Ⓑ Ⓒ Ⓓ Ⓔ	147. Ⓐ Ⓑ Ⓒ Ⓓ Ⓔ
78. Ⓐ Ⓑ Ⓒ Ⓓ Ⓔ	113. Ⓐ Ⓑ Ⓒ Ⓓ Ⓔ	148. Ⓐ Ⓑ Ⓒ Ⓓ Ⓔ
79. Ⓐ Ⓑ Ⓒ Ⓓ Ⓔ	114. Ⓐ Ⓑ Ⓒ Ⓓ Ⓔ	149. Ⓐ Ⓑ Ⓒ Ⓓ Ⓔ
80. Ⓐ Ⓑ Ⓒ Ⓓ Ⓔ	115. Ⓐ Ⓑ Ⓒ Ⓓ Ⓔ	150. Ⓐ Ⓑ Ⓒ Ⓓ Ⓔ
81. Ⓐ Ⓑ Ⓒ Ⓓ Ⓔ	116. Ⓐ Ⓑ Ⓒ Ⓓ Ⓔ	151. Ⓐ Ⓑ Ⓒ Ⓓ Ⓔ
82. Ⓐ Ⓑ Ⓒ Ⓓ Ⓔ	117. Ⓐ Ⓑ Ⓒ Ⓓ Ⓔ	152. Ⓐ Ⓑ Ⓒ Ⓓ Ⓔ
83. Ⓐ Ⓑ Ⓒ Ⓓ Ⓔ	118. Ⓐ Ⓑ Ⓒ Ⓓ Ⓔ	153. Ⓐ Ⓑ Ⓒ Ⓓ Ⓔ
84. Ⓐ Ⓑ Ⓒ Ⓓ Ⓔ	119. Ⓐ Ⓑ Ⓒ Ⓓ Ⓔ	154. Ⓐ Ⓑ Ⓒ Ⓓ Ⓔ
85. Ⓐ Ⓑ Ⓒ Ⓓ Ⓔ	120. Ⓐ Ⓑ Ⓒ Ⓓ Ⓔ	155. Ⓐ Ⓑ Ⓒ Ⓓ Ⓔ
86. Ⓐ Ⓑ Ⓒ Ⓓ Ⓔ	121. Ⓐ Ⓑ Ⓒ Ⓓ Ⓔ	156. Ⓐ Ⓑ Ⓒ Ⓓ Ⓔ
87. Ⓐ Ⓑ Ⓒ Ⓓ Ⓔ	122. Ⓐ Ⓑ Ⓒ Ⓓ Ⓔ	157. Ⓐ Ⓑ Ⓒ Ⓓ Ⓔ
88. Ⓐ Ⓑ Ⓒ Ⓓ Ⓔ	123. Ⓐ Ⓑ Ⓒ Ⓓ Ⓔ	158. Ⓐ Ⓑ Ⓒ Ⓓ Ⓔ
89. Ⓐ Ⓑ Ⓒ Ⓓ Ⓔ	124. Ⓐ Ⓑ Ⓒ Ⓓ Ⓔ	159. Ⓐ Ⓑ Ⓒ Ⓓ Ⓔ
90. Ⓐ Ⓑ Ⓒ Ⓓ Ⓔ	125. Ⓐ Ⓑ Ⓒ Ⓓ Ⓔ	160. Ⓐ Ⓑ Ⓒ Ⓓ Ⓔ
91. Ⓐ Ⓑ Ⓒ Ⓓ Ⓔ	126. Ⓐ Ⓑ Ⓒ Ⓓ Ⓔ	161. Ⓐ Ⓑ Ⓒ Ⓓ Ⓔ
92. Ⓐ Ⓑ Ⓒ Ⓓ Ⓔ	127. Ⓐ Ⓑ Ⓒ Ⓓ Ⓔ	162. Ⓐ Ⓑ Ⓒ Ⓓ Ⓔ
93. Ⓐ Ⓑ Ⓒ Ⓓ Ⓔ	128. Ⓐ Ⓑ Ⓒ Ⓓ Ⓔ	163. Ⓐ Ⓑ Ⓒ Ⓓ Ⓔ
94. Ⓐ Ⓑ Ⓒ Ⓓ Ⓔ	129. Ⓐ Ⓑ Ⓒ Ⓓ Ⓔ	164. Ⓐ Ⓑ Ⓒ Ⓓ Ⓔ
95. Ⓐ Ⓑ Ⓒ Ⓓ Ⓔ	130. Ⓐ Ⓑ Ⓒ Ⓓ Ⓔ	165. Ⓐ Ⓑ Ⓒ Ⓓ Ⓔ
96. Ⓐ Ⓑ Ⓒ Ⓓ Ⓔ	131. Ⓐ Ⓑ Ⓒ Ⓓ Ⓔ	166. Ⓐ Ⓑ Ⓒ Ⓓ Ⓔ
97. Ⓐ Ⓑ Ⓒ Ⓓ Ⓔ	132. Ⓐ Ⓑ Ⓒ Ⓓ Ⓔ	167. Ⓐ Ⓑ Ⓒ Ⓓ Ⓔ
98. Ⓐ Ⓑ Ⓒ Ⓓ Ⓔ	133. Ⓐ Ⓑ Ⓒ Ⓓ Ⓔ	168. Ⓐ Ⓑ Ⓒ Ⓓ Ⓔ
99. Ⓐ Ⓑ Ⓒ Ⓓ Ⓔ	134. Ⓐ Ⓑ Ⓒ Ⓓ Ⓔ	169. Ⓐ Ⓑ Ⓒ Ⓓ Ⓔ
100. Ⓐ Ⓑ Ⓒ Ⓓ Ⓔ	135. Ⓐ Ⓑ Ⓒ Ⓓ Ⓔ	170. Ⓐ Ⓑ Ⓒ Ⓓ Ⓔ
101. Ⓐ Ⓑ Ⓒ Ⓓ Ⓔ	136. Ⓐ Ⓑ Ⓒ Ⓓ Ⓔ	171. Ⓐ Ⓑ Ⓒ Ⓓ Ⓔ
102. Ⓐ Ⓑ Ⓒ Ⓓ Ⓔ	137. Ⓐ Ⓑ Ⓒ Ⓓ Ⓔ	172. Ⓐ Ⓑ Ⓒ Ⓓ Ⓔ
103. Ⓐ Ⓑ Ⓒ Ⓓ Ⓔ	138. Ⓐ Ⓑ Ⓒ Ⓓ Ⓔ	173. Ⓐ Ⓑ Ⓒ Ⓓ Ⓔ
104. Ⓐ Ⓑ Ⓒ Ⓓ Ⓔ	139. Ⓐ Ⓑ Ⓒ Ⓓ Ⓔ	174. Ⓐ Ⓑ Ⓒ Ⓓ Ⓔ
105. Ⓐ Ⓑ Ⓒ Ⓓ Ⓔ	140. Ⓐ Ⓑ Ⓒ Ⓓ Ⓔ	175. Ⓐ Ⓑ Ⓒ Ⓓ Ⓔ
106. Ⓐ Ⓑ Ⓒ Ⓓ Ⓔ	141. Ⓐ Ⓑ Ⓒ Ⓓ Ⓔ	176. Ⓐ Ⓑ Ⓒ Ⓓ Ⓔ
107. Ⓐ Ⓑ Ⓒ Ⓓ Ⓔ	142. Ⓐ Ⓑ Ⓒ Ⓓ Ⓔ	177. Ⓐ Ⓑ Ⓒ Ⓓ Ⓔ
108. Ⓐ Ⓑ Ⓒ Ⓓ Ⓔ	143. Ⓐ Ⓑ Ⓒ Ⓓ Ⓔ	178. Ⓐ Ⓑ Ⓒ Ⓓ Ⓔ
109. Ⓐ Ⓑ Ⓒ Ⓓ Ⓔ	144. Ⓐ Ⓑ Ⓒ Ⓓ Ⓔ	179. Ⓐ Ⓑ Ⓒ Ⓓ Ⓔ
110. Ⓐ Ⓑ Ⓒ Ⓓ Ⓔ	145. Ⓐ Ⓑ Ⓒ Ⓓ Ⓔ	180. Ⓐ Ⓑ Ⓒ Ⓓ Ⓔ

181. Ⓐ Ⓑ Ⓒ Ⓓ Ⓔ   216. Ⓐ Ⓑ Ⓒ Ⓓ Ⓔ
182. Ⓐ Ⓑ Ⓒ Ⓓ Ⓔ   217. Ⓐ Ⓑ Ⓒ Ⓓ Ⓔ
183. Ⓐ Ⓑ Ⓒ Ⓓ Ⓔ   218. Ⓐ Ⓑ Ⓒ Ⓓ Ⓔ
184. Ⓐ Ⓑ Ⓒ Ⓓ Ⓔ   219. Ⓐ Ⓑ Ⓒ Ⓓ Ⓔ
185. Ⓐ Ⓑ Ⓒ Ⓓ Ⓔ   220. Ⓐ Ⓑ Ⓒ Ⓓ Ⓔ
186. Ⓐ Ⓑ Ⓒ Ⓓ Ⓔ   221. Ⓐ Ⓑ Ⓒ Ⓓ Ⓔ
187. Ⓐ Ⓑ Ⓒ Ⓓ Ⓔ   222. Ⓐ Ⓑ Ⓒ Ⓓ Ⓔ
188. Ⓐ Ⓑ Ⓒ Ⓓ Ⓔ   223. Ⓐ Ⓑ Ⓒ Ⓓ Ⓔ
189. Ⓐ Ⓑ Ⓒ Ⓓ Ⓔ   224. Ⓐ Ⓑ Ⓒ Ⓓ Ⓔ
190. Ⓐ Ⓑ Ⓒ Ⓓ Ⓔ   225. Ⓐ Ⓑ Ⓒ Ⓓ Ⓔ
191. Ⓐ Ⓑ Ⓒ Ⓓ Ⓔ   226. Ⓐ Ⓑ Ⓒ Ⓓ Ⓔ
192. Ⓐ Ⓑ Ⓒ Ⓓ Ⓔ   227. Ⓐ Ⓑ Ⓒ Ⓓ Ⓔ
193. Ⓐ Ⓑ Ⓒ Ⓓ Ⓔ   228. Ⓐ Ⓑ Ⓒ Ⓓ Ⓔ
194. Ⓐ Ⓑ Ⓒ Ⓓ Ⓔ   229. Ⓐ Ⓑ Ⓒ Ⓓ Ⓔ
195. Ⓐ Ⓑ Ⓒ Ⓓ Ⓔ   230. Ⓐ Ⓑ Ⓒ Ⓓ Ⓔ
196. Ⓐ Ⓑ Ⓒ Ⓓ Ⓔ
197. Ⓐ Ⓑ Ⓒ Ⓓ Ⓔ
198. Ⓐ Ⓑ Ⓒ Ⓓ Ⓔ
199. Ⓐ Ⓑ Ⓒ Ⓓ Ⓔ
200. Ⓐ Ⓑ Ⓒ Ⓓ Ⓔ
201. Ⓐ Ⓑ Ⓒ Ⓓ Ⓔ
202. Ⓐ Ⓑ Ⓒ Ⓓ Ⓔ
203. Ⓐ Ⓑ Ⓒ Ⓓ Ⓔ
204. Ⓐ Ⓑ Ⓒ Ⓓ Ⓔ
205. Ⓐ Ⓑ Ⓒ Ⓓ Ⓔ
206. Ⓐ Ⓑ Ⓒ Ⓓ Ⓔ
207. Ⓐ Ⓑ Ⓒ Ⓓ Ⓔ
208. Ⓐ Ⓑ Ⓒ Ⓓ Ⓔ
209. Ⓐ Ⓑ Ⓒ Ⓓ Ⓔ
210. Ⓐ Ⓑ Ⓒ Ⓓ Ⓔ
211. Ⓐ Ⓑ Ⓒ Ⓓ Ⓔ
212. Ⓐ Ⓑ Ⓒ Ⓓ Ⓔ
213. Ⓐ Ⓑ Ⓒ Ⓓ Ⓔ
214. Ⓐ Ⓑ Ⓒ Ⓓ Ⓔ
215. Ⓐ Ⓑ Ⓒ Ⓓ Ⓔ

GRE LITERATURE
IN ENGLISH

Practice Test 2
Answer Sheet

1. Ⓐ Ⓑ Ⓒ Ⓓ Ⓔ
2. Ⓐ Ⓑ Ⓒ Ⓓ Ⓔ
3. Ⓐ Ⓑ Ⓒ Ⓓ Ⓔ
4. Ⓐ Ⓑ Ⓒ Ⓓ Ⓔ
5. Ⓐ Ⓑ Ⓒ Ⓓ Ⓔ
6. Ⓐ Ⓑ Ⓒ Ⓓ Ⓔ
7. Ⓐ Ⓑ Ⓒ Ⓓ Ⓔ
8. Ⓐ Ⓑ Ⓒ Ⓓ Ⓔ
9. Ⓐ Ⓑ Ⓒ Ⓓ Ⓔ
10. Ⓐ Ⓑ Ⓒ Ⓓ Ⓔ
11. Ⓐ Ⓑ Ⓒ Ⓓ Ⓔ
12. Ⓐ Ⓑ Ⓒ Ⓓ Ⓔ
13. Ⓐ Ⓑ Ⓒ Ⓓ Ⓔ
14. Ⓐ Ⓑ Ⓒ Ⓓ Ⓔ
15. Ⓐ Ⓑ Ⓒ Ⓓ Ⓔ
16. Ⓐ Ⓑ Ⓒ Ⓓ Ⓔ
17. Ⓐ Ⓑ Ⓒ Ⓓ Ⓔ
18. Ⓐ Ⓑ Ⓒ Ⓓ Ⓔ
19. Ⓐ Ⓑ Ⓒ Ⓓ Ⓔ
20. Ⓐ Ⓑ Ⓒ Ⓓ Ⓔ
21. Ⓐ Ⓑ Ⓒ Ⓓ Ⓔ
22. Ⓐ Ⓑ Ⓒ Ⓓ Ⓔ
23. Ⓐ Ⓑ Ⓒ Ⓓ Ⓔ
24. Ⓐ Ⓑ Ⓒ Ⓓ Ⓔ
25. Ⓐ Ⓑ Ⓒ Ⓓ Ⓔ

26. Ⓐ Ⓑ Ⓒ Ⓓ Ⓔ
27. Ⓐ Ⓑ Ⓒ Ⓓ Ⓔ
28. Ⓐ Ⓑ Ⓒ Ⓓ Ⓔ
29. Ⓐ Ⓑ Ⓒ Ⓓ Ⓔ
30. Ⓐ Ⓑ Ⓒ Ⓓ Ⓔ
31. Ⓐ Ⓑ Ⓒ Ⓓ Ⓔ
32. Ⓐ Ⓑ Ⓒ Ⓓ Ⓔ
33. Ⓐ Ⓑ Ⓒ Ⓓ Ⓔ
34. Ⓐ Ⓑ Ⓒ Ⓓ Ⓔ
35. Ⓐ Ⓑ Ⓒ Ⓓ Ⓔ
36. Ⓐ Ⓑ Ⓒ Ⓓ Ⓔ
37. Ⓐ Ⓑ Ⓒ Ⓓ Ⓔ
38. Ⓐ Ⓑ Ⓒ Ⓓ Ⓔ
39. Ⓐ Ⓑ Ⓒ Ⓓ Ⓔ
40. Ⓐ Ⓑ Ⓒ Ⓓ Ⓔ
41. Ⓐ Ⓑ Ⓒ Ⓓ Ⓔ
42. Ⓐ Ⓑ Ⓒ Ⓓ Ⓔ
43. Ⓐ Ⓑ Ⓒ Ⓓ Ⓔ
44. Ⓐ Ⓑ Ⓒ Ⓓ Ⓔ
45. Ⓐ Ⓑ Ⓒ Ⓓ Ⓔ
46. Ⓐ Ⓑ Ⓒ Ⓓ Ⓔ
47. Ⓐ Ⓑ Ⓒ Ⓓ Ⓔ
48. Ⓐ Ⓑ Ⓒ Ⓓ Ⓔ
49. Ⓐ Ⓑ Ⓒ Ⓓ Ⓔ
50. Ⓐ Ⓑ Ⓒ Ⓓ Ⓔ

51. Ⓐ Ⓑ Ⓒ Ⓓ Ⓔ
52. Ⓐ Ⓑ Ⓒ Ⓓ Ⓔ
53. Ⓐ Ⓑ Ⓒ Ⓓ Ⓔ
54. Ⓐ Ⓑ Ⓒ Ⓓ Ⓔ
55. Ⓐ Ⓑ Ⓒ Ⓓ Ⓔ
56. Ⓐ Ⓑ Ⓒ Ⓓ Ⓔ
57. Ⓐ Ⓑ Ⓒ Ⓓ Ⓔ
58. Ⓐ Ⓑ Ⓒ Ⓓ Ⓔ
59. Ⓐ Ⓑ Ⓒ Ⓓ Ⓔ
60. Ⓐ Ⓑ Ⓒ Ⓓ Ⓔ
61. Ⓐ Ⓑ Ⓒ Ⓓ Ⓔ
62. Ⓐ Ⓑ Ⓒ Ⓓ Ⓔ
63. Ⓐ Ⓑ Ⓒ Ⓓ Ⓔ
64. Ⓐ Ⓑ Ⓒ Ⓓ Ⓔ
65. Ⓐ Ⓑ Ⓒ Ⓓ Ⓔ
66. Ⓐ Ⓑ Ⓒ Ⓓ Ⓔ
67. Ⓐ Ⓑ Ⓒ Ⓓ Ⓔ
68. Ⓐ Ⓑ Ⓒ Ⓓ Ⓔ
69. Ⓐ Ⓑ Ⓒ Ⓓ Ⓔ
70. Ⓐ Ⓑ Ⓒ Ⓓ Ⓔ
71. Ⓐ Ⓑ Ⓒ Ⓓ Ⓔ
72. Ⓐ Ⓑ Ⓒ Ⓓ Ⓔ
73. Ⓐ Ⓑ Ⓒ Ⓓ Ⓔ
74. Ⓐ Ⓑ Ⓒ Ⓓ Ⓔ
75. Ⓐ Ⓑ Ⓒ Ⓓ Ⓔ

76. Ⓐ Ⓑ Ⓒ Ⓓ Ⓔ	111. Ⓐ Ⓑ Ⓒ Ⓓ Ⓔ	146. Ⓐ Ⓑ Ⓒ Ⓓ Ⓔ
77. Ⓐ Ⓑ Ⓒ Ⓓ Ⓔ	112. Ⓐ Ⓑ Ⓒ Ⓓ Ⓔ	147. Ⓐ Ⓑ Ⓒ Ⓓ Ⓔ
78. Ⓐ Ⓑ Ⓒ Ⓓ Ⓔ	113. Ⓐ Ⓑ Ⓒ Ⓓ Ⓔ	148. Ⓐ Ⓑ Ⓒ Ⓓ Ⓔ
79. Ⓐ Ⓑ Ⓒ Ⓓ Ⓔ	114. Ⓐ Ⓑ Ⓒ Ⓓ Ⓔ	149. Ⓐ Ⓑ Ⓒ Ⓓ Ⓔ
80. Ⓐ Ⓑ Ⓒ Ⓓ Ⓔ	115. Ⓐ Ⓑ Ⓒ Ⓓ Ⓔ	150. Ⓐ Ⓑ Ⓒ Ⓓ Ⓔ
81. Ⓐ Ⓑ Ⓒ Ⓓ Ⓔ	116. Ⓐ Ⓑ Ⓒ Ⓓ Ⓔ	151. Ⓐ Ⓑ Ⓒ Ⓓ Ⓔ
82. Ⓐ Ⓑ Ⓒ Ⓓ Ⓔ	117. Ⓐ Ⓑ Ⓒ Ⓓ Ⓔ	152. Ⓐ Ⓑ Ⓒ Ⓓ Ⓔ
83. Ⓐ Ⓑ Ⓒ Ⓓ Ⓔ	118. Ⓐ Ⓑ Ⓒ Ⓓ Ⓔ	153. Ⓐ Ⓑ Ⓒ Ⓓ Ⓔ
84. Ⓐ Ⓑ Ⓒ Ⓓ Ⓔ	119. Ⓐ Ⓑ Ⓒ Ⓓ Ⓔ	154. Ⓐ Ⓑ Ⓒ Ⓓ Ⓔ
85. Ⓐ Ⓑ Ⓒ Ⓓ Ⓔ	120. Ⓐ Ⓑ Ⓒ Ⓓ Ⓔ	155. Ⓐ Ⓑ Ⓒ Ⓓ Ⓔ
86. Ⓐ Ⓑ Ⓒ Ⓓ Ⓔ	121. Ⓐ Ⓑ Ⓒ Ⓓ Ⓔ	156. Ⓐ Ⓑ Ⓒ Ⓓ Ⓔ
87. Ⓐ Ⓑ Ⓒ Ⓓ Ⓔ	122. Ⓐ Ⓑ Ⓒ Ⓓ Ⓔ	157. Ⓐ Ⓑ Ⓒ Ⓓ Ⓔ
88. Ⓐ Ⓑ Ⓒ Ⓓ Ⓔ	123. Ⓐ Ⓑ Ⓒ Ⓓ Ⓔ	158. Ⓐ Ⓑ Ⓒ Ⓓ Ⓔ
89. Ⓐ Ⓑ Ⓒ Ⓓ Ⓔ	124. Ⓐ Ⓑ Ⓒ Ⓓ Ⓔ	159. Ⓐ Ⓑ Ⓒ Ⓓ Ⓔ
90. Ⓐ Ⓑ Ⓒ Ⓓ Ⓔ	125. Ⓐ Ⓑ Ⓒ Ⓓ Ⓔ	160. Ⓐ Ⓑ Ⓒ Ⓓ Ⓔ
91. Ⓐ Ⓑ Ⓒ Ⓓ Ⓔ	126. Ⓐ Ⓑ Ⓒ Ⓓ Ⓔ	161. Ⓐ Ⓑ Ⓒ Ⓓ Ⓔ
92. Ⓐ Ⓑ Ⓒ Ⓓ Ⓔ	127. Ⓐ Ⓑ Ⓒ Ⓓ Ⓔ	162. Ⓐ Ⓑ Ⓒ Ⓓ Ⓔ
93. Ⓐ Ⓑ Ⓒ Ⓓ Ⓔ	128. Ⓐ Ⓑ Ⓒ Ⓓ Ⓔ	163. Ⓐ Ⓑ Ⓒ Ⓓ Ⓔ
94. Ⓐ Ⓑ Ⓒ Ⓓ Ⓔ	129. Ⓐ Ⓑ Ⓒ Ⓓ Ⓔ	164. Ⓐ Ⓑ Ⓒ Ⓓ Ⓔ
95. Ⓐ Ⓑ Ⓒ Ⓓ Ⓔ	130. Ⓐ Ⓑ Ⓒ Ⓓ Ⓔ	165. Ⓐ Ⓑ Ⓒ Ⓓ Ⓔ
96. Ⓐ Ⓑ Ⓒ Ⓓ Ⓔ	131. Ⓐ Ⓑ Ⓒ Ⓓ Ⓔ	166. Ⓐ Ⓑ Ⓒ Ⓓ Ⓔ
97. Ⓐ Ⓑ Ⓒ Ⓓ Ⓔ	132. Ⓐ Ⓑ Ⓒ Ⓓ Ⓔ	167. Ⓐ Ⓑ Ⓒ Ⓓ Ⓔ
98. Ⓐ Ⓑ Ⓒ Ⓓ Ⓔ	133. Ⓐ Ⓑ Ⓒ Ⓓ Ⓔ	168. Ⓐ Ⓑ Ⓒ Ⓓ Ⓔ
99. Ⓐ Ⓑ Ⓒ Ⓓ Ⓔ	134. Ⓐ Ⓑ Ⓒ Ⓓ Ⓔ	169. Ⓐ Ⓑ Ⓒ Ⓓ Ⓔ
100. Ⓐ Ⓑ Ⓒ Ⓓ Ⓔ	135. Ⓐ Ⓑ Ⓒ Ⓓ Ⓔ	170. Ⓐ Ⓑ Ⓒ Ⓓ Ⓔ
101. Ⓐ Ⓑ Ⓒ Ⓓ Ⓔ	136. Ⓐ Ⓑ Ⓒ Ⓓ Ⓔ	171. Ⓐ Ⓑ Ⓒ Ⓓ Ⓔ
102. Ⓐ Ⓑ Ⓒ Ⓓ Ⓔ	137. Ⓐ Ⓑ Ⓒ Ⓓ Ⓔ	172. Ⓐ Ⓑ Ⓒ Ⓓ Ⓔ
103. Ⓐ Ⓑ Ⓒ Ⓓ Ⓔ	138. Ⓐ Ⓑ Ⓒ Ⓓ Ⓔ	173. Ⓐ Ⓑ Ⓒ Ⓓ Ⓔ
104. Ⓐ Ⓑ Ⓒ Ⓓ Ⓔ	139. Ⓐ Ⓑ Ⓒ Ⓓ Ⓔ	174. Ⓐ Ⓑ Ⓒ Ⓓ Ⓔ
105. Ⓐ Ⓑ Ⓒ Ⓓ Ⓔ	140. Ⓐ Ⓑ Ⓒ Ⓓ Ⓔ	175. Ⓐ Ⓑ Ⓒ Ⓓ Ⓔ
106. Ⓐ Ⓑ Ⓒ Ⓓ Ⓔ	141. Ⓐ Ⓑ Ⓒ Ⓓ Ⓔ	176. Ⓐ Ⓑ Ⓒ Ⓓ Ⓔ
107. Ⓐ Ⓑ Ⓒ Ⓓ Ⓔ	142. Ⓐ Ⓑ Ⓒ Ⓓ Ⓔ	177. Ⓐ Ⓑ Ⓒ Ⓓ Ⓔ
108. Ⓐ Ⓑ Ⓒ Ⓓ Ⓔ	143. Ⓐ Ⓑ Ⓒ Ⓓ Ⓔ	178. Ⓐ Ⓑ Ⓒ Ⓓ Ⓔ
109. Ⓐ Ⓑ Ⓒ Ⓓ Ⓔ	144. Ⓐ Ⓑ Ⓒ Ⓓ Ⓔ	179. Ⓐ Ⓑ Ⓒ Ⓓ Ⓔ
110. Ⓐ Ⓑ Ⓒ Ⓓ Ⓔ	145. Ⓐ Ⓑ Ⓒ Ⓓ Ⓔ	180. Ⓐ Ⓑ Ⓒ Ⓓ Ⓔ

181. Ⓐ Ⓑ Ⓒ Ⓓ Ⓔ
182. Ⓐ Ⓑ Ⓒ Ⓓ Ⓔ
183. Ⓐ Ⓑ Ⓒ Ⓓ Ⓔ
184. Ⓐ Ⓑ Ⓒ Ⓓ Ⓔ
185. Ⓐ Ⓑ Ⓒ Ⓓ Ⓔ
186. Ⓐ Ⓑ Ⓒ Ⓓ Ⓔ
187. Ⓐ Ⓑ Ⓒ Ⓓ Ⓔ
188. Ⓐ Ⓑ Ⓒ Ⓓ Ⓔ
189. Ⓐ Ⓑ Ⓒ Ⓓ Ⓔ
190. Ⓐ Ⓑ Ⓒ Ⓓ Ⓔ
191. Ⓐ Ⓑ Ⓒ Ⓓ Ⓔ
192. Ⓐ Ⓑ Ⓒ Ⓓ Ⓔ
193. Ⓐ Ⓑ Ⓒ Ⓓ Ⓔ
194. Ⓐ Ⓑ Ⓒ Ⓓ Ⓔ
195. Ⓐ Ⓑ Ⓒ Ⓓ Ⓔ
196. Ⓐ Ⓑ Ⓒ Ⓓ Ⓔ
197. Ⓐ Ⓑ Ⓒ Ⓓ Ⓔ
198. Ⓐ Ⓑ Ⓒ Ⓓ Ⓔ
199. Ⓐ Ⓑ Ⓒ Ⓓ Ⓔ
200. Ⓐ Ⓑ Ⓒ Ⓓ Ⓔ
201. Ⓐ Ⓑ Ⓒ Ⓓ Ⓔ
202. Ⓐ Ⓑ Ⓒ Ⓓ Ⓔ
203. Ⓐ Ⓑ Ⓒ Ⓓ Ⓔ
204. Ⓐ Ⓑ Ⓒ Ⓓ Ⓔ
205. Ⓐ Ⓑ Ⓒ Ⓓ Ⓔ
206. Ⓐ Ⓑ Ⓒ Ⓓ Ⓔ
207. Ⓐ Ⓑ Ⓒ Ⓓ Ⓔ
208. Ⓐ Ⓑ Ⓒ Ⓓ Ⓔ
209. Ⓐ Ⓑ Ⓒ Ⓓ Ⓔ
210. Ⓐ Ⓑ Ⓒ Ⓓ Ⓔ
211. Ⓐ Ⓑ Ⓒ Ⓓ Ⓔ
212. Ⓐ Ⓑ Ⓒ Ⓓ Ⓔ
213. Ⓐ Ⓑ Ⓒ Ⓓ Ⓔ
214. Ⓐ Ⓑ Ⓒ Ⓓ Ⓔ
215. Ⓐ Ⓑ Ⓒ Ⓓ Ⓔ

216. Ⓐ Ⓑ Ⓒ Ⓓ Ⓔ
217. Ⓐ Ⓑ Ⓒ Ⓓ Ⓔ
218. Ⓐ Ⓑ Ⓒ Ⓓ Ⓔ
219. Ⓐ Ⓑ Ⓒ Ⓓ Ⓔ
220. Ⓐ Ⓑ Ⓒ Ⓓ Ⓔ
221. Ⓐ Ⓑ Ⓒ Ⓓ Ⓔ
222. Ⓐ Ⓑ Ⓒ Ⓓ Ⓔ
223. Ⓐ Ⓑ Ⓒ Ⓓ Ⓔ
224. Ⓐ Ⓑ Ⓒ Ⓓ Ⓔ
225. Ⓐ Ⓑ Ⓒ Ⓓ Ⓔ
226. Ⓐ Ⓑ Ⓒ Ⓓ Ⓔ
227. Ⓐ Ⓑ Ⓒ Ⓓ Ⓔ
228. Ⓐ Ⓑ Ⓒ Ⓓ Ⓔ
229. Ⓐ Ⓑ Ⓒ Ⓓ Ⓔ
230. Ⓐ Ⓑ Ⓒ Ⓓ Ⓔ

GRE LITERATURE IN ENGLISH

Practice Test 3
Answer Sheet

1. Ⓐ Ⓑ Ⓒ Ⓓ Ⓔ	26. Ⓐ Ⓑ Ⓒ Ⓓ Ⓔ	51. Ⓐ Ⓑ Ⓒ Ⓓ Ⓔ	
2. Ⓐ Ⓑ Ⓒ Ⓓ Ⓔ	27. Ⓐ Ⓑ Ⓒ Ⓓ Ⓔ	52. Ⓐ Ⓑ Ⓒ Ⓓ Ⓔ	
3. Ⓐ Ⓑ Ⓒ Ⓓ Ⓔ	28. Ⓐ Ⓑ Ⓒ Ⓓ Ⓔ	53. Ⓐ Ⓑ Ⓒ Ⓓ Ⓔ	
4. Ⓐ Ⓑ Ⓒ Ⓓ Ⓔ	29. Ⓐ Ⓑ Ⓒ Ⓓ Ⓔ	54. Ⓐ Ⓑ Ⓒ Ⓓ Ⓔ	
5. Ⓐ Ⓑ Ⓒ Ⓓ Ⓔ	30. Ⓐ Ⓑ Ⓒ Ⓓ Ⓔ	55. Ⓐ Ⓑ Ⓒ Ⓓ Ⓔ	
6. Ⓐ Ⓑ Ⓒ Ⓓ Ⓔ	31. Ⓐ Ⓑ Ⓒ Ⓓ Ⓔ	56. Ⓐ Ⓑ Ⓒ Ⓓ Ⓔ	
7. Ⓐ Ⓑ Ⓒ Ⓓ Ⓔ	32. Ⓐ Ⓑ Ⓒ Ⓓ Ⓔ	57. Ⓐ Ⓑ Ⓒ Ⓓ Ⓔ	
8. Ⓐ Ⓑ Ⓒ Ⓓ Ⓔ	33. Ⓐ Ⓑ Ⓒ Ⓓ Ⓔ	58. Ⓐ Ⓑ Ⓒ Ⓓ Ⓔ	
9. Ⓐ Ⓑ Ⓒ Ⓓ Ⓔ	34. Ⓐ Ⓑ Ⓒ Ⓓ Ⓔ	59. Ⓐ Ⓑ Ⓒ Ⓓ Ⓔ	
10. Ⓐ Ⓑ Ⓒ Ⓓ Ⓔ	35. Ⓐ Ⓑ Ⓒ Ⓓ Ⓔ	60. Ⓐ Ⓑ Ⓒ Ⓓ Ⓔ	
11. Ⓐ Ⓑ Ⓒ Ⓓ Ⓔ	36. Ⓐ Ⓑ Ⓒ Ⓓ Ⓔ	61. Ⓐ Ⓑ Ⓒ Ⓓ Ⓔ	
12. Ⓐ Ⓑ Ⓒ Ⓓ Ⓔ	37. Ⓐ Ⓑ Ⓒ Ⓓ Ⓔ	62. Ⓐ Ⓑ Ⓒ Ⓓ Ⓔ	
13. Ⓐ Ⓑ Ⓒ Ⓓ Ⓔ	38. Ⓐ Ⓑ Ⓒ Ⓓ Ⓔ	63. Ⓐ Ⓑ Ⓒ Ⓓ Ⓔ	
14. Ⓐ Ⓑ Ⓒ Ⓓ Ⓔ	39. Ⓐ Ⓑ Ⓒ Ⓓ Ⓔ	64. Ⓐ Ⓑ Ⓒ Ⓓ Ⓔ	
15. Ⓐ Ⓑ Ⓒ Ⓓ Ⓔ	40. Ⓐ Ⓑ Ⓒ Ⓓ Ⓔ	65. Ⓐ Ⓑ Ⓒ Ⓓ Ⓔ	
16. Ⓐ Ⓑ Ⓒ Ⓓ Ⓔ	41. Ⓐ Ⓑ Ⓒ Ⓓ Ⓔ	66. Ⓐ Ⓑ Ⓒ Ⓓ Ⓔ	
17. Ⓐ Ⓑ Ⓒ Ⓓ Ⓔ	42. Ⓐ Ⓑ Ⓒ Ⓓ Ⓔ	67. Ⓐ Ⓑ Ⓒ Ⓓ Ⓔ	
18. Ⓐ Ⓑ Ⓒ Ⓓ Ⓔ	43. Ⓐ Ⓑ Ⓒ Ⓓ Ⓔ	68. Ⓐ Ⓑ Ⓒ Ⓓ Ⓔ	
19. Ⓐ Ⓑ Ⓒ Ⓓ Ⓔ	44. Ⓐ Ⓑ Ⓒ Ⓓ Ⓔ	69. Ⓐ Ⓑ Ⓒ Ⓓ Ⓔ	
20. Ⓐ Ⓑ Ⓒ Ⓓ Ⓔ	45. Ⓐ Ⓑ Ⓒ Ⓓ Ⓔ	70. Ⓐ Ⓑ Ⓒ Ⓓ Ⓔ	
21. Ⓐ Ⓑ Ⓒ Ⓓ Ⓔ	46. Ⓐ Ⓑ Ⓒ Ⓓ Ⓔ	71. Ⓐ Ⓑ Ⓒ Ⓓ Ⓔ	
22. Ⓐ Ⓑ Ⓒ Ⓓ Ⓔ	47. Ⓐ Ⓑ Ⓒ Ⓓ Ⓔ	72. Ⓐ Ⓑ Ⓒ Ⓓ Ⓔ	
23. Ⓐ Ⓑ Ⓒ Ⓓ Ⓔ	48. Ⓐ Ⓑ Ⓒ Ⓓ Ⓔ	73. Ⓐ Ⓑ Ⓒ Ⓓ Ⓔ	
24. Ⓐ Ⓑ Ⓒ Ⓓ Ⓔ	49. Ⓐ Ⓑ Ⓒ Ⓓ Ⓔ	74. Ⓐ Ⓑ Ⓒ Ⓓ Ⓔ	
25. Ⓐ Ⓑ Ⓒ Ⓓ Ⓔ	50. Ⓐ Ⓑ Ⓒ Ⓓ Ⓔ	75. Ⓐ Ⓑ Ⓒ Ⓓ Ⓔ	

76. Ⓐ Ⓑ Ⓒ Ⓓ Ⓔ
77. Ⓐ Ⓑ Ⓒ Ⓓ Ⓔ
78. Ⓐ Ⓑ Ⓒ Ⓓ Ⓔ
79. Ⓐ Ⓑ Ⓒ Ⓓ Ⓔ
80. Ⓐ Ⓑ Ⓒ Ⓓ Ⓔ
81. Ⓐ Ⓑ Ⓒ Ⓓ Ⓔ
82. Ⓐ Ⓑ Ⓒ Ⓓ Ⓔ
83. Ⓐ Ⓑ Ⓒ Ⓓ Ⓔ
84. Ⓐ Ⓑ Ⓒ Ⓓ Ⓔ
85. Ⓐ Ⓑ Ⓒ Ⓓ Ⓔ
86. Ⓐ Ⓑ Ⓒ Ⓓ Ⓔ
87. Ⓐ Ⓑ Ⓒ Ⓓ Ⓔ
88. Ⓐ Ⓑ Ⓒ Ⓓ Ⓔ
89. Ⓐ Ⓑ Ⓒ Ⓓ Ⓔ
90. Ⓐ Ⓑ Ⓒ Ⓓ Ⓔ
91. Ⓐ Ⓑ Ⓒ Ⓓ Ⓔ
92. Ⓐ Ⓑ Ⓒ Ⓓ Ⓔ
93. Ⓐ Ⓑ Ⓒ Ⓓ Ⓔ
94. Ⓐ Ⓑ Ⓒ Ⓓ Ⓔ
95. Ⓐ Ⓑ Ⓒ Ⓓ Ⓔ
96. Ⓐ Ⓑ Ⓒ Ⓓ Ⓔ
97. Ⓐ Ⓑ Ⓒ Ⓓ Ⓔ
98. Ⓐ Ⓑ Ⓒ Ⓓ Ⓔ
99. Ⓐ Ⓑ Ⓒ Ⓓ Ⓔ
100. Ⓐ Ⓑ Ⓒ Ⓓ Ⓔ
101. Ⓐ Ⓑ Ⓒ Ⓓ Ⓔ
102. Ⓐ Ⓑ Ⓒ Ⓓ Ⓔ
103. Ⓐ Ⓑ Ⓒ Ⓓ Ⓔ
104. Ⓐ Ⓑ Ⓒ Ⓓ Ⓔ
105. Ⓐ Ⓑ Ⓒ Ⓓ Ⓔ
106. Ⓐ Ⓑ Ⓒ Ⓓ Ⓔ
107. Ⓐ Ⓑ Ⓒ Ⓓ Ⓔ
108. Ⓐ Ⓑ Ⓒ Ⓓ Ⓔ
109. Ⓐ Ⓑ Ⓒ Ⓓ Ⓔ
110. Ⓐ Ⓑ Ⓒ Ⓓ Ⓔ

111. Ⓐ Ⓑ Ⓒ Ⓓ Ⓔ
112. Ⓐ Ⓑ Ⓒ Ⓓ Ⓔ
113. Ⓐ Ⓑ Ⓒ Ⓓ Ⓔ
114. Ⓐ Ⓑ Ⓒ Ⓓ Ⓔ
115. Ⓐ Ⓑ Ⓒ Ⓓ Ⓔ
116. Ⓐ Ⓑ Ⓒ Ⓓ Ⓔ
117. Ⓐ Ⓑ Ⓒ Ⓓ Ⓔ
118. Ⓐ Ⓑ Ⓒ Ⓓ Ⓔ
119. Ⓐ Ⓑ Ⓒ Ⓓ Ⓔ
120. Ⓐ Ⓑ Ⓒ Ⓓ Ⓔ
121. Ⓐ Ⓑ Ⓒ Ⓓ Ⓔ
122. Ⓐ Ⓑ Ⓒ Ⓓ Ⓔ
123. Ⓐ Ⓑ Ⓒ Ⓓ Ⓔ
124. Ⓐ Ⓑ Ⓒ Ⓓ Ⓔ
125. Ⓐ Ⓑ Ⓒ Ⓓ Ⓔ
126. Ⓐ Ⓑ Ⓒ Ⓓ Ⓔ
127. Ⓐ Ⓑ Ⓒ Ⓓ Ⓔ
128. Ⓐ Ⓑ Ⓒ Ⓓ Ⓔ
129. Ⓐ Ⓑ Ⓒ Ⓓ Ⓔ
130. Ⓐ Ⓑ Ⓒ Ⓓ Ⓔ
131. Ⓐ Ⓑ Ⓒ Ⓓ Ⓔ
132. Ⓐ Ⓑ Ⓒ Ⓓ Ⓔ
133. Ⓐ Ⓑ Ⓒ Ⓓ Ⓔ
134. Ⓐ Ⓑ Ⓒ Ⓓ Ⓔ
135. Ⓐ Ⓑ Ⓒ Ⓓ Ⓔ
136. Ⓐ Ⓑ Ⓒ Ⓓ Ⓔ
137. Ⓐ Ⓑ Ⓒ Ⓓ Ⓔ
138. Ⓐ Ⓑ Ⓒ Ⓓ Ⓔ
139. Ⓐ Ⓑ Ⓒ Ⓓ Ⓔ
140. Ⓐ Ⓑ Ⓒ Ⓓ Ⓔ
141. Ⓐ Ⓑ Ⓒ Ⓓ Ⓔ
142. Ⓐ Ⓑ Ⓒ Ⓓ Ⓔ
143. Ⓐ Ⓑ Ⓒ Ⓓ Ⓔ
144. Ⓐ Ⓑ Ⓒ Ⓓ Ⓔ
145. Ⓐ Ⓑ Ⓒ Ⓓ Ⓔ

146. Ⓐ Ⓑ Ⓒ Ⓓ Ⓔ
147. Ⓐ Ⓑ Ⓒ Ⓓ Ⓔ
148. Ⓐ Ⓑ Ⓒ Ⓓ Ⓔ
149. Ⓐ Ⓑ Ⓒ Ⓓ Ⓔ
150. Ⓐ Ⓑ Ⓒ Ⓓ Ⓔ
151. Ⓐ Ⓑ Ⓒ Ⓓ Ⓔ
152. Ⓐ Ⓑ Ⓒ Ⓓ Ⓔ
153. Ⓐ Ⓑ Ⓒ Ⓓ Ⓔ
154. Ⓐ Ⓑ Ⓒ Ⓓ Ⓔ
155. Ⓐ Ⓑ Ⓒ Ⓓ Ⓔ
156. Ⓐ Ⓑ Ⓒ Ⓓ Ⓔ
157. Ⓐ Ⓑ Ⓒ Ⓓ Ⓔ
158. Ⓐ Ⓑ Ⓒ Ⓓ Ⓔ
159. Ⓐ Ⓑ Ⓒ Ⓓ Ⓔ
160. Ⓐ Ⓑ Ⓒ Ⓓ Ⓔ
161. Ⓐ Ⓑ Ⓒ Ⓓ Ⓔ
162. Ⓐ Ⓑ Ⓒ Ⓓ Ⓔ
163. Ⓐ Ⓑ Ⓒ Ⓓ Ⓔ
164. Ⓐ Ⓑ Ⓒ Ⓓ Ⓔ
165. Ⓐ Ⓑ Ⓒ Ⓓ Ⓔ
166. Ⓐ Ⓑ Ⓒ Ⓓ Ⓔ
167. Ⓐ Ⓑ Ⓒ Ⓓ Ⓔ
168. Ⓐ Ⓑ Ⓒ Ⓓ Ⓔ
169. Ⓐ Ⓑ Ⓒ Ⓓ Ⓔ
170. Ⓐ Ⓑ Ⓒ Ⓓ Ⓔ
171. Ⓐ Ⓑ Ⓒ Ⓓ Ⓔ
172. Ⓐ Ⓑ Ⓒ Ⓓ Ⓔ
173. Ⓐ Ⓑ Ⓒ Ⓓ Ⓔ
174. Ⓐ Ⓑ Ⓒ Ⓓ Ⓔ
175. Ⓐ Ⓑ Ⓒ Ⓓ Ⓔ
176. Ⓐ Ⓑ Ⓒ Ⓓ Ⓔ
177. Ⓐ Ⓑ Ⓒ Ⓓ Ⓔ
178. Ⓐ Ⓑ Ⓒ Ⓓ Ⓔ
179. Ⓐ Ⓑ Ⓒ Ⓓ Ⓔ
180. Ⓐ Ⓑ Ⓒ Ⓓ Ⓔ

181. Ⓐ Ⓑ Ⓒ Ⓓ Ⓔ
182. Ⓐ Ⓑ Ⓒ Ⓓ Ⓔ
183. Ⓐ Ⓑ Ⓒ Ⓓ Ⓔ
184. Ⓐ Ⓑ Ⓒ Ⓓ Ⓔ
185. Ⓐ Ⓑ Ⓒ Ⓓ Ⓔ
186. Ⓐ Ⓑ Ⓒ Ⓓ Ⓔ
187. Ⓐ Ⓑ Ⓒ Ⓓ Ⓔ
188. Ⓐ Ⓑ Ⓒ Ⓓ Ⓔ
189. Ⓐ Ⓑ Ⓒ Ⓓ Ⓔ
190. Ⓐ Ⓑ Ⓒ Ⓓ Ⓔ
191. Ⓐ Ⓑ Ⓒ Ⓓ Ⓔ
192. Ⓐ Ⓑ Ⓒ Ⓓ Ⓔ
193. Ⓐ Ⓑ Ⓒ Ⓓ Ⓔ
194. Ⓐ Ⓑ Ⓒ Ⓓ Ⓔ
195. Ⓐ Ⓑ Ⓒ Ⓓ Ⓔ
196. Ⓐ Ⓑ Ⓒ Ⓓ Ⓔ
197. Ⓐ Ⓑ Ⓒ Ⓓ Ⓔ
198. Ⓐ Ⓑ Ⓒ Ⓓ Ⓔ
199. Ⓐ Ⓑ Ⓒ Ⓓ Ⓔ
200. Ⓐ Ⓑ Ⓒ Ⓓ Ⓔ
201. Ⓐ Ⓑ Ⓒ Ⓓ Ⓔ
202. Ⓐ Ⓑ Ⓒ Ⓓ Ⓔ
203. Ⓐ Ⓑ Ⓒ Ⓓ Ⓔ
204. Ⓐ Ⓑ Ⓒ Ⓓ Ⓔ
205. Ⓐ Ⓑ Ⓒ Ⓓ Ⓔ
206. Ⓐ Ⓑ Ⓒ Ⓓ Ⓔ
207. Ⓐ Ⓑ Ⓒ Ⓓ Ⓔ
208. Ⓐ Ⓑ Ⓒ Ⓓ Ⓔ
209. Ⓐ Ⓑ Ⓒ Ⓓ Ⓔ
210. Ⓐ Ⓑ Ⓒ Ⓓ Ⓔ
211. Ⓐ Ⓑ Ⓒ Ⓓ Ⓔ
212. Ⓐ Ⓑ Ⓒ Ⓓ Ⓔ
213. Ⓐ Ⓑ Ⓒ Ⓓ Ⓔ
214. Ⓐ Ⓑ Ⓒ Ⓓ Ⓔ
215. Ⓐ Ⓑ Ⓒ Ⓓ Ⓔ

216. Ⓐ Ⓑ Ⓒ Ⓓ Ⓔ
217. Ⓐ Ⓑ Ⓒ Ⓓ Ⓔ
218. Ⓐ Ⓑ Ⓒ Ⓓ Ⓔ
219. Ⓐ Ⓑ Ⓒ Ⓓ Ⓔ
220. Ⓐ Ⓑ Ⓒ Ⓓ Ⓔ
221. Ⓐ Ⓑ Ⓒ Ⓓ Ⓔ
222. Ⓐ Ⓑ Ⓒ Ⓓ Ⓔ
223. Ⓐ Ⓑ Ⓒ Ⓓ Ⓔ
224. Ⓐ Ⓑ Ⓒ Ⓓ Ⓔ
225. Ⓐ Ⓑ Ⓒ Ⓓ Ⓔ
226. Ⓐ Ⓑ Ⓒ Ⓓ Ⓔ
227. Ⓐ Ⓑ Ⓒ Ⓓ Ⓔ
228. Ⓐ Ⓑ Ⓒ Ⓓ Ⓔ
229. Ⓐ Ⓑ Ⓒ Ⓓ Ⓔ
230. Ⓐ Ⓑ Ⓒ Ⓓ Ⓔ

REA's Test Prep Books Are The Best!
(a sample of the <u>hundreds of letters</u> REA receives each year)

" What I found in your book was a wealth of information sufficient to shore up my basic skills in math and verbal... The section on analytical ability was excellent. The practice tests were challenging and the answer explanations most helpful. It certainly is the *Best Test Prep for the GRE*! "

Student, Pullman, WA

" I am writing to thank you for your test preparation... Your book helped me immeasurably, and I have nothing but praise for your GRE preparation. "

Student, Benton Harbor, MI

" My students report your chapters of review as the most valuable single resource they used for review and preparation. "

Teacher, American Fork, UT

" Your book was such a better value and was so much more complete than anything your competition has produced (and I have them all!). "

Teacher, Virginia Beach, VA

" Compared to the other books that my fellow students had, your book was the most useful in helping me get a great score. "

Student, North Hollywood, CA

" Your book was responsible for my success on the exam, which helped me get into the college of my choice... I will look for REA the next time I need help. "

Student, Chesterfield, MO